학습 진도표와 함께 목표를 달성해 보세요.

_____의 Grammar Gateway Intermediate 학습 진도표

목표와 다짐을 적어보세요.

나는 _____을 하기 위해

_____년 _____월 _____일까지 이 책을 끝낸다.

학습플랜을 선택하세요.

☐ 하루에 Lesson 4개씩 **한 달** 안에 완성

☐ 하루에 Lesson 2개씩 **두 달** 안에 완성

☐ 하루에 Lesson _____ 개씩 _____ 안에 완성

학습을 마친 Lesson의 번호에 색칠해 보세요. 복습이 필요한 Lesson은 별도로 표시하고, 꼭 복습하세요.

	2	3	4	5	6	7	8	9	10	11	12	13	14	15	16	17	18	19	20
21	22	23	24	25	26	27	28	29	30	31	32	33	34	35	36	37	38	39	40
41	42	43	44	45	46	47	48	49	50	51	52	53	54	55	56	57	58	59	60
61	62	63	64	65	66	67	68	69	70	71	72	73	74	75	76	77	78	79	80
81	82	83	84	85	86	87	88	89	90	91	92	93	94	95	96	97	98	99	100
101	102	103	104	105	106	107	108	109	110										

|H|A|C|K|E|R|S|

Grammar
Gateway
Intermediate

해커스 어학연구소

GRAMMAR
GATEWAY
INTERMEDIATE

www.Hackers.co.kr

PREFACE

Grammar Gateway Intermediate은
영문법의 기초를 다진 학습자들이 보다 심도 있는 문법 학습을 통해 한 단계 높이 도약할
수 있는 중급 영어 문법서입니다.

본 교재는 영어를 모국어로 사용하는 사람들이 어떻게 말하고 쓰는지 분석·관찰하여
가장 중요한 문법 포인트를 총 110개의 레슨으로 담아냈습니다. 한 레슨을 2페이지로 구성
하여, 왼쪽 페이지에서 쉽고 명확하게 설명되어 있는 문법 사항들을 학습한 후 곧바로 오른
쪽 페이지에서 배운 내용을 연습해 볼 수 있습니다. 영문법에 두려움을 가진 학습자를 위해
어려운 문법 용어 대신 쉬운 문법 설명과 다양한 삽화를 통해 재미있게 공부할 수 있도
록 하였습니다. 나아가 실생활에서 바로 사용할 수 있는 예문과 다양한 유형의 연습문
제를 통해 문법뿐만 아니라 말하기와 쓰기 능력도 기를 수 있습니다. 해커스인강(www.
HackersIngang.com)에서 무료로 제공하는 'Grammar Gateway Intermediate 스피킹·라
이팅 훈련 워크북'을 이용하면 보다 효과적인 말하기·쓰기 훈련이 가능합니다.

동영상강의를 들으면서 공부하고 싶은 학습자들은 해커스 동영상강의 포털 해커스인강
(www.HackersIngang.com)에서 해커스 선생님들의 명쾌한 강의와 함께 학습이 가능합니다.
더불어, 실시간 토론과 정보 공유의 장인 해커스영어 사이트(www.Hackers.co.kr)와 점프해
커스(www.JumpHackers.com)에서 교재 학습 중 궁금한 점을 다른 학습자들과 나누고, 다
양한 무료 영어 학습 자료를 이용할 수 있습니다.

Grammar Gateway Intermediate을 통해 막연하고 어렵게만 여겨지는 영문법에 한걸음
더 가까이 다가설 수 있으리라 확신합니다. 여러분의 꿈을 이루는 길에 Grammar Gateway
Intermediate이 함께하기를 기원합니다.

해커스 어학연구소

CONTENTS

CONTENTS

책의 특징

쉽게 이해할 수 있는 문법책

- 이해하기 어려운 문법 용어를 사용하지 않고 쉬운 말로 설명을 풀어 써서 누구든지 쉽게 이해할 수 있습니다.
- 표와 그래프를 사용하여 보다 효과적으로 문법 설명을 이해할 수 있습니다.

재미있게 공부할 수 있는 문법책

- 실제 상황을 보는 듯 생생하고 재미있는 삽화가 그려져 있어 영문법을 보다 효과적이고 재미있게 공부할 수 있습니다.
- 삽화 문제, 대화문 등 다양한 유형의 연습문제가 수록되어 있어 보다 흥미롭게 영문법을 공부할 수 있습니다.

끝까지 볼 수 있는 문법책

- 초중급 학습자가 꼭 알아야 할 문법 포인트와 궁금해하는 문법 포인트만을 엄선, 110개 레슨으로 구성하여 빠르게 학습을 마칠 수 있습니다.
- 문법 학습 후 바로 옆 페이지에서 문제풀이로 연습해 볼 수 있도록 한 레슨을 두 페이지로 간단하게 구성하여 부담없이 학습을 마칠 수 있습니다.
- 학습 진도표를 통해 스스로 학습 진도를 점검하며 꾸준히 공부하면 책을 끝까지 마칠 수 있습니다.

스피킹·라이팅에 활용할 수 있는 문법책

- 실생활에서 사용할 수 있는 예문들이 수록되어 있어 실제 말하기·쓰기에 바로 적용할 수 있습니다.
- 문장과 대화를 직접 완성해보는 연습을 통해 학습한 내용이 실생활에서 어떻게 활용될 수 있는지 확인할 수 있고, 말하기·쓰기 실력 또한 향상시킬 수 있습니다.

책 의 구 성

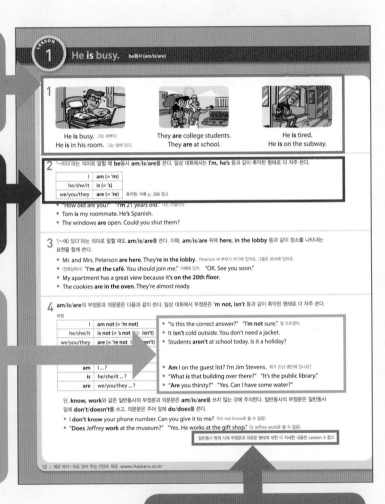

PRACTICE

A. 그림을 보고 주어진 표현들을 하나씩 사용하여 예시와 같이 문장을 완성하세요.

a painter a reporter a soldier	+	at the airport in a cafeteria in a helicopter
baseball players nurses		on a bench on a hill

DANIEL   SARAH and JULIA   BETTY   MARVIN   JIM and ALAN

1. _Daniel is a painter. He's_ OR _He is on a hill_ .
2. _____ .
3. _____ .
4. _____ .
5. _____ .

B. 주어진 표현과 am/is/are를 사용하여 문장을 완성하세요. 필요한 경우 부정문으로 쓰세요.

at the theater   Chinese   happy   in my bag   on 2nd Avenue   twins

1. "The post office _is on 2nd Avenue_ ." "OK. Thanks."
2. I can't find my keys. They _____ .
3. "What's wrong?" "I _____ with my exam results."
4. Jane _____ . She is watching a movie with her friends.
5. Ella and Emma _____ , but they don't look the same.
6. David _____ . He's from Korea.

C. 괄호 안에 주어진 표현들과 am/is/are를 적절히 배열하여 문장을 완성하세요.

1. (17 years / old / he) My brother is in high school. _He's 17 years old_ OR _He is 17 years old_ .
2. (in Seattle / Johnny and Robert) _____ right now.
3. (the bathroom) "Where _____ ?" "It's around that corner."
4. (not / I / familiar) _____ with this neighborhood.
5. (a photographer / you) "_____ ?" "Yes, I am."
6. (expensive / not / this necklace) _____ . I should buy it.

D. 괄호 안에 주어진 표현들과 am/is/are를 사용하여 Linda와 James의 대화를 완성하세요. 필요한 경우 부정문으로 쓰세요.

LINDA: 1. Dinner _is ready_ . Where are the kids? (ready)
2. _____ Chris _____ ? (in his room)
JAMES: Yes. I think he has a lot of work. 3. He _____ . (busy)
LINDA: How about Justin and Amy?
JAMES: They're not home yet.
4. Amy _____ with Kate, and Justin _____ . (at school, back from the library)
LINDA: Well, it's 7 o'clock. 5. _____ you _____ ? (hungry)
JAMES: Not really. 6. I _____ for now. (OK)
LINDA: Then let's wait for the kids.

정답 p.306 Check-Up Test 1 p.234
본 교재 동영상강의 www.ChampStudy.com | 13

문제
재미있고 다양한 문제를 풀어보며 공부한 내용을 바로 연습할 수 있어요.

실용지문 문제
대화문, 이메일, 에세이, 광고 등 실생활에서 볼 수 있는 지문을 통해 공부한 내용을 연습해 볼 수 있어요.

Check-Up Test 링크
링크를 따라가면 여러 Lesson의 내용을 종합적으로 점검해볼 수 있는 Check-Up Test를 풀어볼 수 있어요.

현재진행 현재진행형
1
Grammar Gateway Intermediate

1

He **is** busy. 그는 바쁘다.
He **is** in his room. 그는 방에 있다.

They **are** college students.
They **are** at school.

He **is** tired.
He **is** on the subway.

2 '~이다'라는 의미로 말할 때 be동사 **am/is/are**를 쓴다. 일상 대화에서는 **I'm, he's** 등과 같이 축약된 형태로 더 자주 쓴다.

I	am (= 'm)
he/she/it	is (= 's)
we/you/they	are (= 're)

축약형: 부록 p. 286 참고

- "How old are you?" "I'**m** 21 years old." 나는 21살이다.
- Tom **is** my roommate. He'**s** Spanish.
- The windows **are** open. Could you shut them?

3 '(~에) 있다'라는 의미로 말할 때도 **am/is/are**를 쓴다. 이때, **am/is/are** 뒤에 **here, in the lobby** 등과 같이 장소를 나타내는 표현을 함께 쓴다.

- Mr. and Mrs. Peterson **are** here. They'**re in the lobby.** Peterson 씨 부부가 여기에 있어요. 그들은 로비에 있어요.
- (전화상에서) "I'**m at the café.** You should join me." 카페에 있어. "OK. See you soon."
- My apartment has a great view because it'**s on the 20th floor.**
- The cookies **are in the oven.** They're almost ready.

4 **am/is/are**의 부정문과 의문문은 다음과 같이 쓴다. 일상 대화에서 부정문은 **'m not, isn't** 등과 같이 축약된 형태로 더 자주 쓴다.

부정

I	am not (= 'm not)
he/she/it	is not (= 's not 또는 isn't)
we/you/they	are not (= 're not 또는 aren't)

- "Is this the correct answer?" "I'**m not** sure." 잘 모르겠어.
- It **isn't** cold outside. You don't need a jacket.
- Students **aren't** at school today. Is it a holiday?

의문

am	I ... ?
is	he/she/it ... ?
are	we/you/they ... ?

- **Am** I on the guest list? I'm Jim Stevens. 제가 손님 명단에 있나요?
- "What **is** that building over there?" "It's the public library."
- "**Are** you thirsty?" "Yes. Can I have some water?"

단, **know, work**와 같은 일반동사의 부정문과 의문문은 **am/is/are**를 쓰지 않는 것에 주의한다. 일반동사의 부정문은 일반동사 앞에 **don't/doesn't**를 쓰고, 의문문은 주어 앞에 **do/does**를 쓴다.

- I **don't know** your phone number. Can you give it to me? (I'm not know로 쓸 수 없음)
- "**Does** Jeffrey **work** at the museum?" "Yes. He works at the gift shop."
  (Is Jeffrey work로 쓸 수 없음)

일반동사 현재 시제 부정문과 의문문 형태에 대한 더 자세한 내용은 Lesson 3 참고

PRACTICE

A. 그림을 보고 주어진 표현들을 하나씩 사용하여 예시와 같이 문장을 완성하세요.

| ~~a painter~~   a reporter   a soldier | + | at the airport   in a cafeteria   in a helicopter |
| baseball players   nurses | | on a bench   ~~on a hill~~ |

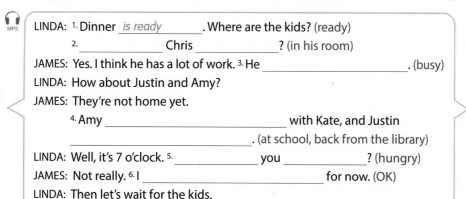

1. *Daniel is a painter. He's* OR *He is on a hill* .
2. _____ .
3. _____ .
4. _____ .
5. _____ .

B. 주어진 표현과 am/is/are를 사용하여 문장을 완성하세요. 필요한 경우 부정문으로 쓰세요.

| at the theater   Chinese   happy   in my bag   ~~on 2nd Avenue~~   twins |

1. "The post office *is on 2nd Avenue* ." "OK. Thanks."
2. I can't find my keys. They _____ .
3. "What's wrong?" "I _____ with my exam results."
4. Jane _____ . She is watching a movie with her friends.
5. Ella and Emma _____ , but they don't look the same.
6. David _____ . He's from Korea.

C. 괄호 안에 주어진 표현들과 am/is/are를 적절히 배열하여 문장을 완성하세요.

1. (17 years / old / he) My brother is in high school. *He's 17 years old* OR *He is 17 years old* .
2. (in Seattle / Johnny and Robert) _____ right now.
3. (the bathroom) "Where _____ ?" "It's around that corner."
4. (not / I / familiar) _____ with this neighborhood.
5. (a photographer / you) "_____ ?" "Yes, I am."
6. (expensive / not / this necklace) _____ . I should buy it.

D. 괄호 안에 주어진 표현들과 am/is/are를 사용하여 Linda와 James의 대화를 완성하세요. 필요한 경우 부정문으로 쓰세요.

LINDA: 1. Dinner *is ready* . Where are the kids? (ready)
2. _____ Chris _____ ? (in his room)
JAMES: Yes. I think he has a lot of work. 3. He _____ . (busy)
LINDA: How about Justin and Amy?
JAMES: They're not home yet.
4. Amy _____ with Kate, and Justin _____ . (at school, back from the library)
LINDA: Well, it's 7 o'clock. 5. _____ you _____ ? (hungry)
JAMES: Not really. 6. I _____ for now. (OK)
LINDA: Then let's wait for the kids.

1

She is at the table.

She is selling books.

그녀는 책을 팔고 있다.

'책을 팔고 있다'라는 의미로 지금 하고 있는 행동에 대해 말하기 위해 현재진행 시제
is selling을 썼다.

2

'~하고 있다, ~하는 중이다'라는 의미로 말하고 있는 시점인 지금 하고 있는 행동이나 일어나고 있는 일에 대해 말할 때 현재진행 시제를
쓴다. 현재진행 시제는 **am/is/are + -ing**로 쓴다.

긍정 · 부정

I	am		washing
he/she/it	is	(not)	playing
we/you/they	are		watching

의문

am	I	washing … ?
is	he/she/it	playing … ?
are	we/you/they	watching … ?

동사의 형태 변화: 부록 p. 280 참고

I**'m washing** the dishes.

과거　　　　　지금　　　　　미래

- Sophia, can you answer the phone? I**'m washing** the dishes. 설거지를 하고 있어.
- Mike **isn't playing** video games anymore. He**'s watching** TV. Mike는 더 이상 비디오 게임을 하고 있지 않아. TV를 보고 있어.
- "**Are** you **using** that pen? May I borrow it?" "Sure. Here you go."
- It**'s not snowing** a lot outside. Just a little.

3

말하고 있는 시점인 지금 하고 있거나 일어나고 있는 일이 아닐지라도, 요즘 하고 있는 행동이나 일어나고 있는 일에 대해 말할 때도
현재진행 시제를 쓸 수 있다.

We**'re planning** a Christmas party.

과거　　　　　지금　　　　　미래

- "We**'re planning** a Christmas party. Do you want to come?" "Sure."
  (지금 하고 있는 것은 아니지만 요즘 파티를 계획하고 있음)
- I'm very busy this week. I**'m writing** a report for my English class. (지금 하고 있는 것은 아니지만 요즘 보고서를 쓰고 있음)
- Ann **isn't living** in the dorm this semester. She**'s staying** at her aunt's house.
- What **are** you **doing** these days? **Are** you **practicing** for the soccer match?

4

현재진행 시제는 다음과 같은 표현과 자주 함께 쓴다.

(right) now (바로) 지금	**at the moment** 지금. 요즘
these days 요즘	**this week/month/year** 등 이번 주/이번 달/올해 등

- I can't go out with you. I**'m studying right now**. 지금 공부하고 있어.
- Our website **isn't working at the moment**. We need to find the problem. 우리 웹사이트가 지금 작동하고 있지 않아.
- "Michelle! You look great!" "Thanks. I**'m exercising** more **these days**."
- "**Are** the stores **having** big sales **this week**?" "Yes. Let's go shopping tomorrow!"

PRACTICE

A. 그림을 보고 주어진 표현을 사용하여 예시와 같이 문장을 완성하세요.

hold a cup	read a book	ride bikes	~~run~~

1. Dogs _are running_ by the lake.
2. Frank _____.
3. Olivia _____.
4. Nick and Harry _____.

clean the desk	fix a photocopier	move a plant	stand at the door

5. Brian and Donald _____.
6. Mary _____.
7. Kevin _____.
8. Anna and Joseph _____.

B. 괄호 안에 주어진 단어들을 사용하여 예시와 같이 토크쇼 진행자와 영화 배우 Johnny의 대화를 완성하세요. 필요한 경우 부정문으로 쓰세요.

Host: 1. _Are you working_ these days? (you, work)
JOHNNY: 2. No, _____ at the moment. (I, act)
3. _____ a break. (I, take)
Host: I see. 4. And what _____ with your time? (you, do)
JOHNNY: 5. Well, _____ my son about acting. (I, teach)
He wants to become an actor.
Host: Oh, that sounds nice. 6. _____ acting in college? (he, study)
JOHNNY: 7. Yes, but _____ classes this year. (he, attend)
He's taking a year off.
Host: Well, your son is lucky! 8. _____ from the best! (he, learn)

C. 주어진 표현들을 사용하여 문장을 완성하세요. 필요한 경우 부정문으로 쓰세요.

bake	change	date	hire	listen	sleep	spend	~~wear~~

1. (he) "Which person is John?" " _He's wearing_ OR _He is wearing_ a blue sweater."
2. (I) Can you be quiet, please? _____ to the radio.
3. (they) "Bella and David are always together. _____?" "I think so."
4. (She) "Nicole looks so tired."
   "_____ much these days because she's busy at work."
5. (we) "Are there any jobs at your company?" "No, _____ right now."
6. (Mom) "_____ cupcakes?" "No. Muffins."
7. (I) _____ a lot of money this month. I'm saving for a new car.
8. (the leaves) _____ colors. The weather will be cold soon.

He **works** at a bank. 현재 시제 (1)

1

He **works** at a bank. 그는 은행에서 일한다.

He **meets** new people every day. 그는 매일 새로운 사람들을 만난다.

'은행에서 일한다', '(매일) 새로운 사람들을 만난다'라는 의미로 일반적으로 사실인 일과
반복적으로 일어나는 일에 대해 말하기 위해 현재 시제 works와 meets를 썼다.

2 일반적으로 사실인 일이나 반복적으로 일어나는 일에 대해 말할 때 현재 시제를 쓴다. 또한 과학적인 법칙과 같이 변하지 않는 사실에
대해 말할 때도 현재 시제를 쓴다.

I/we/you/they	live	clean	cover	brush
he/she/it	lives	cleans	covers	brushes

I **live** in Los Angeles.

과거 　　　　　 지금 　　　　　 미래

- I **live** in Los Angeles. 나는 로스앤젤레스에 산다.
- We **clean** our house on Saturdays. 우리는 매주 토요일에 집을 청소한다.
- Water **covers** 72 percent of the Earth.
- Susan **brushes** her teeth after every meal.

  he/she/it 등을 주어로 쓰는 경우, 동사원형에 **(e)s**를 붙이는 것에 주의한다. 단, **have**는 **has**로 쓴다.

  - Claire **enjoys** cooking. She also **has** many cookbooks. (Claire enjoy, She also have로 쓸 수 없음)
  - I have a history lecture on Thursdays. It **finishes** at 5 o'clock. (It finish로 쓸 수 없음)

  동사의 형태 변화: 부록 p.280 참고

3 현재 시제의 부정문과 의문문은 다음과 같이 쓴다.

부정

I/we/you/they	don't	go
he/she/it	doesn't	take

의문

do	I/we/you/they	go … ?
does	he/she/it	take … ?

- I **don't go** out much on weekdays. 평일에는 많이 외출하지 않는다.
- "**Does** that store **take** credit cards?" "No, it **doesn't accept** them."
- "What **do** you **wear** to work?" "Suits."

  이때, 주어가 **he/she/it** 등이라도 동사 끝에 **(e)s**를 붙이지 않는 것에 주의한다.

  - Mr. Warren lived in Japan, but he **doesn't speak** Japanese. (he doesn't speaks로 쓸 수 없음)
  - "That movie looks good. **Does** it **seem** OK to you?" "Sure." (Does it seems로 쓸 수 없음)

4 현재 시제는 반복적으로 일어나는 일에 대해 말할 때 쓴다. 따라서 어떤 일이 얼마나 자주 일어나는지를 나타내는 **always/
sometimes/never** 등과 같은 빈도부사와 자주 함께 쓴다. 이때 빈도부사는 **walk, drive** 등과 같은 일반동사 앞에 주로 쓴다.

- "Do you **always walk** to school?" 항상 걸어서 학교에 가니?
  "No, I **sometimes drive**." 아니, 가끔 운전해.
- My friends **never forget** my birthday. They send me gifts every year. 내 친구들은 내 생일을 절대 잊어버리지 않는다.
- Betty **often goes** to parties on weekends.
- Mark doesn't **usually read** newspapers in the morning.

  빈도부사에 대한 더 자세한 내용은 Lesson 71 참고

PRACTICE

A. 주어진 동사를 사용하여 문장을 완성하세요.

| cost | eat | fix | ~~play~~ | see | teach | travel | wake |

1. On Sundays, Nick _plays_ basketball with Ronald.
2. My brother lives in San Diego, so we only _____ each other twice a year.
3. "Do you always get up early?" "Yes. I _____ up at 6 every day."
4. John is often out of town. He _____ almost every month.
5. "How much are tickets to the amusement park?" "They _____ $40."
6. My sister _____ English at my school. All of the students like her.
7. My computer breaks down sometimes, and Chloe _____ it. She's very helpful.
8. I _____ a lot of vegetables because they are good for my health.

B. 주어진 표현을 사용하여 문장을 완성하세요.

fall in the rainforest	•		•	1. The sun _sets in the west_ .
fly south in the winter	•		•	2. Pine trees _____ .
not have flowers	•		•	3. Oil _____ .
not mix with water	•		•	4. A lot of rain _____ .
~~set in the west~~	•		•	5. Many birds _____ .

C. 괄호 안에 주어진 표현들을 사용하여 대화를 완성하세요.

1. A: (you, take) _Do you take_ a lot of pictures?
   B: (I, bring) Yes. _____ my camera with me everywhere.

2. A: (you and your friends, go) How often _____ to the mall?
   B: A few times each month.

3. A: (this bus, stop) _____ at Rose Park?
   B: (it, turn) No. _____ before Rose Park.

4. A: (Jennifer, enjoy) _____ swimming?
   B: No. She's scared of water.

5. A: (you, spell) How _____ your last name?
   B: C-H-O.

6. A: (Peter, send) _____ you e-mails often?
   B: (he, call) No, but _____ me every week.

D. 괄호 안에 주어진 단어들을 사용하여 Justin과 Linda의 대화를 완성하세요. 필요한 경우 부정문으로 쓰세요.

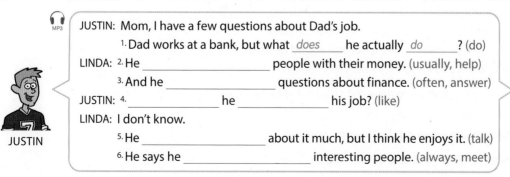

JUSTIN: Mom, I have a few questions about Dad's job.
   1. Dad works at a bank, but what _does_ he actually _do_ ? (do)
LINDA: 2. He _____ people with their money. (usually, help)
   3. And he _____ questions about finance. (often, answer)
JUSTIN: 4. _____ he _____ his job? (like)
LINDA: I don't know.
   5. He _____ about it much, but I think he enjoys it. (talk)
   6. He says he _____ interesting people. (always, meet)

JUSTIN

LINDA

He knows her. 현재 시제 (2) 현재진행 시제로 쓰지 않는 동사

1

He is waving at her.

He knows her.
그는 그녀를 안다.

현재진행 시제는 어떤 동작이 지금 일어나고 있다고 말할 때 쓴다. 그러나 know(알다)와 같이 동작을 나타내지 않는 다음과 같은 동사들은 현재진행 시제로 쓰지 않고 주로 현재 시제로 쓴다.

know	remember	understand	believe	agree
want	need	love	like	hate
own	possess	belong	contain	

- I **remember** you! You're Helen, right? (I'm remembering으로 쓸 수 없음)
- Max **doesn't want** a watch for Christmas. He **wants** a new computer. (Max isn't wanting, He's wanting으로 쓸 수 없음)
- "**Do** Mr. and Mrs. Jackson **own** a house in Hawaii?" "Yes. It's very close to the sea."
- "I **don't understand** this menu. Can you read Italian?" "A little."

2 **have**를 '~을 가지고 있다'라는 의미로 말할 때는 현재진행 시제로 쓰지 않고 현재 시제로 쓴다.

- Diane **has** a cute dog. His name is Rocky. Diane은 귀여운 강아지를 가지고 있다. (Diane is having으로 쓸 수 없음)
- I can't think of anything good. **Do** you **have** any ideas? 무슨 아이디어를 가지고 있니? (Are you having으로 쓸 수 없음)

단, 다음과 같이 **have**를 '(음식을) 먹다', '(행사 등을) 하다', '(시간을) 보내다'라는 의미로 말할 때는 현재진행 시제와 현재 시제를 둘 다 쓸 수 있다.

have salad/a hamburger 등 샐러드/햄버거 등을 먹다	have breakfast/lunch/dinner 아침/점심/저녁을 먹다
have a meeting/party 회의/파티를 하다	have a good time/nice day 좋은 시간/좋은 하루를 보내다

- Julie often **has salad** for lunch, but she**'s having a hamburger** today.
  Julie는 보통 점심에 샐러드를 먹지만, 오늘은 햄버거를 먹고 있다.
- "**Is** Mr. Walker **having a meeting**?" Walker 씨는 회의를 하고 있나요?
  "Yes. He **has a meeting** every Monday at 2 o'clock." 그는 매주 월요일 2시에 회의를 해요.
- I usually **have a good time** at parties. At this one, I**'m not having a good time**.

3 다음과 같이 감각을 나타내는 동사들도 주로 현재 시제로 쓴다.

look 보이다	**sound** 들리다	**taste** 맛이 나다	**smell** 냄새가 나다	**feel** 느껴지다

- Tim isn't wearing his glasses today. He **looks** different. 그는 달라 보인다.
- "Do you know this song?" "No. It **doesn't sound** familiar." 익숙하게 들리지 않아.
- These strawberries **taste** so fresh. Let's buy some.

단, '맛을 보다', '냄새를 맡다'라는 의미로 동작을 나타내기 위해 **taste, smell**을 쓸 때는 현재진행 시제로 쓸 수 있다.

- Charles **is tasting** the pasta. (파스타를 맛보고 있음)
- The children **are smelling** the flowers. (꽃 냄새를 맡고 있음)

look과 **feel**은 현재진행 시제로도 쓸 수 있다. 이때, 현재 시제로 썼을 때와 의미 차이가 거의 없다.

- You**'re looking** lovely tonight. 또는 You **look** lovely tonight. 오늘밤 사랑스러워 보여.
- "I**'m feeling** sick." 또는 "I **feel** sick." "Maybe you should go home early, then."

PRACTICE

A. 주어진 동사를 사용하여 현재 시제 또는 현재진행 시제 문장을 완성하세요. 필요한 경우 부정문으로 쓰세요.

agree	belong	go	have	have	lie	~~need~~	plant

1. Can I talk to you? I _____need_____ your advice.
2. I respect your opinion. However, I _____ with you.
3. Greg is in the garden with his dad. He _____ a tree with him.
4. "_____ Sarah _____ a car?" "No. She uses public transportation."
5. "Where _____ you _____ now?" "To the dentist. I have an appointment."
6. This pen _____ to me. Is it yours?
7. Jessica _____ on the beach right now. She's swimming.
8. My parents _____ dinner at a nice restaurant. Today is their wedding anniversary.

B. 괄호 안에 주어진 동사를 사용하여 현재 시제 또는 현재진행 시제 문장을 완성하세요. 필요한 경우 부정문으로 쓰세요.

1. (smell) "What are you doing?" "I _'m smelling_ this perfume. It has lovely scent."
2. (sound) My computer is making a strange noise. It _____ terrible.
3. (feel) "_____ you _____ nervous?" "Yes. I'm really worried about my speech."
4. (taste) This cherry pie looks tasty, but it _____ very good.
5. (smell) These socks seem dirty, but they _____ bad.
6. (taste) "Is the soup ready?" "Almost. The chef _____ it right now."

C. 다음 문장을 읽고 틀린 부분이 있으면 바르게 고치세요. 틀린 부분이 없으면 ○로 표시하세요.

1. Each box is containing 20 pieces of chocolate.   _is containing → contains_
2. The neighbors have a party. Can you hear the music? _____
3. The hotel room doesn't look clean. Let's ask for a different room. _____
4. Ms. Brown tastes some new wines right now. _____
5. "What's your favorite kind of movie?" "Well, I really like action films." _____
6. I'm not believing Jerry. He often tells lies. _____
7. Derek is a great golf player. He is possessing a lot of talent. _____
8. "Are you having a nice day?" "Yes. Thank you!" _____

D. 괄호 안에 주어진 동사를 현재 시제 또는 현재진행 시제로 사용하여 Chris와 Rachel의 대화를 완성하세요.

CHRIS: Hi, Rachel. 1. _Do_ you _remember_ me? (remember)
     We went to high school together.
RACHEL: Of course! Don't tell me . . . 2. I _____ your name! (know)
     You're Chris, right?
CHRIS: Yes. It's nice to see you again. 3. You _____ great! (look)
RACHEL: Thanks! You too!
     4. What _____ you _____ these days? (do)
CHRIS: 5. I _____ for a job. (search)
RACHEL: I see. How about getting some coffee together? Do you have time?
CHRIS: 6. Sure, that _____ great! (sound)

CHRIS

RACHEL

LESSON 5

I'm doing vs. I do 현재진행 시제와 현재 시제

1

She **is watching** TV now. 그녀는 지금 TV를 보고 있다.

She **studies** art. 그녀는 미술을 공부한다.

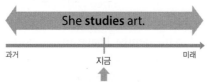

She **studies** art.

과거　　　　지금　　　　미래

She **is watching** TV now.

'TV를 보고 있다'라는 의미로 지금 일어나고 있는 일에 대해 말하기 위해 현재진행 시제 is watching을 쓴 반면, '미술을 공부한다'라는 의미로 일반적으로 사실인 일에 대해 말하기 위해 현재 시제 studies를 썼다.

2 현재진행 시제

말하고 있는 시점인 지금 하고 있는 행동이나 일어나고 있는 일에 대해 말할 때 현재진행 시제를 쓴다.

- Please be quiet. The babies **are sleeping**.
  (지금 아기들이 자고 있음)
- (전화상에서) Can I call you later? I**'m driving** right now.
  (지금 운전을 하고 있음)
- The wind **is blowing** hard tonight.
- "Is Professor Jones in her office?"
  "No. She**'s teaching** a class downstairs."

현재 시제

일반적으로 사실인 일이나 반복적으로 일어나는 일, 또는 변하지 않는 사실에 대해 말할 때 현재 시제를 쓴다.

- Babies **sleep** about 13 hours a day.
  (아기들은 일반적으로 하루에 약 13시간씩 잠)
- I **drive** an hour to my office every morning.
  (매일 아침 사무실까지 1시간씩 운전함)
- The wind **blows** hard during a thunderstorm.
- Professor Jones **teaches** politics at my university.
  Her lectures are a little boring.

3 일시적으로 일어나고 있는 일에 대해 말할 때는 현재진행 시제를 쓰고, 지속적으로 일어나는 일에 대해 말할 때는 현재 시제를 쓴다.

- I**'m living** in Paris at the moment. I really enjoy it. (지금 일시적으로 파리에서 거주하고 있음)
  I **live** in France. I'm French. (지속적으로 프랑스에서 거주함)
- Kathy **is working** as a volunteer at a hospital this summer.
  "What does Kathy do?"　"She **works** in a hospital. She's a doctor."

4 사람의 일시적인 행동에 대해 말할 때 be동사를 현재진행 시제(am/is/are + being)로 쓴다. 그러나 사람의 성격과 같은 지속적인 특징에 대해 말할 때는 be동사를 현재 시제(am/is/are)로 주로 쓴다.

- "Why **are** you **being** so kind today?"　"What do you mean? I'm always nice."
  (오늘 일시적으로 친절하게 행동하고 있음)

  Dorothy always helps other people. She**'s** very kind.
  (지속적으로 친절한 성격임)
- I usually clean my room every day, but I**'m being** lazy right now.
  My brother never cleans his room. He**'s** so lazy.

PRACTICE

A. 주어진 동사를 사용하여 현재진행 시제 또는 현재 시제 문장을 완성하세요.

bring	freeze	look	run	shop	sing	smoke	~~wait~~

1. "Can I help you with anything?" "I _'m waiting_ to see Dr. Bowman."
2. _____ you usually _____ your lunch to work?
3. "_____ Jenny _____ at the mall?" "Yes. She wants new curtains."
4. Kent _____ in a marathon every year.
5. Listen! Rosa and Cindy _____. They sound beautiful together.
6. "_____ Mr. Johnson _____ cigarettes?" "No. Not anymore."
7. Water _____ at zero degrees Celsius.
8. I'm really hungry. _____ you still _____ at the menu?

B. 괄호 안에 주어진 동사를 사용하여 현재진행 시제 또는 현재 시제 문장을 완성하세요.

1. John is still not home.	(come) Really? He usually _comes_ early.
2. When is your concert?	(practice) Next week. I _____ hard for it.
3. Is Ted your best friend?	(see) Yes. We _____ each other every day.
4. How is your business?	(grow) Good. It _____ a lot.
5. Where is your hotel room?	(stay) We _____ at the Plaza Hotel.
6. Is Carol a guitarist?	(play) No. She _____ the drums.

C. 적절한 be동사를 사용하여 문장을 완성하세요. 현재진행 시제 또는 현재 시제로 쓰세요.

1. Melissa doesn't like meeting new people because she _'s_ shy.
2. Our neighbors _____ very polite. They always say hello to us.
3. Patricia _____ silly at the moment. She's not usually so childish.
4. "What is Julie's boyfriend like?" "He _____ very intelligent."
5. Don't eat all the cake! You _____ really selfish right now.
6. "Walk slowly. The floor is very slippery." "I know. I _____ careful."

D. Amy와 Kate가 통화 중입니다. 주어진 동사를 현재진행 시제 또는 현재 시제로 사용하여 Amy와 Kate의 대화를 완성하세요.

be	~~do~~	meet	take	want	watch

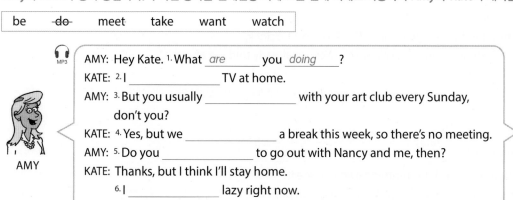

MP3

AMY: Hey Kate. ¹·What _are_ you _doing_ ?
KATE: ²·I _____ TV at home.
AMY: ³·But you usually _____ with your art club every Sunday, don't you?
KATE: ⁴·Yes, but we _____ a break this week, so there's no meeting.
AMY: ⁵·Do you _____ to go out with Nancy and me, then?
KATE: Thanks, but I think I'll stay home.
⁶·I _____ lazy right now.
AMY: All right.

AMY

KATE

LESSON

6 Her parents first **met** 30 years ago. 과거 시제

1

Her parents first met 30 years ago.
그녀의 부모님은 30년 전에 처음 만났다.

They had a wedding in Paris in 1989.
그들은 1989년에 파리에서 결혼식을 올렸다.

'30년 전에 처음 만났다', '1989년에 결혼식을 올렸다'라는 의미로 과거에 했던 일에 대해 말하기 위해 과거 시제 **met**과 **had**를 썼다.

2

'~했다'라는 의미로 과거에 했거나 일어났던 일에 대해 말할 때 과거 시제를 쓴다. 과거 시제는 **boiled**와 같이 주로 동사원형에 **(e)d**를 붙인다. 그러나 **began, bought**와 같이 불규칙적으로 변하는 동사들도 있다.

동사원형	boil	receive	end	begin	buy	eat
과거 시제	**boiled**	**received**	**ended**	**began**	**bought**	**ate**

동사의 형태 변화: 부록 p. 280 참고
불규칙 동사: 부록 p. 283 참고

- I **boiled** water to make tea. 차를 만들기 위해 물을 끓였다.
- "Christina **received** a letter from Jeff." Christina가 Jeff로부터 편지를 받았어. "Really? When?"
- World War I **began** in 1914 and **ended** in 1918.
- "Is that a new hat?" "Yes. I **bought** it a week ago."
- We **ate** at that Chinese restaurant last time. Let's try somewhere different.

3

과거 시제 부정문은 **did not + 동사원형**으로 쓴다.

I/we/you/they	**did not**	**see**
he/she/it	**(= didn't)**	**play**

- "I **didn't see** you at the meeting yesterday." 어제 회의에서 당신을 못 봤어요. "I had a lunch appointment."
- We **didn't play** golf last weekend because of the rain.
- Ten years ago, our town **didn't have** any tall buildings.

과거 시제 의문문은 **did + 주어 + 동사원형**으로 쓴다.

did	I/we/you/they	**get ... ?**
	he/she/it	**go ... ?**

- "**Did** you **get** my message?" 내 메시지 받았니? "Yes, I did."
- "When **did** the children **go** to sleep?" "Around 11 o'clock."
- "**Did** Matt **tell** you about his accident?" "Yes. He already told me about it."

4

am/is/are의 과거 시제는 **was/were**로 쓴다. **was/were**는 '~이었다, (~에) 있었다'라는 의미이다.

긍정 · 부정

I/he/she/it	**was**	**(not)**
we/you/they	**were**	

의문

was	I/he/she/it	**... ?**
were	we/you/they	

- The sky **was** beautiful this morning. Did you see it? 하늘이 아름다웠다.
- We **were** at the library with Tim. We had a group project. 우리는 Tim과 함께 도서관에 있었다.
- "**Was** the musical good?" "No, it **wasn't**."
- Where **were** you earlier? You **weren't** in your office.

PRACTICE

A. 그림을 보고 주어진 표현을 사용하여 지난 일요일에 Brad가 한 일에 대한 문장을 완성하세요.

| exercise at a gym | get a haircut | go to a restaurant | ~~have a sandwich~~ | watch a movie |

1. In the morning, Brad _had a sandwich_ for breakfast.
2. After that, he _____.
3. In the afternoon, he _____.
4. In the evening, he _____.
5. Later that night, he _____.

B. 주어진 동사를 사용하여 과거 시제 문장을 완성하세요. 필요한 경우 부정문으로 쓰세요.

| ~~be~~ | be | be | hear | join | swim | write |

1. "Did you talk to your parents?" "No. I called them, but they _weren't_ OR _were not_ home."
2. I _____ the book club two months ago. It's a lot of fun.
3. I don't think the doorbell rang. I _____ anything.
4. Sandra brought two friends to the party on Saturday. Their names _____ Bill and Helen.
5. Josh _____ at the beach last weekend. He said the water was too cold.
6. William Shakespeare _____ *Romeo and Juliet* in the late 16th century.
7. "I'm sorry about the delay." "It's OK. It _____ your fault."

C. 괄호 안에 주어진 단어들을 사용하여 대화를 완성하세요.

1. A: (we, have) _We had_ a family picnic yesterday.
   B: (it, be) _____ fun?

2. A: (you, be) _____ on time for your meeting?
   B: (I, arrive) No. _____ after it started.

3. A: (Roy, play) _____ tennis in college?
   B: (he, be) Yes. In fact, _____ the university champion in 2012.

4. A: (I, work) _____ late last night.
   B: (you, leave) Really? What time _____ the office?

D. 괄호 안에 주어진 동사를 사용하여 과거 시제 또는 현재 시제 문장을 완성하세요. 필요한 경우 부정문으로 쓰세요.

Love at the Eiffel Tower
By Amy Wilson

1. (grow up) My father was born in the US, but he _grew up_ in France.
2. (be) He _____ just a baby when his parents moved to Paris.
3. (meet, fall) Thirty years ago, he _____ my mother near the Eiffel Tower and _____ in love at first sight.
4. (give up) My mother didn't like him much at the time, but my father _____.
5. (get) Eventually, they became a couple, and they _____ married a year later.
6. (live, visit) Now they _____ in the US, but they _____ Paris every year.

과거와 과거진행

LESSON 6

Grammar Gateway Intermediate

1 Someone knocked on his door at 2 p.m. yesterday.

He **was reading** a book.
그는 책을 읽고 있었다.

'책을 읽고 있었다'라는 의미로 어제 오후 2시에 그가 하고 있었던 일에 대해 말하기 위해
과거진행 시제 was reading을 썼다.

어제 오후 2시

2 '~하고 있었다, ~하는 중이었다'라는 의미로 과거의 특정한 시점에 진행 중이었던 일에 대해 말할 때 과거진행 시제를 쓴다. 과거진행
시제는 **was/were** + **-ing**로 쓴다.

긍정 · 부정

I/he/she/it	was	(not)	talking
we/you/they	were		doing

의문

was	I/he/she/it	talking ... ?
were	we/you/they	doing ... ?

I **was talking** on the phone.

통화를 시작함   어제 저녁 6시   통화를 끝냄   지금

- At 6 o'clock last night, I **was talking** on the phone with my boyfriend.
  어제 저녁 6시에 남자친구와 통화를 하고 있었다.

- My roommate **wasn't doing** anything when I got home. He **was** just **lying** on the sofa.
  내가 집에 도착했을 때, 내 룸메이트는 아무것도 하고 있지 않았다. 그는 그냥 소파 위에 누워 있었다.

- "Who **were** you **waiting** for this morning?" "My friend Jack."

- Paula **was printing** something when the power went out.

3 과거 시제

어떤 일이 과거에 이미 끝났다는 의미로 말할 때 과거 시제를
쓴다.

- "What did you do last summer?"
  "I **traveled** around Europe."
  (지난 여름에 유럽 여행이 끝났음)

- Jerry and Cindy **had** pizza for lunch.
  (점심 때 피자를 먹는 것이 끝났음)

- Tim **rode** his bike to the park. He needed some
  fresh air.

- We **climbed** the mountain yesterday. Luckily, it
  didn't rain.

과거진행 시제

과거의 특정한 시점에 어떤 일이 끝나지 않고 진행 중이었다는
의미로 말할 때 과거진행 시제를 쓴다.

- "Where were you on New Year's Day?"
  "I **was traveling** in Europe."
  (새해 첫날에 유럽 여행을 하는 중이었음)

- I saw Jerry and Cindy at the restaurant.
  They **were having** pizza. (피자를 먹는 중이었음)

- Tim **was riding** his bike in the park at 8:30
  yesterday.

- We **were climbing** the mountain when the rain
  started.

단, **know, believe** 등과 같이 동작을 나타내지 않는 동사들은 과거진행 시제로 쓰지 않고 과거 시제로 주로 쓴다.

- I **knew** everyone at the party, so I felt comfortable. (과거진행 시제 I was knowing으로 쓸 수 없음)

- "**Did** you **believe** in ghosts when you were young?" "No, I didn't." (과거진행 시제 Were you believing으로 쓸 수 없음)

진행 시제로 쓰지 않는 동사에 대한 더 자세한 내용은 Lesson 4 참고

PRACTICE

A. 그림을 보고 괄호 안에 주어진 동사를 사용하여 과거진행 시제 문장을 완성하세요. 필요한 경우 부정문으로 쓰세요.

At 3:00 p.m. yesterday,

1. (work) Jason _wasn't working_ OR _was not working_ on the computer.
2. (attend) He _____ a meeting.
3. (hold) He _____ a pen.
4. (give) He _____ a presentation.

When Lucy arrived at the restaurant,

5. (sit) Mary and Eve _____ at a table.
6. (talk) Mary _____ to a waiter.
7. (look) Eve _____ at a menu.
8. (eat) They _____ anything.

B. 주어진 동사를 사용하여 과거진행 시제 문장을 완성하세요. 필요한 경우 부정문으로 쓰세요.

argue	carry	~~change~~	hide	pay	wear

1. Rick _was changing_ his clothes when his mom walked in his room. He was embarrassed.
2. The police officer gave us tickets because we _____ seatbelts.
3. Sorry , I _____ attention. What did you say?
4. I saw you in the lobby earlier. Why _____ you _____ a huge suitcase?
5. Perry _____ with the taxi driver. They both looked very upset.
6. Where did you find the cat? _____ it _____ under the sofa again?

C. 괄호 안에 주어진 표현들을 사용하여 과거진행 시제 또는 과거 시제 문장을 완성하세요.

1. A: (Mr. Kent, leave) _Did Mr. Kent leave_ the office?
   B: (he, meet) I don't think so. _____ with a client a minute ago.

2. A: (you, drive) _____ when I called?
   B: (I, go) Yes. _____ to the mall.

3. A: (you, not exercise) _____ at the gym when I got there at 8.
   B: (I, walk) Oh, _____ my dog.

4. A: (you, know) _____ Christy in college?
   B: (we, be) Yes. _____ classmates.

5. A: (you, turn) Why _____ off the TV?
   B: (you, watch) Oh, sorry. _____ it?

6. A: (you, show) _____ everyone the picture?
   B: (they, like) I did. _____ it.

D. 괄호 안에 주어진 동사와 과거진행 시제 또는 과거 시제를 사용하여 Paul과 Chris의 대화를 완성하세요. 필요한 경우 부정문으로 쓰세요.

PAUL: ¹·What _were_ you _doing_ yesterday at 2 p.m.? (do)
CHRIS: ²·I _____ a book in my room. Why? (read)
PAUL: ³·I _____ over to meet Amy and I _____ to say hi to you. (come, want) I knocked on your door but you didn't answer.
CHRIS: I'm sorry. ⁴·I _____ you. (hear)
⁵·I _____ to music. (listen)
PAUL: Oh. ⁶·I thought maybe you _____ . (sleep)

PAUL

CHRIS

LESSON 8 | **I did vs. I was doing** 과거 시제와 과거진행 시제

1 다음과 같이 과거 시제와 과거진행 시제를 함께 쓸 수 있다.

When she **was dancing**, he **entered** her room.

(그녀가 춤을 추는 도중에 그가 들어왔음)

'~하는 중이었다'라는 의미로 진행되고 있던 일에 대해 말할 때는 **was dancing**과 같이 과거진행 시제를 쓴다. 반면 '~했다'라는 의미로 도중에 일어난 일에 대해 말할 때는 **entered**와 같이 과거 시제를 쓴다.

- When we **met** Jenny in China, we **were traveling**.
  (중국을 여행하는 도중에 Jenny를 만났음)

- I **was driving**, so I **didn't answer** my phone.
  (운전하는 도중에 전화를 받지 않았음)

- Julie **was** still **working** in the office when somebody **turned** off the lights.

- Max **spilled** some of his coffee. He **was walking** too fast with it.

  과거 시제와 과거진행 시제를 함께 쓰는 경우, 진행되고 있던 일을 나타내는 과거진행 시제는 **while**과 자주 함께 쓴다.

  - **While** we **were going** home, the fireworks **began**.
    집으로 가는 도중에, 불꽃놀이가 시작되었다.

  - "How did you hurt your arm?" "I **fell while** I **was getting** off the bus."
    버스에서 내리던 도중에 넘어졌어.

  - **While** Ms. Johnson **was cleaning** her house, she **found** some old photos.

2 과거에 순서대로 일어난 두 가지 일에 대해 말할 때는 두 가지 일 모두 과거 시제로 쓴다.

When he **entered** her room, she **turned** off the music.

(그가 들어온 후에 그녀가 음악을 껐음)

- Last night we **wrapped** all the presents and **put** them under the Christmas tree.
  (선물을 포장한 후에 크리스마스트리 아래에 놓았음)

- When Andy and Robert **finished** dinner, they **went** to get ice cream.
  (저녁을 먹은 후에 아이스크림을 먹으러 갔음)

- After I **moved** to Chicago, I **got** a job as a news reporter.

- The crowd **cheered** when the singer **stepped** onto the stage.

P R A C T I C E

A. 그림을 보고 괄호 안에 주어진 동사들을 사용하여 과거 시제 또는 과거진행 시제 문장을 완성하세요.

1. (call, shave) Somebody _called_ while he _was shaving_ .
2. (jump, swim) He _____ in the water while she _____ .
3. (pay, leave) She _____ the bill and _____ the restaurant.
4. (lose, jog) He _____ his keys while he _____ .
5. (land, get) When the plane _____, the passengers _____ off.
6. (snow, go) It _____ when they _____ outside.

B. 괄호 안에 주어진 동사들을 사용하여 과거 시제 또는 과거진행 시제 문장을 완성하세요.

1. (invite) Last Friday, my wife Carla and I _invited_ our friends to dinner.
2. (get, cook) When I _____ home from work, Carla _____ in the kitchen. I decided to help her.
3. (prepare, put) While she _____ the salad, I _____ the chicken in the oven. Then, I fell asleep on the sofa.
4. (sleep, go) While I _____, Carla _____ out to buy drinks. When she returned, she was shocked.
5. (ring) The smoke alarm _____!
6. (have) The chicken was badly burned, so we _____ dinner at a restaurant nearby.

C. 괄호 안에 주어진 표현들을 적절히 배열하여 과거 시제 또는 과거진행 시제 문장을 완성하세요.

1. (Samantha / while / hike) _While Samantha was hiking_ in the woods, she saw a deer.
2. (give / I / my presentation / while) I made some errors _____.
3. (the rain / when / stop) The rainbow appeared _____.
4. (I / park / while) _____, I hit my neighbor's car.
5. (watch / we / while / TV) The deliveryman arrived _____.
6. (wake up / Maria / when)
   _____, she made some coffee and toast.
7. (when / shut down / his computer)
   Steve was writing a report _____.
8. (the glass / when / drop / the child) _____, it broke.

과거 → 지금

1 She drives a car now.

She used to take the bus every day.
(과거에는 매일 버스를 탔지만 지금은 아님)

'(과거에는) 매일 버스를 탔다 (지금은 아니다)'라는 의미로 말하기 위해
used to take를 썼다.

2 과거에는 자주 또는 습관적으로 하곤 했지만 지금은 더 이상 하지 않는 일에 대해 말할 때 **used to** + 동사원형을 쓴다.

I/we/you/they he/she/it	used to	study call

- I **used to study** German, but I don't study it anymore. (과거에는) 독일어를 공부했다. (지금은 아니다)
- Nora **used to call** me once a week. She doesn't call me often anymore.

  부정문은 **didn't use to** + 동사원형이나 **never used to** + 동사원형으로 쓴다.

  - I **didn't use to listen** to classical music. I started liking it only a few months ago.
    (과거에는) 클래식 음악을 듣지 않았다. (지금은 아니다)
  - My mother **never used to work** on weekends. Now she often works on Saturdays.

  의문문은 **did** + 주어 + **use to** + 동사원형으로 쓴다.

  - "**Did** you **use to eat** at Jimmy's Burgers in college?" (과거에는) Jimmy's Burgers에서 식사했니? "Yes! I miss that place."

3 과거에는 사실이었지만 지금은 더 이상 사실이 아닌 일에 대해 말할 때도 **used to** + 동사원형을 쓴다.

- This bookstore just moved here. It **used to be** on Carson Street. (과거에는) Carson가에 있었다. (지금은 아니다)
- Eddie and I **didn't use to like** each other. Lately, we've become good friends. (과거에는) 서로 좋아하지 않았다. (지금은 아니다)
- Wild lions **used to live** in Europe too. They are only in Africa and Asia nowadays.
- I bought this laptop recently. I **didn't use to have** one.

4 **used to**는 과거 시제, 현재 시제와 다음과 같은 의미 차이가 있다.

used to ● I **used to work** out at the gym every weekend. I'm too busy these days.
(과거에는 주말마다 체육관에서 운동했지만 지금은 아님)

과거 시제 ● I **worked** out at the gym on weekends last year.
(작년에는 주말마다 체육관에서 운동했음. 현재는 주말에 운동을 하는지 알 수 없음)

현재 시제 ● I **work** out at the gym every weekend.
(현재 주말마다 체육관에서 운동하고 있음)

5 **used to** + 동사원형과 **be used to** + **-ing**의 의미 차이에 주의한다. **be used to** + **-ing**는 '~하는 데 익숙하다'라는 의미이다.

- I **used to wake** up early, but these days I usually sleep until noon.
  (과거에는) 일찍 일어났지만, 요즘에는 보통 정오까지 잔다.

  I have class at 7 o'clock every morning, so I**'m used to waking** up early.
  매일 아침 7시에 수업이 있어서 일찍 일어나는 데 익숙하다.

- I **used to share** clothes with my sister when we were the same size.

  My sister and I **are used to sharing** clothes. We often wear each other's shirts and pants.

PRACTICE

A. 그림을 보고 **used to**를 사용하여 예시와 같이 문장을 완성하세요. 필요한 경우 부정문으로 쓰세요.

I live in London.
1·2
I never wear skirts.
10 years ago

I live in Beijing.
I enjoy wearing skirts.
now

I'm a college student.
3-4
I never grow a beard.
30 years ago

I'm a professor.
I love my beard.
now

1. She _used to live_ _____ in London. 3. He _____ a college student.
2. She _____ skirts. 4. He _____ a beard.

B. 주어진 동사와 **used to**를 사용하여 문장을 완성하세요. 필요한 경우 부정문으로 쓰세요.

bake	be	belong	check	drink	have	~~visit~~

1. I _used to visit_ _____ my parents every weekend. These days, I see them only once a month.
2. "_____ you _____ a lot of soda?" "Yes, I usually had five cans every day."
3. Mary _____ much free time. She was always so busy.
4. We _____ bread when we had an oven at home. It was so delicious.
5. Your dad is in a sailor's uniform in the photo. _____ he _____ a sailor?
6. I _____ my e-mail very often. I do it at least three times a day now.
7. This desk _____ to my grandfather. He gave it to me last year as a gift.

C. 괄호 안에 주어진 동사와 **used to** 또는 **be used to -ing**를 사용하여 문장을 완성하세요.

1. (fly) Alison travels a lot for her job, so she _'s used to flying_ _____ in airplanes.
2. (run) I _____ long distances because I often compete in marathons.
3. (be) Alaska _____ part of Russia. Then, the US bought it in 1867.
4. (take) I _____ care of children. I have two younger sisters.
5. (ski) When Jim and Ray lived in Switzerland, they _____ a lot.
   They don't ski much anymore.

D. 괄호 안에 주어진 동사와 **used to** 또는 현재 시제를 사용하여 Amy와 Kate의 대화를 완성하세요.

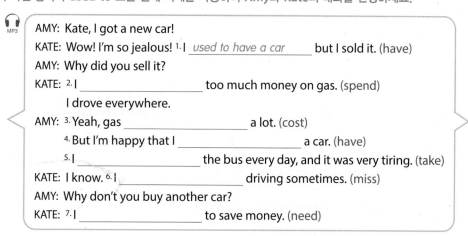

AMY: Kate, I got a new car!
KATE: Wow! I'm so jealous! 1. I _used to have a car_ but I sold it. (have)
AMY: Why did you sell it?
KATE: 2. I _____ too much money on gas. (spend)
   I drove everywhere.
AMY: 3. Yeah, gas _____ a lot. (cost)
   4. But I'm happy that I _____ a car. (have)
   5. I _____ the bus every day, and it was very tiring. (take)
KATE: I know. 6. I _____ driving sometimes. (miss)
AMY: Why don't you buy another car?
KATE: 7. I _____ to save money. (need)

AMY

KATE

과거와 과거진행

LESSON
9

Grammar Gateway Intermediate

It **has snowed** for three days. 현재완료 시제 (1) 계속

1   It started snowing two days ago. It's still snowing.

It has snowed for three days.
3일 동안 눈이 오고 있다.

'(계속) 눈이 오고 있다'라는 의미로 과거에 시작해서 지금까지 계속되는
일에 대해 말하기 위해 현재완료 시제 has snowed를 썼다.

그제   어제   지금

2   과거에 시작해서 지금까지 계속되는 일에 대해 말할 때 현재완료 시제 **have/has + 과거분사**를 쓴다. 이때, **for** 또는 **since**와 자주
함께 쓴다.

긍정 · 부정

I/we/you/they	have	(not)	lived
he/she/it	has		seen

의문

have	I/we/you/they	lived ... ?
has	he/she/it	seen ... ?

불규칙 동사: 부록 p. 283 참고
축약형: 부록 p. 286 참고

I have lived in this city for 15 years.

과거   지금
(이 도시에서 살기 시작함)   (지금도 살고 있음)

- I **have lived** in this city **for 15 years**. (15년 동안 계속 이 도시에 살아왔음)
- Jim is studying abroad. He **hasn't seen** his family **since last year**. (지난해부터 가족을 보지 못해왔음)
- "This tree is huge! How long **has** it **been** here?"   "For a century."

3   **for**와 **since**는 다음과 같은 차이가 있다.

for + 일이 지속된 기간 (four years, a few days 등)
: (지금까지) ~ 동안

- I**'ve owned** this camera **for four years**.
  (지금까지) 4년 동안 이 카메라를 소유해왔다.
- Luke **hasn't watched** TV **for a few days**. He's been
  busy with final exams.
- Cindy **has studied** cancer **for decades**.

since + 일이 시작된 시점 (2010, Tuesday 등)
: ~부터 (지금까지)

- I**'ve owned** this camera **since 2010**.
  2010년부터 (지금까지) 이 카메라를 소유해왔다.
- Mary is on vacation. She **hasn't attended** classes
  since Tuesday.
- Bob **has felt** sick **since lunchtime**.

4   **since** 다음에 **주어 + 동사**도 쓸 수 있다. 이때, 동사를 과거 시제로 쓰는 것에 주의한다.

- Robert **has wanted** to be a lawyer **since he was** a little boy.
  Robert는 어린 소년이었을 때부터 (지금까지) 변호사가 되길 원해왔다.
- **Since we had** our baby, we **haven't slept** very well. She cries a lot at night.
- I always take my bike to work. I**'ve ridden** it to the office every day **since I bought** it.

5   과거부터 지금까지 계속되는 일에 대해 말할 때 과거 시제를 쓰지 않는 것에 주의한다.

- Ken and I first met at a tennis club. I**'ve known** him for over seven years.
  (과거부터 지금까지 계속 그를 알고 있으므로 과거 시제 I knew로 쓸 수 없음)
- We don't have many customers these days. We **haven't been** busy since January.
  (과거부터 지금까지 계속 바쁘지 않으므로 과거 시제 We weren't로 쓸 수 없음)

PRACTICE

A. 주어진 동사를 사용하여 문장을 완성하세요. 필요한 경우 부정문으로 쓰세요.

check	have	make	~~play~~	visit	work

1. Mike _has played_ football for three hours. He's really tired now.
2. "_____ Ms. Ross _____ here for a long time?" "Yes. She's the manager now."
3. I _____ our hometown since 2007. I miss it.
4. Since our marriage, my husband and I _____ all of our decisions together.
5. Penny _____ her e-mail for a few months and now she's forgotten the password.
6. How long _____ you _____ this MP3 player? It looks quite old.

B. 그림을 보고 주어진 표현들과 for 또는 since를 사용하여 문장을 완성하세요. 필요한 경우 부정문으로 쓰세요.

~~be in Hawaii~~	brush my hair	come	do the laundry	drive that car	teach here

1. (five months) We _'ve OR have been in Hawaii for five months_.
2. (last week) I _____ _____.
3. (last semester) She _____ _____.
4. (a month) I _____ _____.
5. (30 minutes) The taxi _____ _____.
6. (1995) He _____ _____.

C. 괄호 안에 주어진 동사들을 사용하여 현재완료 시제 또는 과거 시제 문장을 완성하세요.

1. (open, become) Since the restaurant _opened_, it _____ very popular.
2. (not go) We _____ to the gym for weeks. We should go more often.
3. (be, be) Donna and I _____ best friends since I _____ eight.
4. (sell) Brian works at a furniture store. He _____ furniture for 12 years.
5. (not listen, break) I _____ to the radio since my brother _____ it on Friday.

D. 주어진 그래프를 보고 since를 함께 사용하여 예시와 같이 문장을 완성하세요.

1 like that artist	2 not smoke	3 meet many people	4 not speak
see the exhibit → now	get married → now	move to LA → now	have an argument → now

1. Erica _has liked that artist since she saw the exhibit_.
2. Mr. Evans _____.
3. We _____.
4. Kimberly and Lisa _____.

LESSON 11

She **has worked** at a library before. 현재완료 시제 (2) 경험

1 '~해본 적이 있다'라는 의미로 과거부터 지금까지의 경험에 대해 말할 때도 현재완료 시제를 쓴다.

과거

- She **has worked** at a library before. 그녀는 전에 도서관에서 일해본 적이 있다.
- "Excuse me. **Have** we **met**?" 우리가 만난 적이 있나요? "Yes, I think we have."
- Is the new mall nice? I **haven't visited** it yet.
- We **have eaten** sushi a few times. We didn't like it.

2 지금까지 살아오면서 어떤 일을 해본 경험에 대해 말할 때 현재완료 시제와 **ever** 또는 **never**를 자주 함께 쓴다.

ever는 '지금까지 (한 번이라도)'라는 의미로 어떤 일을 해본 경험이 있는지 물을 때 자주 쓴다.

- "**Have** you **ever read** *Romeo and Juliet*?" '로미오와 줄리엣'을 읽어본 적 있니? "Yes. Have you?"
- "Tina has lived alone for years." "**Has** she **ever wanted** a roommate?"
- "**Have** you **ever baked** muffins?" "No, I haven't."

never는 '~해본 적이 전혀 없다'라는 의미로 어떤 일을 해본 경험이 없다는 것을 강조해서 말할 때 쓴다.

- I**'ve never climbed** this mountain. It's beautiful. 나는 이 산을 올라본 적이 전혀 없다.
- Our children are excited about going to the zoo. They**'ve never seen** a panda.
- Jane **has never watched** an opera, but she has attended many musicals.

3 **have/has been (to)**는 '(~에) 가본 적이 있다'라는 의미로 말할 때 쓸 수 있다.

- "I want to go to Paris one day." "I**'ve been** there. It's amazing." 나는 거기에 가본 적이 있어.
- Tony **has been to** the new stadium. Let's ask him for directions.
- I **haven't been to** campus for a while because I'm taking a year off.

'(~에) 가본 적이 있다'라는 의미로 말할 때 **have/has gone (to)**를 쓰지 않는 것에 주의한다. **have/has gone (to)**는 '(~에) 가고 없다'라는 의미이다.

- Terry**'s gone to** Denmark. He's not here anymore. Terry는 덴마크에 가고 없다. (덴마크에 가본 적이 있다는 의미가 아님)
- "Is Betty in her office?" "She**'s gone**. She'll be back tomorrow."
- Luke and Barbara **have gone to** the park. They like to take walks there.

4 경험의 횟수를 말할 때 다음과 같은 표현을 현재완료 시제와 함께 쓸 수 있다.

once 한 번	**twice** 두 번	**three/four/…/many times** 세/네/…/여러 번

- I**'ve worn** a tuxedo **once**. It was at my sister's wedding. 턱시도를 입어본 적이 한 번 있다.
- Dan **has skied** only **twice**, but he's quite good at it.
- We**'ve made** this same mistake **many times**. Let's focus.

5 **the best ~ I've ever** …: 지금까지 내가 …해본 최고의 ~

- Thanks so much for the new watch. It's **the best present I've ever received**! 지금까지 내가 받아본 최고의 선물이야!
- **The best pizza I've ever tasted** was at Gusto Pizzeria.
- Rick, that's **the best story I've ever heard**. You should write a book about it!

P R A C T I C E

A. 주어진 동사를 사용하여 현재완료 시제 문장을 완성하세요. 필요한 경우 부정문으로 쓰세요.

give	listen	live	receive	~~ride~~	use

1. We _'ve ridden_____ on a camel once. It was a wonderful experience.
2. Kevin _____ in a foreign country, but he wants to try it one day.
3. "_____ you _____ to Alisha Rose's new song yet?" "No. Is it good?"
4. "Do you need some help with the photocopier?" "Yes. I _____ it before."
5. Eddie is the best runner at this school. He _____ many trophies.
6. "_____ Richard ever _____ you flowers?" "No, never."

B. 주어진 표현을 사용하여 자신의 경험에 대해 말해보세요. 필요한 경우 never를 함께 쓰세요.

1. study Chinese
2. break a bone
3. try scuba diving
4. make bread at home

1. _I've (never) studied Chinese_____.
2. _____.
3. _____.
4. _____. You

ever를 사용하여 Pam에게 위의 경험에 대해 질문해보세요.

5. _____ ?
6. _____ ?
7. _____ ?
You 8. _____ ?

No, I haven't.
Yes, twice.
No, have you?
Yes, but only once.

PAM

C. have been 또는 have gone을 적절한 형태로 써넣으세요.

1. I _'ve been_____ to the dentist twice this year.
2. "Where's Susan?" "She _____ out with her friends."
3. _____ we _____ to that restaurant? It looks familiar.
4. "_____ the children _____ to school?" "Yes. They left a few minutes ago."
5. Karen is interested in art. She _____ to many art exhibitions.

D. 괄호 안에 주어진 표현들과 현재완료 시제를 사용하여 Kate와 Amy의 대화를 완성하세요.

KATE

KATE: Vacation is almost here. Do you have any plans, Amy?
AMY: Not yet. 1. But I want to do something _I've never done_____ . (I, never, do)
KATE: 2. _____ any volunteer work? (you, ever, do)
AMY: 3. _____ at a library before. (I, volunteer)
　　How about you?
KATE: 4. _____ to help children. (I, be, to Africa once)
　　5. It was the best experience _____ . (I, ever, have)
　　Why don't you try it?
AMY: 6. _____ about going to Africa. (I, never, think)
　　But maybe I should consider it. Thanks!

AMY

현재완료와 과거완료

LESSON
11

Grammar Gateway Intermediate

LESSON 12

I have done vs. I did 현재완료 시제와 과거 시제

1 현재완료 시제는 과거에 일어난 일을 현재의 사실과 관련지어 말할 때 쓴다.

- The train **has arrived** at the station.
  (기차가 도착해서 지금 역에 있음)
- We **have moved** the bookshelf upstairs.
  (책장을 옮겨서 지금 위층에 있음)
- I **have deleted** the file from my computer.

과거 시제는 과거에 끝난 일이나 상황 자체에 대해서만 말할 때 쓴다.

- The train **arrived** at the station two minutes ago.
  (2분 전에 기차가 도착했음)
- We **moved** the bookshelf upstairs yesterday.
  (어제 책장을 위층으로 옮겼음)
- I **deleted** the file after I printed it.

2 다음과 같은 경우에는 현재완료 시제 또는 과거 시제만 쓰는 것에 주의한다.

현재까지 계속되는 과거의 일에 대해 말할 때는 현재완료 시제만 쓴다.

- Anna **has used** the same cell phone for six years. It's so old.
  (지금도 계속 같은 휴대전화를 사용하고 있으므로 과거 시제 Anna used로 쓸 수 없음)
- My wife and I are vegetarians. We **haven't eaten** meat since 2003.
  (2003년부터 지금까지 계속 고기를 먹지 않고 있으므로 과거 시제 We didn't eat으로 쓸 수 없음)

현재와 관련이 없거나 지금은 계속되지 않는 과거의 일에 대해 말할 때는 과거 시제만 쓴다.

- I don't have a pet now, but I **raised** a cat when I was young.
  (어렸을 때 고양이를 키웠다는 과거의 사실은 현재와 관련이 없으므로 현재완료 시제 I have raised로 쓸 수 없음)
- Mr. Parker **was** one of my employees a year ago. Now he owns a business.
  (지금은 Parker 씨가 직원이 아니므로 현재완료 시제 Mr. Parker has been으로 쓸 수 없음)

3 이미 지나가 버린 과거 시간을 나타내는 다음과 같은 표현들은 현재완료 시제와는 함께 쓸 수 없고 과거 시제와 함께 쓰는 것에 주의한다.

yesterday	last night/week/month
~ ago (five minutes ago 등)	in + 과거시점 (in 1492, in the 17th century 등)

- **Did** you **check** the mail **yesterday**? (Have you checked the mail yesterday로 쓸 수 없음)
- I'm tired because I **didn't sleep** well **last night**. (I haven't slept well last night으로 쓸 수 없음)
- We're late. The movie **began five minutes ago**.
- Columbus **discovered** America **in 1492**.

today, this morning/week/month 등이 나타내는 시점이 아직 끝나지 않은 경우에는 현재완료 시제와 함께 쓸 수 있다.

- "**Have** you **checked** the mail **today**?" "Not yet." (아직 오늘이 끝나지 않았음)
- I'm so upset. My car **has broken** down twice **this week**. (아직 이번 주가 끝나지 않았음)

4 just (방금, 막), already (이미, 벌써), yet (아직)은 현재완료 시제와 과거 시제 모두와 함께 쓸 수 있다. 이때, 의미 차이가 거의 없다.

- Our team **has just won** the game! 또는 Our team **just won** the game! 우리 팀이 방금 경기에서 이겼어!
- Steve **has already opened** his birthday presents. 또는 Steve **already opened** his birthday presents.
- **Have** you **met** your new boss **yet**? 또는 **Did** you **meet** your new boss **yet**?

yet은 부정문과 의문문에 주로 쓴다.

- I **haven't made** my vacation plans **yet**. 또는 I **didn't make** my vacation plans **yet**.
  아직 휴가 계획을 세우지 않았어.
- **Have** you **finished** cleaning your room **yet**? 또는 **Did** you **finish** cleaning your room **yet**?

P R A C T I C E

A. 주어진 동사를 사용하여 현재완료 시제 또는 과거 시제 문장을 완성하세요.

go	lose	paint	play	~~publish~~	visit	wake	want

1. Ben and Frank _have published_ a magazine for 12 years. It's very popular.
2. Josh looks thinner. _____ he _____ weight since we last saw him?
3. The storm last night was so loud. I _____ up in the middle of the night.
4. We _____ Vietnam when we were traveling in Asia.
5. "_____ Monet _____ *Sunflowers*?" "No. The artist was Van Gogh."
6. Sharon _____ that hat since she saw it in the store.
7. "Sara and Tim are our guitarists." "How long _____ they _____ in your band?"
8. "Why _____ you _____ home early yesterday?" "My son was sick."

B. 괄호 안에 주어진 표현들을 사용하여 결혼을 앞두고 있는 Jane과 친구 Sue의 대화를 완성하세요. 과거 시제 또는 현재완료 시제로 쓰세요.

SUE: Hi Jane! 1. _I received_ your wedding invitation yesterday. (I, receive)
2. _____?
(you, choose a wedding dress, yet)
JANE: 3. Yes. _____ a beautiful one two days ago. (I, buy)
SUE: That's great! How about the honeymoon?
4. _____ to go?
(you, already, find a place)
JANE: Yes. 5. _____.
(we, just, make reservations)
SUE: I'm so happy for you. I can't wait to see you in your dress!

C. 다음 문장을 읽고 틀린 부분이 있으면 바르게 고치세요. 틀린 부분이 없으면 ○로 표시하세요.

1. Mr. Jenkins has started taking guitar lessons last month. _has started → started_
2. I exercised at that gym for a week now. I like it a lot. _____
3. "Is dinner ready?" "No. We haven't cooked it yet." _____
4. "Patrick didn't smoke a cigarette since January." "Good for him!" _____
5. "Did you already wash the dishes?" "Yes. There weren't very many." _____
6. "Have you gone to the concert yesterday?" "No. I had to work." _____

D. 괄호 안에 주어진 표현과 현재완료 시제 또는 과거 시제를 사용하여 Chris와 Justin의 대화를 완성하세요.

CHRIS: 1. I _called_ you earlier, but you didn't answer. (call)
2. Where _____ you? (be)
JUSTIN: I was at work. I got a job at a fast-food restaurant.
CHRIS: Really? 3. How long _____ you _____ there? (work)
JUSTIN: 4. I _____ yesterday. (start) Please don't tell Mom, though.
5. I _____ her yet. (not tell)
CHRIS: Why?
JUSTIN: I want to surprise her with a gift when I get my first pay.

CHRIS

JUSTIN

현재완료와 과거완료

LESSON
12

Grammar Gateway Intermediate

1 She arrived an hour ago.

She **has been waiting** for an hour.

그녀는 한 시간 동안 기다려오고 있다.

'(한 시간 전부터 지금까지) 기다려오고 있다'라는 의미로 한 시간 전에 시작해서 지금도 진행 중인 일에 대해 말하기 위해 현재완료진행 시제 **has been waiting**을 썼다.

한 시간 전 　　　 지금

2 과거에 시작해서 지금도 진행 중인 일에 대해 말할 때 현재완료진행 시제 **have/has been + -ing**를 쓴다. 현재완료진행 시제는 '(과거부터 지금까지) ~해오고 있다'라는 의미이다.

긍정 · 부정

I/we/you/they	have			talking
he/she/it	has	(not)	been	saving

의문

have	I/we/you/they		talking ... ?
has	he/she/it	been	saving .... ?

동사의 형태 변화: 부록 p. 280 참고

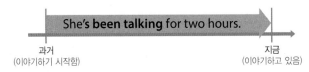

She's **been talking** for two hours.

과거　　　　　　　　　　　　　　　　　　지금
(이야기하기 시작함)　　　　　　　　　　　(이야기하고 있음)

- Nancy is still on the phone. She**'s been talking** for two hours. (2시간 전부터 지금까지) 이야기해오고 있다.
- We **have been saving** a lot of money since last year. We want to buy a new house.
  (작년부터 지금까지) 저축해오고 있다.
- I **haven't been working** for the past few days. I caught a bad cold.
- "What **has** Kevin **been doing** lately?" "I don't know. I haven't seen him for six months."

3 어떤 일을 얼마나 오랫동안 지속해오고 있는지 나타내기 위해 현재완료진행 시제와 **for, since, how long** 등을 자주 함께 쓴다.

- Let's go to the mall. I **haven't been shopping for four weeks**. (4주 전부터 지금까지) 쇼핑을 하지 않았어.
- My neighbor's dog **has been barking since 6 a.m.** It's so annoying!
- "**How long have** you **been attending** the art school?" "For about three years."

4 과거에 시작해서 진행되어 오다가 방금 전에 끝난 일에 대해 말할 때도 현재완료진행 시제를 쓸 수 있다. 이때, 현재완료진행 시제는 방금 전에 끝난 일이 지금까지도 영향을 미치고 있음을 의미한다.

- "Your eyes are red. **Have** you **been crying**?" "Yes. I failed my exam again." (방금 전까지 울어서 지금 눈이 빨개져 있음)
- The children **have been playing** in the mud. Their shoes are dirty. (방금 전까지 진흙에서 놀아서 신발이 더러움)
- "Why is Scott upset?" "He **has been arguing** with his roommate."
- "You're sweating." "I**'ve been exercising**."

5 **know, believe** 등과 같이 동작을 나타내지 않는 동사들은 현재완료진행 시제로 쓰지 않고 현재완료 시제로 주로 쓴다.

- Patricia and I **have known** each other since high school. (현재완료진행 시제 Patricia and I have been knowing으로 쓸 수 없음)
- My mother **has** always **believed** in me. She always supports my decisions.
  (현재완료진행 시제 My mother has always been believing으로 쓸 수 없음)

진행 시제로 쓸 수 없는 동사에 대한 자세한 내용은 Lesson 4 참고

PRACTICE

A. 그림을 보고 주어진 표현을 사용하여 현재완료진행 시제 문장을 완성하세요.

| clean the windows | listen to | paint a picture | run | sit | ~~speak~~ |

1-3

10 minutes ago → now

4-6

one hour ago → now

1. A woman _has been speaking_ at a meeting.
2. Three people _____ a presentation.
3. A man _____.
4. A man _____.
5. A woman _____ on a blanket.
6. Two people _____.

B. 주어진 문장을 보고 현재완료진행 시제와 **for** 또는 **since**를 사용하여 예시와 같이 다시 말해보세요.

1. Nate is camping by the river. He went there on Friday.
   → _He's been camping by the river since Friday_ OR _He has been camping by the river since Friday_.

2. Eve is cooking dinner. She began cooking at 5 o'clock.
   → _____.

3. The workers are building a bridge. The project began six months ago.
   → _____.

4. Tina and Kim are playing tennis. They started at noon.
   → _____.

5. Jack is using his laptop. He turned it on an hour ago.
   → _____.

C. 그림을 보고 주어진 동사를 사용하여 현재완료진행 시제 문장을 완성하세요.

| climb | ~~eat~~ | pack | sleep | swim |

1. She _'s been eating_ OR _has been eating_.
2. They _____.
3. He _____.
4. She _____.
5. They _____.

D. 괄호 안에 주어진 표현들을 사용하여 예시와 같이 의문문을 완성하세요.

1. (Liz and Ron, date) _Have Liz and Ron been dating_ for a long time?
2. (how long, you, watch) _____ TV?
3. (where, John, stay) _____ this week?
4. (you, enjoy) _____ the book club?
5. (how long, Lucy, plan) _____ her trip?

Yes. For several years.
About two hours.
At his friend's house.
Yes. I love it.
For a month.

1

He started fixing his computer at 2 p.m. It is now 4 p.m.

He **has fixed** his computer.
It works now. 컴퓨터를 고쳤다. (지금은 잘 작동한다)

He **has been fixing** his computer for two hours.
He is tired. (2시간 전부터 지금까지) 컴퓨터를 고쳐오고 있다.

과거에 컴퓨터를 고치기 시작해서 지금은 컴퓨터가 고쳐졌다는 것을 강조하기 위해 현재완료 시제 **has fixed**를 쓴 반면,
두 시간 전에 시작해서 지금까지 고쳐왔다는 것을 강조하기 위해 현재완료진행 시제 **has been fixing**을 썼다.

2

현재완료 시제

현재완료 시제는 과거에 시작해서 지금은 끝난 일의 결과를 강조할 때 쓴다.

- Finally I**'ve done** my homework. Now I can help you with the laundry.
  (과거에 숙제를 시작해서 지금은 숙제가 끝났다는 결과를 강조함)
- Elizabeth **has made** some delicious tomato soup. Would you like to try some?
  (과거에 수프를 만들기 시작해서 지금은 수프가 완성되었다는 결과를 강조함)
- The workers **have completed** the construction. We can use that road now.

현재완료진행 시제

현재완료진행 시제는 어떤 일을 과거에 시작해서 지금까지 진행해왔다는 것을 강조할 때 쓴다.

- I**'ve been doing** my homework since 3 o'clock. I need a break.
  (3시부터 지금까지 숙제를 해왔다는 것을 강조함)
- Maria **has been cleaning** the house all morning and she's still not finished.
  (아침 내내 청소를 해왔다는 것을 강조함)
- "Why are you and Jane laughing?"
  "Oh. We**'ve been watching** a comedy show."

3

live, study, work 등과 같은 동사들은 현재완료 시제로 썼을 때와 현재완료진행 시제로 썼을 때 의미 차이가 없다.

- I **have lived** in this house for a long time. 또는 I **have been living** in this house for a long time.
  이 집에서 오랫동안 살아왔다.
- **Have** you **studied** Russian for many years? 또는 **Have** you **been studying** Russian for many years?

4

과거부터 지금까지 어떤 일을 얼마나 많이 또는 몇 번 했는지를 말할 때는 현재완료 시제를 쓴다. 이때, 현재완료진행 시제를 쓰지 않는 것에 주의한다.

- "Do you want some more wine?" "No. I**'ve had three glasses** already."
  이미 세 잔 마셨어. (I've been having three glasses로 쓸 수 없음)
- "**How many times has** Peter **run** a marathon?" "Just twice so far."
  Peter는 마라톤을 몇 번 뛰었니? (How many times has Peter been running으로 쓸 수 없음)

어떤 일을 지금까지 얼마나 오래 했는지를 말할 때는 현재완료 시제와 현재완료진행 시제를 모두 쓸 수 있다. 이때, 현재완료진행 시제를 더 자주 쓴다.

- I**'ve taken** this medicine **for several days**. 또는 I**'ve been taking** this medicine **for several days**.
  (지금까지) 이 약을 며칠간 먹어왔다.
- **How long has** Gina **practiced** ballet? 또는 **How long has** Gina **been practicing** ballet?

P R A C T I C E

A. 그림을 보고 주어진 표현을 사용하여 예시와 같이 현재완료 시제 문장을 완성하세요.

| bake eight muffins | drive 90 miles | have three cups of coffee |
| ~~miss five calls~~ | pick a basket of oranges | |

1. She *'s missed five calls* _____.
2. He _____ so far.
3. They _____.
4. He _____.
5. She _____.

B. Judy가 하는 말을 보고 for 또는 since를 함께 사용하여 예시와 같이 현재완료진행 시제 문장을 완성하세요.

JUDY

1. I'm working now. I began at 9 a.m.
2. I keep a diary. I started it when I was 10.
3. My dogs are sleeping. They fell asleep an hour ago.
4. I wear glasses. I got them five years ago.
5. My parents are renovating the house. They started in May.

1. She *'s been working since 9 a.m.* _____.
2. She _____.
3. Her dogs _____.
4. She _____.
5. Her parents _____.

C. 괄호 안에 주어진 표현들을 사용하여 현재완료 시제 또는 현재완료진행 시제 문장을 완성하세요.

1. (we, live) My husband and I love our house. *We've lived* OR *We've been living* _____ in it since we got married.
2. (I, call, her) Can you call Julie? _____ twice already but she didn't answer.
3. (I, read, this book) _____ three times. It's really good.
4. (it, sell) That shoe store is old. _____ shoes in this town for many years.
5. (Sandra, spend) Tom is moving soon, so _____ a lot of time with him recently.
6. (Sue, visit) _____ the museum five times. She's interested in history.
7. (Ken and Mark, not work) _____ at our company long, so they still have much to learn.
8. (they, have) This isn't Jill and Ian's first date. _____ dinner a few times before.
9. (you, go out for drinks) "How many times _____ this week?"
   "Only once."
10. (you, design, clothes) "How long _____?"
    "I started when I was in college."

1 When he got to the bus stop, the bus **had** already **left.**
그가 버스 정류장에 도착했을 때, 버스가 이미 떠났다.

과거에 버스 정류장에 도착했던 것을 기준으로 그 전에 버스가 떠났다는 것을 말하기 위해
과거완료 시제 had left를 썼다.

2 과거에 일어난 어떤 일을 기준으로 그 전에 일어난 일에 대해 말할 때 과거완료 시제 **had + 과거분사**를 쓴다.

긍정·부정

| I/we/you/they | had | (not) | ended |
| he/she/it | | | fixed |

불규칙 동사: 부록 p. 283 참고
축약형: 부록 p. 286 참고

The show **had ended.**

과거 기준시점
(TV를 켰음)

지금

- When we turned on the TV, the show **had** already **ended.**
  (과거에 TV를 켠 것을 기준으로 그 전에 쇼가 끝났음)
- The mechanics still **hadn't fixed** my car when I returned to the repair shop.
  (수리점에 돌아간 것을 기준으로 그 전에 차를 고치지 않았음)
- Jack found his hat, but he **had** already **bought** a new one.
- My parents went to India last year. They **hadn't been** there before.
- According to the news, the thief **had robbed** six banks when the police finally caught him.

3 과거에 일어난 어떤 일을 기준으로 그 전에 일어난 일에 대해 말할 때는 과거완료 시제를 쓴다. 그러나 과거의 기준 시점 이후에 일어난 일에 대해 말할 때는 과거 시제를 쓴다.

The rain **had stopped.**   I **saw** a rainbow.

과거 기준시점
(밖에 나갔음)

지금

- When I **went** outside, I noticed that the rain **had** already **stopped.** (밖에 나가기 전에 비가 그쳤음)
  When I **went** outside, I **saw** a rainbow. (밖에 나간 후에 무지개를 보았음)
- We **had** already **been** married for a year when we **graduated** from college.
  We **graduated** from college and then we **got** jobs.

4 before, after 등을 쓰면 과거완료 시제를 쓰지 않아도 어떤 일이 먼저 일어났는지가 명확해진다. 따라서 이 경우에는 과거완료 시제 대신 과거 시제를 쓸 수 있다.

- I **had called** Dave **before** I went to his house.
  또는 I **called** Dave **before** I went to his house. (Dave의 집에 가기 전에 그에게 전화했음)
- **After** the guests **had finished** their steak, the waiters served dessert.
  또는 **After** the guests **finished** their steak, the waiters served dessert. (손님들이 식사한 후에 웨이터가 디저트를 내왔음)

PRACTICE

A. 그림을 보고 주어진 표현을 사용하여 과거완료 시제 문장을 완성하세요.

break the lamp	~~deliver a package~~	eat all the cookies	go to bed	leave a note

When Stacy got home yesterday,

1. Someone *had delivered a package*   .
2. Her dog   .
3. Her parents   .
4. Her mom   .
5. Her brother   .

B. 괄호 안에 주어진 동사를 사용하여 과거완료 시제 문장을 완성하세요. 필요한 경우 부정문으로 쓰세요.

1. (melt) I wanted to go skiing last month, but the snow *had melted*   .
2. (see) Carol realized that she _____ her cousin for three years. She decided to call him.
3. (order) When I arrived, everybody _____ and some people were already eating.
4. (expect) The actor was surprised about the award. He _____ to win it.
5. (open) The bank _____ when I got there, so I had to wait.
6. (practice) We _____ enough for the match. We didn't need to be worried.

C. 주어진 동사를 사용하여 과거완료 시제 또는 과거 시제 문장을 완성하세요.

answer	~~buy~~	go	reach	save	watch

1. I needed a new dress, so I *bought*   one.
2. Paula _____ only half of her exam questions when the bell rang.
3. Scott's computer stopped working suddenly, but luckily he _____ his files already.
4. I met Karen and we _____ a scary movie.
5. When we _____ the beach, the sun had already gone down.
6. "Was Ben at the party when you got there?" "No. He _____ home."

D. 괄호 안에 주어진 동사를 사용하여 선생님과 Justin의 대화를 완성하세요. 과거완료 시제 또는 과거 시제로 쓰세요.

Teacher

JUSTIN

Teacher: Why are you late, Justin?

JUSTIN: I'm sorry. 1. I *woke*   up late this morning. (wake)
2. When I _____ at the bus stop, the bus
_____. (arrive, already leave)
I thought my brother could drive me.
3. But when I _____ back home, he
_____ to work. (get, already go)

Teacher: 4. Why _____ you _____ up so late? (get)

JUSTIN: I didn't sleep much last night.
5. I _____ coffee before I went to bed. (drink)

Teacher: I see. Well, please be more careful next time.

1

She **will become** a famous painter one day.
그녀는 언젠가 유명한 화가가 될 것이다.

She **will take** art classes in Italy.
그녀는 이탈리아에서 미술 수업을 들을 것이다.

'유명한 화가가 될 것이다'라는 의미로 미래에 일어날 일을 예측하기 위해 **will** become을 썼고, '미술 수업을 들을 것이다'라는 의미로 미래에 하겠다고 결정한 일을 말하기 위해 **will** take를 썼다.

2   '~할 것이다'라는 의미로 미래에 어떤 일이 일어날 것이라고 예측할 때 **will + 동사원형**을 쓴다.

긍정 · 부정

I/we/you/they	**will** (= **'ll**)	have
he/she/it	**will not** (= **won't**)	see

의문

will	I/we/you/they	have ... ?
	he/she/it	see ... ?

축약형: 부록 p. 286 참고

- I'm excited about camping this weekend. We**'ll have** so much fun. 우리는 즐거운 시간을 보낼 것이다.
- Julie is moving abroad. I **won't see** her very often now. 이제 그녀를 자주 보지 못할 것이다.
- "**Will** the new city hall **be** open next weekend?" "I don't think so."
- Tom **will love** this chocolate cake. He really likes chocolate.

3   미래에 어떤 일을 하겠다고 결정할 때도 **will**을 쓴다.

- "You need to return these DVDs." "OK. I**'ll return** them today." 오늘 반납할게.
- This milk smells bad. I **won't drink** it.
- (전화상에서) "I miss you and Tom." "We miss you too. We**'ll visit** you soon."

상대방에게 어떤 일을 해주겠다고 제안하거나 약속할 때도 **will**을 쓸 수 있다.

- "I need to get to the train station." "I**'ll give** you a ride." 내가 태워줄게.
- I **won't forget** your birthday again. I'm so sorry.
- "Can someone set the table, please?" "I**'ll do** it."

4   **will**은 다음과 같은 표현과 자주 함께 쓴다.

I think / I don't think ~ will … (안) 할 것 같다
I guess ~ will …할 것 같다
I'm sure ~ will 분명 …할 것이다
I'm afraid ~ will (유감이지만) …할 것 같다

- **I think** you**'ll** enjoy that book. It's great. 네가 그 책을 좋아할 것 같아.
- **I guess** I **won't** find my lost wallet. 잃어버린 지갑을 찾지 못할 것 같아.
- "I can't go to Mike's graduation." "**I'm sure** he**'ll** understand."
- **I'm afraid** I **won't** be on time for the meeting.

I think 뒤에는 **won't**를 잘 쓰지 않는다. **I don't think ~ will**을 주로 쓴다.

- "Can Emily help us with our homework?" "**I don't think** she**'ll** have time." 그녀는 시간이 없을 것 같아.
- **I don't think** we**'ll** stay at that hotel again. It wasn't very nice.

PRACTICE

A. 주어진 동사와 will을 사용하여 문장을 완성하세요. 필요한 경우 부정문으로 쓰세요.

arrive	be	buy	call	have	help	hurt	~~lend~~

1. "My laptop isn't working, but I need to write a report." "I _ˈll lend_ OR _will lend_ you mine."
2. I'm sure Jack _____ you soon. Stop looking at your phone.
3. I want to wear my new miniskirt. _____ the weather _____ warm tomorrow?
4. "Mom, I don't want to go to the dentist." "Don't worry. It _____ much."
5. "May I take your order?" "Yes. I want the shrimp and my wife _____ the fish."
6. When _____ the pizza _____? I ordered it an hour ago.
7. "I can't open this jar." "Let me see it. I _____ you."
8. The clock seems cheaper at that store across the street. I _____ it here.

B. 그림을 보고 주어진 동사와 will을 사용하여 대화를 완성하세요. 필요한 경우 부정문으로 쓰세요.

~~cook~~	eat	explain	play

1. I _ˈll cook_ OR _will cook_ something for you.
2. We _____ too long. Don't worry.
3. All right. I _____ it.
4. I _____ it to you.

C. 주어진 표현과 I think ~ will 또는 I don't think ~ will을 사용하여 예시와 같이 자신에 대해 말해보세요.

1. wake up early tomorrow
2. get a haircut next week
3. see a movie next weekend
4. travel abroad next year
5. go to the beach next summer

1. _I (don't) think I'll wake up early tomorrow_ .
2. _____ .
3. _____ .
4. _____ .
5. _____ .

You

D. 괄호 안에 주어진 표현들과 will을 사용하여 교수님과 Kate의 대화를 완성하세요. 필요한 경우 부정문으로 쓰세요.

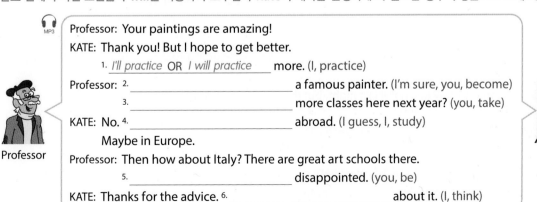

Professor: Your paintings are amazing!
KATE: Thank you! But I hope to get better.
1. _I'll practice_ OR _I will practice_ more. (I, practice)
Professor: 2. _____ a famous painter. (I'm sure, you, become)
3. _____ more classes here next year? (you, take)
KATE: No. 4. _____ abroad. (I guess, I, study)
Maybe in Europe.
Professor: Then how about Italy? There are great art schools there.
5. _____ disappointed. (you, be)
KATE: Thanks for the advice. 6. _____ about it. (I, think)

미래, 미래진행과 미래완료

LESSON **16**

Grammar Gateway Intermediate

I'm going to look beautiful in this dress. am/is/are going to

1 '~할 것이다'라는 의미로 미래에 어떤 일이 일어날 것이라고 예측할 때 **am/is/are going to** + 동사원형을 쓸 수 있다.

긍정 · 부정

I	am			look
he/she/it	is	(not)	going to	let
we/you/they	are			stop

의문

am	I		look ... ?
is	he/she/it	going to	let ... ?
are	we/you/they		stop ... ?

- **I'm going to look** beautiful in this dress. It's lovely! 이 드레스를 입으면 아름다워 보일 거야.
- "My parents **aren't going to let** me travel abroad alone." "They might. You should ask them."
- "**Is** it **going to stop** raining soon?" "Maybe."

미래에 일어날 일을 예측할 때 **will** + 동사원형도 쓸 수 있다.

- Jeff **won't come** for dinner this evening. Jeff는 저녁을 먹으러 오지 않을 거야. (= Jeff is not going to come.)

단, 현재의 상황을 근거로 하여 미래에 일어날 일을 예측할 때는 **will**을 쓰지 않고 **am/is/are going to**를 쓰는 것에 주의한다.

He's going to cry.

- The baby **is going to cry**.
  (현재 아기의 표정을 근거로 울 것이라고 예측하고 있으므로 The baby will cry로 쓸 수 없음)
- The traffic is really bad. I'm **going to be** late for work.
  (현재 교통체증이 심한 것을 근거로 직장에 지각할 것이라고 예측하고 있으므로 I will be로 쓸 수 없음)

2 어떤 일을 하겠다고 결정한 것에 대해 말할 때 **am/is/are going to**를 쓸 수 있다. 단, **will**과는 다음과 같은 차이가 있다.

말하고 있는 시점 이전에 이미 결정해둔 일에 대해 말할 때는 **am/is/are going to**를 주로 쓴다.

친구들을 만나기로 결정함
과거 　 지금 　 미래
(말하는 시점)

- "Do you have plans tonight?"
  "Yes. **I'm going to meet** some friends at a party."
  (말하고 있는 시점 이전에 이미 만나기로 결정했음)
- Brandon **is going to buy** a bike. He has saved $200 already.
  (말하고 있는 시점 이전에 이미 사기로 결정했음)

말하고 있는 시점인 지금 결정한 일에 대해 말할 때는 **will**을 주로 쓴다.

친구들을 만나기로 결정함
과거 　 지금 　 미래
(말하는 시점)

- "Do you want to go to the party with us tonight?"
  "Sure. **I'll meet** you there after work."
  (말하고 있는 시점인 지금 만나기로 결정함)
- "This bike costs only $250."
  "Really? **I'll buy** it, then."
  (말하고 있는 시점인 지금 사기로 결정함)

3 **am/is/are going to**의 과거는 **was/were going to**로 쓴다. **was/were going to**는 하려고 결정은 했지만 실제로는 하지 않은 일에 대해 말할 때 자주 쓴다.

- Bob **was going to stay** at a hotel last night, but there were no rooms available.
  Bob은 어젯밤 호텔에서 지내려 했지만, 이용 가능한 방이 없었다. (실제로는 호텔에서 지내지 않았음)
- We **were going to study** at the library yesterday, but it was closed.
  어제 도서관에서 공부하려 했지만, 도서관이 닫혀 있었다. (실제로는 도서관에서 공부하지 않았음)

일어날 것이라고 예측했던 일에 대해 말할 때도 **was/were going to**를 쓸 수 있다.

- Jane was confident. She was sure she **was going to get** the scholarship. 그녀는 장학금을 받을 것이라고 확신했다.
- "I thought the exhibits **were going to start** on June 21." "Yes, but the schedule changed."

PRACTICE

A. 그림을 보고 주어진 표현과 am/is/are going to를 사용하여 문장을 완성하세요.

~~blow out the candles~~	fall into the box	melt	sleep on the sofa	wash the dog

1. He *'s going to blow out the candles* .
2. The oranges _____ .
3. She _____ .
4. They _____ .
5. The ice _____ .

B. 괄호 안에 주어진 동사와 am/is/are going to 또는 will을 사용하여 문장을 완성하세요.

1. (be) I broke the window again. I *'m going to be* in big trouble!
2. (help) "What do you think of the new website?"
   "I like it. I think it _____ our business."
3. (have) My sister is at the hospital. She _____ her baby very soon.
4. (find) "I lost my dog. I'm so sad." "Don't worry. You _____ him."
5. (learn) I _____ a lot at the workshop. I'm excited about it.
6. (complete) Bob and Joe are near the finish line! They _____ the marathon!

C. 주어진 상황을 보고 괄호 안에 주어진 단어들과 am/is/are going to 또는 will 중 더 적절한 것을 사용하여 예시와 같이 문장을 완성하세요. 필요한 경우 부정문으로 쓰세요.

1. Sarah asks you to help her move this weekend, and you are free.
   YOU: (I, help) Sure. *I'll help* you this weekend. What time should I be there?
2. Kyle asks you why Peter is taking Chinese lessons lately. It is because his New Year's plan was to visit China.
   YOU: (he, visit) _____ China this year, so he needs to study a lot.
3. You are in the restroom washing your hands. Somebody knocks on the door.
   YOU: (I, be) Wait a second. _____ out soon.
4. Jessie and you just arrived at an Italian restaurant. She tells you that she doesn't like mushrooms.
   YOU: (I, order) OK. _____ mushroom pizza then. Do you like pepperoni?
5. Mr. Brown wants to have a lunch meeting with your boss, but she already has a doctor's appointment.
   YOU: (she, be) _____ in the office at lunch. She'll be back around 3 o'clock.

D. 주어진 동사와 was/were going to를 사용하여 문장을 완성하세요.

attend	give	~~make~~	wait

1. Hi kids,
I *was going to make* spaghetti for dinner, but there was no pasta! I'll be home from the supermarket soon.

2. Dear Kelly,
Happy Birthday!
We _____ you a scarf, but we bought something else. I hope you like it.

3. Marcia,
I'm sorry I wasn't at your wedding.
I _____, but unfortunately I had to work that weekend.

4. Jason,
We've gone to the mall.
We _____ for you, but the mall closes at 8 o'clock. Sorry!

정답 **p. 309** / Check-Up Test 4 **p. 240**

미래, 미래진행과 미래완료

LESSON **17**

Grammar Gateway Intermediate

They **are watching** a soccer game tonight.

1

They **are watching** a soccer game tonight.
그들은 오늘 밤 축구 경기를 볼 것이다.

The game **starts** at 7 p.m.
경기는 오후 7시에 시작할 것이다.

are watching과 starts는 각각 현재진행과 현재 시제의 형태이지만 '볼 것이다',
'시작할 것이다'라는 의미로 둘 다 미래의 일에 대해 말하기 위해 썼다.

2

구체적으로 약속을 했거나 계획을 세워 둔 미래의 일에 대해 말할 때 현재진행 시제를 쓸 수 있다.

• "Are you doing anything this weekend?"   "Yes. **I'm meeting** Josh."   Josh를 만날 거야.
• We **aren't returning** from Mexico until next Wednesday.   다음 주 수요일까지는 Mexico에서 돌아오지 않을 것이다.
• Why are we hiring a new secretary? **Is** Ms. Rogers **retiring**?
• **I'm seeing** the doctor today. I made an appointment for 6 o'clock.
• "When **are** you **moving** out?"   "In three months."

이때, 현재진행 시제 대신 **am/is/are going to + 동사원형**도 쓸 수 있다.

• We**'re having** a company picnic on Monday.
  또는 We**'re going to have** a company picnic on Monday.
  월요일에 회사 야유회를 할 거예요.
• **Is** Andy **spending** his summer vacation with his family?
  또는 **Is** Andy **going to spend** his summer vacation with his family?

3

대중교통, 영화, 수업 시간 등 이미 짜여 있는 시간표, 일정표 상의 일에 대해 말할 때는 미래의 일이라 할지라도 현재 시제를 쓸 수 있다.

• The train to Rome **departs** at 9 p.m. tonight.   로마행 열차는 오늘 밤 9시에 출발할 것이다.
• "The movie **finishes** at midnight."   영화가 자정에 끝나.   "It will be late when we get home."
• Anna's yoga class **starts** on September 5th.
• We don't have time to go to the bank. It **closes** soon.
• Each interview **lasts** for 20 minutes, and you will have a short break after each one.

  그러나 개인의 계획에 대해 말할 때는 현재진행 시제를 주로 쓴다.

  • **I'm speaking** at a meeting next Saturday.   다음 주 토요일에 회의에서 발언을 할 것이다.
  • My daughter **is taking** her driving test next week. She's excited about getting her license.

4

am/is/are about to + 동사원형: 막 ~하려고 하다

매우 가까운 미래에 어떤 일이 일어날 것이라고 말할 때 **am/is/are about to + 동사원형**을 쓸 수 있다.

• The presentation **is about to begin**. Please take your seats.   발표가 막 시작하려고 합니다.
• We have been awake all night. The sun **is about to come** up!   해가 막 떠오르려고 해!
• Stop! You**'re about to hit** that car!
• "Do you want to have some coffee?"   "No, thanks. I**'m about to go** to bed."
• Jake, put on your coat. We**'re about to leave**.

P R A C T I C E

A. 그림을 보고 주어진 표현을 사용하여 예시와 같이 문장을 완성하세요.

| ~~attend a seminar~~ | get married | meet | open a bakery | run in a marathon |

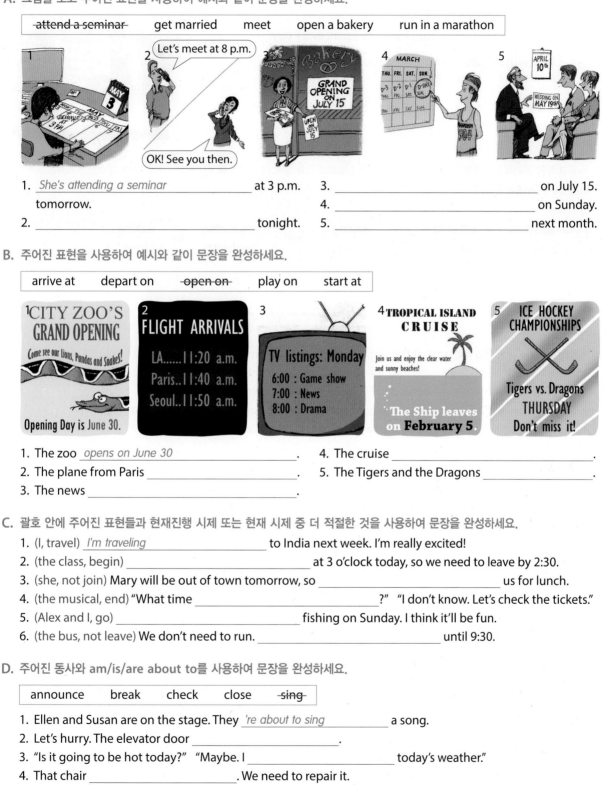

1. *She's attending a seminar* _____ at 3 p.m. tomorrow.
2. _____ tonight.
3. _____ on July 15.
4. _____ on Sunday.
5. _____ next month.

B. 주어진 표현을 사용하여 예시와 같이 문장을 완성하세요.

| arrive at | depart on | ~~open on~~ | play on | start at |

1. The zoo *opens on June 30* _____ .
2. The plane from Paris _____ .
3. The news _____ .
4. The cruise _____ .
5. The Tigers and the Dragons _____ .

C. 괄호 안에 주어진 표현들과 현재진행 시제 또는 현재 시제 중 더 적절한 것을 사용하여 문장을 완성하세요.

1. (I, travel) *I'm traveling* _____ to India next week. I'm really excited!
2. (the class, begin) _____ at 3 o'clock today, so we need to leave by 2:30.
3. (she, not join) Mary will be out of town tomorrow, so _____ us for lunch.
4. (the musical, end) "What time _____ ?"   "I don't know. Let's check the tickets."
5. (Alex and I, go) _____ fishing on Sunday. I think it'll be fun.
6. (the bus, not leave) We don't need to run. _____ until 9:30.

D. 주어진 동사와 **am/is/are about to**를 사용하여 문장을 완성하세요.

| announce | break | check | close | ~~sing~~ |

1. Ellen and Susan are on the stage. They *'re about to sing* _____ a song.
2. Let's hurry. The elevator door _____ .
3. "Is it going to be hot today?"   "Maybe. I _____ today's weather."
4. That chair _____ . We need to repair it.
5. Attention, please. Mr. and Mrs. Robbins _____ the winner of the art contest.

1 There is a Spanish class from 7 p.m. to 9 p.m. every day.

They **will be studying** at 8 p.m. tomorrow.
그들은 내일 오후 8시에 공부하고 있을 것이다.

'공부하고 있을 것이다'라는 의미로 내일 오후 8시 이전에 시작되어 8시에도 계속 진행되고 있을 일에 대해 말하기 위해 미래진행 시제 will be studying을 썼다.

2 '~하고 있을 것이다'라는 의미로 미래의 특정한 시점에 진행되고 있을 일에 대해 말할 때 미래진행 시제를 쓴다. 미래진행 시제는 **will be + -ing**로 쓴다.

긍정 · 부정

I/we/you/they	will (= 'll)	be	waiting
he/she/it	will not (= won't)		taking

의문

will	I/we/you/they	be	waiting … ?
	he/she/it		taking … ?

We **will be waiting** for Janet at the station.

지금	기다리기 시작함	내일 5시	미래

- We **will be waiting** for Janet at the station at 5 o'clock tomorrow. 내일 5시에 역에서 Janet을 기다리고 있을 것이다.
- Mandy **won't be taking** exams next week. Her last exam is this Thursday. Mandy는 다음 주에 시험을 치고 있지 않을 것이다.
- Can I use the computer in 10 minutes? Or **will** you still **be using** it then?
- That band **won't be performing** in July. They're taking a break from June to August.
- Peter can't go skiing with us on Saturday because he**'ll be working** then.

3 미래진행 시제와 미래 시제는 다음과 같은 차이가 있다.

- "I'll be home at 7." "OK. I**'ll be making** dinner when you arrive." (도착했을 때 요리를 하고 있을 것임)
  "I'll be home at 5." "OK. We**'ll make** dinner together when you arrive." (도착하면 요리를 시작할 것임)
- The girls **will be singing** when the bride enters.
  The girls **will sing** after the bride enters.

  know, believe 등과 같이 동작을 나타내지 않는 동사들은 미래진행 시제로 쓰지 않고 미래 시제로 주로 쓴다.

- "Doctor, will Melissa be all right?" "We**'ll know** more when we get the test results."
  (미래진행 시제 We'll be knowing으로 쓸 수 없음)
- "I broke John's camera, but it was an accident." "Tell him that. I'm sure he**'ll believe** you."
  (미래진행 시제 he'll be believing으로 쓸 수 없음)

진행 시제로 쓰지 않는 동사에 대한 더 자세한 내용은 Lesson 4 참고

4 미래의 어떤 시점에 진행되고 있지 않더라도, 그 시점에 할 것으로 확정된 일이나 당연히 일어날 것으로 예상되는 일에 대해 말할 때도 미래진행 시제를 쓸 수 있다.

- I**'ll be leaving** for Hawaii on April 7. I'm so excited! 4월 7일에 하와이로 갈 거야.
- "**Will** the guests **be arriving** soon?" "No, they **won't be arriving** until 1 o'clock."

  이때, 미래진행 시제와 비슷한 의미로 **am/is/are going to**를 쓸 수도 있다.

- I**'m going to leave** for Hawaii on April 7. I'm so excited! (= I'll be leaving)

PRACTICE

A. Claire는 다음 주 금요일에 이사할 예정입니다. 다음 주 계획표를 보고 예시와 같이 문장을 완성하세요.

MON	TUE	WED	THU	FRI
6:00-8:00 clean the new house	12:00-2:00 buy some furniture	10:00-2:00 paint the new house	10:00-4:00 pack / 4:00-8:00 have a farewell party	2:00-6:00 move into the new house

1. Claire _will be cleaning the new house_ at 7 on Monday.
2. She _____ at 1 on Thursday.
3. She _____ on Wednesday at 10:30.
4. She _____ at 1:30 on Tuesday.
5. She _____ at 5 on Friday.

B. 괄호 안에 주어진 동사를 사용하여 미래진행 시제 또는 미래 시제 문장을 완성하세요. 필요한 경우 부정문으로 쓰세요.

1. (drive) "Do you want to go for a walk at 7 tonight?"
   "I can't. I _'ll be driving_ OR _will be driving_ to my grandmother's house then."
2. (remember) Jennifer _____ my birthday. She always forgets it.
3. (sleep) "I'll be home around midnight. _____ you _____?"
   "I don't think so. I'll probably be reading my book."
4. (go) I need some cash. Let's stop by the bank first, and then we _____ shopping.
5. (prepare) "Are you doing something after lunch?" "Yes. I _____ for a presentation."
6. (attend) Ray _____ the workshop at 3. He has an appointment at the same time.
7. (show) "I can't open this lock. _____ you _____ me how it works?"
   "Sure. Let me see it."
8. (play) "Can we have dinner at 6?"
   "No. The children _____ soccer. Their game doesn't finish until 6:30 today."

C. 주어진 동사와 미래진행 시제를 사용하여 대화를 완성하세요. 필요한 경우 부정문으로 쓰세요.

come	~~receive~~	stay	volunteer

1. A: _Will_ I _be receiving_ the delivery soon?
   B: Yes. You'll get them this Friday.

2. A: Are your parents visiting you this week?
   B: No, they _____. Maybe I'll see them next week.

3. A: We _____ at the children's hospital this weekend.
   B: That's a very kind thing to do.

4. A: I'm going on a business trip next month.
   B: Where _____ you _____? At a hotel?

D. 괄호 안에 주어진 단어들과 미래진행 시제를 사용하여 Sara와 Linda의 대화를 완성하세요. 필요한 경우 부정문으로 쓰세요.

SARA: 1. Linda, _will you be taking_ your Spanish class tonight? (you, take)
LINDA: 2. No, _____ to class this evening. (I, go)
SARA: 3. What _____? (you, do)
LINDA: 4. _____ dinner with James. (I, have)
SARA: I see. I was going to have dinner with you. Maybe next time.
LINDA: 5. _____ anything after work tomorrow. (I, do) How about tomorrow night?
SARA: Great! 6. _____ for you at the gate at 6. (I, wait)

SARA

LINDA

미래, 미래진행과 미래완료

LESSON 19

Grammar Gateway Intermediate

She **will have graduated** by this time next year. 미래완료 시제

1 She is in her last year of high school.

She **will have graduated** by this time next year.
그녀는 내년 이맘때까지는 졸업했을 것이다.

'졸업했을 것이다'라는 의미로 내년 이맘때까지는 완료되었을 일에 대해 말하기 위해
미래완료 시제 **will have graduated**를 썼다.

올해　　　　　내년

2 미래의 특정한 시점까지는 어떤 일이 완료되었을 것이라고 말할 때 미래완료 시제 **will have + 과거분사**를 쓴다.

긍정 · 부정

| I/we/you/they | will (= 'll) | have | climbed |
| he/she/it | will not (= won't) | | left |

의문

| will | I/we/you/they | have | climbed … ? |
| | he/she/it | | left … ? |

불규칙 동사: 부록 p. 283 참고

- We **will have climbed** to top of the mountain by noon. 정오까지는 산 정상에 올라 있을 것이다.
- "Will you be home at 6 p.m.?"
  "No. I **won't have left** campus by then. I have evening classes." 그때까지는 교정을 떠나지 않았을 거야.
- "**Will** Flight BK702 **have landed** at 11 o'clock?" "Yes. There's no delay."
- On January 15, Mr. Jones **will have worked** at the company for a year.
- "By the end of your trip, how many countries **will** you **have visited**?" "Six."

　미래완료 시제는 **by + 미래 시점**과 자주 함께 쓴다. **by + 미래 시점**은 '~까지는'이라는 의미이다.
  - The leaves **will have changed** color **by the end of October**. 10월 말까지는 나뭇잎 색깔이 바뀌어 있을 것이다.
  - "**Will** you **have fixed** the printer **by lunchtime**?" "Maybe."

3 '~할 때쯤'이라는 의미의 **by the time**도 미래완료 시제와 자주 함께 쓴다. **by the time**은 뒤에 **주어 + 동사**를 쓴다.
- I'**ll have learned** a lot **by the time I complete** this course. 이 과정을 마칠 때쯤 많은 것을 배웠을 것이다.
- **By the time the meeting starts**, we **won't have prepared** the sales report. Let's put off the meeting.
  회의가 시작할 때쯤, 우리는 판매 보고서를 준비하지 못했을 것이다.
- **By the time I see** Mila again, she **will have had** her baby.
- Steve **will have retired by the time he turns** 65.

　이때, **by the time** 뒤에는 현재 시제를 쓴다. **will**이나 **am/is/are going to**를 쓰지 않는 것에 주의한다.
  - I'**ll have made** coffee for you **by the time** you **wake** up tomorrow morning.
    네가 내일 아침 일어날 때쯤이면 내가 널 위해 커피를 만들어두었을 거야. (by the time you will wake로 쓸 수 없음)
  - **By the time** my children **are** in college, tuition fees **will have increased** a lot.
    아이들이 대학에 갈 때쯤이면 등록금이 많이 올라 있을 것이다. (By the time my children are going to be로 쓸 수 없음)

4 미래완료 시제와 미래 시제는 다음과 같은 의미 차이가 있다.
- By January, I **will have moved** to Florida. (1월까지는 이사를 완료했을 것임)
  In January, I'**m going to move** to Florida. (1월에 이사할 것임)
- Tom will be very late. By the time he checks in at the hotel, we **will have toured** the city.
  When Tom checks in at the hotel, we'**ll tour** the city. Let's wait for him in the room.

P R A C T I C E

A. 앞으로 일어날 일들을 예측한 다음의 그래프를 보고 주어진 동사를 사용하여 예시와 같이 문장을 완성하세요.

drop	~~increase~~	lose	produce	save

1 Gold Price Forecast
($) 2,000 / 1,800 / 1,600
Apr. Aug. Dec.

2 Greg's Savings
($) 1,500 / 1,000 / 500
Sept. 1 Sept. 15 Sept. 30

3 Total Weekly Production
250 / 200 / 150 / 100 / 50
MON TUE WED THU FRI

4 Country's Population
million 55 / 50 / 45
2030 2040 2050

5 Leo's weight
kg 90 / 88 / 85
June 1 June 15 June 30

1. The price of gold _will have increased_ $400 by December.
2. Greg _____ $1,500 by September 30.
3. The company _____ 250 cars by the end of the week.
4. The population of the country _____ to 45 million by 2050.
5. Leo _____ 5 kilograms by the end of this month.

B. 괄호 안에 주어진 표현들과 미래완료 시제 또는 현재 시제를 사용하여 문장을 완성하세요.

1. (get, find) It _will have gotten_ dark by the time Kyle _____ the station.
2. (not finish) Can we change our date to 8:30? I _____ work by 8.
3. (melt, get) Let's eat the ice cream here. It _____ by the time we _____ home.
4. (reach, walk) By the time we _____ the park, we _____ 5 kilometers.
5. (not read, return) I _____ the entire book by the time I _____ it to the library.
6. (wait) If the package doesn't come by tomorrow, I _____ for three weeks.

C. 주어진 동사와 will을 사용하여 미래완료 시제 또는 미래 시제 문장을 완성하세요.

call	clean	live	pass	pay	~~receive~~

1. I sent you a postcard. By next weekend, you _will have received_ it.
2. " _____ Mr. Riley _____ the driving test this time?" "I hope so."
3. "Here's my phone number." "OK. I _____ you tonight."
4. The kitchen is a mess now, but we _____ it by the time the guests arrive.
5. Our family _____ in this house for 10 years next month.
6. I have no money right now. But when I get my paycheck, I _____ my electricity bill.

D. 다음 Sandy의 인생 계획을 보고 예시와 같이 문장을 완성하세요.

SANDY'S FUTURE PLANS
○ By this time next year...
   graduate from high school
○ By 2017...
   complete college
○ By 2020...
   direct several movies
○ By the time
   I'm 45... win a big award

1. By this time next year, _I'll have graduated from high school_ .
2. By 2017, _____ with a degree in film.
3. If I'm lucky, by 2020 _____ .
4. Hopefully, _____ by the time I'm 45.

SANDY

LESSON
21
He will call her **when he leaves** the house.

시간, 조건을 나타내는
문장에서의 미래

1

They are going on a picnic tomorrow.

He will call her **when he leaves** the house.
그는 집을 떠날 때 그녀에게 전화할 것이다.

집을 떠나는 것은 미래에 일어날 일이지만 when 다음에 미래 시제가 아니라 현재 시제
leaves를 썼다.

I'll call you **when I leave**.

2 다음과 같이 시간을 나타내는 표현 다음에 미래에 일어날 일에 대해 말할 때 **주어 + 현재 시제**를 쓴다. 이때, **will**이나
am/is/are going to 등을 쓰지 않는 것에 주의한다.

when ~할 때	**while** ~하는 동안	**before** ~하기 전에	**after** ~한 후에	**until** ~할 때까지

주어 + 현재 시제

- We will go fishing | **when** | **the weather gets** | nicer. (when the weather will get 등으로 쓸 수 없음)
- Let's get some popcorn | **before** | **the movie starts.** (before the movie is going to start 등으로 쓸 수 없음)
- Will you check my e-mail | **after** | **you come** | back from lunch?
- Please do not stand up | **until** | **the bus stops.**

주어 + 현재 시제

- **While** | **we're** | in Germany next month, we are going to visit Berlin.
- **Before** | **you exercise,** | you should stretch.
- **After** | **we eat** | dinner, can you clean the table?
- **Until** | **she feels** | better, Sally will not be attending class.

이때, **when, before** 등의 다음에 **he/she/it** 등을 주어로 쓰는 경우, 동사원형에 **(e)s**를 붙이는 것에 주의한다.

- **When Rob saves** enough money, he'll open a restaurant. (주어가 Rob이므로 saves를 썼음)
- Kara will stop at the bank **before she goes** to the supermarket. (주어가 she이므로 goes를 썼음)

3 '~한다면'이라는 의미로 조건을 나타내는 **if** 다음에도 미래에 일어날 일에 대해 말할 때 **주어 + 현재 시제**를 쓴다. 이때, **will**이나
am/is/are going to 등을 쓰지 않는 것에 주의한다.

- **If Bill wins** the contest, we're going to celebrate. (If Bill will win 등으로 쓸 수 없음)
- I'm having trouble with my homework. Will you help me **if you have** time later?
  (if you're going to have 등으로 쓸 수 없음)
- **If I don't find** my car key, Shannon is going to give me a ride home.
- Can you buy some stamps on your way home **if the post office is** still open?

4 **when, while, if** 등의 다음에 미래진행(will be + -ing), 미래완료(will have + 과거분사) 시제도 쓰지 않는 것에 주의한다. 미래진
행 대신 현재진행 시제를 쓰고, 미래완료 대신 현재완료 시제를 쓴다.

- We're going to discuss our vacation plan **while** we**'re having** coffee.
  커피를 마시는 동안 우리의 휴가 계획에 대해 논의할 것이다. (while we will be having으로 쓸 수 없음)
- If Danny **hasn't prepared** the report by 1 o'clock, we'll cancel the meeting.
  Danny가 1시까지 보고서를 준비하지 않으면, 회의를 취소할 것이다. (If Danny won't have prepared로 쓸 수 없음)

PRACTICE

A. when을 사용하여 주어진 두 문장을 예시와 같이 한 문장으로 바꾸어 쓰세요.

1. Tammy will choose a wedding date. She will send us an invitation.
   → *When Tammy chooses a wedding date* _____, she will send us an invitation.

2. I'm going to move to New York City. I'm going to rent an apartment.
   → _____, I'm going to rent an apartment.

3. Brian will buy a present for his wife. He will get a bonus next month.
   → Brian will buy a present for his wife _____.

4. I'll order pizza. Lisa and Jake will feel hungry.
   → I'll order pizza _____.

5. Mr. Harris is going to retire next year. He's going to write a book.
   → _____, he's going to write a book.

B. 괄호 안에 주어진 표현들을 사용하여 문장을 완성하세요. 현재 시제로 쓰거나 will을 함께 쓰세요.

1. (cook, make) Steve _will cook_ the steak while I _____ the salad.
2. (not pay, charge) If we _____ our bill on time, the credit card company _____ a fee.
3. (travel, study) Before I _____ to China, I _____ Chinese.
4. (be, not come) I _____ sad if Natalie _____ to my party.
5. (buy, give) If my brother _____ a new laptop, he _____ me his old one.
6. (not start, arrive) We _____ the seminar until you _____.
7. (become, receive) _____ Tara _____ a professor after she _____ her degree?

C. 다음 문장을 읽고 틀린 부분이 있으면 바르게 고치세요. 틀린 부분이 없으면 ○로 표시하세요.

1. I'll set the alarm before I will sleep. I have to wake up early.   *will sleep → sleep*
2. Will you excuse me while I go to the restroom?   _____
3. Tom will lend me his camera next week if he won't be using it.   _____
4. If you haven't found a good hairdresser, I'll take you to mine.   _____
5. Gina will watch the kids until their mother will return home.   _____
6. When you will have completed the application, give it to me.   _____

D. 괄호 안에 주어진 동사들을 사용하여 Rachel과 Chris의 대화를 완성하세요. 현재 시제로 쓰거나 will을 함께 쓰세요.

RACHEL: I'm so excited about our trip tomorrow.
  1. _Will_ you _call_ me when you _____ the house? (call, leave)

CHRIS: Sure! But I'll have to go to the mechanic first.
  2. After he _____ my car, I _____ you up. (fix, pick)

RACHEL: Great. By the way, we'll need some snacks for our trip.
  3. _____ you _____ at the grocery store before you _____ to the repair shop? (stop, go)

CHRIS: I don't think I'll have enough time to do that.
  4. If you _____ time today, _____ you _____ the shopping? (have, do)

RACHEL: OK. But I'll need to borrow my mom's car.
  5. I _____ her when she _____ home. (ask, come)

RACHEL

CHRIS

미래, 미래진행과 미래완료

21

Grammar Gateway Intermediate

1 Justin has two cousins.

Lisa **can walk.** Lisa는 걸을 수 있다.

Denny **can't walk.** Denny는 걸을 수 없다.

'걸을 수 있다', '걸을 수 없다'라는 의미로 능력에 대해 말하기 위해 can walk, can't walk를 썼다.

2 '~할 수 있다'라는 의미로 어떤 일을 할 수 있는 능력을 가지고 있거나 어떤 일을 하는 것이 가능하다고 말할 때 can을 쓴다.

긍정·부정

| I/we/you/they | **can** | **ride** |
| he/she/it | **cannot (= can't)** | **move** |

의문

| **can** | I/we/you/they | **ride … ?** |
| | he/she/it | **move … ?** |

- My son **can ride** a bicycle now. He really enjoys it. 내 아들은 이제 자전거를 탈 수 있다.
- Carla broke her arm. She **can't move** it at the moment.
- "**Can** penguins **fly**?" "No, but they **can swim** very well."

can과 같은 의미로 **am/is/are able to**를 쓸 수 있다. 단, 일상 대화에서는 **can**을 주로 쓴다.

- I'm **able to visit** my grandparents often because I live near them. (= can visit)
- Many Americans **aren't able to use** chopsticks, but some can. (= can't use)

3 과거에 대해 말할 때는 **could**를 쓴다. 이때, **could** 대신 **was/were able to**를 쓸 수도 있다.

- I **could read** some words when I was two years old.
  또는 I **was able to read** some words when I was two years old. 나는 2살이었을 때 몇몇 단어를 읽을 수 있었다.
- In Miami, we **could jog** on the beach every day. 또는 In Miami, we **were able to jog** on the beach every day.

단, 과거의 특정한 상황에 실제로 어떤 일을 해냈다고 말할 때는 **could**를 쓸 수 없고 **was/were able to**만 쓰는 것에 주의한다.

- There were lots of cars on the road, but Matt **was able to get** to the movies on time.
  (실제로 영화관에 정시에 도착해냈다는 의미이므로 could get으로 쓸 수 없음)
- We **were able to clean** our messy house before the guests arrived.
  (실제로 손님이 도착하기 전에 청소를 해냈다는 의미이므로 could clean으로 쓸 수 없음)

couldn't와 **wasn't/weren't able to**는 차이 없이 쓸 수 있다.

- We **couldn't go** to the party. 또는 We **weren't able to go** to the party. 우리는 파티에 갈 수 없었다.
- Brent **couldn't dance** well in the past. 또는 Brent **wasn't able to dance** well in the past.

4 다음과 같은 경우에는 **can**은 쓸 수 없고 **be able to**만 쓸 수 있는 것에 주의한다.

will/might/should 등 + be able to

- I **won't be able to meet** you this Saturday. I have an appointment. (won't can meet으로 쓸 수 없음)
- Laura **might be able to join** our book club. She'll let us know soon. (might can join으로 쓸 수 없음)

have/has been able to

- Peter **has been able to work** faster since he got a new laptop. 새 노트북 컴퓨터를 산 이후로 Peter는 일을 더 빨리 할 수 있었다.
- My friend is in town this week, so we**'ve been able to spend** some time together.

P R A C T I C E

A. 주어진 동사와 **can**을 사용하여 대화를 완성하세요. 필요한 경우 부정문으로 쓰세요.

do	~~drive~~	eat	pay	play	reach

1. A: I need to go to the supermarket.
   B: I _can drive_____ you there. I'll get my key.

2. A: I _____ that book. It's too high.
   B: Here, let me try.

3. A: _____ your dog _____ any tricks?
   B: Yes. I'll show you.

4. A: Steve _____ the violin very well.
   B: I know. He's really good at it.

5. A: _____ we _____ with a credit card?
   B: I'm sorry, but we only accept cash.

6. A: Do you want some more pasta?
   B: No. I _____ anymore. I'm full.

B. 괄호 안에 주어진 단어들과 **can** 또는 **could**를 사용하여 문장을 완성하세요. 필요한 경우 부정문으로 쓰세요.

1. (we, buy) There's a café across the street. _We can buy_____ some coffee there.
2. (I, type) In college, _____ 80 words in one minute, but I can't now.
3. (they, get) Mike and Ann bought the tickets too late, so _____ good seats.
4. (I, run) "Can we stop for a break? _____ anymore." "Sure. Let's sit here."
5. (he, throw) That pitcher has been training hard. Now _____ a baseball much faster.
6. (Josh, afford) _____ a house at the moment. He doesn't have enough money.
7. (you, read) "I have to wear my glasses when I read now."
   "I know. _____ without them in the old days."
8. (Kelly, ski) _____ well before she took the lessons last year. But now she's quite good.

C. **could** 또는 **was/were able to**를 써넣으세요. 필요한 경우 부정문으로 쓰세요.

1. Lucas _could OR was able to_____ make bread at home after he took a baking class.
2. Although no one helped her, Mia _____ finish the project without any problem.
3. We _____ complete the puzzle because some pieces were missing.
4. Our best player didn't play, but we _____ win the game anyway.
5. I _____ remove the lid from the jar. It was too tight.
6. Jeff was very strong when he was young. He _____ lift 150 kilos.

D. 다음은 Clara의 일기입니다. 괄호 안에 주어진 동사와 **can** 또는 **be able to**를 적절한 형태로 사용하여 문장을 완성하세요. 필요한 경우 부정문으로 쓰세요.

Clara's Diary
August 01, 2016

I enjoy learning new languages. Right now, I'm taking a French class.
1. (speak) At first, I _couldn't OR wasn't able to speak_____ French very well.
2. (speak) But now I _____ it much better.
3. (learn) The teacher always explains everything clearly, so I have _____ it quickly.

This summer, I'm going to take a Japanese class.
Judy recently introduced me to Japanese music.
4. (understand) Although I _____ the words, the music was beautiful.
5. (sing) Maybe I'll _____ these songs in Japanese after taking the class.

LESSON 23 · It **could** belong to James. could (추측)

1

She found a cell phone.

It **could belong** to James. James의 것일지도 모른다.

It **couldn't belong** to James. James의 것일 리 없다.

'James의 것일지도 모른다', 'James의 것일 리 없다'라는 의미로 추측한
내용을 말하기 위해 could belong, couldn't belong을 썼다.

2 could + 동사원형: ~할지도 모른다

현재나 미래의 확실하지 않은 일에 대해 추측할 때 **could**를 쓸 수 있다. 이때, **could**는 과거의 의미가 아니다.

- I think the rain **could stop** soon. The sky looks brighter. 비가 곧 그칠지도 몰라.
- "Where's Emma?" "She **could be** in her room."
- I probably won't win the lottery, but it **could happen**!

3 couldn't + 동사원형: ~할 리 없다

사실상 어떤 일이 일어나는 것이 불가능하다고 강하게 추측할 때는 **couldn't**를 쓴다.

- "Is that Pete over there?" "It **couldn't be** Pete. He went to Tokyo this morning." Pete일 리 없어.
- My dog **couldn't** possibly **jump** over the fence. It is 3 meters tall.
- People **couldn't live** on Mars because there's no oxygen.

  이때, **couldn't** 대신 **can't**도 쓸 수 있다.

  - "Is that a real diamond ring?" "It **can't be**. It's only $25." 그럴 리 없어. (= couldn't be)
  - It's only 4 o'clock. The store **can't close** so early. 가게가 이렇게 일찍 닫을 리 없다. (= couldn't close)

4 could have + 과거분사: (과거에) ~했을지도 모른다

과거의 확실하지 않은 일에 대해 추측할 때는 **could have + 과거분사**를 쓴다.

- "Mr. Rogers wasn't in his office." "He **could have gone** out to meet a customer." 고객을 만나러 나갔을지도 몰라요.

  could have + 과거분사는 '(과거에) ~할 수도 있었다 (그러나 하지 않았다)'라는 의미로도 자주 쓴다.

  - We **could have stayed** at the beach longer, but we came back. (해변에 더 오래 머물 수도 있었지만 그러지 않았음)
  - "Sorry I'm late." "You **could have called**. We were waiting for you." (전화할 수도 있었지만 하지 않았음)

5 couldn't have + 과거분사: (과거에) ~했을 리 없다

과거에 어떤 일이 일어나는 것이 불가능했다고 강하게 추측할 때는 **couldn't have + 과거분사**를 쓴다.

- Jenny **couldn't have moved** this desk by herself. It's too heavy. Jenny가 이 책상을 혼자서 옮겼을 리 없다.
- Nobody told my brother about the surprise party. He **couldn't have known** about it.

  이때, **couldn't have + 과거분사** 대신 **can't have + 과거분사**도 쓸 수 있다.

  - Greg and Jay **can't have drunk** all of the wine. There were four bottles! (= couldn't have drunk)

PRACTICE

A. 주어진 동사와 could 또는 couldn't를 사용하여 문장을 완성하세요.

~~be~~	be	have	join	see	tell

1. We should check the chicken in the oven. It _could be_____ ready.
2. You _____ all of Rome in two days. There are so many places to visit.
3. "That store doesn't sell cranberry juice." "The one across the street _____ some."
4. "How do we get to the bank?" "Let's ask that man. He _____ us."
5. Charles _____ the ski club. He hates going outside in the winter.
6. "Why isn't Angela in class today?" "I'm not sure. She _____ sick."

B. 괄호 안에 주어진 동사와 couldn't 또는 couldn't have + 과거분사를 사용하여 문장을 완성하세요.

1. (be) That _couldn't be_____ Nate's glove. His is black, but that one is brown.
2. (fly) The storm is too strong right now. Planes _____ in this weather.
3. (do) Katie finished all of her work in just one day. She _____ it alone.
4. (know) Your wife _____ me. We've never met before.
5. (write) Mike _____ this letter. His handwriting is completely different.
6. (get) Jack _____ his new shoes there. That store was closed yesterday.
7. (eat) Let's order a medium pizza. We _____ a large one by ourselves.
8. (arrive) My parents _____ home already. They left here 10 minutes ago.

C. 주어진 문장을 보고 could have + 과거분사를 사용하여 예시와 같이 다시 말해보세요.

1. I didn't take a train to Geneva even though there was one.
   → _I could have taken a train to Geneva_____ .
2. We didn't visit the Great Wall even though we were in China.
   → _____ .
3. Bill and Helen didn't sell their old car even though a few people wanted to buy it.
   → _____ .
4. You didn't go shopping with me although you had free time.
   → _____ .

D. 괄호 안에 주어진 동사와 could 또는 could have + 과거분사를 사용하여 Linda와 James의 대화를 완성하세요. 필요한 경우 부정문으로 쓰세요.

LINDA: I found your phone in the garage, honey.
JAMES: ¹·It _couldn't be_____ mine. (be) Mine is here.
LINDA: Then whose is it?
JAMES: Isn't it Chris's?
         ²·He _____ it in the garage yesterday. (drop)
LINDA: ³·He _____ that. (do)
         He went camping yesterday and called us when he got there.
JAMES: Oh, that's right.
LINDA: ⁴·It _____ to Amy. (belong)
         She always loses her things.
JAMES: I think you're right.

LINDA

JAMES

He **might** eat at the restaurant.   might와 may (추측)

1   He **might eat** at the restaurant.
그는 식당에서 먹을지도 모른다.

He **might not eat** at the restaurant.
그는 식당에서 먹지 않을지도 모른다.

'식당에서 먹을지도 모른다', '식당에서 먹지 않을지도 모른다'라는 의미로 추측한 내용을
말하기 위해 might eat, might not eat을 썼다.

2   '~할지도 모른다'라는 의미로 현재나 미래의 확실하지 않은 일에 대해 추측할 때 **might** 또는 **may**를 쓸 수 있다. 이때, **might**는
과거의 의미가 아니며, 일상 대화에서는 **may**보다 **might**를 더 자주 쓴다.

긍정 · 부정

| I/we/you/they | **might** | (not) | **be** |
| he/she/it | **may** | | **sell** |

- The seminar **might be** interesting. 또는 The seminar **may be** interesting. 세미나가 재미있을지도 모른다.
- I **might not sell** my motorcycle. 또는 I **may not sell** my motorcycle. I'm still thinking about it.

3   **might/may**와 **could**는 '~할지도 모른다'라는 비슷한 의미로 쓴다.

- "There's someone at the door." "It **might/may be** Ben." 또는 "It **could be** Ben." Ben일지도 몰라.

그러나 **might/may not**과 **couldn't**는 다음과 같은 의미 차이가 있다.

| **might/may not** + 동사원형 | • Matthew doesn't have much experience, so he **might not get** that job. |
| ~하지 않을지도 모른다 (그러나 ~할 가능성도 있다) | Matthew는 그 일자리를 얻지 못할지도 모른다. (그러나 일자리를 얻을 가능성도 있음) |

| **couldn't** + 동사원형 | • Matthew has no experience at all. He **couldn't** possibly **get** that job. |
| ~할 리 없다 (~하는 것이 사실상 불가능하다) | Matthew는 그 일자리를 도저히 얻을 리 없다. (일자리를 얻는 것이 사실상 불가능함) |

4   과거의 확실하지 않은 일에 대해 추측할 때는 **might/may have** + 과거분사를 쓴다.

might/may have + 과거분사: (과거에) ~했을지도 모른다

- "Who turned off the heater?" "It wasn't me. Alex **might/may have done** it." Alex가 그랬을지도 몰라.
- I haven't seen my neighbors for a few days. They **might/may have gone** on a vacation.

might/may not have + 과거분사: (과거에) ~하지 않았을지도 모른다.

- I **might/may not have locked** the door. I'll go back and check. 문을 잠그지 않았을지도 몰라.
- Jason **might/may not have been** to the exhibit yet. Let's ask him to go with us.

5   '(과거에) ~했을지도 모른다'라는 의미로 **could have** + 과거분사도 쓸 수 있다. 일상 대화에서는 **might/may have** + 과거분사를
더 자주 쓴다.

- The exam wasn't hard, but I **could have made** a few mistakes. 실수를 약간 했을지도 모른다. (= might/may have made)

단, **couldn't have** + 과거분사와는 다음과 같은 의미 차이가 있다.

- The man **couldn't have stolen** the car. He was in another city. 그 남자가 차를 훔쳤을 리 없다. (사실상 불가능함)
  The man **might/may not have stolen** the car. We don't really know.
  그 남자가 차를 훔치지 않았을지도 모른다. (훔쳤을 가능성도 있음)

PRACTICE

A. 그림을 보고 **might**를 사용하여 예시와 같이 문장을 완성하세요. 필요한 경우 부정문으로 쓰세요.

1	Are you going to stay home tonight? — Possibly.	4	Will the package arrive today? — Perhaps.
2	Will you help Jo with her presentation? — I don't know if I can.	5	Will you go to the festival next week? — Maybe not.
3	Are you going to buy that shirt? — I'm not sure.	6	Are we going to have dinner with Tom? — Possibly. I'll ask him.

1. _He might stay home tonight_ .
2. _____ .
3. _____ .
4. _____ .
5. _____ .
6. _____ .

B. 주어진 동사와 **might** 또는 **might have + 과거분사**를 사용하여 문장을 완성하세요. 필요한 경우 부정문으로 쓰세요.

attend	~~be~~	hear	know	leave	miss	order	wear

1. A: I don't want to go bowling.
   B: Why not? It _might be_ _____ fun.

2. A: Where do we keep the files?
   B: Ask Ross. He _____
      where they are.

3. A: I _____ a coat tonight.
   B: But you should. It's going to get cold later.

4. A: I called Mary's name, but she ignored me.
   B: Well, she _____ you.

5. A: Where did Edward get his new hat?
   B: I'm not sure. He _____ it online.

6. A: I _____ the meeting. I have a lot
      of work.
   B: Oh. John and I probably aren't going either.

7. A: We _____ the bus.
   B: I guess so. We got here too late.

8. A: I wanted to say goodbye to Tom, but I couldn't.
   B: He _____ yet. Let's call him.

C. 괄호 안에 주어진 동사와 **might not** 또는 **couldn't**를 사용하여 문장을 완성하세요. 필요한 경우 동사를 **have + 과거분사**로 쓰세요.

1. (rain) The ground is so dry. It _couldn't have rained_ last night.
2. (feel) "Why did Sara leave the concert early?" "She didn't tell me. She _____ well."
3. (be) "That man looks like Jim." "Yes, but it _____ him. Jim is much taller."
4. (have) "Tom _____ a pet. He is scared of animals." "Then, whose cat is that in his yard?"
5. (provide) Maybe we should take some shampoo for our trip. The hotel _____ it.
6. (begin) The show _____ already. It starts at 7:30, but it's only 7:15 now.
7. (work) You can use the printer, but it _____. I haven't used it in months.
8. (wake) Jessie _____ up yet. She sometimes sleeps late on Sunday mornings.

1

He **must be** scared.
그는 분명히 두려울 것이다.

He **must not want** to enter.
그는 분명히 들어가는 것을 원하지 않을 것이다.

'분명히 두려울 것이다', '분명히 들어가는 것을 원하지 않을 것이다'라는 의미로 강하게
추측한 내용을 말하기 위해 must be, must not want를 썼다.

2

'분명히 ~할 것이다'라는 의미로 현재나 미래의 일에 대해서 강하게 추측할 때 **must**를 쓴다.

긍정 · 부정

I/we/you/they he/she/it	must	(not)	listen use

- Terry **must listen** to a lot of music. His apartment is full of CDs. Terry는 분명히 음악을 많이 들을 것이다.
- Your laptop still looks new. You **must not use** it much.
- The children **must be** excited about their trip. They've been talking about it all morning.

3

과거의 일에 대해 강하게 추측할 때는 **must have + 과거분사**를 쓴다.

must have + 과거분사: (과거에) 분명히 ~했을 것이다

- Mark is covered in mud! He **must have slipped**. 그는 분명히 미끄러졌을 것이다.
- "Wendy is still not here." "She **must have gotten** lost. She doesn't know this area very well."

must not have + 과거분사: (과거에) 분명히 ~하지 않았을 것이다

- This shirt is dirty. I **must not have washed** it. 분명히 그것을 빨지 않았을 것이다.
- My roommate **must not have paid** the electricity bill. The lights won't turn on.

4

must/might/could는 모두 추측할 때 쓴다. 이때, 다음과 같은 의미 차이가 있다.

must + 동사원형 분명히 ~할 것이다 (~할 것이라고 거의 확신한다)	• Steve **must be** very busy. He has worked late a lot this week. (Steve가 바쁠 것이라고 거의 확신함)
might, could + 동사원형 ~할지도 모른다 (그러나 ~하지 않을 가능성도 있다)	• "Steve isn't answering his phone." "Well, he **might be** busy." 또는 "Well, he **could be** busy." (Steve가 바쁘지 않을 가능성도 있음)

must not과 **might not, couldn't**는 다음과 같은 의미 차이가 있다.

must not + 동사원형 분명히 ~하지 않을 것이다 (~하지 않을 것이라고 거의 확신한다)	• Andrea always drives her dad's car. She **must not own** one. (Andrea가 차를 소유하고 있지 않을 것이라고 거의 확신함)
might not + 동사원형 ~하지 않을지도 모른다 (그러나 ~할 가능성도 있다)	• Andrea **might not own** a car now. She said she wanted to **sell** it. (Andrea가 차를 소유하고 있을 가능성도 있음)
couldn't + 동사원형 ~할 리 없다 (~하는 것이 사실상 불가능하다)	• Andrea **couldn't own** a car. She can't drive. (Andrea가 차를 소유하는 것이 사실상 불가능함)

PRACTICE

A. 주어진 동사와 must를 사용하여 대화를 완성하세요. 필요한 경우 부정문으로 쓰세요.

~~be~~	be	cook	have	know	play

1. It's midnight but I think I'll keep reading.
2. Peter's fridge is usually empty.
3. Tom said hello to Jane.
4. I have won several piano competitions.
5. Only a few people are watching that movie.
6. Julia is coughing a lot.

You _must not be_ _____ sleepy.
He _____ at home often.
They _____ each other.
You _____ the piano well.
It _____ very good.
She _____ a cold.

B. 괄호 안에 주어진 동사와 must 또는 must have + 과거분사를 사용하여 문장을 완성하세요.

1. (be) Ben seems very nervous today. He _must be_ _____ worried about something.
2. (get) Joanna _____ a haircut. Her hair looks shorter today.
3. (enjoy) "I've worked for the same company for 20 years." "You _____ your job."
4. (exercise) Karen _____ a lot these days. She's in great shape.
5. (come) "There's a package at the door." "Oh, it _____ while we were out."
6. (drink) Somebody _____ all of the beer. There's none in the kitchen.

C. 주어진 표현과 must 또는 must have + 과거분사를 사용하여 예시와 같이 문장을 완성하세요. 필요한 경우 부정문으로 쓰세요.

be married	~~be twins~~	learn Italian there	like chicken	ride it to school	sleep enough

1. Don and Dan look exactly alike. _They must be twins_ _____.
2. Andrea hasn't eaten any of her food. _____.
3. Eric seems tired. _____.
4. Nancy and Robert went to college in Rome. _____.
5. Tina doesn't wear a wedding ring. _____.
6. Jim's bicycle isn't in the garage. _____.

D. Jenny와 Lucas가 영화를 보며 대화 중입니다. must 또는 might를 써넣으세요. 필요한 경우 부정문으로 쓰세요.

JENNY: Who stole Mrs. Parker's necklace?
LUCAS: I'm not sure. 1. It _might_ _____ have been Ms. Johnson.
I think she wanted the necklace.
JENNY: True. 2. But she was out of town, so it _____ have been her.
LUCAS: You're right. So who's left?
JENNY: 3. Well, Jack _____ have stolen it. What do you think?
LUCAS: Hmm. Maybe you're right, but I'm not sure...
4. Jack _____ have stolen it because he didn't seem very interested.
JENNY: Wait a minute. The cook was home alone!
5. He _____ have taken it!
LUCAS: You're right! Nobody knew he was home.
6. Mr. and Mrs. Parker _____ have thought it was him!

조동사

LESSON 25

Grammar Gateway Intermediate

She **must follow** the rules. must와 have to (의무)

1
She must follow the rules.
그녀는 반드시 규칙을 지켜야 한다.

She must not feed the animals.
그녀는 동물들에게 먹이를 주어서는 안 된다.

'반드시 규칙을 지켜야 한다', '동물들에게 먹이를 주어서는 안 된다'라는 의미로 의무에 대해 말하기 위해 must follow, must not feed를 썼다.

You must follow the rules.

2
must + 동사원형: 반드시 ~해야 한다

반드시 해야 하는 일, 즉 의무에 대해 말할 때 **must**를 쓴다. **must**는 공식적인 글에서 규정, 규칙에 대해 말할 때 자주 쓴다.

- Cars **must stop** at the red traffic light. 차는 빨간 신호에서 멈춰야 한다.
- I **must pay** rent at the end of every month.

must not + 동사원형: ~해서는 안 된다

해서는 안 되는 일, 즉 금지의 의미를 나타낼 때는 **must not**을 쓴다.

- Please be quiet. You **must not make** noise in the library. 도서관에서 소음을 내서는 안 된다.
- Students **must not be** late to the exam. They cannot come in after 10 a.m.

3
'~해야 한다'라는 의미로 말할 때 **have/has to**도 쓸 수 있다. 일상 대화에서는 **must**보다 **have/has to**를 더 자주 쓴다.

긍정	
I/we/you/they	**have to**
he/she/it	**has to**

부정		
I/we/you/they	**don't**	**have to**
he/she/it	**doesn't**	

의문		
do	I/we/you/they	**have to ... ?**
does	he/she/it	

- I don't have any clean clothes. I **have to do** my laundry soon. 곧 빨래를 해야 한다.
- Your dog **doesn't have to wait** outside. Dogs are welcome in this store.
- "**Do** I **have to apply** for the scholarship by tomorrow?" "No. The deadline is next Friday."

don't/doesn't have to는 '~할 필요가 없다'라는 의미이다. **must not**과의 의미 차이에 주의한다.

- You **don't have to call** Mr. Watson again. I already did. (Watson 씨에게 전화할 필요가 없음)
  You **mustn't call** Mr. Watson. He's in an important meeting right now. (Watson 씨에게 전화해서는 안 됨)

4
과거에 대해 말할 때는 **had to**를 쓴다. **must**는 과거형이 없다.

- I **had to finish** my homework first, so I arrived at the party late yesterday. 먼저 숙제를 끝내야 해서 어제 파티에 늦게 도착했다.
- Ms. Morgan isn't in her office. She **had to leave** for a doctor's appointment.

had to의 부정문은 **didn't have to**로 쓰고, 의문문은 **did ~ have to**로 쓴다.

- I **didn't have to worry** about the test. It was easy. 시험에 대해 걱정하지 않아도 되었다.
- "We went to the Chinese restaurant last week." "**Did** you **have to make** a reservation?"

5
will/might 등의 다음에는 **must**를 쓸 수 없고 **have to**만 쓰는 것에 주의한다.

- The bank isn't open yet. We**'ll have to come** back later. (will must come으로 쓸 수 없음)
- I **might have to borrow** your tent to go camping. I don't own one. (might must borrow로 쓸 수 없음)

PRACTICE

A. 그림을 보고 주어진 동사와 **must**를 사용하여 문장을 완성하세요. 필요한 경우 부정문으로 쓰세요.

~~bring~~	drive	show	take	touch	wear

🏛 **Rules for Museum Visitors**

1. You _must not bring_ in food or beverages.

2. You _____ the artwork.

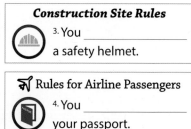

Construction Site Rules

3. You _____ a safety helmet.

✈ **Rules for Airline Passengers**

4. You _____ your passport.

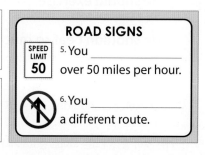

ROAD SIGNS

SPEED LIMIT **50**

5. You _____ over 50 miles per hour.

6. You _____ a different route.

B. 괄호 안에 주어진 단어들과 **have/has to**를 적절한 형태로 사용하여 문장을 완성하세요. 필요한 경우 부정문으로 쓰세요.

1. (we, be) "Our plane leaves at 8:30." " _We have to be_ _____ at the airport by 7 o'clock, then."
2. (She, take) Megan is better now. _____ her medicine anymore.
3. (we, work) "_____ late again tonight?" "I'm afraid so."
4. (the mayor, give) "_____ a speech at the ceremony?" "Yes. It's a tradition."
5. (you, walk) _____ to the grocery store. I'll give you a ride.
6. (he, pass) Tim is studying hard. _____ his science exam to graduate.

C. 괄호 안에 주어진 동사와 **must not** 또는 **don't have to**를 사용하여 문장을 완성하세요.

Hadley Park - General Information

1. (smoke) You _must not smoke_ _____ within the park. It's a no-smoking area.
2. (bring) You can rent tennis rackets. You _____ yours.
3. (fish) You _____ in the pond. It is not allowed.
4. (carry) There's a locker room. You _____ heavy bags around.
5. (pay) You _____ a parking fee. Parking is free.
6. (feed) You _____ bread to the ducks. It's bad for them.

D. 주어진 동사와 **must** 또는 **have to**를 적절한 형태로 사용하여 문장을 완성하세요. 필요한 경우 부정문으로 쓰세요.

apologize	hire	move	revise	sleep	~~stay~~	teach	tell

1. Stacey _had to stay_ _____ home last night because her baby was sick.
2. Professor Franklin is absent. Professor Taylor might _____ our class today.
3. I _____ to Roy after the fight. He said he was sorry first.
4. "Tara left her car keys here." "You _____ her. She could be looking for them."
5. Jeff _____ his seat closer to the front. He couldn't see very well.
6. "_____ you _____ your article?" "Yes. It still had some errors."
7. Sara and Eric had an extra bedroom, so I _____ on the sofa.
8. One of our employees suddenly quit, so now we _____ a new one.

조동사

LESSON **26**

Grammar Gateway Intermediate

1 He **should** exercise.
그는 운동하는 것이 좋겠다.

He **shouldn't eat** so much.
그는 너무 많이 먹지 않는 것이 좋겠다.

You **should** exercise.

'운동하는 것이 좋겠다', '너무 많이 먹지 않는 것이 좋겠다'라는 의미로 충고하기 위해
should exercise, shouldn't eat을 썼다.

---

2 '~하는 것이 좋겠다'라는 의미로 충고하거나 의견을 말할 때 **should**를 쓴다.

긍정 · 부정

I/we/you/they he/she/it	should	(not)	sleep drive

- "I sleep only three hours every night." "You **should sleep** more!" 잠을 더 자는 것이 좋겠어!
- It's snowing hard. I **shouldn't drive** tonight. 오늘 밤 운전하지 않는 것이 좋겠다.
- You **should say** "thank you" when people help you.
- "I don't think Kim **should drink** so much coffee." "I agree."
- Tommy, you **should be** nice to your brother. You **shouldn't fight** with him.

   should와 같은 의미로 **ought to**도 쓸 수 있다. 단, 일상 대화에서는 **should**를 주로 쓴다.

   - You **ought to stop** smoking. It's bad for you. (= should stop)

---

3 **should I/we ~?**: ~하는 것이 좋을까요?

상대방의 조언이나 의견을 구할 때는 **should I/we ~?**를 쓴다.

- "**Should I bring** anything to the party?" 파티에 무엇인가를 가져가는 것이 좋을까? "Maybe some wine."
- We've been practicing our dance for two hours. **Should we take** a break?
- "Where **should I put** the Christmas tree?" "In front of the window."

---

4 과거의 일에 대한 후회나 유감을 나타낼 때 **should have + 과거분사**를 쓴다.

should have + 과거분사: (과거에) ~했어야 했다 (그러나 하지 않았다)

- I told Julia's secret to Tina by accident. I **should have been** more careful. 더 조심했어야 했어. (그러나 조심하지 않았음)
- We **should have taken** the subway. The traffic is horrible today.

shouldn't have + 과거분사: (과거에) ~하지 말았어야 했다 (그러나 했다)

- Jim lost my camera. I **shouldn't have lent** it to him. 그에게 빌려주지 말았어야 했다. (그러나 빌려주었음)
- "Do you like your new apartment?" "Not really. I **shouldn't have moved**."

---

5 **should**와 **must/have to**는 다음과 같은 의미 차이가 있다.

- We **should attend** the seminar. It'll be interesting. (세미나에 참석하는 것이 좋지만 반드시 참석해야 하는 것은 아님)
   All employees **must attend** the seminar. It's required. (반드시 세미나에 참석해야 함)
- You **should wear** that blue tie. It looks nice on you.
   You **have to wear** a uniform to school. It's a rule.

PRACTICE

A. 주어진 동사와 should를 사용하여 대화를 완성하세요. 필요한 경우 부정문으로 쓰세요.

| give | leave | listen | open | ~~visit~~ | worry |

1. I haven't seen Derek for so long.
2. I'm nervous about my interview.
3. Let's get Ellen some roses!
4. Jason is always giving me advice.
5. Mr. Brown isn't answering his phone.
6. What's in this box? Can I see?

I think you _should visit_____ him.
You _____. You'll do fine.
We _____ her flowers. She's allergic.
He's smart. I think you _____ to him.
We _____ him a message.
It's Tom's. You _____ it.

B. 주어진 단어들과 should I ~?를 사용하여 문장을 완성하세요.

| ~~cut~~ | hang | meet | order | plan | throw |

1. " _Should I cut_____ my hair?" "Yes. I think you will look great with short hair."
2. "When _____ you at the café?" "How about in an hour?"
3. I bought a new painting to put on our wall. Where _____ it?
4. "I'm hungry." "Oh, _____ some food?"
5. "_____ away these old receipts?" "Sure. You don't need them."
6. Don and Lisa are coming to see me. What activities _____ for their visit?

C. 괄호 안에 주어진 표현들과 should have + 과거분사를 사용하여 예시와 같이 문장을 완성하세요. 필요한 경우 부정문으로 쓰세요.

1. (I, prepare more) I did badly on my presentation. _I should have prepared more_____.
2. (Jack, play) _____ the music so loudly. The neighbors complained.
3. (I, ask you first) "Did you use my bike this morning?" "Yes. Sorry. _____."
4. (we, help her) We didn't help Jill clean the house, so she's mad at us. _____.
5. (she, sell it) "Tracy sold her guitar. She regrets it." "That's too bad. _____."
6. (you, scare your little sister) Tony, _____. She was crying for hours.
7. (you, come with us) _____. The tour was a lot of fun.

D. 괄호 안에 주어진 동사와 should 또는 should have + 과거분사를 사용하여 James와 Linda의 대화를 완성하세요. 필요한 경우 부정문으로 쓰세요.

JAMES: I don't feel well.
  1. I think I _should lie_____ down for a while. (lie)
LINDA: What's wrong? Do you have a cold?
JAMES: No, I have a stomachache.
LINDA: Oh no. 2. You _____ so much at lunch. (eat)
JAMES: I know. 3. I _____ more French fries. (order)
LINDA: And you haven't exercised for weeks.
  4. You _____ a walk or go jogging later. (take)
JAMES: You're right. 5. I _____ exercising. (stop)
  6. I _____ so lazy from now on! (be)

JAMES

LINDA

1 Chris might fall off the ladder.

He **had better be** careful.
그는 조심하는 것이 좋겠다.

You**'d better be** careful!

'조심하는 것이 좋겠다'라는 의미로 강하게 충고하기 위해 had better be를 썼다.

---

2 '~하는 것이 좋겠다'라는 의미로 강하게 충고하거나 의견을 말할 때 **had better**를 쓴다. 일상 대화에서는 **we'd better**나 **you'd better** 등과 같이 축약된 형태를 더 자주 쓴다.

I/we/you/they	had better	hurry
he/she/it	(= 'd better)	start

- "The train will arrive soon." "We**'d better hurry**." 서두르는 것이 좋겠어.
- You**'d better start** on that report now. You only have a few days before the deadline.
  지금 보고서를 시작하는 것이 좋겠다.
- I**'d better change** my shirt. I dropped ketchup on it.
- "Smoke is coming out of the photocopier." "You**'d better call** the technician."

---

3 had better의 부정은 **had better not**으로 쓴다. **had better not**은 '~하지 않는 것이 좋겠다'라는 의미이다.

I/we/you/they	had better	not	stay
he/she/it	(= 'd better)		touch

- I have to wake up early tomorrow, so I**'d better not stay** up late. 늦게까지 깨어있지 않는 것이 좋겠어.
- The wall has just been painted. You**'d better not touch** it. 만지지 않는 것이 좋겠어.
- We**'d better not park** here. That sign says "No Parking."
- Frank **had better not jump** on the bed. He might damage it.

이때, **had not better**로 쓰지 않는 것에 주의한다.
- You**'d better not sit** there. That's Carla's seat. 거기에 앉지 않는 게 좋겠다. (You'd not better sit으로 쓸 수 없음)
- I promised Dave that I will write to him. I**'d better not forget**. (I'd not better forget으로 쓸 수 없음)

---

4 어떤 일을 하는 것이 좋겠다고 말할 때 **should**도 쓸 수 있다. 단, **had better**와 **should**는 다음과 같은 의미 차이가 있다.

had better는 어떤 일을 하지 않으면 좋지 않은 결과가 생길 것이라고 경고할 때 주로 쓴다.

- Tickets will be sold out soon. You**'d better buy** some today.
  (오늘 사지 않으면 표가 매진될 수 있음)
- "We**'d better take** the pie out of the oven now." "You're right! It might burn."
  (오븐에서 지금 꺼내지 않으면 파이가 탈 수 있음)
- I**'d better follow** you, or I might get lost.

should는 반드시 해야 하는 것은 아니지만 어떤 일을 하는 것이 좋겠다는 의견을 말할 때 주로 쓴다.

- You **should buy** those tickets. The seats are closer to the stage.
  (반드시 사야 하는 것은 아니지만 그 표를 사는 것이 좋겠음)
- "We **should take** a pie to the party tonight." "Good idea."
  (반드시 가져가야 하는 것은 아니지만 파이를 가져가는 것이 좋겠음)
- Mr. Park **should join** our golf club. He enjoys golf.

PRACTICE

A. 그림을 보고 주어진 표현과 **had better**를 사용하여 문장을 완성하세요.

close the window	keep quiet here	slow down
stay away	wash your hands	~~wear a helmet~~

1. You _'d better wear a helmet_
   OR _had better wear a helmet_ .

2. You _____
   _____ .

3. We _____
   _____ .

4. I _____
   _____ .

5. We _____
   _____ .

6. You _____
   _____ .

B. 주어진 동사와 **had better**를 사용하여 문장을 완성하세요. 필요한 경우 부정문으로 쓰세요.

arrive	forget	play	quit	register	~~rest~~	sweep	turn

1. "My feet hurt. We've been hiking all morning."   "We _'d better rest_ OR _had better rest_ under this tree."
2. "The floor in your room is very dirty."   "Oh, you're right. I _____ it."
3. You _____ with that knife, Sally. It's not a toy and you could get hurt.
4. Ms. Miller's class is almost full. If students want to take her class, they _____ now.
5. "Max got a warning about coming to work late."   "Well, he _____ late anymore."
6. I _____ to pay the credit card bill or I'll get another late fee.
7. You _____ off the music. I'm taking an important phone call.
8. "I heard Patrick may stop playing volleyball."   "He _____ the team! We need him!"

C. 주어진 상황을 보고 예시와 같이 **had better**를 사용해서 충고해보세요.

1. John is crossing a busy intersection. You think he should watch out.
   YOU: _You'd better watch out_ OR _You had better watch out_ .
2. There is a bad storm and you and Amanda are going outside. You think You and Amanda shouldn't.
   YOU: _____ .
3. The children might break the vase. You think you and your wife should put the vase on the top shelf.
   YOU: _____ .
4. Your employees are working very slowly. You think they shouldn't miss the deadline.
   YOU: _____ .
5. Joe wants to take a vacation next month. You think he shouldn't spend a lot of money this month.
   YOU: _____ .

1 be/have/can/do 등의 의문문은 다음과 같이 쓴다.

의문사	be/have/can/do 등	주어	
	Is	**it**	raining outside? 밖에 비가 오고 있니?
"**What**	**has**	**Tim**	been doing lately?" Tim은 요즘 뭐하고 지내? "Mostly looking for a new job."
	Can	**you**	call me later? I'm busy at the moment.
"**How**	**did**	**Jen**	get home?" "She took a taxi."

2 의문사가 있는 의문문에서 다음과 같이 의문사 뒤에 명사 또는 형용사/부사를 쓸 수도 있다.

what/which/whose + 명사 (time, tie 등)

what/which/whose	명사	
"**What**	**time**	is it right now?" 지금 몇 시니? "It's 10:45."
"**Which**	**tie**	should I wear?" 어떤 넥타이를 매는 것이 좋을까? "That red one."
"**Whose**	**laptop**	did you borrow?" "Martin's."
"**What**	**year**	was your sister born?" "1995."

how + 형용사/부사 (tall, fast 등)

how	형용사/부사	
"**How**	**tall**	is Tokyo Tower?" 도쿄 타워는 얼마나 높니? "It's over 2,000 feet."
"**How**	**fast**	can you type?" "Around 40 words a minute."
"**How**	**long**	have you been teaching art?" "For five years."

3 의문사가 있는 의문문에서 다음과 같이 전치사를 문장의 맨 끝에 쓸 수 있다.

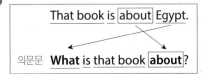

That book is about Egypt.

의문문 **What** is that book **about**?

- "**Who** did you go to the beach **with**?" 누구와 해변에 갔니? "I went alone."
- "**Where** are you walking **to**?" 어디로 걸어가는 중이니? "The grocery store."
- "Ann has been standing there for a while. **Who** is she waiting **for**?" "Her boyfriend."
- "I need a hobby." "Well, **what** kinds of things are you interested **in**?"

4 **What ~ for?**: ~은 무엇을 위한 것인가요?, 무엇 때문에 ~하나요?

사물의 용도나 사람의 행동의 목적을 묻기 위해 **What ~ for?**를 쓸 수 있다.

- "**What**'s this button **for**?" 이 버튼은 무엇을 위한 것인가요? "It turns on the printer."
- "Ouch! **What** did you hit me **for**?" "Sorry. It was an accident!"

What ~ like?: ~은 어떤가요?

사람이나 사물이 어떠한지 그 특징을 묻기 위해 **What ~ like?**를 쓸 수 있다.

- "**What** are your bosses **like**?" 네 상사들은 어떠니? "They are usually friendly."
- "I went to the new restaurant last night." "Really? **What** is it **like**?"

PRACTICE

A. 괄호 안에 주어진 표현들을 적절히 배열하여 의문문을 완성하세요.

1. (David / how / preparing / is) *How is David preparing* _____ for his interview?
2. (you / will / when / return home) _____ ?
3. (has / sent / Jenny / the documents) _____ yet?
4. (have / your neighbor / does) _____ a garden?
5. (your friends / are / graduating) _____ tomorrow?
6. (have / traveled / where / you) _____ in Canada?
7. (visit / Sarah / who / did) _____ last weekend?

B. 주어진 단어와 what/whose/how를 사용하여 의문문을 완성하세요.

car	idea	~~instrument~~	languages	much	often

1. " *What instrument* _____ do you play?" "I play the piano."
2. This is a brilliant suggestion! _____ was it?
3. "_____ can you speak?" "English and Korean."
4. "_____ do you see your parents?" "A few times a year."
5. We have a lot of luggage. _____ has the biggest trunk?
6. "An economy ticket is $300." "Then _____ is a business class ticket?"

C. 그림을 보고 주어진 표현과 what을 사용하여 의문문을 완성하세요. 현재진행 시제로 쓰세요.

apologize for	argue about	hide from	laugh at	reach for	~~think about~~

1. *What are you thinking about* ?
2. _____ ?
3. _____ ?
4. _____ ?
5. _____ ?
6. _____ ?

I'm sorry.

D. 괄호 안에 주어진 단어들과 What ~ for/like?를 사용하여 의문문을 완성하세요. 현재 시제 또는 과거 시제로 쓰세요.

1. (these balloons, be) *What are these balloons for* ?
2. (your roommate, be) _____ ?
3. (your first date, be) _____ ?
4. (the cake, be) _____ ?
5. (this big bowl, be) _____ ?

They're for my nephew's visit.
He's very nice. And he's funny.
It was really boring.
It was my mom's birthday.
It's for fruit.

LESSON 29

Grammar Gateway Intermediate

1

Rachel invited <u>someone</u>.
목적어

Who did Rachel invite?

Rachel이 누구를 초대했니?

'누구를'이라는 의미로 Who를 의문문의 목적어로 썼다.

<u>Someone</u> invited Chris.
주어

Who invited Chris?

누가 Chris를 초대했니?

'누가'라는 의미로 Who를 의문문의 주어로 썼다.

2

who/what/which는 의문문의 목적어로 쓸 수 있다.

- "**Who is Lucas helping**?" "An old lady."
  Lucas가 누구를 도와주고 있니? (동사 is helping의 목적어로 Who를 썼음)

- "**What did you buy** at the mall?" "A wallet."
  쇼핑몰에서 무엇을 샀니? (동사 buy의 목적어로 What을 썼음)

- "**Which does Jim prefer**, steak or pasta?"
  "He prefers steak."

- "**Who can we ask** about gardening?"
  "Let's ask Nina. She knows a lot."

- "**What did Emily bring** to class?"
  "It's a violin. She's going to play it for us."

이때, 일반동사 의문문에서는 주어 앞에 **do/does/did**를 쓰는 것에 주의한다.

- "**Who did you call** last night?" "I called Mike."
  어젯밤에 누구에게 전화했니?

- "**What do you want** for breakfast?"
  "How about an omelet?"

who/what/which는 의문문의 주어로도 쓸 수 있다.

- "**Who is helping** the old lady?" "Lucas."
  누가 저 노부인을 도와주고 있니? (동사 is helping의 주어로 Who를 썼음)

- "**What's** in that box?" "It's a new wallet."
  상자 안에 무엇이 들어있니? (동사 is의 주어로 What을 썼음)

- "I've eaten the steak and the pasta here."
  "**Which is** better?"

- "**Who has taught** you to dance?"
  "My sister has. She's a dance teacher."

- "**What caused** the accident?"
  "A deer jumped in front of the car."

이때, 일반동사 의문문에서도 주어 앞에 **do/does/did**를 쓰지 않는 것에 주의한다.

- "**Who called** you last night?" "Richard did."
  어젯밤에 누가 너에게 전화했니?

- "**Which travels** faster? Sound or light?"
  "Light."

3

의문문에서 **who** 대신 **whom**도 목적어로 쓸 수 있다. 그러나 일상 대화에서는 **who**를 더 자주 쓴다.

- **Who** did you meet yesterday? 또는 **Whom** did you meet yesterday? 어제 누구를 만났니?

- "**Who** is Tony marrying?" 또는 "**Whom** is Tony marrying?" "I don't know."

4

의문사 (what/which/whose/how many 등) + 명사도 의문문의 목적어나 주어로 쓸 수 있다.

- **What sports do you play**?
  어떤 운동을 하나요? (동사 play의 목적어로 What sports를 썼음)

- **Which camera should I buy**? I can't decide.
  어느 카메라를 살까? (동사 buy의 목적어로 Which camera를 썼음)

- "**Whose classes are you taking** next semester?"
  "Mr. Peterson's."

- "**How many people have you hired** this
  month?" "We've hired ten so far."

- **What sports are** popular in Brazil?
  브라질에선 어떤 운동이 인기가 있나요? (동사 are의 주어로 What sports를 썼음)

- **Which camera costs** less? I want the cheaper one.
  어느 카메라가 값이 더 적게 드나요? (동사 costs의 주어로 Which camera를 썼음)

- "**Whose classes are** the most interesting?"
  "Professor Kent's. His classes are always full."

- "**How many people have visited** the Grand Canyon
  this year?" "A few million."

P R A C T I C E

A. 그림을 보고 괄호 안에 주어진 대상과 who를 사용하여 의문문을 완성하세요.

1. (Craig) A: *Who told Craig the secret* ?
   B: Anna told him the secret.

2. (Craig) A: _____ to?
   B: He told Bill the secret.

3. (the Bears) A: _____ ?
   B: The Lions beat them.

4. (the Owls) A: _____ ?
   B: They beat the Dragons.

B. 주어진 문장을 보고 who 또는 what을 사용하여 보이지 않는 정보에 대해 질문하세요.

 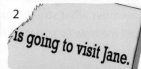  

  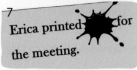

1. *Who did Samantha meet at the park* ?
2. _____ ?
3. _____ ?
4. _____ ?
5. _____ ?
6. _____ ?
7. _____ ?
8. _____ ?

C. 괄호 안에 주어진 표현들을 적절히 배열하여 Chris와 Paul의 대화를 완성하세요.

CHRIS: Hey Paul. I'm going to a party tonight.
1. *Which shirt looks better* on me? (looks / shirt / which / better)

PAUL: A party? 2. _____ to a party?
(you / who / invited)

CHRIS: Rachel. It's her birthday.

PAUL: Oh, that will be fun. 3. _____ ?
(people / are coming / how many)

CHRIS: Around 10, I think. 4. _____ for a gift?
(give / should / I / what / her)

PAUL: Maybe flowers or a cake. 5. _____ more?
(she / will / like / which)

CHRIS: I don't know. I'll just get both.

CHRIS

PAUL

LESSON 30

Grammar Gateway Intermediate

Do you know **where the dog is?** 간접의문문

1 Where is the dog?

Do you know **where the dog is**?
　　　　　　　　　간접의문문

개가 어디 있는지 아세요?

Where is the dog?이라는 의문문을 Do you know ~?에 포함시켜 말하기 위해
where the dog is로 썼다. 이때, where the dog is는 간접의문문이다.

Do you know **where the dog is?**

2 의문문을 다른 문장 안에 포함시켜 말할 때 간접의문문을 쓴다. 간접의문문은 다음과 같이 쓴다.

의문사가 있는 의문문을 간접의문문으로 쓸 때는 **의문사 + 주어 + 동사** 순서로 쓴다.

Who is our new teacher?
　의문사 동사　　주어

Do you know **who our new teacher is**?
　　　　　　　　의문사　　　주어　　　동사

- Do you know **who our new teacher is**? 새로 온 선생님이 누구인지 아니?
- I'm not sure **where Lily has gone**. Lily가 어디 갔는지 잘 모르겠어.
- I don't remember **what street Frank lives** on.
- Can you tell me **how I can get** to Herald Square?

단, **who/what/which**를 주어로 쓰는 경우에는 **who/what/which + 동사** 순서로 쓴다.

- I wonder **who is going to sing** at Cindy's wedding. 누가 Cindy의 결혼식에서 노래를 부를지 궁금하다.
- This story is a mystery. I don't know **what will happen** next.
- Can you tell me **which store sells** baby clothes?

의문사가 없는 의문문을 간접의문문으로 쓸 때는 **if/whether + 주어 + 동사** 순서로 쓴다. 이때, **if/whether**는 '~인지 (아닌지)'라는
의미이다.

Is Bill in his office?
동사　주어

I wonder **if Bill is** in his office.
　　　　　주어　동사

- I wonder **if Bill is** in his office. Bill이 사무실에 있는지 궁금해요.
- I don't remember **whether I saw** that movie. 저 영화를 봤는지 기억이 안 난다.
- I'm not sure **if I'll have** time to meet you tonight.
- Do you know **whether Julie has finished** the assignment?

3 간접의문문에서는 일반동사를 쓰는 경우에도 **do/does/did**를 쓰지 않는 것에 주의한다.

When did Sue go to lunch?	→	- I don't know **when Sue went to lunch**. (when Sue did go로 쓸 수 없음)
Do students receive a discount?	→	- Can you tell me **if students receive a discount**? (if students do receive으로 쓸 수 없음)
What time does Jim's flight arrive?	→	- I wonder **what time Jim's flight arrives**.

4 간접의문문은 다음과 같은 표현과 자주 함께 쓴다.

I don't know …	- **I don't know** if I've studied enough for the exam. 시험 공부를 충분히 했는지 모르겠어.
Do you know … ?	- **Do you know** how many lakes are in this city? 이 도시에 호수가 몇 개 있는지 아니?
I wonder …	- **I wonder** who will become class president this year.
I'm not sure …	- **I'm not sure** which way the post office is. Do you know?
I don't remember …	- **I don't remember** whether I turned off the stove.
Can you tell me … ?	- "**Can you tell me** what your phone number is?" "Of course. It's 555-6400."

P R A C T I C E

A. 각 사람이 궁금해하는 내용을 보고 간접의문문을 사용하여 문장을 완성하세요.

1. Do you know *when Joseph will come home* ?

2. I wonder _____ .

3. Can you tell me _____ ?

4. Do you know _____ ?

B. 괄호 안에 주어진 표현들을 적절히 배열하여 문장을 완성하세요. 과거 시제로 쓰세요.

1. (what time / go to school / Mandy) I don't remember *what time Mandy went to school* _____ yesterday.
2. (in Lucy's backpack / what / be) I wonder _____ . It seemed heavy.
3. (get into / how / the thief) I don't know _____ our house.
4. (who / this file / leave) Do you know _____ in the meeting room?
5. (stay in LA / where / you) Can you tell me _____ ? I'm going there soon.
6. (which sandwich / want / Laura) I wasn't sure _____ , so I just ordered.

C. 주어진 의문문을 사용하여 대화를 완성하세요.

| Are these shoes on sale? | Did I tell you about the art exhibit? | Does the bus to Oak Park stop here? |
| ~~Has Henry read my e-mail?~~ | Is someone sitting here | |

1. I wonder *if/whether Henry has read my e-mail* .
2. I'm not sure _____ .
3. I don't know _____ .
4. Do you know _____ ?
5. Can you tell me _____ ?

He said he'll check.
Let's ask the salesman.
You did. Let's go see it.
No. The seat is empty.
Yes. It will arrive in a bit.

D. 주어진 표현들을 사용하여 문장을 완성하세요.

| ~~Has Todd had lunch yet?~~ | Should I believe her? | Was it a dog or a cat? |
| What is it called? | When will my suit be ready? | Who did Christine call? |

1. (I'm not sure) *I'm not sure if/whether Todd has had lunch yet* _____ . I want to eat with him.
2. (do you know) I can't remember the name of this plant. _____ ?
3. (I don't know) Kayla lies sometimes. _____ .
4. (can you tell me) _____ ? I need it before Sunday.
5. (I don't remember) Karen had a pet, but _____ .
6. (I wonder) _____ . She was on the phone for a long time.

LESSON **31**

Grammar Gateway Intermediate

1 상대방에게 동의를 구하거나, 자신의 말이 맞는지 물을 때 문장 끝에 부가의문문을 쓴다. 긍정문 뒤에는 부정 부가의문문을 쓰고, 부정문 뒤에는 긍정 부가의문문을 쓴다. 부가의문문의 주어는 항상 대명사로 쓴다.

긍정문 + 부정 부가의문문

- Rita's birthday is tomorrow, **isn't it?** Rita의 생일은 내일이야, 그렇지 않니?
- "We have been to that restaurant before, **haven't we?**" "We might have."
- "You can help me move tomorrow, **can't you?**" "Sorry, I can't. I'll be busy."

부정문 + 긍정 부가의문문

- "Nick isn't quitting his job, **is he?**" Nick은 일을 그만두지 않을 거야, 그렇지 않니? "I don't think so."
- "You haven't done the laundry yet, **have you?**" "No, but I'll do it soon."
- "Your dog won't bite, **will he?**" "No. He's friendly."

  앞서 말한 동사가 일반동사인 경우, 부가의문문에 **do/does/did**를 쓰는 것에 주의한다.

  - You play golf, **don't you?** (play가 일반동사이므로 don't you를 썼음)
  - Jessica didn't enjoy the movie, **did she?** (didn't enjoy가 일반동사이므로 did she를 썼음)

2 자신의 의견이 옳다고 생각하여 상대방이 동의하기를 바랄 때는 주로 부가의문문의 끝을 내려서 말한다.

- "Jonathan's house is beautiful, **isn't it?**" "Yes, it is." (Jonathan의 집이 아름답다는 의견에 대해 상대방이 동의하기를 바람)
- "This assignment doesn't look easy, **does it?**" "No, it looks quite difficult."
  (과제가 쉬워 보이지 않는다는 의견에 대해 상대방이 동의하기를 바람)

자신의 말이 맞는지 아닌지를 상대방에게 확인할 때는 주로 부가의문문의 끝을 올려서 말한다.

- "These are your gloves, **aren't they?**" "Oh, yes. Thanks."
  (장갑의 주인이 맞는지 확인함)
- "We don't have to work on Christmas Day, **do we?**" "Of course not."
  (크리스마스에 일을 하지 않아도 되는 것이 맞는지 확인함)

3 상대방이 동의하기를 바라거나, 어떤 사실에 대한 놀라움을 나타낼 때 부정의문문을 쓴다. 부정의문문은 다음과 같이 쓴다.

Isn't/Aren't/Wasn't/Weren't … ?	Haven't/Hasn't … ?
Don't/Doesn't/Didn't … ?	Won't/Wouldn't/Can't/Couldn't … ?

- **Wasn't that** a great performance? 정말 훌륭한 공연이지 않니? (훌륭한 공연이었다는 생각에 대해 상대방이 동의하기를 바람)
- "Is Santana Park nice?" "It's great! **Haven't you** been there before?" 그곳에 가본 적이 없니? (가본 적이 없다는 사실에 놀람)
- **Don't you** remember my phone number? We have been friends for three years!
- "I think I'll buy this shirt for Jessica. **Won't she** love it?" "I think so."

4 부가의문문과 부정의문문에 답할 때, **Yes**와 **No**의 사용에 주의한다. '~하다/이다'라는 긍정의 의미로 답할 때는 **Yes**를 쓰고, '~하지 않다/아니다'라는 부정의 의미로 답할 때는 **No**를 쓴다.

- "That soup tastes salty, **doesn't it?**" "**Yes**, it does." 응. 짜. (= Yes, it tastes salty.)
- "**Aren't you** excited about your vacation?" "**Yes**, I am."
- "Gina hasn't left yet, **has she?**" "**No**, she hasn't." 아니, 아직 떠나지 않았어. (= No, she hasn't left yet.)
- "**Can't Mike** drive?" "**No**, he can't."

PRACTICE

A. Jennifer와 Sam은 수영하러 가는 것에 대해 대화 중입니다. 부가의문문을 사용하여 대화를 완성하세요.

> JENNIFER: 1. The weather is great today, *isn't it* _____?
>
> SAM: It's perfect! 2. We should do something outside, _____?
>
> JENNIFER: How about swimming?
>
>   Oh, wait. 3. You can't swim, _____?
>
> SAM: No, but you can teach me.
>
>   4. You've taken swimming lessons before, _____?
>
> JENNIFER: Yes, I have.
>
> SAM: Great. But I don't have a swimsuit.
>
>   5. You don't mind if we stop by the store, _____?
>
> JENNIFER: Not at all. Let's go!

B. 괄호 안에 주어진 표현들을 적절히 배열하여 문장을 완성하세요. 부가의문문을 함께 쓰세요.

1. (you / will / me / call / later) *You will call me later, won't you* _____?
2. (take / me / can't / to the concert / you) _____?
3. (rides / her bike / Melissa / to work) _____?
4. (on a business trip / is going / Chad) _____?
5. (haven't / we / hiking / gone / together) _____?

C. 주어진 상황을 보고 예시와 같이 부정의문문을 사용해서 말해보세요.

1. You think the pie is delicious. You want your friend to agree with you.
   YOU: *Isn't the pie delicious* _____?
2. You're surprised that Lucas wasn't waiting for his sister at the airport.
   YOU: _____?
3. You think you look good in blue jeans. You want your friend to agree with you.
   YOU: _____?
4. You're surprised that Melanie didn't leave for work yet.
   YOU: _____?
5. You think you and your friend will have fun at the beach. You want your friend to agree with you.
   YOU: _____?
6. You're surprised that Roger hasn't had a girlfriend before.
   YOU: _____?

D. 주어진 문장을 보고 상황에 맞게 Yes 또는 No를 써넣으세요.

1. Eric isn't coming over for dinner, is he?	*Yes*_____, he is. And he's bringing his wife.
2. Don't you have an interview this morning?	_____. It was yesterday.
3. Graham doesn't have a brother, does he?	_____. He's an only child.
4. Didn't Shelley look pretty at her wedding?	_____. She was very beautiful.
5. Can't you play the guitar?	_____. I've never learned how to play.
6. Jenny will graduate from university next week, won't she?	_____. Her graduation is next Saturday.

1

능동태   He **painted** the fence.
목적어

수동태   The fence **was painted** .
주어
울타리가 페인트칠 되었다.

'울타리가 페인트칠 되었다'라는 의미로 말하기 위해 수동태 was painted를 썼다.
이때, 주어 The fence는 페인트칠의 대상이다.

2 주어가 어떤 일의 대상일 때 수동태를 쓴다. 수동태는 **be동사 + 과거분사**로 쓴다.

(현재) **am/is/are** + 과거분사
- Salt **is used** in almost every dish. 소금은 거의 모든 요리에 사용된다.
- Cameras **are not allowed** inside the museum. 카메라는 박물관 안에서 허용되지 않는다.

(과거) **was/were** + 과거분사
- Donna **was taken** to the hospital. She had a bad stomachache.
- "Where **were** these grapes **grown**?" "Chile."

주어가 어떤 일을 하는 사람이나 사물일 때는 능동태를 쓴다. 능동태와 수동태는 다음과 같은 차이가 있다.

능동태 • **We planned** the party a month ago. (우리가 파티를 계획했음)
수동태 • **The party was planned** a month ago. (파티가 계획되었음)

3 다음과 같이 수동태를 다양한 형태로 쓸 수 있다.

현재진행, 과거진행 시제 수동태는 **be동사 + being + 과거분사**로 쓴다.

	능동태	수동태
(현재진행)	A bird **is building** a nest.	→ A nest **is being built**.
(과거진행)	Workers **were making** shoes at the factory.	→ Shoes **were being made** at the factory.

- "Did you buy all the presents?" "Yes. They**'re being wrapped** right now." 그것들은 지금 포장되고 있어.
- "The elevators **were being repaired**." "Did you take the stairs, then?"
- I turned off the TV because it **wasn't being watched**.

현재완료, 과거완료 시제 수동태는 **have/has/had been + 과거분사**로 쓴다.

	능동태	수동태
(현재완료)	Mr. Smith **has changed** the meeting time.	→ The meeting time **has been changed**.
(과거완료)	They **had delivered** the groceries when we got home.	→ The groceries **had been delivered** when we got home.

- The prices of all products **have been reduced**. The store is having a sale. 모든 상품들의 가격이 인하되었다.
- The piano in my room **hasn't been played** for years.
- When I came back from my vacation, the office building **had been renovated**.

will/can/must 등과 함께 쓸 때는 **will/can/must** 등 + **be** + 과거분사로 쓴다.

능동태	수동태
They **will serve** dinner soon.	→ Dinner **will be served** soon.
You **can purchase** tickets online.	→ Tickets **can be purchased** online.

- All refunds **must be requested** within 90 days. 모든 환불은 90일 이내에 요구되어야 한다.
- We're working on a huge project. It **won't be completed** until next year.

PRACTICE

A. 그림을 보고 주어진 표현들을 하나씩 사용하여 예시와 같이 문장을 완성하세요. 과거 시제로 쓰세요.

the juice	the letters	the onion		cut	~~make~~	send
~~the statue~~	the windows		+	spill	wash	

1. _The statue was made_____ in 1892.
2. _____ over the keyboard.
3. _____ into four pieces.
4. _____.
5. _____ to Michael.

B. 주어진 동사를 적절한 형태로 사용하여 능동태 또는 수동태 문장을 완성하세요.

cancel	carry	cook	include	join	know	~~speak~~	wear

1. In Canada, both English and French _are spoken_____. They are the national languages.
2. Mark _____ a book club last month. He's enjoying it very much.
3. Tomorrow's baseball game might _____ because of the storm.
4. "These boxes are so heavy." "Give them to me. I'll _____ them for you."
5. That singer is famous. She _____ around the world.
6. These noodles should _____ for at least 10 minutes in boiling water.
7. Samantha always _____ pants. I've never seen her in a skirt.
8. Meals _____ in the travel package. We didn't have to pay extra for them.

C. 괄호 안에 주어진 동사를 사용하여 수동태 문장을 완성하세요. 현재진행 시제 또는 과거진행 시제로 쓰세요.

1. (fix) "Why is it so cold in here?" "Our heater _is being fixed_____ at the moment."
2. (plant) When I went to the farm last spring, potatoes _____.
3. (not use) Those chairs _____ right now. We can sit there.
4. (not clean) The pool _____ this morning, so we went swimming.
5. (develop) New cancer drugs _____ at the moment. This gives hope to patients.
6. (perform) We got to the theater late. The play _____ when we arrived.
7. (not help) That old lady _____ right now. Let's go and help her get on the bus.
8. (print) While our wedding invitations _____, we waited at a coffee shop.

D. 괄호 안에 주어진 표현들을 사용하여 수동태 문장을 완성하세요. 현재완료 시제 또는 과거완료 시제로 쓰세요.

1. (the deadline, move) I have to work all night tonight. _The deadline has been moved_____ to tomorrow.
2. (North America, not discover) _____ before Columbus found it in 1492.
3. (my purse, take) When I returned to the café, _____ already.
4. (it, update) My computer was slow for months, but _____ recently. Now it's very fast.
5. (we, introduce) "Have you met Ms. Paulson?" "Yes, _____."
6. (the ring, sell) _____ when I visited the store the next day.
7. (it, close) There was a big fire at the museum last Friday. _____ since then.
8. (all of the things, pack) _____. Finally, we can leave now!

수동태

LESSON 33

Grammar Gateway Intermediate

The new city hall will be designed by a French architect. 수동태 (2)

1 수동태를 쓸 때 누구 또는 무엇에 의해서 일어나는 일인지를 말하기 위해 **by**를 쓸 수 있다.

- The new city hall **will be designed by a French architect**. 새 시청은 프랑스인 건축가에 의해 설계될 것이다.
- *A Christmas Carol* **was written by Charles Dickens**.
- The security system in this building **is controlled by computers**.

누구 또는 무엇에 의해서 일어나는 일인지를 말하지 않아도 알 수 있거나, 누가 하는지가 중요하지 않은 경우에는 **by**를 쓰지 않는다.

- Rice **is eaten** in many countries around the world. (누가 먹는지는 말하지 않아도 알 수 있음)
- The winners of the contest **were announced** yesterday. (누가 발표했는지는 중요하지 않음)
- "I like your sweater. **Is** it **made** of wool?" "Yes, it is."

2 다음과 같은 동사는 수동태로 쓰지 않는다.

seem/appear ~인 것처럼 보이다	**happen/occur** 일어나다, 벌어지다	**belong** 속하다	**consist** 구성되다

- I met John's girlfriend yesterday. She **seems** nice. 친절한 것처럼 보인다. (She is seemed로 쓸 수 없음)
- What **happened**? The window is broken. 무슨 일이 일어났던 거야? (What was happened로 쓸 수 없음)
- "Whose car is that?" "It **belongs** to Mr. Bradley."
- This survey **consists** of 12 questions. Please answer all of them.

3 다음과 같이 수동태로 쓰는 표현들이 있다.

be married 기혼이다	**be born** 태어나다	**be done/finished** 끝내다, 마치다	**be lost** 길을 잃다

- "Is Charlie single?" "No. He**'s married**." 그는 기혼이야.
- "I **was born** in Toronto." 나는 토론토에서 태어났어. "Really? Me too!"
- "**Are** you **finished** with your homework?" "Yes, I**'m done**."
- "Where are we?" "I'm not sure. I think we**'re lost**."

4 다음과 같이 **get + 과거분사**로 쓰는 수동태 표현이 있다. **get + 과거분사** 표현들은 격식을 갖춘 대화보다는 일상 대화에서 주로 쓴다.

get married 결혼하다	**get invited** 초대받다	**get dressed** 옷을 입다	**get caught** 잡히다
get paid 봉급을 받다	**get promoted** 승진하다	**get hired** 채용되다	**get fired** 해고되다
get hit 맞다, 치이다	**get hurt** 다치다	**get burned** 화상을 입다	**get broken** 깨지다, 망가지다

- My wife and I **got married** in 2012. 아내와 나는 2012년에 결혼했다.
- We usually go out for a beer when we **get paid**. 우리는 봉급을 받으면 맥주를 마시러 간다.
- Tony **got hit** by the baseball during practice yesterday.
- "Do you want to see a movie?" "Sounds great. I'll **get dressed**."

get + 과거분사의 부정문은 **don't/doesn't/didn't get + 과거분사**로 쓰고, 의문문은 **do/does/did ~ get + 과거분사**로 쓴다.

- These wine glasses **don't get broken** easily. They're quite strong. 이 와인 잔들은 쉽게 깨지지 않는다.
- "I **didn't get promoted**. I heard the news this morning." "That's too bad."
- "**Did** you **get invited** to Amanda's birthday party?" Amanda의 생일 파티에 초대받았니? "Yes, but I can't go."
- "How **did** Maria **get burned**?" "She spilled hot coffee on her arm."

PRACTICE

A. 첫 번째 괄호 안에 주어진 동사를 사용하여 문장을 완성하세요. 두 번째 괄호 안에 주어진 표현은 꼭 필요한 경우에만 by와 함께 쓰세요. 현재 시제 또는 과거 시제로 쓰세요.

1. (invent) (Chester Carlson) The photocopier *was invented by Chester Carlson*   .
2. (bake) (a baker) The bread at that bakery _____ every day, so it's always fresh.
3. (cause) (a tornado) The damage to the house _____ .
4. (deliver) (a postman) These packages are for Sara. They _____ this morning.
5. (prepare) (Antonio Bruno) Now our meals _____ . He's our new chef.
6. (arrest) (the police) Frank _____ because he was driving without a license.

B. 다음 문장을 읽고 틀린 부분이 있으면 바르게 고치세요. 틀린 부분이 없으면 ○로 표시하세요.

1. The cereal is consisted of natural ingredients.   *is consisted → consists*
2. The actress is surrounded photographers.   _____
3. A cat suddenly was appeared in the doorway.   _____
4. "Was this book published last year?" "Yes, it was."   _____
5. Olivia got burned while she was cooking, but she's OK now. _____
6. That jacket isn't belonged to me.   _____
7. We were lost in a strange place and didn't have a map.   _____
8. Some trains delayed by an accident yesterday.   _____

C. 다음은 작가 Michelle O'Neal에 대한 기사입니다. 수동태로 쓰는 표현을 사용하여 문장을 완성하세요.

1. Michelle O'Neal, a romance novelist, *was born* in Canada in 1976.
2. She _____ to a Japanese man and has two kids.
Michelle met her husband when she was visiting Japan.
3. She _____ and he helped her to find her hotel.
Michelle is currently writing a book about their love story.
4. By next month, she will _____ with it.
There's more good news. Michelle is expecting her third child.
5. The baby will _____ in November.

D. 주어진 동사와 get을 사용하여 대화를 완성하세요. 필요한 경우 부정문으로 쓰세요. 과거 시제로 쓰세요.

break	catch	dress	fire	hurt	~~invite~~

1. A: Taylor *got invited* _____ to the White House.
   B: Wow! That's amazing!

2. A: These dishes _____ during delivery.
   B: Oh, no. Those were really expensive.

3. A: Some men robbed a bank downtown today.
   B: _____ they _____ yet?

4. A: The bus crashed, but the passengers _____ .
   B: They were very lucky.

5. A: _____ you _____ ?
   We need to go.
   B: OK. I'm putting on my coat now.

6. A: Dave was worried about losing his job.
   B: Fortunately, he _____ .

1

They gave Justin a skateboard.
 사람   사물

Justin was given a skateboard.
 주어
Justin은 스케이트보드를 받았다.

A skateboard was given to Justin.
 주어
스케이트보드가 Justin에게 주어졌다.

Justin(사람)과 a skateboard(사물)는 모두 동사 gave의 목적어이다. 두 개의 목적어를 각각 주어로 하여 두 개의 수동태 문장을 썼다.

2 다음의 동사들 뒤에 사람과 사물 두 개의 목적어를 쓸 수 있다. 따라서 이 동사들을 수동태로 쓸 때는 두 개의 목적어를 각각 주어로 하여 두 가지 형태의 수동태 문장을 쓸 수 있다.

give	offer	send	lend	tell	show	teach	ask	pay

능동태
Ms. Williams offered **the guests tea**.
 사람   사물

→ (사람) ● **The guests were offered** tea by Ms. Williams.
손님들은 Williams 씨에 의해 차를 제공받았다.

(사물) ● **Tea was offered** to the guests by Ms. Williams.
차는 Williams 씨에 의해 손님들에게 제공되었다.

Readers send **the editor letters** every day. →
 사람   사물

(사람) ● **The editor is sent** letters by readers every day.

(사물) ● **Letters are sent** to the editor by readers every day.

3 사람을 주어로 수동태 문장을 쓸 때는 **be동사 + 과거분사** 뒤에 사물을 쓴다.

사람	be동사 + 과거분사	사물	
●	I	was asked	some questions	by the police officer. 나는 경찰관에 의해 몇 가지 질문을 받았다.
●	The children	are shown	a video	once a week.
●	Jane	will be paid	$50	for babysitting.

사물을 주어로 수동태 문장을 쓸 때는 **be동사 + 과거분사** 뒤에 **to + 사람**을 쓴다.

사물	be동사 + 과거분사	to + 사람	
●	Headphones	were lent	to passengers	during the flight. 비행 중 탑승객들에게 헤드폰이 대여되었다.
●	Art history	is taught	to all students	at our school.

일반적으로 사물을 주어로 한 수동태 문장보다는 사람을 주어로 한 수동태 문장을 더 자주 쓴다.

● **Ms. Ross was given** earrings on Valentine's Day. Ross 씨는 밸런타인데이에 귀걸이를 받았다.
● **We were told** the news about Gary's accident today.

PRACTICE

A. 그림을 보고 주어진 표현과 give를 사용하여 문장을 완성하세요. 과거 시제로 쓰세요.

a gold medal	a good grade	a package	balloons
cards	some cookies	some medicine	~~some money~~

1. He _was given some money_ .
2. He _____ .
3. They _____ .
4. She _____ .
5. They _____ .
6. She _____ .
7. They _____ .
8. He _____ .

B. 주어진 문장을 보고 밑줄 친 대상을 주어로 하는 수동태 문장으로 다시 말해보세요. 필요한 경우 to를 함께 쓰세요.

1. The store sends <u>customers</u> calendars every year. → _Customers are sent calendars_ by the store every year.
2. Bob paid <u>me</u> $50 for my old bike. → _____ for my old bike.
3. That bank lends foreign residents <u>money</u>. → _____ by that bank.
4. Ms. Sanders will show <u>visitors</u> the gardens. → _____ .
5. Mr. Harrison told his grandchildren <u>the story</u>. → _____ by Mr. Harrison.
6. The clerk offered <u>us</u> a discount. → _____ by the clerk.
7. Ashley teaches <u>students</u> yoga twice a week. → _____ by Ashley twice a week.
8. The reporter will ask the movie star <u>some questions</u>. → _____ .

C. 주어진 수동태 문장을 보고 예시와 같이 주어진 주어에 맞는 수동태 문장으로 다시 말해보세요.

1. A joke was told to the audience by the comedian.
   → The audience _was told a joke by the comedian_ .
2. The driver will be paid a delivery fee.
   → A delivery fee _____ .
3. Passports must be shown to the security guard.
   → The security guard _____ .
4. Manners are taught to children by their parents.
   → Children _____ .
5. The girl was sent a box of chocolate by Ned.
   → A box of chocolate _____ .

Playing chess is difficult. 주어로 쓰는 -ing와 It ~ to + 동사원형

Playing chess is difficult.

1 Chess is difficult.

Playing chess is difficult.
체스를 두는 것은 어렵다.

'체스를 두는 것'이라는 의미로 Playing chess를 썼다. 이때, Playing chess는 동사 is의 주어이다.

2 '~하는 것'이라는 의미로 **-ing**를 주어로 쓸 수 있다.
- **Skiing** is exciting. It's my favorite sport! 스키를 타는 것은 신이 난다.
- Let's take a plane to Dallas. **Flying** will save time. 비행기를 타는 것이 시간을 아껴줄 거야.
- **Writing letters** has become less common these days.
- "You have a lot of old coins!" "**Collecting coins** used to be my hobby."

동사의 형태 변화: 부록 p. 280 참고

이때, 다음과 같이 **-ing** 뒤에 여러 단어를 함께 쓸 수 있다.

- **Wearing a seatbelt** can protect you from injury. (안전벨트를 하는 것)
- **Going for a walk** sounds nice. Let's go. (산책하러 가는 것)
- **Dancing at the party last night** was great. I hadn't danced in a long time.

3 **-ing**를 주어로 쓸 때는 뒤에 단수동사를 쓴다.

단수동사
- **Working** from home   **is**   very convenient. 집에서 일하는 것은 매우 편리하다.
- **Driving** a car during rush hour   **wasn't**   a good idea. 혼잡한 시간에 차를 운전하는 것은 좋은 생각이 아니었다.
- **Reducing** the use of paper cups   **has helped**   to decrease waste.
- **Renting** an apartment in this city   **doesn't cost**   much. It's quite cheap.

4 **to + 동사원형**도 '~하는 것'이라는 의미로 주어로 쓸 수 있다. 이때, 뒤에 단수동사를 쓴다.
- **To understand Mr. Bentley's lectures is** easy. (To understand를 주어로 썼으므로 단수동사 is를 썼음)
- **To become a good musician takes** time. (To become을 주어로 썼으므로 단수동사 takes를 썼음)

그러나 일반적으로 **to + 동사원형**보다 **It ~ to + 동사원형**을 주어로 더 자주 쓴다.

It   to + 동사원형
- **It** is easy **to understand Mr. Bentley's lectures.** Bentley 선생님의 강의를 이해하는 것은 쉽다.
- **It** was important **to finish the project on time.** 프로젝트를 제시간에 끝내는 것이 중요했다.
- **It** takes a lot of effort **to achieve success in life.**
- **It** will be fun **to go camping this weekend.**

It ~ to + 동사원형에서 **It**은 **to + 동사원형**을 대신하는 주어이다. '그것'이라는 의미가 아닌 것에 주의한다.

- **It** is impossible **to predict the future.** 미래를 예측하는 것은 불가능하다. ('그것은 불가능하다'라는 의미가 아님)
- **It** seems hard **to find a quiet café around here.**

P R A C T I C E

A. 주어진 표현들을 하나씩 사용하여 예시와 같이 문장을 완성하세요.

cook	find	park	
see	share	~~tell~~	+

a job	a meal at home	a room
on this road	the singer on stage	~~the truth~~

1. _Telling the truth_ isn't always easy, but I always try to be honest.
2. I'm glad I don't live in a dorm now. _____ with someone else gave me stress.
3. _____ often costs less than going to a restaurant.
4. _____ might take time. Not many companies are hiring these days.
5. You must move your car. _____ is not allowed.
6. "Are you excited about the concert tonight?" "Yes. _____ will be great."

B. 괄호 안에 주어진 표현들을 적절히 배열하여 문장을 완성하세요. 필요한 경우 동사를 -ing로 쓰세요.

> ### Dr. Smith Discusses Health Myths
>
> 1. (prevents / vitamin C / take) _Taking vitamin C prevents_ _____ colds.
> 2. (coffee / drink / is) _____ not good for your health.
> 3. (close to the TV / leads / sit) _____ to bad eyesight.
> 4. (fruits / eat / affect / doesn't) _____ your weight.
> 5. (wear / causes / a hat) _____ hair loss.

These ideas are either wrong or not proven yet.

DR. SMITH

C. 주어진 표현들을 적절한 형태로 사용하여 예시와 같이 문장을 완성하세요. 현재 시제로 쓰세요.

become a famous actress	~~learn about other cultures~~	review the article again
ride an elephant	speak in front of people	take care of children

1. (help) _Learning about other cultures_ _helps_ you to understand people from different countries.
2. (require) It's hard to be a parent. _____ _____ patience.
3. (not seem) _____ _____ necessary. I've read it twice already.
4. (be) Carrie is performing in a musical. _____ _____ her dream.
5. (not sound) _____ _____ fun to me. I'm afraid of animals.
6. (not make) I like giving speeches. _____ _____ me nervous.

D. 주어진 표현에 대해 자신의 생각과 가까운 것에 표시하고 It ~ to + 동사원형을 사용하여 예시와 같이 말해보세요.

1. swim in the ocean	☑ exciting	□ scary
2. sleep on a sofa	□ comfortable	□ uncomfortable
3. have a cell phone	□ necessary	□ unnecessary
4. take the bus	□ convenient	□ inconvenient
5. watch movies alone	□ fun	□ boring

1. _It's exciting to swim in the ocean_ .
2. _____ .
3. _____ .
4. _____ .
5. _____ .

-ing와 to + 동사원형

LESSON
36

Grammar Gateway Intermediate

1

They enjoyed the game.

They **enjoyed watching** the game.
그들은 경기를 관람하는 것을 즐겼다.

'경기를 관람하는 것을 즐겼다'라는 의미로 말하기 위해 동사 enjoyed 뒤에 watching을 썼다.

It was a great game.

2

'~하는 것'이라는 의미로 다음과 같은 동사 뒤에 **-ing**를 쓴다.

enjoy	finish	miss	keep	practice	
quit	mind	avoid	deny	risk	**-ing**
suggest	recommend	consider	imagine	admit	(reading, using, going 등)
give up	put off				

- I **finished reading** this book. The ending is so sad. 이 책을 읽는 것을 끝냈다.
- That store **quit using** plastic bags last week. It only provides paper bags now.
  저 상점은 지난 주에 비닐 봉지를 사용하는 것을 중단했다.
- "My friends **suggested going** to Bali for our honeymoon." "Sounds good to me."
- I **gave up looking** for my sunglasses. I guess I lost them.
- "Do you **mind paying** for lunch? I forgot my wallet." "No problem."
- We're going to **put off buying** a house. We can't afford it right now.

3

-ing의 부정은 **not + -ing**로 쓴다. **not + -ing**는 '~하지 않는 것'이라는 의미이다.

- I **recommend not wearing** that tie. It doesn't match your suit. 그 넥타이를 매지 않는 것을 권한다.
- Brad has a lot of work these days. He **misses not working** so much.
- Matt hasn't slept for three days. Can you **imagine not sleeping** for that long?

not + -ing와 일반적인 부정문은 다음과 같은 의미 차이가 있다.

- Sara **considered not attending** the seminar because she had a headache.
  (세미나에 참석하지 않는 것을 고려했음)

  Sara **didn't consider attending** the seminar at all. She just wasn't interested.
  (세미나에 참석할 것인지에 대한 고려 자체를 하지 않았음)

4

-ing를 수동의 의미로 말할 때는 **being + 과거분사**를 쓴다.

- I spilled hot tea, but fortunately, I **avoided being burned**. 데는 것을 피했다.
- We expected the delivery last week, but it **kept being delayed**.
- Let's take the train. I can't **risk being caught** in traffic.

5

동사가 나타내는 어떤 시점을 기준으로 그 전에 일어난 일에 대해 말할 때는 동사 뒤에 **having + 과거분사**를 쓴다.

- The suspect **admitted having committed** the crime. (인정한 시점을 기준으로 그 전에 범죄를 저질렀음)

이때, **having + 과거분사** 대신 **-ing**를 쓸 수도 있다.

- Bill **denied having eaten** my sandwich. 또는 Bill **denied eating** my sandwich. Bill은 내 샌드위치를 먹은 것을 부인했다.
- Jake **admitted having cheated** on the test. 또는 Jake **admitted cheating** on the test.

PRACTICE

A. 괄호 안에 주어진 동사들을 적절히 배열하여 문장을 완성하세요. 필요한 경우 동사를 -ing로 쓰세요.

1. (lie / miss) I _miss lying_ _____ on the beach every weekend. It's too cold now.
2. (lose / risk) Don't take your phone on the rollercoaster. You'll _____ it.
3. (deny / meet) Peter didn't _____ Nancy last night. They went on a date!
4. (walk / keep) If you _____ in that direction, you'll see the bank on the right.
5. (finish / eat) My friends eat so fast. They always _____ before me.
6. (take / suggest) "What airline do you recommend?" "I'd _____ Swift Air."
7. (give up / skate) The skater is going to _____ after the Olympics.

B. Alex의 말을 보고 예시와 같이 문장을 완성하세요. 필요한 경우 not을 함께 쓰세요.

ALEX

> 1. I'm tired. I'll clean the house tomorrow.
> 2. I don't put sugar in my coffee.
> 3. I didn't lock the door. I'm sorry.
> 4. I used to study Spanish, but I changed my major.
> 5. I might not go to Susie's party. I'm busy.

1. Alex put off _cleaning the house_ _____.
2. He avoids _____.
3. He admitted _____.
4. He quit _____.
5. He's considering _____.

C. 주어진 동사를 사용하여 문장을 완성하세요. -ing 또는 being + 과거분사로 쓰세요.

| injure | live | photograph | spend | teach | ~~wash~~ |

1. "I finished _washing_ _____ the dishes." "OK. I'll dry them now."
2. Simon has been in a small town all his life. He can't imagine _____ in a big city.
3. The actress doesn't mind _____. She likes being in front of the cameras.
4. "Why do the students enjoy _____ by Mr. Miller?" "Because he's fun."
5. My best friend moved to Miami. I miss _____ time with her.
6. Fortunately, everyone avoided _____ in the accident.

D. 다음은 여행자들을 위한 정보입니다. 문장을 읽고 틀린 부분이 있으면 바르게 고치세요. 틀린 부분이 없으면 ○로 표시하세요.

> ### World Tour Magazine's Travel Tips!
>
> 1. Don't put off being made hotel reservations. Early reservations are cheaper.
> 2. We suggest read a guidebook before you take a trip.
> 3. Practice speaking the local language before you visit a foreign country.
> 4. Consider having rented a car. You can visit more sites with it.
> 5. When on a group tour, don't risk being left alone. It can be dangerous.
> 6. We recommend carrying not your passport when sightseeing.
>   It might get stolen.

being made → _making_
_____
_____
_____
_____
_____

정답 p. 313 / Check-Up Test 8 p. 248
본 교재 동영상강의 www.ChampStudy.com | 85

1 She wants some coffee.

She wants to drink some coffee.

그녀는 커피를 마시는 것을 원한다.

'커피를 마시는 것'이라는 의미로 말하기 위해 동사 wants 뒤에 **to drink**를 썼다.

I want some coffee.

2 '~하는 것'이라는 의미로 다음과 같은 동사 뒤에 **to + 동사원형**을 쓴다. 이때, **-ing**를 쓰지 않는 것에 주의한다.

want	hope	expect	agree	prepare	
plan	decide	choose	offer	promise	**to + 동사원형**
learn	refuse	fail	manage	intend	(to meet, to invite, to speak 등)
seem	appear	claim	pretend		

- "I **hope to meet** Ken at the party." "I think he's coming."
  파티에서 Ken을 만나는 것을 바라. (hope meeting으로 쓸 수 없음)
- I didn't forget Bob's birthday. I'm **planning to invite** him to dinner.
  저녁 식사에 그를 초대하는 것을 계획 중이다. (planning inviting으로 쓸 수 없음)
- "Where did you **learn to speak** Chinese?" "In Shanghai."
- "Did you give the present to Sam?" "Yes. He **seemed to like** it."

3 **to + 동사원형**의 부정은 **not to + 동사원형**으로 쓴다. **not to + 동사원형**은 '~하지 않는 것'이라는 의미이다.

- My husband and I **agreed not to sell** our car. We're keeping it. 남편과 나는 차를 팔지 않는 것에 동의했다.
- Jake **decided not to join** the football club. He's joining the tennis club instead.
- "I'll tell you what happened if you **promise not to be** angry." "OK, I won't."

  not to + 동사원형과 일반적인 부정문은 다음과 같은 의미 차이가 있다.

  - I thought about taking the writing class, but **chose not to register**. (수업에 등록하지 않는 것을 선택했음)
    I **didn't choose to register** for the writing class. It was required. (수업에 등록할 것인지에 대한 선택 자체를 하지 않았음)

4 **to + 동사원형**을 수동의 의미로 말할 때는 **to be + 과거분사**를 쓴다.

- When I retire from this company, I **want to be remembered** as a good manager. 좋은 매니저로 기억되기를 원한다.
- The band **refused to be interviewed** and left quickly after the concert.
- I was surprised when I was given the award. I didn't **expect to be chosen**!

5 동사가 나타내는 어떤 시점에 진행 중인 일에 대해 말할 때는 동사 뒤에 **to be + -ing**를 쓴다.

- "How is Diane's project going?" "It **appears to be going** OK." 잘 되고 있는 것처럼 보여.
- I didn't want to talk to Beth, so I **pretended to be sleeping**.
- "The kids **seem to be having** fun." "Yes, they like this playground."

  동사가 나타내는 어떤 시점을 기준으로 그 전에 일어난 일에 대해 말할 때는 동사 뒤에 **to have + 과거분사**를 쓴다.

- John **claims to have met** the president. John은 대통령을 만났었다고 주장한다. (주장한 시점을 기준으로 그 전에 대통령을 만났음)
- We **seem to have passed** the park. We should have turned at the traffic light.
- Doris isn't answering the door. She **appears to have gone** out.

PRACTICE

A. 주어진 동사를 사용하여 문장을 완성하세요. **to + 동사원형** 또는 **-ing**로 쓰세요.

allow	catch	finish	live	move	shop	~~visit~~

1. "Why is Greg going to Chicago during the holidays?"   "He wants _to visit_____ his friends."
2. John failed _____ the last bus. He had to walk home.
3. I miss _____ in my old house. I loved it.
4. Your luggage is blocking the way. Would you mind _____ it?
5. We had a lot of work to do, but we managed _____ all of it.
6. The prices at that supermarket are high. I'd suggest _____ at a different store.
7. We can't eat there. That restaurant refuses _____ pets inside.

B. 주어진 동사들과 **to** 또는 **not to**를 사용하여 문장을 완성하세요. 과거 시제로 쓰세요.

arrive	call	hide	~~play~~	ride	share	watch

1. (learn) Shawn is an excellent violinist. He _learned to play_____ the violin at a young age.
2. (expect) We _____ early, but we were just on time.
3. (promise) Jimmy, you _____ TV after 10 o'clock. Please turn it off.
4. (offer) Donald didn't bring his umbrella, so Holly _____ hers with him.
5. (decide) I _____ my bicycle to the office today because it was too cold.
6. (agree) Sally and Brian _____ anything. Now, they tell each other everything.
7. (intend) Ron _____ Mr. Watson, but he dialed someone else's number.

C. 다음은 Pizza Palace의 광고입니다. 괄호 안에 주어진 동사를 사용하여 문장을 완성하세요. **to + 동사원형** 또는 **to be + 과거분사**로 쓰세요.

PIZZA PALACE GRAND OPENING!

1. (open) Pizza Palace plans _to open_____ a restaurant in Jonesville!
2. (build) Our brand new restaurant is expected _____ by the end of May.
3. (provide) Pizza Palace promises _____ good quality food.
4. (use) We choose _____ only the freshest ingredients.
5. (recognize) We hope _____ as the best pizza restaurant in town.
6. (amaze) Prepare _____ by our delicious pizzas!

D. 괄호 안에 주어진 동사를 사용하여 대화를 완성하세요. **to be + -ing** 또는 **to have + 과거분사**로 쓰세요.

1. A: How are Ryan and Melissa these days?
   B: (do) Well, they appear _to be doing_____ OK. Why?

2. A: The photocopier doesn't work.
   B: (fix) Are you sure? The repairman claimed _____.

3. A: (grow) Our new tree in the backyard seems _____ fast.
   B: Yes. It's getting taller every week.

4. A: It's still snowing.
   B: (stop) Still? It appeared _____ earlier.

5. A: (change) Wow! You seem _____ your hairstyle.
   B: Yes, I got my hair cut yesterday.

6. A: I thought the lecture was really boring.
   B: (listen) I totally agree with you. I only pretended _____.

1 다음과 같은 동사 뒤에는 **-ing** 또는 **to + 동사원형**을 모두 쓸 수 있다. 이때, 의미 차이가 거의 없다.

like	love	prefer	hate	bother	**-ing** (working, talking 등)
start	begin	continue	propose		**to + 동사원형** (to work, to talk 등)

- Hannah **likes working** in the garden.
  또는 Hannah **likes to work** in the garden. <small>Hannah는 정원에서 일하는 것을 좋아한다.</small>
- My little brother **started talking** when he was 18 months old.
  또는 My little brother **started to talk** when he was 18 months old.
- Our friends said the movie was terrible, so we didn't **bother seeing** it.
  또는 Our friends said the movie was terrible, so we didn't **bother to see** it.

2 다음과 같은 동사 뒤에도 **-ing** 또는 **to + 동사원형**을 모두 쓸 수 있다. 단, **-ing**를 쓸 때와 **to + 동사원형**을 쓸 때 의미가 다르다.

remember/forget	**-ing** (전에 어떤 일을) 한 것을 기억하다/잊다
	to + 동사원형 (아직 하지 않은 어떤 일을) 할 것을 기억하다/잊다

- I can't find my passport, but I **remember bringing** it. <small>여권을 가져온 것을 기억한다.</small>
  Please **remember to bring** your passport tomorrow. <small>내일 여권을 가져올 것을 기억하세요.</small>
- I'll never **forget meeting** my favorite singer. It was so exciting.
  "Don't **forget to meet** Jane after school." "I won't."

regret	**-ing** (전에 어떤 일을) 한 것을 후회하다
	to + 동사원형 (아직 하지 않은 어떤 일을) 하게 되어 유감이다

- I **regret telling** Max my secret. He told everyone. <small>Max에게 내 비밀을 이야기한 것을 후회한다.</small>
  I **regret to tell** you that no more tickets are available. <small>이용 가능한 표가 더 없다고 말씀드리게 되어 유감입니다.</small>

try	**-ing** (시험 삼아) ~해보다
	to + 동사원형 ~하려고 노력하다

- "I need to lose some weight." "**Try swimming**. It really helps." <small>수영을 해봐.</small>
  I **tried to swim** along the coast, but the waves were too big. <small>해안을 따라 수영하려고 노력했지만 파도가 너무 컸다.</small>

stop	**-ing** ~하는 것을 멈추다
	to + 동사원형 ~하기 위해 (하던 일을) 멈추다

- Joe finally **stopped eating** after he had finished a whole pizza. <small>Joe는 피자 한 판을 끝낸 후에 먹는 것을 멈추었다.</small>
  The pizza arrived when we were cleaning the house. We **stopped to eat**. <small>우리는 먹기 위해 멈추었다.</small>

need	**-ing** ~될 필요가 있다
	to + 동사원형 ~할 필요가 있다

- The sheets on the bed **need changing**. I spilled juice on them. <small>침대 시트는 교체될 필요가 있다.</small>
  I **need to change** the sheets on the bed. They're dirty. <small>침대 시트를 교체할 필요가 있다.</small>

이때, **need + -ing**는 수동의 의미를 나타내므로 **need to be + 과거분사**로도 쓸 수 있다.
  - My camera **needs fixing**. 또는 My camera **needs to be fixed**. <small>내 카메라는 수리될 필요가 있다.</small>
  - We hired some new staff. They **need training**. 또는 They **need to be trained**.

PRACTICE

A. 주어진 동사를 사용하여 문장을 완성하세요. -ing 또는 to + 동사원형으로 쓰세요.

keep	make	quit	~~read~~	rise	work

1. When the teacher began *reading* OR *to read* _____ the book, the children became quiet.
2. "You should stop smoking." "Actually, I plan _____ on January 1."
3. Jane likes group projects. She hates _____ alone.
4. I'd recommend _____ a reservation. That restaurant is always busy.
5. Peter was going to throw away his old computer, but decided _____ it.
6. The temperature will continue _____ all afternoon.

B. 괄호 안에 주어진 동사들을 적절한 순서로 배열하여 문장을 완성하세요. 필요한 경우 동사를 -ing 또는 to + 동사원형으로 쓰세요.

1. (invite / forget) "Don't *forget to invite* _____ Mr. Anderson for lunch." "Don't worry. I won't."
2. (go / remember) "I _____ to the circus when I was young." "Me too. It was always fun."
3. (remember / pick) _____ up my blouse from the dry cleaner's. I need it tomorrow.
4. (regret / buy) I don't like my new hat. I _____ it.
5. (visit / forget) Venice was a wonderful place. I'll never _____ that city.
6. (regret / announce) We _____ that the flight to Sydney has been canceled.
7. (pack / forget) You shouldn't _____ the sunscreen. The sun is really strong at the beach.

C. A에 주어진 표현과 **tried to + 동사원형**을 사용하여 Keith의 말을 완성하고, B에 주어진 표현과 **try -ing**를 사용하여 1–3번에 대한 해결 방법을 제안해보세요.

A	call Sarah	~~learn Arabic~~	B	follow the recipe	send her a text message
	make an omelet			study with a partner	

KEITH

1. I *tried to learn Arabic* _____, but it's a difficult language.
2. Cooking is so hard. I _____, but I couldn't.
3. I _____, but she didn't answer.

4. Why don't you _____?
5. _____ more carefully.
6. You could _____.

You

D. 괄호 안에 주어진 동사와 **stop** 또는 **need**를 사용하여 문장을 완성하세요. 필요한 경우 동사를 -ing 또는 to + 동사원형으로 쓰세요.

1. (go) "Can you stay a little longer?" "No. Unfortunately, I *need to go* _____ now."
2. (check) Let's _____ the tire. I think there's something wrong with it.
3. (spend) Ted always wastes money. He should _____ so much.
4. (sign) These forms _____. I'll put them on your desk.
5. (change) I'm watching that show. _____ the TV channel, please.
6. (take) We _____ out the garbage. It's starting to smell.
7. (update) Those websites _____. The information on them is old.

He wants the clerk to find the book. 동사 + 목적어 + to ~/-ing

1

He wants to buy a book.

He **wants the clerk to find** the book.

그는 점원이 책을 찾아주는 것을 원한다.

'점원이 책을 찾아주는 것을 원한다'라는 의미로 말하기 위해 동사 wants 뒤에
the clerk to find를 썼다.

Could you find a book for me?

2 다음과 같은 동사 뒤에는 **목적어 + to + 동사원형**을 쓸 수 있다.

want	cause	expect	require	force
allow	enable	teach	advise	encourage
tell	invite	ask		

- The storm last night **caused a lot of trees to fall**. 지난밤의 폭풍은 많은 나무들이 쓰러지게 했다.
- The Internet **allows us to share** information very quickly. 인터넷은 우리가 정보를 매우 빠르게 공유하는 것을 가능하게 해준다.
- "What did the doctor **tell Nick to do**?" "He **advised him to drink** less coffee."
- Mike's job **requires him to work** on weekends.
- I got in trouble. My teacher **forced me to remain** after class.

3 다음과 같은 동사 뒤에는 **목적어 + -ing**를 쓸 수 있다.

dislike	remember	imagine	mind	keep	leave

- My parents **dislike me going** out late at night. 부모님은 내가 밤늦게 외출하는 것을 싫어하신다.
- "Did Jeff find a roommate?"
  "I think so. I **remember someone telling** me that." 누군가가 내게 그것에 대해 말해준 것을 기억해.
- "Can you **imagine Monica saying** bad things about people?" "No. She's always so nice."
- "Do you **mind us sitting** here?" "Not at all."
- I'm so tired. Our football coach **kept us running** for hours.

    stop과 **prevent** 뒤에는 **목적어 + from + -ing**를 주로 쓴다.
    - Give the baby some milk. It will **stop her from crying**. 아기가 우는 것을 멈추게 할 거야.
    - The fog **prevented the driver from seeing** the road clearly.

4 **I want to get**과 **I want you to get**

- **I want to get** a haircut.
  나는 (내가) 머리를 자르는 것을 원해.

- **Do you remember dancing** with Sam?
  너는 (네가) Sam과 춤춘 것을 기억하니?

- **Jerry expects to win** the competition.

- **We don't mind staying** in a small room.

- **I can't imagine wearing** that skirt. It's not my
  style.

- **I want you to get** a haircut.
  나는 네가 머리를 자르는 것을 원해.

- **Do you remember me dancing** with Sam?
  너는 내가 Sam과 춤춘 것을 기억하니?

- **Jerry expects Alice to win** the competition.

- **We don't mind you staying** at our house.

- **I can't imagine Liz wearing** that skirt. It's not her
  style.

PRACTICE

A. 주어진 표현과 **want**를 사용하여 예시와 같이 문장을 완성하세요. 현재 시제로 쓰세요.

~~go with them~~　　meet her　　move back　　sell it to him　　take him

LENA

1. My friends are going to a concert tonight. They _want me to go with them_____.
2. Robert asked about my old grill. He _____.
3. My dog _____ to the park. He is bored.
4. I live alone. My parents _____ home.
5. My aunt _____ at the airport. She is coming tomorrow.

B. Ross 씨는 부하직원들에게 여러 가지 일을 지시했습니다. 괄호 안에 주어진 동사와 적절한 목적어를 사용하여 예시와 같이 문장을 완성하세요. 과거 시제로 쓰세요.

Mr. ROSS

1. Bill, can you bring the reports?
2. Prepare for the presentation, Cori.
3. Kevin, do you want to go out for drinks tonight?
4. If you're sick, you can go home early, Denise.
5. You should call the customer soon, Jane.
6. Steve, you should attend the seminar.

1. (ask) He _asked Bill to bring the reports_____.
2. (tell) He _____.
3. (invite) He _____.
4. (allow) He _____.
5. (advise) He _____.
6. (encourage) He _____.

C. 주어진 동사와 적절한 목적어를 사용하여 예시와 같이 문장을 완성하세요. 필요한 경우 **from**을 함께 쓰세요.

join　　laugh　　say　　~~spend~~　　spread　　take　　wait

1. My husband dislikes _me spending_____ too much money on clothes, so I try not to.
2. "Can Josh come with us to the basketball game?"　"Sure. I don't mind _____ us."
3. There was a fire at a hotel, but the firemen prevented _____ to other buildings.
4. "Did Cathy tell you the meeting was canceled?"　"No, I don't remember _____ that."
5. Eric and Ann were upset with Sarah. She left _____ at the station for an hour!
6. We took the camera to the museum, but the guards stopped _____ pictures.
7. Fred often tells me funny jokes. He keeps _____ all the time.

D. 괄호 안에 주어진 동사를 **-ing** 또는 **to + 동사원형**으로 써서 문장을 완성하세요. 필요한 경우 적절한 목적어를 함께 쓰세요.

1. (fish) My grandfather taught _me to fish_____ when I was five years old.
2. (live) "Is Bob moving to Seattle or Portland?"　"He decided _____ in Portland."
3. (go) Olivia and Harry hate winter sports. I can't imagine _____ skiing.
4. (study) Greg wants _____ engineering in college. He enjoys the subject very much.
5. (take) "Did Lisa take her medicine?"　"Yes. I remember _____ it after breakfast."
6. (apologize) Whenever our son says something rude, my wife forces _____.
7. (play) My neighbors kept _____ loud music all night. I called them to complain.
8. (do) We started using a new program at work. It enables _____ our work faster.

정답 **p. 314** / Check-Up Test 8 **p. 248**

-ing와 to + 동사원형

LESSON
40

Grammar Gateway Intermediate

41 He made her laugh. make/help/see 등 + 목적어 + 동사원형

1 **make/have/let** + 목적어 + 동사원형: ∼가 …하게 하다

다른 사람이 어떤 일을 하게 한다고 말할 때 **make/have/let** + 목적어 + 동사원형을 쓴다.

	make/have/let	목적어	동사원형	
• He	**made**	**her**	**laugh.**	그는 그녀가 웃게 했다.
• I	**have**	**a mechanic**	**check**	my car regularly.
•	**Let**	**me**	**pay**	for the coffee today.

make/have/let과 비슷한 의미로 **get**도 쓸 수도 있다. 그러나 **get** 뒤에는 목적어 + **to** + 동사원형을 쓰는 것에 주의한다.

- Ms. Hill always **gets her secretary to reserve** her flights for business trips.
  Hill 씨는 출장을 위한 항공편을 항상 비서가 예약하게 한다. (gets her secretary reserve로 쓸 수 없음)
- I **got Nick to change** his schedule, so now he can go to the concert with us.
  Nick이 일정을 바꾸게 해서, 이제 그는 우리와 콘서트에 갈 수 있다. (got Nick change로 쓸 수 없음)

2 사람 또는 사물에 어떤 일이 일어나게 한다고 말할 때는 **have/get** + 목적어 + 과거분사를 쓴다. 이때, 목적어 뒤에 동사원형을 쓰지 않는 것에 주의한다.

	have/get	목적어	과거분사	
• We	**have**	**our office**	**cleaned**	every Sunday. (have our office clean으로 쓸 수 없음)
• Ron	**will get**	**the invitations**	**printed**	next week. (will get the invitations print로 쓸 수 없음)
• I	**had**	**my hair**	**cut.**	How do I look?

3 **help** + 목적어 + 동사원형: ∼가 …하는 것을 돕다

다른 사람이 어떤 일을 하는 것을 돕는다고 말할 때는 **help** + 목적어 + 동사원형을 쓴다.

	help	목적어	동사원형	
• I	**will help**	**you**	**do**	the laundry. 네가 빨래하는 것을 도와줄게.
• Mistakes	**help**	**people**	**learn.**	

이때, 동사원형 대신 **to** + 동사원형도 쓸 수 있다.

- Will you **help me (to) choose** a birthday present for my mother? 내가 어머니 생신 선물을 고르는 것을 도와주겠니?

4 **see/hear/listen to/feel** 등 + 목적어 + 동사원형: ∼가 …하는 것을 보다/듣다/느끼다

다른 사람이나 사물이 어떤 동작을 하는 것을 보거나 듣거나 느낀다고 말할 때 **see/hear/listen to/feel** 등 + 목적어 + 동사원형을 쓴다.

	see/hear 등	목적어	동사원형	
• She	**saw**	**him**	**fall**	into the water. 그녀는 그가 물에 빠지는 것을 보았다.
• I	**heard**	**the dog**	**bark.**	Is someone outside?
• Ted	**felt**	**something**	**hit**	him on the head. It was an apple.

see/hear/listen to/feel 등 + 목적어 + **-ing**도 쓸 수 있다. 이때, 동사원형을 쓸 때와는 다음과 같은 의미 차이가 있다.

- I **saw Carrie come out** of the house and **get** into a car. (Carrie가 집에서 나와서 차로 들어가는 것을 처음부터 끝까지 보았음)
  I **saw Carrie talking** on the phone when I was on the bus. (Carrie가 통화하는 도중에 보았음)

PRACTICE

A. 그림을 보고 괄호 안에 주어진 동사를 사용하여 예시와 같이 문장을 완성하세요. 과거 시제로 쓰세요.

1. (make) *She made them sit down* .
2. (let) _____ .
3. (have) _____ .

4. (make) _____ .
5. (let) _____ .

B. 괄호 안에 주어진 표현들을 적절히 배열하여 문장을 완성하세요. 필요한 경우 동사를 to + 동사원형 또는 과거분사로 쓰세요.

1. (arrest / had / them) Some people tried to rob the store, and the store owner *had them arrested* .
2. (made / fall / me) The documentary was boring. It _____ asleep.
3. (them / read / get) My children don't like books. I can't _____ anything.
4. (get / take / him) Do you see that man walking toward us? Let's _____ our photo.
5. (your eyes / had / test) "Have you _____ recently?" "No. It has been a while."
6. (let / ride / Phil) Jacob _____ his motorcycle. He really enjoyed it.
7. (pull / a tooth / get) I have a dentist's appointment tomorrow. I'm going to _____ .

C. 주어진 상황을 보고 주어진 동사와 **help**를 사용하여 예시와 같이 문장을 완성하세요.

bake	feel	~~pack~~	solve

1. Your neighbor is moving next week. You offer to help.
   YOU: I'll *help you (to) pack* the boxes.
2. You and your classmate can't answer a math question. You ask a teacher for help.
   YOU: Could you _____ this math question?
3. Your friend has a cold. You offer her some medicine.
   YOU: This medicine will _____ better.
4. You are making a cake, but you are having trouble with it. You ask your sister for help.
   YOU: Will you _____ the cake?

D. 주어진 표현들과 적절한 목적어를 사용하여 예시와 같이 대화를 완성하세요. 과거 시제로 쓰세요.

call	finish	leave	~~ring~~	shake	speak

1. Was that the bell for class?
2. Did Dr. Wall give a speech at the seminar?
3. Where's Mary? Has she gone out?
4. Are Mom and Dad looking for me?
5. Did John complete the marathon?
6. The ground was moving. Did you feel it?

(hear) Yes. I *heard it ring* .
(listen to) Yes, he did. I _____ .
(see) Yes. I _____ a minute ago.
(hear) I think so. I _____ you.
(see) Yes. I _____ it.
(feel) I _____ too. I think it was an earthquake!

정답 **p. 314** / Check-Up Test 8 **p. 248**

-ing와 to + 동사원형

LESSON 41

Grammar Gateway Intermediate

1

He boiled some water.

He boiled some water to make spaghetti.
그는 스파게티를 만들기 위해 물을 끓였다.

'스파게티를 만들기 위해'라는 의미로 물을 끓인 목적에 대해 말하기 위해 **to make**를 썼다.

2 '∼하기 위해'라는 의미로 어떤 일을 하는 목적에 대해 말할 때 **to + 동사원형**을 쓸 수 있다.

- I went to the gym **to exercise**, but it was closed. 운동을 하기 위해 헬스장에 갔지만, 닫혀 있었다.
- "Why did Helen quit her job?" "**To look** after her grandmother."
- We should put this milk in the fridge **to keep** it cool.

이때, **to + 동사원형** 대신 **in order to + 동사원형**도 쓸 수 있다. 단, 일상 대화에서는 **to + 동사원형**을 더 자주 쓴다.

- Plants need water **(in order) to survive**. 식물들은 생존하기 위해 물을 필요로 한다.
- I called the doctor's office **(in order) to cancel** my appointment.

'∼하지 않기 위해'라는 의미로 말할 때는 **in order not to + 동사원형**을 쓸 수 있다. 이때, **not to + 동사원형**은 쓰지 않는 것에 주의한다.

- I ran to the gate **in order not to miss** my flight.
  비행기를 놓치지 않기 위해 탑승구로 뛰어갔다. (not to miss로 쓸 수 없음)
- **In order not to waste** electricity, please turn off the printer when you're not using it.
  전기를 낭비하지 않기 위해, 프린터를 사용하지 않을 때는 전원을 꺼주시기 바랍니다. (Not to waste로 쓸 수 없음)

3 **(in order) to**와 같은 의미로 **so that**도 쓸 수 있다. **so that** 뒤에는 **주어 + 동사**를 쓴다.

- I need to start on the report fast **so that I can meet** the deadline. 마감 기한을 맞추기 위해 보고서를 빨리 시작해야 한다.
- We came home early **so that we could watch** our favorite TV show.
- Jane hired a tutor **so that she would do** better in her physics class.

in order not to와 같은 의미로 말할 때는 **so that ~ not**도 쓸 수 있다. 일상 대화에서는 **so that ~ not**을 더 자주 쓴다.

- Be careful on the ladder **so that you don't fall**. (= in order not to fall)
- We spoke quietly **so that we wouldn't wake** the baby. (= in order not to wake)
- Dry your hair before you go outside **so that you won't catch** a cold.

so that에 대한 더 자세한 내용은 Lesson 93 참고

4 어떤 일을 하는 목적에 대해 말할 때 **for + 명사**도 쓸 수 있다.

- "I'm bored. Let's go **for a drive**." "Sounds good." (드라이브하기 위해)
- After jogging for an hour, we sat down on a bench **for some rest**. (휴식을 취하기 위해)
- Melissa invited us **for dinner** tomorrow. Would you like to go?

5 '∼할/∼하기 위한'이라는 의미로 명사 뒤에 **to + 동사원형**을 쓸 수 있다.

- Many parents don't get much **time to spend** with their children these days. (아이들과 보낼 시간)
- "This is a perfect **place to have** a picnic." "I agree." (소풍을 하기 위한 장소)
- The charity is raising **money to help** poor people. It has raised over $10,000 this week.

P R A C T I C E

A. 그림을 보고 주어진 표현과 **went**를 사용하여 예시와 같이 문장을 완성하세요.

deliver groceries	fly kites	get some cash	listen to the speech	~~pick up Jessica~~

Please put them here.

1. He _went to the airport to pick up Jessica_.
2. They _____.
3. She _____.
4. They _____.
5. He _____.

B. 주어진 문장과 **so that**을 사용하여 문장을 완성하세요. 필요한 경우 부정문으로 쓰세요.

an old lady could sit there	I can look at the stars at night	I would forget
~~we can hear you better~~	we will get hungry later	you injure yourself

1. Could you speak louder _so that we can hear you better_ ?
2. Let's eat something now _____.
3. "I bought a telescope _____." "Really? Can I see it?"
4. Mr. Brown reminded me about the meeting _____.
5. You should stretch before soccer practice _____.
6. Jenny gave up her seat _____.

C. 괄호 안에 주어진 표현과 **to** 또는 **for**를 사용하여 문장을 완성하세요.

1. (attend his graduation) We visited our son's school _to attend his graduation_
2. (a conference) Kevin had to travel to Texas _____.
3. (enter the National Museum) A fee is not required in order _____.
4. (wish her good luck) I called Sally _____ on her interview.
5. (a hammer) My neighbor came by my apartment _____.
6. (help the environment) Some people drive electric cars _____.
7. (my cousin's wedding) I took the day off from work _____.
8. (a drink) Tom and I usually meet on Friday night _____.

D. 주어진 명사와 동사를 하나씩 사용하여 문장을 완성하세요. **to**를 함께 쓰세요.

chance	decision	dress		~~eat~~	listen	make
letter	movies	~~place~~	+	send	watch	wear

1. Let's find a _place to eat_. How about the café over there?
2. Could you get me a stamp from that drawer? I have a _____.
3. Emily bought a nice _____ to the party. She looks so pretty in it.
4. "Have you chosen a college yet?" "No. It's a difficult _____."
5. "Do you know this song?" "No. I haven't had the _____ to it."
6. Would you like to go to the theater tonight? There are some good _____ these days.

I'm happy to be back. 형용사 + to + 동사원형

1 다음과 같이 사람의 감정을 나타내는 형용사 뒤에 **to** + 동사원형을 쓸 수 있다. 이때, **to** + 동사원형은 '～해서'라는 의미이다.

happy	glad	pleased	proud	**to** + 동사원형
afraid	relieved	sorry	surprised	(to be, to receive 등)

- "How was Paris?" "It was good, but I'm **happy to be** back." 돌아와서 기뻐요.
- "Were you **surprised to receive** the news?" 그 소식을 접해서 놀랐니? "A little."
- We are **proud to announce** the winners of this year's contest.
- Ray is **afraid to go** to the hospital tomorrow.

2 다음과 같은 형용사 뒤에도 **to** + 동사원형을 쓸 수 있다. 이때, **to** + 동사원형은 '～하기'라는 의미이다.

easy	cheap	expensive	impossible	**to** + 동사원형
hard	difficult	safe	dangerous	(to cook, to solve 등)

- Pasta is **easy to cook**. I'll teach you. 파스타는 요리하기 쉽다.
- "This puzzle is **hard to solve**." 이 퍼즐은 풀기 어려워. "Let me try."
- Houses weren't **cheap to buy**, so we decided to rent one.
- Our beauty products are **safe to use** on any skin type.

이와 비슷한 의미로 **It is/was** + 형용사 + **to** + 동사원형도 쓸 수 있다.

It is/was	형용사	to + 동사원형	
It's	easy	to cook	pasta. I'll teach you. 파스타를 요리하는 것은 쉽다.
"It's	hard	to solve	this puzzle." 이 퍼즐을 푸는 것은 어려워. "Let me try."
It was	impossible	to read	John's handwriting. It was so messy.
It wasn't	expensive	to stay	at the hotel. It was only $20 per night.

이때, **to** + 동사원형 앞에 **for** + 사람을 쓸 수 있다.

	for + 사람	to + 동사원형	
This book is difficult	**for me**	**to understand.**	이 책은 내가 이해하기 어렵다.
It's dangerous	**for women**	**to travel**	alone. 여자가 혼자 여행하는 것은 위험하다.
It was impossible	**for the scientists**	**to do**	the experiment due to the weather.
This medicine is safe	**for children**	**to take.**	

3 다음과 같이 사람의 성품을 나타내는 형용사는 **It is/was** + 형용사와 **to** + 동사원형 사이에 **of** + 사람을 쓴다. 이때, **for** + 사람을 쓰지 않는 것에 주의한다.

kind	nice	brave	generous	careless	selfish

It is/was	형용사	of + 사람	to + 동사원형	
It was	kind	of Lynn	to bring	us flowers. Lynn이 우리에게 꽃을 준 것은 친절했다.
It isn't	brave	of Jed	to lie	about his mistakes. Jed가 실수에 대해 거짓말한 것은 용감하지 못하다.
It's	generous	of Cindy	to forgive	you for forgetting the appointment.
"It was	careless	of you	to leave	the door unlocked." "I'm sorry."

P R A C T I C E

A. 주어진 문장을 보고 **to + 동사원형**을 사용하여 예시와 같이 다시 말해보세요.

1. Steve met Stacy. He was pleased. → _Steve was pleased to meet Stacy_____.
2. Maria missed the phone call. She was sorry. → _____.
3. I found my credit card! I was relieved. → _____.
4. I got so many presents for my birthday. I was surprised. → _____.
5. Don helped his wife with the housework. He was glad. → _____.

B. 괄호 안에 주어진 단어들을 사용하여 예시와 같이 자신의 생각에 대해 말해보세요. 필요한 경우 부정문으로 쓰세요.

1. (safe, drive) Race cars _are safe to drive_ OR _aren't safe to drive_____.
2. (difficult, learn) Languages _____.
3. (expensive, own) A car _____.
4. (hard, get) A good job _____.
You 5. (easy, grow) Plants _____.

It is ~ to + 동사원형을 사용하여 예시와 같이 1–5번의 문장을 바꾸어 쓰세요.

6. _It is safe to drive race cars_ OR _It isn't safe to drive race cars_____.
7. _____.
8. _____.
9. _____.
10. _____. **You**

C. 주어진 단어들과 **to**를 사용하여 문장을 완성하세요. **for** 또는 **of**를 함께 쓰세요.

(cheap, me, get)	(dangerous, beginners, try)	(generous, him, lend)
(impossible, us, carry)	~~(nice, you, say)~~	(selfish, Evan, eat)

1. "You look lovely in that dress!" "It is _nice of you to say_____ so."
2. I work for an airline, so it's _____ plane tickets. I get a 50 percent discount!
3. Could you help us? This heavy luggage is _____.
4. "Mr. Franklin is going to let us borrow $1,000!" "Really? It is _____ us money."
5. Rock climbing is _____ without enough training. They could hurt themselves.
6. It was _____ all of the cookies last night. He didn't share them.

D. 주어진 단어들과 **to**를 사용하여 Dan과 Linda의 대화를 완성하세요. 필요한 경우 **for** 또는 **of**를 함께 쓰세요.

DAN: 1. I'm _glad to see_____ you, Linda! Thanks for coming. (glad, see)
LINDA: 2. I'm _____ here. Your house is lovely! (happy, be)
DAN: Thanks. 3. Was it _____ here? (difficult, you, get)
LINDA: No. 4. You gave me good directions, so it wasn't _____ your house. (hard, me, find)
DAN: 5. I'm _____ that. (relieved, hear)
LINDA: 6. Anyway, it was really _____ me. (nice, you, invite)
DAN: Not at all!

DAN   LINDA

1 다음과 같이 의문사 **what/who/where/when/how** 뒤에 **to** + 동사원형을 쓸 수 있다.

> **what to + 동사원형** 무엇을 ~할지, ~할 것

- I don't know **what to do** during my vacation. 휴가 동안 무엇을 할지 모르겠다.
- There are so many good movies. I can't decide **what to watch**.

> **who to + 동사원형** 누구를/누구에게 ~할지, ~할 사람

- I'm not sure **who to take** to the dance party. 무도회에 누구를 데려가야 할지 잘 모르겠다.
- Would you let me know **who to contact** for more information?

> **where to + 동사원형** 어디에서 ~할지, ~할 장소

- "Have you asked Nancy **where to meet?**" Nancy에게 어디에서 만날지 물어봤니? "Not yet."
- "Could you tell me **where to find** a cheap hotel?" "Try Main Street."

> **when to + 동사원형** 언제 ~할지, ~할 시간

- We haven't decided **when to move**. Maybe in August or September. 우리는 언제 이사할지 아직 결정하지 않았다.
- Jane and David are still discussing **when to send** their wedding invitations.

> **how to + 동사원형** 어떻게 ~할지, ~하는 방법

- I used to take piano lessons, but I've forgotten **how to play**. 피아노 레슨을 받았었지만, 어떻게 연주하는지 잊어버렸다.
- My mother taught me **how to make** delicious chicken soup. She is a good cook.

  why 뒤에는 **to** + 동사원형을 쓰지 않고 주어 + 동사를 쓰는 것에 주의한다.

  - Sam didn't tell me **why he was** upset this morning. Did he tell you? (why to be로 쓸 수 없음)
  - "Do you have any idea **why Liz left** early?" "She had to meet a client." (why to leave로 쓸 수 없음)

2 what/which/whose + 명사 뒤에도 **to** + 동사원형을 쓸 수 있다.

> **what/which + 명사 + to + 동사원형** 어떤 ~을 ···할지

- I've finally decided **what major to choose**. I'm going to study biology. 어떤 전공을 선택할지 드디어 결정했다.
- Derrick has looked at three cars so far, but he isn't certain **which car to buy**.
- Jamie and I have picked **which city to visit** on our trip to Europe.

> **whose + 명사 + to + 동사원형** 누구의 ~을 ···할지

- Rick couldn't choose **whose gift to open** first. Rick은 누구의 선물을 먼저 개봉할지 선택할 수 없었다.
- Two of my best friends were arguing and I wasn't sure **whose side to take**.
- My favorite bands are performing on the same night. I can't decide **whose concert to attend**.

3 whether 뒤에도 **to** + 동사원형을 쓸 수 있다.

> **whether to + 동사원형** ~할지 말지

- I don't know **whether to help** Jim with his homework. Maybe he should do it himself.
  Jim의 숙제를 도와줘야 할지 말지 모르겠어.
- Neil is going to be late. I'm not sure **whether to wait** for him.
- The company is considering **whether to build** a new factory.

P R A C T I C E

A. 그림을 보고 **to + 동사원형**을 사용하여 예시와 같이 문장을 완성하세요.

What should we order?

Who should I date?

Where should I hang my shirt?

When should we meet again?

How should I change the light bulb?

1. They aren't sure _what to order_____.
2. She doesn't know _____.
3. He's wondering _____ his shirt.
4. They're deciding _____ again.
5. She's asking _____ the light bulb.

B. 주어진 단어들을 하나씩 사용하여 예시와 같이 문장을 완성하세요.

how	when	where	+	come	hire	join
~~whether~~	whether	who		play	put	~~shave~~

1. "I'm still thinking about _whether to shave_____ my beard." "I think you look better with it."
2. "Could you tell me _____ these boxes?" "Just leave them on that table."
3. Can you teach me the rules again? I don't remember _____ this game.
4. "Did Tara say _____ to her house?" "No, but let's go around 8 o'clock."
5. We interviewed several people, but we still aren't sure _____.
6. I'm considering _____ the tennis club next month. I might not have time.

C. Eddie가 하는 말을 보고 **to + 동사원형**을 사용하여 예시와 같이 문장을 완성하세요.

1. What gift should I buy for Grace?
2. Whose story should I believe?
3. Which book am I going to read first?

EDDIE

4. What color should I paint the wall?
5. Which way should I go?
6. Whose advice should I follow?

1. He doesn't know _what gift to buy for Grace_____.
2. He's confused about _____.
3. He hasn't decided _____ first.
4. He isn't sure _____.
5. He has no idea _____.
6. He's uncertain _____.

D. 괄호 안에 주어진 단어들과 **what/who/where/how/whether**를 사용하여 Justin과 Chris의 대화를 완성하세요.

JUSTIN

JUSTIN: 1. I want to throw a party, but I don't know _what to do_____! (do)

CHRIS: That's easy. 2. First, pick _____ the party. (have)
The place is the most important thing.
3. Then, choose _____. (invite)
4. Oh, and decide _____ the food or make it. (buy)

JUSTIN: 5. Well, I don't know _____. (cook)
I've never tried. I guess I'll buy something.

CHRIS: OK. 6. And think about _____ at the party. (do)
Let me know if you need any help.

CHRIS

-ing와 to + 동사원형

LESSON 44

Grammar Gateway Intermediate

I'm thinking **about moving** to a bigger apartment. 전치사 + -ing

1 **about/in/on/without** 등과 같은 전치사 뒤에는 **-ing**를 쓴다. 이때, 동사원형이나 **to** + 동사원형을 쓸 수 없는 것에 주의한다.

- I'm thinking **about moving** to a bigger apartment.
  더 큰 아파트로 이사 가는 것에 대해 생각 중이다. (about move 또는 about to move로 쓸 수 없음)

- I lent Mark a book, but he wasn't interested **in reading** it.
  Mark에게 책을 빌려줬는데 그는 그것을 읽는 데 관심이 없었어. (in read 또는 in to read로 쓸 수 없음)

- "When are you planning **on traveling** to Africa?" "In October."

- Don't swim in the lake **without wearing** a life jacket. It's dangerous.

2 다음과 같은 표현 뒤에도 동사원형이나 **to** + 동사원형을 쓰지 않고 **-ing**를 쓴다.

in favor of ~에 찬성하는	**in spite of** ~임에도 불구하고	**instead of** ~ 대신에
as a result of ~의 결과로	**in addition to** ~에 더해서	

- Most people are **in favor of building** a new mall in town. 대부분의 사람들이 시내에 새 쇼핑몰을 짓는 것에 찬성한다.

- I was late for work yesterday **in spite of leaving** home early. 어제 집에서 일찍 출발했음에도 불구하고 직장에 늦었다.

- It's a nice day. Let's go outside **instead of staying** inside.

- **As a result of losing** his passport, Robert could not board the plane.

- **In addition to buying** jeans and a shirt, Lucy also got a new hat.

- Rick usually uses cash **instead of paying** with his credit card.

3 다음과 같이 **to**로 끝나는 표현 뒤에도 **-ing**를 쓴다.

be used to + -ing ~하는 데 익숙하다

- **I'm used to having** my camera with me all the time. 카메라를 항상 갖고 다니는 데 익숙하다.

- Cathy recently got her license, so she**'s not used to driving** yet.

look forward to + -ing ~하기를 기대하다

- I **look forward to hearing** from you soon. 너에게 곧 소식을 듣기를 기대해.

- "Are you **looking forward to meeting** Julie's family?" "Yes, but I'm a little nervous."

object to + -ing ~하는 데 반대하다

- I **object to having** the meeting on the weekend. 주말에 회의를 하는 것에 반대해요.

- My wife didn't **object to getting** a new TV, so I bought one.

when it comes to + -ing ~하는 것에 관한 한, ~하는 것에 대해서라면

- **When it comes to studying**, I prefer going to the library. 공부하는 것에 관한 한, 나는 도서관에 가는 것을 선호한다.

- Jim is the best **when it comes to fixing** things.

  이때 **to**는 전치사이므로, 뒤에 동사원형을 쓰지 않고 **-ing**를 쓰는 것에 주의한다.

  - **I'm used to living** alone. I rarely feel lonely.
    (I'm used to live로 쓸 수 없음)

  - It was nice doing business with you. We **look forward to working** with you again.
    (We look forward to work로 쓸 수 없음)

PRACTICE

A. 주어진 단어들을 사용하여 예시와 같이 광고를 완성하세요.

call	clean	cook	leave	make	~~write~~

1 Essay Help
(about) Are you worried
about writing your next essay?
Come to the Learning Center
for help.

2 MAKE YOUR SINKS SHINE!
(for) Shine Bright products
are perfect _____
_____
kitchens and bathrooms.

3 Home-Shop.com
(without) Shop any time
_____
your home!
Visit our website.

4 Become a master chef!
(at) If you are bad _____
_____, try our
online programs. You'll become
an expert chef in two months!

5 Watkins Institute
(by) Get more information
about our great art classes
_____
555-9867.

6 J&T Financial Group
(on) Do you want to be
rich? We offer seminars
_____
money.

B. 주어진 표현들을 하나씩 사용하여 문장을 완성하세요.

as a result of	in addition to	in favor of		celebrate	change	have
in spite of	~~instead of~~	instead of	+	offer	train	~~use~~

1. I want to lose weight, so I usually walk up the stairs _instead of using_ _____ an elevator.
2. _____ every day, Sam won the race.
3. The employees are _____ the business hours during the holidays.
4. _____ discounts, the store also gives free gifts.
5. Carla still went to school _____ a cold.
6. "Why did you stay home _____ Kim's birthday with us?"   "I was sick."

C. 주어진 표현들을 적절한 형태로 사용하여 문장을 완성하세요.

be used to	look forward to	object to	~~when it comes to~~	when it comes to

1. (give) Ben is great _when it comes to giving_ _____ advice. His opinion is always helpful.
2. (speak) Ms. Clark gives lectures every week. She _____ in front of people.
3. (stay) I _____ at that hotel again. The room was so dirty last time.
4. (build) Turner Construction has the most experience _____ bridges.
5. (take) "Are you _____ Mr. Wallace's class?"   "Yes. It will be interesting."

D. 다음 문장을 읽고 틀린 부분이 있으면 바르게 고치세요. 틀린 부분이 없으면 ○로 표시하세요.

1. I never go to bed without brush my teeth.   _brush → brushing_
2. In addition to have a big lunch, I ate a huge dinner too.   _____
3. When the dog saw the mailman, it began to bark loudly.   _____
4. I'd like to begin the interview by ask you a personal question.   _____
5. I look forward to start a new project. It'll be exciting!   _____
6. I go to the gym every day, so I'm used to exercising regularly.   _____

46 She **spent** two hours **getting** ready. -ing와 to + 동사원형을 사용한 다양한 표현들

1 다음과 같은 표현에 **-ing**를 쓴다.

spend/waste ⋯ -ing ~하는 데 (시간/돈/노력 등)을 쓰다/낭비하다

- She **spent two hours getting** ready. 그녀는 준비하는 데 두 시간을 썼다.
- We **waste too much money eating** out. We should cook more.

feel like -ing ~하고 싶다

- This song is so good! I **feel like dancing**! 춤 추고 싶어!
- "I don't **feel like driving**. Can we take a taxi?" "Sure."

be busy -ing ~하느라 바쁘다

- I haven't seen you much lately. Have you **been busy working**? 일하느라 바빴니?
- Joan and Jackie **are busy making** plans for the holidays.

have trouble/difficulty -ing ~하는 데 어려움을 겪다

- I'm **having trouble using** this photocopier. Can you help me? 이 복사기를 사용하는 데 어려움을 겪고 있어요.
- "Do you **have difficulty sleeping** at night?" "Yes, sometimes."

can't help -ing ~할 수밖에 없다

- Jane is in love with Pete. She **can't help thinking** about him. 그를 생각할 수밖에 없다.
- I **couldn't help buying** this jacket. It looked so good on me.

be (not) worth -ing ~할 가치가 있다(없다)

- "I didn't get the job." "Well, it **was worth trying**." 시도할 가치는 있었어.
- "The problems aren't serious. They**'re not worth arguing** about." "I guess you're right."

Would/Do you mind -ing ~? ~해주시겠어요?

- "I'm a bit cold. **Would you mind turning** off the fan?" 선풍기를 꺼주시겠어요? "Of course not."
- "**Do you mind getting** some orange juice from the store?" "Not at all."

2 다음과 같은 표현에는 **to + 동사원형**을 쓴다.

It takes/costs ⋯ + to + 동사원형 ~하는 데 (시간/비용 등)이 걸리다/들다

- **It took 30 minutes to get** to work. 출근하는 데 30분이 걸렸다.
- I like that hotel, but **it costs too much to stay** there.

  이때, **takes/costs** 뒤에 사람을 쓸 수도 있다.

  - **It didn't cost Marie** much money **to renovate** her kitchen. Marie가 부엌을 보수하는 데 돈이 많이 들지 않았다.

can/can't afford to + 동사원형 ~할 여유가 있다/없다

- I **can't afford to buy** that laptop. It's too expensive. 저 노트북을 살 여유가 없다.
- After saving up for three years, I **could afford to rent** a small apartment downtown.

can't wait to + 동사원형 너무 ~하고 싶다

- I **can't wait to play** this video game. I heard it's really good! 이 비디오 게임을 너무 하고 싶다.
- Peter got promoted. He **can't wait to tell** everybody.

PRACTICE

A. 괄호 안에 주어진 단어들을 적절히 배열하여 문장을 완성하세요. 필요한 경우 동사를 -ing로 바꾸어 쓰세요.

1. (you / mind / would / change) " _Would you mind changing_ the channel?" "No. Which channel?"
2. (have / like / felt) Jason _____ a beer, so he went out for a drink.
3. (push / do / mind / you) I'm going to the ninth floor. _____ the button for me?
4. (was / clean / busy) Sorry I missed your call. I _____ the house.
5. (difficulty / understand / have) Troy and I _____ each other sometimes.
6. (worth / was / read) The novel _____. I enjoyed it.

B. 주어진 문장을 보고 -ing를 쓰는 표현(feel like -ing, be busy -ing 등)을 사용하여 다시 말해보세요.

1. Danny wants to go to the beach this weekend.
   → Danny _feels like going to the beach this weekend_ .
2. I fixed my car. It cost a lot of money.
   → I _____ .
3. Ms. Carson is busy because she is preparing for her presentation.
   → Ms. Carson _____ .
4. Parents worry about their children all the time. They can't stop.
   → Parents _____ .
5. Melissa can't see very well without her glasses.
   → Melissa _____ .

C. 그림을 보고 괄호 안에 주어진 동사와 It took/cost + 사람 ~을 사용하여 예시와 같이 문장을 완성하세요.

1. (wash) _It took him 30 minutes to wash_ the dishes.
2. (make) _____ the sweater.
3. (buy) _____ a new phone.
4. (watch) _____ the movie.
5. (see) _____ the concert.
6. (get) _____ to the hotel.

D. 주어진 동사와 can't help/can(can't) afford/can't wait를 사용하여 예시와 같이 문장을 완성하세요.

feel	laugh	leave	meet	~~pay~~	stay

1. Jack _can't afford to pay_ tuition this year, so he's taking a year off.
2. "Are you excited about your trip to Russia?" "Yes! I _____!"
3. I _____ bad for Sarah. She is sick right now.
4. I'm sorry, but I _____. You look so funny in that costume.
5. "Do you have to go home now?" "No. I think we _____ a little longer."
6. "I want to introduce you to my friends." "I _____ them!"

-ing와 to + 동사원형

LESSON **46**

Grammar Gateway Intermediate

1 명사는 셀 수 있는 명사와 셀 수 없는 명사로 나뉜다.

다음과 같은 명사는 셀 수 있는 명사이다.

cup	chair	store	dog	ant
singer	teacher	orange	apple	flower

- There's **a cup** on the table.
  식탁 위에 컵 하나가 있다.
- Two **singers** are on stage.
  가수 두 명이 무대 위에 있다.
- I bought **an orange** and three **apples**.
- Smell these **flowers**, Mary! They're so nice.

다음과 같은 명사는 셀 수 없는 명사이다.

water	oil	rice	salt	rain
love	air	weather	music	traffic

- There's **water** in the cup.
  컵 안에 물이 있다.
- **Love** is the greatest gift.
  사랑은 가장 위대한 선물이다.
- Many people around the world eat **rice**.
- **Traffic** is terrible on the weekends.

2 셀 수 있는 명사는 단수 또는 복수로 쓸 수 있다. 사람 또는 사물이 하나인 경우를 **단수**, 둘 이상인 경우를 **복수**라고 한다.

단수	a brother	the room	my bag	the child
복수	two brothers	the rooms	my bags	children

명사의 형태 변화: 부록 p. 281 참고

- Ryan has **a brother**. His name is Nick. Ryan은 형이 한 명 있다.
- **The rooms** at that hotel aren't very clean. Don't go there. 저 호텔의 방들은 매우 깨끗하지 않아.
- Can you hold **my bag** please? I need to tie my shoes.
- **Children** are chasing **butterflies**. They are trying to catch them.

단수명사는 앞에 **a/an**/**the**/**my**(소유격) 등을 항상 함께 쓴다.

- "Can I borrow **a pencil**?" "Sure. Look in **the drawer**." (Can I borrow pencil? 또는 Look in drawer로 쓸 수 없음)
- Rita isn't going to sell **her car** until next year. (Rita isn't going to sell car로 쓸 수 없음)

복수명사는 앞에 **숫자**/**the**/**my** 등을 함께 쓰거나, 단독으로 쓸 수도 있다. 단, 복수명사 앞에는 **a/an**을 쓸 수 없는 것에 주의한다.

- "Where can we hang **our coats**?" "Over there." (a coats로 쓸 수 없음)
- Matt gave me **flowers** and **two tickets** to the ballet for my birthday. (a flowers, a tickets로 쓸 수 없음)
- **The artists** are going to open a gallery together.

3 셀 수 없는 명사에는 단수와 복수의 개념이 없다. 따라서 셀 수 없는 명사는 앞에 **a/an**이나 숫자를 쓸 수 없고, 복수로도 쓸 수 없다.

- Some people believe that true **happiness** comes from helping others. (a happiness 또는 happinesses로 쓸 수 없음)
- I usually use **oil** to fry eggs, but sometimes I use **butter**. (an oil, two butters 등으로 쓸 수 없음)

  단, **the**/**my** 등을 함께 쓰거나, 단독으로 쓸 수도 있다.

  - I hope **the weather** doesn't get worse this week. 이번 주에 날씨가 더 나빠지지 않기를 바란다.
  - **My coffee** needs **sugar**. It's not sweet at all.

4 단수명사 또는 셀 수 없는 명사를 주어로 쓸 때는 단수동사를 쓰고, 복수명사를 주어로 쓸 때는 복수동사를 쓴다.

- This **sofa costs** too much. I don't think I can buy it. (This sofa가 단수명사이므로 단수동사 costs를 썼음)
- Those **gloves aren't** big enough for my hands. (Those gloves가 복수명사이므로 복수동사 aren't를 썼음)
- **Honesty is** important between friends.

주어와 동사의 수 일치: 부록 p. 276 참고

PRACTICE

A. 그림을 보고 주어진 명사와 a/an 또는 two/three/four 등을 사용하여 예시와 같이 문장을 완성하세요.

bicycle	bird	book	calendar	~~girl~~	umbrella

1. _There are two girls_ on the bench.
2. _____ under the tree.
3. _____ in the sky.
4. _____ on the desk.
5. _____ by the door.
6. _____ on the wall.

B. 주어진 명사를 사용하여 문장을 완성하세요. 필요한 경우 a/an을 함께 쓰거나 복수로 쓰세요.

air	apartment	athlete	~~knowledge~~	novel	rain	table	tourist

1. Your _knowledge_ of computers will be useful for this job.
2. "Do many _____ come here?" "Yes. The streets are full of visitors in spring."
3. I'd like to reserve _____ for tonight. Could I get one by the window?
4. My tire is almost flat. It needs _____ .
5. Many _____ from around the world compete in the Olympics.
6. We got so much _____ last night. The roads are still wet.
7. Jackie moved to _____ close to her university. Now, she can walk to campus.
8. "What _____ did you borrow from the library?" "Moby-Dick and Little Women."

C. 괄호 안에 주어진 표현들을 적절한 형태로 사용하여 문장을 완성하세요. 현재 시제로 쓰세요.

1. (climate, be) In the Sahara desert, the _climate is_ _____ very dry.
2. (movie, look) "These three _____ interesting." "Then let's watch one of them."
3. (juice, contain) This _____ a lot of vitamin C.
4. (museum, display) The _____ a lot of paintings. It has various statues, too.
5. (cookie, have) You aren't allergic to nuts, are you? These _____ nuts in them.
6. (delivery truck, bring) A _____ fresh ingredients to our bakery each day.

D. 다음 문장을 읽고 틀린 부분이 있으면 바르게 고치세요. 틀린 부분이 없으면 ○로 표시하세요.

1. I think a salt makes food taste better. I put it on everything.   _a salt → salt_
2. "Music aren't very creative these days." "Yes. I agree."   _____
3. My sister had baby yesterday. It's a girl.   _____
4. A people are using public transportation more because it is convenient.   _____
5. The trees in my yard aren't oaks. They're maples.   _____
6. Some dishes at this restaurant are served with rices.   _____
7. The key to success is hard work.   _____
8. "I got two new video game." "Really? Can we play them?"   _____
9. This street have no space for more buildings. It's full.   _____

This **bread** has **cheese** in it. 셀 수 있는 명사와 셀 수 없는 명사 (2)

1 다음과 같이 의미상 셀 수 있을 것 같지만 셀 수 없는 명사가 있다.

bread	cheese	chocolate	meat	food	ice
paper	wood	information	advice	news	

- This **bread** has **cheese** in it. 이 빵에는 치즈가 들어있다.
- **Paper** is usually made from **wood**. 종이는 보통 나무로 만들어진다.
- There's so much **information** on the Internet.
- My cousin just told me great **news**. She's getting married!

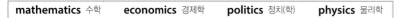

bread   cheese

다음과 같은 학과명은 **-s**로 끝나서 복수명사처럼 보이지만, 셀 수 없는 명사이다.

mathematics 수학	**economics** 경제학	**politics** 정치(학)	**physics** 물리학

- **Mathematics** is important in most fields of science. 수학은 대부분의 과학 분야에서 중요하다.
- I don't understand **economics**. It's too hard for me.

2 셀 수 없는 명사 앞에 **a cup of/two slices of** 등과 같이 단위를 나타내는 표현을 함께 쓸 수 있다.

- I had **a cup of coffee** and **two slices of toast** for breakfast today. 오늘 아침으로 커피 한 잔과 토스트 두 조각을 먹었다.
- "May I offer you **a piece of advice**?" 충고 한 마디를 해드려도 될까요? "Sure."
- There is going to be 50 guests, so we need about **five kilos of rice**.
- "A **bottle of water** costs $5 at this resort." "That seems expensive."

3 다음과 같이 의미에 따라서 셀 수 없는 명사로 쓸 수도 있고, 셀 수 있는 명사로 쓸 수도 있는 명사가 있다.

light	빛 – 셀 수 없는 명사
	전등 – 셀 수 있는 명사

- We get a lot of **light** in the hallway. 복도에 빛이 많이 들어온다.
- The **lights** in the hallway are on. 복도의 전등이 켜져 있다.

paper	종이 – 셀 수 없는 명사
	신문 – 셀 수 있는 명사

- That shop sells **paper** and office supplies.
- I read **a paper** on the plane this morning.

room	공간 – 셀 수 없는 명사
	방 – 셀 수 있는 명사

- There's no **room** in the fridge.
- Our house has three **rooms** and a kitchen.

time	시간 – 셀 수 없는 명사
	횟수, ~ 번 – 셀 수 있는 명사

- Kenny didn't have **time** to do his homework yesterday.
- "Have you been to Japan?" "Yes. Four **times**."

glass	유리 – 셀 수 없는 명사
	유리잔 – 셀 수 있는 명사

- This bowl is made of **glass**.
- "Could you get some **glasses** from the cabinet?" "Sure."

work	일 – 셀 수 없는 명사
	작품 – 셀 수 있는 명사

- "Let's meet this weekend." "Sorry, I have too much **work**."
- *Oliver Twist* is one of Dickens's greatest **works**.

4 hair는 '머리카락 전체'라는 의미로 쓸 때는 셀 수 없는 명사이지만, '머리카락 한 올'이라는 의미로 쓸 때는 셀 수 있는 명사이다.

- Everyone in Jenny's family has blond **hair**.
  ('머리카락 전체'를 의미하므로 셀 수 없음)

  The restaurant gave me a free meal because I found **a hair** in my soup.
  ('머리카락 한 올'을 의미하므로 셀 수 있음)

hair   a hair

PRACTICE

A. 주어진 명사를 사용하여 문장을 완성하세요. 필요한 경우 a/an을 함께 쓰세요.

engineer	~~food~~	ice	news	tie

1. You can't eat here, sir. *Food*_____ isn't allowed in the museum.
2. Evan was always interested in machines. When he grew up, he became _____.
3. In Sweden, there is a hotel made of _____. It's only open during the winter.
4. Bill couldn't find _____ to match his shirt.
5. Did you hear the _____ about John? He's moving to LA.

envelope	information	meat	picture	politics

6. Do you have _____? I need something to put this document in.
7. If you major in _____, you can learn a lot about social issues and policies.
8. "This is _____ of me a few years ago." "You look very young."
9. "What kind of _____ is this?" "I think it's beef."
10. This magazine contains a lot of _____ about cars.

B. 그림을 보고 주어진 단어들을 적절한 형태로 사용하여 예시와 같이 문장을 완성하세요.

(bar, soap)	(bottle, beer)	(jar, jam)	(kilo, cheese)	~~(sheet, paper)~~

1. She's holding *a sheet of paper*_____.
2. There are _____ in the cabinet.
3. There's _____ on the sink.
4. _____ costs $20.
5. He's carrying _____.

C. 괄호 안에 주어진 명사를 사용하여 문장을 완성하세요. 필요한 경우 a를 함께 쓰거나 복수로 쓰세요.

(paper) 1. "Can you pick up *a paper*_____ for me? I want to read the news." "Sure. I'll get one."
2. We are trying to use less _____ in our office. We print on both sides now.

(time) 3. This is my favorite book. I've read it several _____.
4. "Do we have _____ to stop at the mall?" "Yes. What do you need?"

(light) 5. "Let's turn on the _____. It's dark in here." "OK. I'll turn them on."
6. Bright _____ came in through my window this morning. It woke me up.

(glass) 7. Most tall buildings today are made of steel and _____.
8. The _____ in the sink need to be washed. They're dirty.

(room) 9. I reserved _____ with an ocean view. You'll like it.
10. There isn't enough _____ to put the sofa here. It's too big.

(hair) 11. You have _____ on your sweater. I'll remove it for you.
12. The hairdresser cut off too much _____. Now it's too short.

LESSON 48

명사

Grammar Gateway Intermediate

1 furniture(가구류), jewelry(보석류)와 같이 종류 전체를 의미하는 명사는 셀 수 없다. 그러나 **chair, earring**과 같이 어느 한 종류에 포함되는 구체적인 품목들은 셀 수 있다.

셀 수 없는 명사 (종류 전체)	셀 수 있는 명사 (포함되는 품목)			
furniture (가구류)	a chair	a desk	a bed	a table
jewelry (보석류)	an earring	a necklace	a ring	a bracelet
baggage/luggage (수화물류)	a bag	a backpack	a suitcase	a handbag
money (화폐류)	a dollar	a coin	a penny	a bill
mail (우편물류)	a letter	a card	a postcard	an e-mail

- We bought some new **furniture**. It's for our living room.   우리는 새 가구를 샀다.
  I need **a chair** and **a desk** for my bedroom.   내 침실에 의자 하나와 책상 하나가 필요하다.
- "Do you usually wear **jewelry**?"   "No."
  There's **an earring** under the table. Is it yours?
- "Could you lend me some **money**?"   "How much do you need?"
  I found a couple of **dollars** and a few **coins** in my pocket.

furniture

a chair   a desk

2 **work**(일, 직장)와 **a job**(일자리, 직업)은 비슷한 의미이지만, **work**는 셀 수 없는 명사이고 **a job**은 셀 수 있는 명사이다.

- "How's **work** these days?"   "Good, but busy."   요즘 일은 어떠니? (work – 셀 수 없는 명사)
  "Have you found **a job** yet?"   "Yes! Just yesterday."   일자리는 찾았니? (a job – 셀 수 있는 명사)

다음과 같은 명사들도 비슷한 의미이지만 셀 수 없는 명사와 셀 수 있는 명사로 각각 다르게 쓴다.

vocabulary	어휘 – 셀 수 없는 명사	• I need to study **vocabulary** for my Italian test. 이탈리아어 시험을 위해 어휘를 공부할 필요가 있다.
a word	단어 – 셀 수 있는 명사	• Shakespeare created more than a thousand **words**. 셰익스피어는 천 개 이상의 단어들을 만들어냈다.
travel	여행, 이동 – 셀 수 없는 명사	• "Where can I find books on **travel**?" "On the second floor."
a trip	여행, 관광 – 셀 수 있는 명사	• Dana's family took **a trip** to India last year.
homework	숙제 – 셀 수 없는 명사	• Mr. Larson gives his students a lot of **homework**.
an assignment	과제 – 셀 수 있는 명사	• These two **assignments** must be finished by Friday.
advice	조언 – 셀 수 없는 명사	• Tim always gives me **advice**, but it's not helpful.
a suggestion	제안 – 셀 수 있는 명사	• Kim made some **suggestions** for my wedding.
news	소식, 뉴스 – 셀 수 없는 명사	• "I heard you got promoted!" "Wow, **news** travels fast!"
an article	기사 – 셀 수 있는 명사	• There were many interesting **articles** in today's newspaper.
scenery	풍경 – 셀 수 없는 명사	• The **scenery** in Switzerland was amazing.
a view	전망 – 셀 수 있는 명사	• Look outside! There's **a** lovely **view** of the sunset.
food	음식 – 셀 수 없는 명사	• I ordered Chinese **food**. Do you want some?
a meal	식사, 끼니 – 셀 수 있는 명사	• We're having **a meal** with Phillip next week.

PRACTICE

A. 괄호 안에 주어진 명사들을 순서대로 사용하여 문장을 완성하세요. 필요한 경우 복수로 쓰세요.

1

AA Jewelry Store

(necklace, earring, bracelet, jewelry)

You can get 50% off on all our

necklaces _____ , _____ ,

and _____ . Come see

our fine _____ !

2

Looking for Collectors

(money, coin, penny)

I would like to sell some old

_____ . I have many

rare _____ . In fact,

two of the _____ are

from the early 1900s!

3

For Sale

(table, chair, furniture)

I'm moving, and I have a

_____ , and four

_____ for sale.

If you are interested in

buying my _____ ,

give me a call.

---

4 **Postage Rates Increase**

(mail, regular letter, postcard)

Postage rates for _____

have increased. All _____

and _____ are now 48

cents.

---

5 *Found*

(luggage, brown suitcase, backpack)

I found some _____ near my

apartment. There's a _____

and two _____ .

I'm in apartment 102.

B. 주어진 명사를 사용하여 문장을 완성하세요. 필요한 경우 a/an을 함께 쓰거나 복수로 쓰세요.

big meal	~~homework~~	news	suggestion	travel	word

1. I forgot to do my *homework* _____ again. The teacher is going to be angry.
2. You can learn a lot of new _____ while watching foreign films.
3. Can I make _____ ? I have an idea about how we can improve sales.
4. _____ costs money, but sometimes you can find cheap flights online.
5. We rarely hear any _____ from Timothy. He hasn't called any of us in years.
6. I had _____ at lunch, but I'm already hungry again.

C. 주어진 명사를 사용하여 Justin과 James의 대화를 완성하세요. 필요한 경우 복수로 쓰세요.

article	job	~~postcard~~	scenery	trip	work

JUSTIN: What are you reading, Dad?

JAMES: 1. It's a *postcard* _____ from your uncle Nick.

2. You know, his company sent him to Belgium for _____ .

JUSTIN: What does he do?

JAMES: 3. He writes _____ for a travel magazine.
You can read them online.

JUSTIN: Is he a reporter? 4. That sounds like a fun _____ !

JAMES: Yeah. 5. He takes many _____ and experiences many cultures.

6. He also sees a lot of beautiful _____ .

JUSTIN: Wow. He's so lucky!

LESSON 49

명사

Grammar Gateway Intermediate

Can you pass me those **scissors**? 단수, 복수에 주의해야 할 명사

1 다음과 같이 두 개의 부분이 모여 하나의 사물을 이루는 명사는 항상 복수로 쓴다.

scissors	jeans	pants	shorts	pajamas	glasses	binoculars

- "Can you pass me the **scissors**?" 저 가위를 건네줄래? "Sure."
- These **pants** feel really comfortable. You should buy these too. 이 바지는 정말 편해.
- "I didn't know you wore **glasses**." "Only for reading."
- I have had my blue **jeans** since I was in high school.

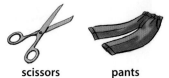

scissors   pants

이 명사들을 주어로 쓸 때는 항상 복수동사를 쓴다. 단수동사를 쓰지 않는 것에 주의한다.

- "Your **shorts look** nice. Where did you get them?" "At the department store." (Your shorts looks로 쓸 수 없음)
- **Pajamas were** on sale at L-Mart. They only cost $20. (Pajamas was로 쓸 수 없음)

이 명사들을 셀 때는 앞에 **a/an**이나 숫자를 쓸 수 없고, **a pair of/two pairs of**와 같은 표현을 쓰는 것에 주의한다.

- He brought **two pairs of binoculars** to the football game.
  축구 경기에 쌍안경 두 개를 가져왔다. (two binoculars로 쓸 수 없음)
- Doris gave her sister **a pair of jeans** because they didn't fit her anymore.
  Doris는 여동생에게 청바지 한 벌을 주었다. (a jeans로 쓸 수 없음)

two pairs of binoculars

2 다음과 같은 명사는 항상 복수로 쓴다.

belongings 소지품	clothes 옷	congratulations 축하	goods 상품	surroundings 주위 환경

- Make sure to take all your **belongings** with you when you exit the train. 기차에서 내릴 때 소지품을 모두 챙겼는지 확인하세요.
- Your room is a mess. Please put away your **clothes**. 네 옷을 치우렴.
- "Jim and Lisa are having a baby." "Give them my **congratulations**."
- This lake is beautiful. The **surroundings** seem perfect for hiking.

이 명사들을 주어로 쓸 때는 항상 복수동사를 쓴다. 단수동사를 쓰지 않는 것에 주의한다.

- The **goods were** imported from China. They are sold for 5 dollars. (The goods was로 쓸 수 없음)
- Phil's apartment is great, but the **surroundings are** noisy. It's by a highway. (the surroundings is로 쓸 수 없음)

3 다음과 같은 명사는 여러 구성원들이 모인 집단을 의미하지만 주로 단수로 쓴다. 이 명사들을 주어로 쓸 때는 단수동사를 주로 쓴다.

family 가족	class 학급	team 팀	staff 직원	audience 청중	crowd 무리	committee 위원회

- My **family is** going to Greece next summer. 우리 가족은 내년 여름에 그리스에 갈 예정이다.
- Jerry's **class has** only 12 students in it. He goes to a very small school. Jerry의 학급엔 열두 명의 학생밖에 없다.
- The city's baseball **team hasn't** improved much over the past two years.
- You should stay at Hotel Valencia. The **staff** there **provides** excellent service.

4 **police**는 복수명사이다. 따라서 **police**를 주어로 쓸 때는 항상 복수동사를 쓰는 것에 주의한다.

- The **police have** been looking for a man in a red jacket. (The police has been looking으로 쓸 수 없음)
- "Why **are** the **police** standing outside?" "There was a robbery." (Why is the police standing으로 쓸 수 없음)

경찰관 한 명을 말할 때는 **a police officer**를 쓴다.

- Maria didn't want her son to become **a police officer**. She thought the job was too dangerous.
  Maria는 그녀의 아들이 경찰관이 되는 것을 원하지 않았다.

PRACTICE

A. 다음은 Jamie 상점 고객들의 주문 목록입니다. 다음 주문서를 보고 one/two 또는 a pair of/two pairs of 등을 함께 사용하여 문장을 완성하세요.

		ANDY	JENNY	DAVID	TINA
Jamie's Closet	SHIRT	/		////	
	PANTS	//		/	
	CAP				///
ORDER LIST	SUNGLASSES		/		
	SKIRT		//		/
	SHORTS				///

1. Andy ordered _one shirt_____ and _____.
2. Jenny wants _____ and _____.
3. David is getting _____ and _____.
4. Tina will buy _____, _____, and _____.

B. 주어진 표현들을 사용하여 문장을 완성하세요. 현재 시제로 쓰세요.

a museum ticket   binoculars   my vocabulary   ~~the post office~~   the surroundings   these pants

1. (be) You can't send mail today. _The post office is_____ closed because of the holiday.
2. (help) _____ you see things from far away.
3. (improve) _____ every day. I'm always learning new words.
4. (be) The temple is in the mountains. _____ very peaceful.
5. (seem) "_____ too big for me?" "No, I think they're OK."
6. (cost) _____ $6. It includes a free coffee from our cafeteria.

my son   pajamas   personal belongings   these shoes   time   your steak

7. (feel) _____ soft because they are for sleeping.
8. (be) _____ precious. We should spend every minute wisely.
9. (play) _____ the drums quite well. He wants to join a band.
10. (make) "_____ my feet hurt." "Maybe they're too small for you."
11. (need) The gym is not responsible for stolen items. _____ to be watched carefully.
12. (smell) "_____ delicious." "It's tasty. Here, try some!"

C. 다음 문장을 읽고 틀린 부분이 있으면 바르게 고치세요. 틀린 부분이 없으면 ○로 표시하세요.

1. Your jeans is in the washing machine.   _is → are_
2. "I won the art competition!" "Congratulation!"   _____
3. "Whose scissors are these?" "They're mine."   _____
4. These shoes is new. They were a gift from my boyfriend.   _____
5. "How often does your committee meet?" "Once a week."   _____
6. "The police still hasn't arrived." "But you called hours ago!" _____
7. There is a pair of glass on the desk. Are they yours?   _____
8. It's too hot to wear pants today. I should have worn a shorts. _____
9. "What good do you sell at your store?" "We sell phones."   _____
10. The crowd was excited to see the rock star.   _____

명사

LESSON 50

Grammar Gateway Intermediate

1

Which one should we watch?

They want to watch **a movie.**
(특별히 정해지지 않은) 영화를 한 편 보기를 원한다.

막연한 영화 한 편을 의미하므로 movie 앞에 a를 썼다.

Let's watch this one.

They want to watch **the movie.**
(특정한) 그 영화를 보기를 원한다.

특정한 영화를 의미하므로 movie 앞에 the를 썼다.

2 특별히 정해지지 않은 막연한 사람이나 사물 하나를 말할 때는 명사 앞에 **a/an**을 쓴다.

- I need **a lawyer**. Do you know one?
  (특별히 정해지지 않은 변호사 한 명)
- Can I borrow **a pencil**? I forgot to bring one.
  (특별히 정해지지 않은 연필 한 자루)
- "I'd like to buy **an alarm clock**."
  "How about this one?"

특정한 사람이나 사물을 말할 때는 명사 앞에 **the**를 쓴다.

- I know **the lawyer** that Jim hired. I went to law school with him. (Jim이 고용한 특정한 변호사)
- Here is **the pencil** I borrowed. Thanks for letting me use it. (내가 빌린 특정한 연필)
- **The alarm clock** I just bought is very loud. It will wake my whole family up.

상대방이 모르는 어떤 대상을 처음 말할 때는 명사 앞에 **a/an**을 쓰고, 그 대상을 다시 말할 때는 **the**를 쓴다.

- Mike sent me **a rose** and **a cake**. **The rose** was beautiful, and **the cake** was delicious.
  Mike가 장미 한 송이와 케이크를 보냈다. 장미는 아름다웠고, 케이크는 맛있었다.
- "I have to write **an essay**." "Oh, what's the topic of **the essay**? Maybe I can help."
- If you see **a man** with **a boy**, please contact the police. **The man** is wearing a brown hat, and **the boy** is wearing blue shorts.

3 상황상 누구 또는 무엇을 가리키는지 명확히 알 수 있는 경우에는 명사 앞에 **the**를 쓴다.

- "Where are **the children**?" "They're playing outside."
  (말하는 사람과 듣는 사람이 모두 알고 있는 아이들로 누구를 가리키는지가 명확하므로 the를 썼음)
- "I think I just heard **the bell** ring." "Me too. I'll go and check **the door**."
  (말하는 사람과 듣는 사람이 모두 알고 있는 초인종과 문으로 무엇을 가리키는지가 명확하므로 the를 썼음)
- We should fix **the dishwasher**. We haven't been able to use it for weeks.

4 **a/an**은 셀 수 있는 명사의 단수 앞에 쓴다. 복수명사나 셀 수 없는 명사 앞에는 **a/an**을 쓰지 않는 것에 주의한다.

- I took **a picture** of my **friends** on the beach. The sun was setting behind them.
  해변에서 친구들의 사진을 찍었다. (friends는 복수명사이므로 a friends로 쓸 수 없음)
- "How is the salmon?" "It needs **salt**." 소금이 필요해. (salt는 셀 수 없는 명사이므로 a salt로 쓸 수 없음)

the는 셀 수 있는 명사의 단수와 복수 그리고 셀 수 없는 명사 모두와 함께 쓸 수 있다.

- "Where did you get your jewelry? I really like it."
  "Thanks. **The necklace** was a gift, but I bought **the earrings**." 목걸이는 선물 받았지만, 귀걸이는 내가 샀어.
- Fred got a bonus at work. He spent **the money** on a new stereo.

PRACTICE

A. 괄호 안에 주어진 표현과 a/an 또는 the를 사용하여 문장을 완성하세요.

1. (score) "What's _the score_ _____ of the baseball game?" "It's 6 to 3."
2. (newspaper) "Could I get _____ for the flight?" "Sure. Which one?"
3. (dream) "I had a bad dream." "Really? What was _____ about?"
4. (bike) _____ with a flat tire belongs to Adam.
5. (umbrella) "Can you lend me _____?" "Sorry. I don't have an extra."
6. (vase) "I broke a vase today." "Was it _____ you got from your mom?"
7. (old man) There's _____ trying to carry boxes. Let's help him.
8. (store) "Is there _____ nearby? I want a snack." "There's one around the corner."

B. a/an 또는 the를 써넣으세요.

1. A: Can I borrow _a_ hammer?
   B: Sure. We keep one in _____ garage.

2. A: They're building _____ café across _____ street.
   B: Really? When will _____ café open?

3. A: We saw _____ accident on the road this morning.
   B: Oh no. Was anyone hurt in _____ accident?

4. A: I had _____ question but the speaker's gone.
   B: You could send him _____ question by e-mail.

5. A: I didn't see you at _____ dorm. Where were you?
   B: I went to _____ library to study.

6. A: I need _____ bowl for _____ grapes we bought.
   B: OK. I'll bring you one.

C. 다음 문장을 읽고 틀린 부분이 있으면 바르게 고치세요. 틀린 부분이 없으면 ○로 표시하세요.

1. "Do you see the taxi anywhere?" "Yes, there's one over there!" _____ _the taxi → a taxi_ _____
2. How many a bathrooms does the apartment have? _____
3. A mayor of our city is traveling to Asia. _____
4. Jessica couldn't move the furniture by herself. _____
5. "Did you put a sugar on the grocery list?" "Yes." _____
6. I sent you a postcard. Did you get it? _____
7. "I'm bored." "I have the idea. Let's go to the amusement park!" _____

D. 다음은 Sandy가 쓴 영화 감상문입니다. 주어진 표현과 a/an 또는 the를 사용하여 문장을 완성하세요.

| ~~action movie~~ | city | city | enemy | enemy | motorcycle | superhero |

Clone Man – A Great Movie!

By Sandy Smith

1. If you are in the mood for _an action movie_ , I recommend *Clone Man*.
2. It is a movie about _____.
3. Clone Man is his name, and he lives in _____ with a lot of criminals.
4. Every night, he drives _____ around the city to fight crime.
5. He also has _____ who is trying to destroy the city.
6. But in the end, Clone Man saves _____ and everybody is happy.
7. My favorite part was when Clone Man defeated _____.
It was amazing! Go watch *Clone Man* today!

A baby needs more sleep than an adult. a/an과 the (2)

1 a/an은 일반적인 사람 또는 사물에 대해 말할 때도 쓴다.

- **A baby** needs more sleep than **an adult**. 아기는 성인보다 더 많은 수면을 필요로 한다. (일반적인 아기, 일반적인 성인)
- **A bicycle** is a convenient way to get around this town. 자전거는 이 마을에서 이동하기에 편리한 수단이다. (일반적인 자전거)
- "How many legs does **a spider** have?" "Eight."
- **An egg** consists of an egg white and a yolk.

  단, 일반적인 것에 대해 말할 때에라도 셀 수 없는 명사 앞에는 **a/an**을 쓰지 않는 것에 주의한다.

  - **Honesty** is the most important thing in a relationship.
    (Honesty는 셀 수 없는 명사이므로 An honesty로 쓸 수 없음)
  - Some students love doing **homework**. Other students don't like it.
    (Homework은 셀 수 없는 명사이므로 a homework으로 쓸 수 없음)

2 일반적인 사람 또는 사물에 대해 말할 때 복수명사도 쓸 수 있다. a/an + 단수명사보다는 복수명사를 더 자주 쓴다.

- **Children** can learn **foreign languages** easily. 아이들은 외국어를 쉽게 배운다. (일반적인 아이들, 일반적인 외국어)
- How do **bees** make honey? 벌은 어떻게 꿀을 만드나요? (일반적인 벌)
- "Do you enjoy watching **operas**?" "No. I prefer **plays**."
- **Oranges** are rich in **vitamins**.

3 일반적인 사람 또는 사물에 대해 말할 때 **the**를 쓰지 않는 것에 주의한다. **the**는 특정한 사람 또는 사물에 대해 말할 때 쓴다.

- **An architect** designs buildings. 건축가는 건물을 디자인한다. (일반적인 건축가)
  "Who is **the architect** for this building?" "Mr. Duval." 이 건물의 건축가가 누구니? (특정한 건축가)
- **Backpacks** are useful for hiking and camping.
  The backpacks designed by Jimmy King are on sale.
- "What is **cheese** made from?" "Milk."
  "When did you buy **the cheese** in the refrigerator?" "I just got it yesterday."

4 일반적인 사람 또는 사물에 대해 말할 때는 **the**를 쓰지 않지만, 일반적인 동식물, 기계류, 악기에 대해 말할 때는 a/an + 단수명사 또는 복수명사 대신 the + 단수명사도 쓸 수 있다.

- **The lion** is commonly known as "the king of the jungle."
  사자는 흔히 '밀림의 왕'으로 알려져있다. (= A lion, Lions)
- **The sunflower** turns toward the sun.
  해바라기는 태양을 향해 돈다. (= A sunflower, Sunflowers)
- "When was **the telescope** invented?" "In the early 1600s."
- In jazz music, you can often hear **the saxophone**.

5 사람의 직업이 무엇인지 또는 사물이 어떤 종류인지를 말할 때는 a/an을 주로 쓴다.

- Craig is **an editor** for a fashion magazine. He's great at his job. Craig는 패션 잡지의 편집자이다.
- Monaco is **a country**. It's near France. 모나코는 나라이다.
- The woman standing over there is **an illustrator**. She's very talented.
- "What is your hometown like?" "Well, it isn't **a large town**. It's very quiet."

PRACTICE

A. 주어진 표현들을 사용하여 괄호 안의 명사에 대해 예시와 같이 설명해보세요.

be great for breakfast or as a snack	be words for people, places, or things
~~create paintings and sculptures~~	help you keep in touch with friends
provide space to park cars	travel on ships

1. (artist) *Artists create paintings and sculptures* .
2. (muffin) _____ .
3. (garage) _____ .
4. (cell phone) _____ .
5. (noun) _____ .
6. (sailor) _____ .

B. 다음은 쌍둥이 형제 Fred와 Peter의 블로그입니다. 필요한 경우 a/an 또는 the를 써넣고, 필요하지 않은 경우에는 – 로 표시하세요.

◀ ▶ + ● http:// Fred.foodblog.com ↻

Fred .blog

1. I'm a good cook and I love ___ – ___ food!
2. I especially like _____ sandwiches.
3. _____ good sandwich needs good bread.
4. _____ bread in my sandwiches is delicious, and it's homemade. I have a great recipe.
5. If you want my recipe, send me _____ e-mail.

◀ ▶ + ● http:// Peter.myblog.com ↻

Peter .blog

6. I think cooking is a waste of _____ time.
7. My brother Fred cooks all the time, but I prefer going out to eat at _____ restaurants.
8. Near my house, there's _____ Thai restaurant.
9. _____ food there is really good!
10. I especially like _____ spicy soup on their menu.

C. 주어진 명사를 단수 또는 복수로 사용하여 문장을 완성하세요. 필요한 경우 the를 함께 쓰세요.

~~bed~~	blue whale	bone	judge	microscope	tile

1. I like _the bed_____ in this hotel room. It's very comfortable.
2. _____ can be 30 meters long. That's longer than all other animals.
3. It was not possible to see very small things before _____ .
4. _____ break more easily as you get older because they become weaker.
5. I like _____ in this catalog. They seem perfect for our bathroom.
6. Being fair is an important quality for _____ . They must not be affected by their own opinions.

D. 괄호 안에 주어진 표현들과 a/an을 적절히 배열하여 문장을 완성하세요.

1. (Bill's wife / newspaper reporter / is) *Bill's wife is a newspaper reporter* .
2. (the tomato / vegetable / is) _____ that is often used in pasta.
3. (is / excellent singer / Todd) _____ . I love his voice.
4. (is / Judy / lawyer in Florida) _____ .
5. (old desk / this / is) _____ . It was my grandmother's.
6. (the cactus / tough plant / is)

_____ . It grows in deserts and requires little water.

1 다음과 같은 명사는 보통 **the**와 함께 쓴다.

유일한 것	the sun	the moon	the earth	the world	the universe
자연환경	the sea	the ocean	the sky	the ground	
	the rain	the wind	the environment		

- **The sun** is at the center of our solar system. 해는 우리 태양계의 중심에 있다.
- **The sky** became cloudy and **the rain** began to fall.
- Mr. Watson owns one of the biggest computer manufacturers in **the world**.

극장	the theater	the cinema	the movies
방송, 매체	the Internet	the radio	

- **The theater** offers discount tickets on Tuesdays. 그 극장은 화요일마다 할인된 표를 제공한다.
- "Where did you buy those gloves?" "On **the Internet**."

TV를 '방송'이라는 의미로 쓸 때는 **the**를 쓰지 않지만 'TV'라는 기계 자체에 대해 말할 때는 **the**를 쓸 수 있다.
- I don't watch **TV**. I prefer reading books. (TV 방송을 의미하므로 the를 쓰지 않았음)
  Sitting close to **the TV** is bad for your eyes. (TV라는 기계 자체를 의미하므로 the를 썼음)

movies를 일반적인 '영화'라는 의미로 쓸 때는 **the**를 쓰지 않는다. 단, '극장'이라는 의미로 말할 때는 **the**를 쓰는 것에 주의한다.
- I like **movies**. I watch them often. (영화를 의미하므로 the를 쓰지 않았음)
  I haven't been to **the movies** in months. I've been very busy. (극장을 의미하므로 the를 썼음)

정부 집단	the police	the government	the army

- We called **the police** right after we saw the traffic accident. 교통사고를 본 후 즉시 경찰에 전화했다.
- My brother works for **the government**. He's in **the army**.

2 다음과 같은 표현도 보통 **the**와 함께 쓴다.

the only + 명사: 유일한 ~
- Kelly is **the only woman** in our department. Kelly는 우리 부서에서 유일한 여자이다.
- "Do you play tennis, too?" "No. Badminton is **the only sport** I play."

the same + 명사: 같은 ~
- "Are we wearing **the same dress**?" 우리가 같은 드레스를 입고 있는거야? "Yes. We look like twins!"
- Karen and I have been in love with **the same man** since college.

the first/second/third 등 (서수) + 명사: 첫 번째/두 번째/세 번째 ~
- "Who was **the first president** of the United States?" 미국의 첫 번째 대통령이 누구였니?
  "George Washington."
- Our seats for the concert are in **the fifth row**.

the best/worst/fastest 등 (최상급) + 명사: 가장 좋은/나쁜/빠른 ~
- "I had **the worst day** of my life today!" 오늘 내 인생에서 가장 나쁜 하루를 보냈어! "Why? What happened?"
- "How do I get to Wentworth Tower?" "**The fastest way** is by subway."

PRACTICE

A. 예시와 같이 필요한 곳에 **the**를 써넣으세요.

1. Look! <u>The</u> Moon is full tonight!

2. TV uses a lot of electricity.

3. In 2010, China had largest population in world.

4. Sky is beautiful. There are so many stars.

5. We go to movies a lot. We enjoy it.

6. I use Internet every day for research.

7. Do you prefer listening to radio or watching TV?

8. "I hope rain stops soon." "I do too."

9. Government passed a new child protection law.

10. Ronald and I went fishing in ocean yesterday.

B. 괄호 안에 주어진 명사를 사용하여 문장을 완성하세요. 필요한 경우 **the**를 함께 쓰세요.

1. (TV) Michael moved <u>the TV</u> . It's in the living room now.

2. (cinema) "Are there any good movies at _____?" "I don't know. Let's check."

3. (books) Paula likes reading _____ in her free time.

4. (flour) _____ is an important ingredient for baking.

5. (wind) _____ is perfect for flying kites today.

6. (universe) Scientists are searching for life on other planets in _____.

7. (TV) There are so many advertisements on _____ these days. I get tired of watching them.

8. (songs) I need to choose music for my wedding. Can you recommend _____ about love?

C. 괄호 안에 주어진 표현들과 **the**를 적절히 배열하여 문장을 완성하세요.

1. (is / museum / The Central Gallery / only) <u>The Central Gallery is the only museum</u> in this city.

2. (fourth / April / month / is) _____ of the year.

3. (oldest / child / is / who) _____ in your family?

4. (best / serves / Brad's Café / coffee) _____ in town.

5. (person / my class / in / I'm / only) _____ without a cell phone.

6. (Matthew / same / in / house / has lived) _____ all his life.

D. 다음은 Justin이 쓴 학교 신문 기사입니다. 예시와 같이 필요한 곳에 **the**를 써넣으세요.

1. **Protect** <u>the</u> **Earth!**

By Justin Wilson

2. It is very important to save environment.

The earth gives us food and water, so we must protect it.

3. Plants and animals living on the land and in ocean need a clean environment, too.

So what is the solution?

4. Recycling is first thing we can do. And it's easy!

5. Second thing is reducing pollution.

6. There are many ways to help, but best way is to do something right now before it's too late.

정답 **p. 316** / Check-Up Test 10 **p. 252**

관사

LESSON
53

Grammar Gateway Intermediate

1 **home, work, bed**를 포함한 다음과 같은 표현에는 **the**를 쓰지 않는다.

at home	go/come home	leave home
at work	go to work	leave work
in bed	go to bed	

- "I'm here to see Mr. Smith. Is he **at home?**" 그가 집에 있나요? "No. He's **at work.**" 아뇨. 회사에 있어요.
- "Why is Pete still **in bed?**" "He didn't **go to bed** until midnight last night."
- (전화상에서) "When are you **coming home?**" "In about an hour. I'll be **leaving work** soon."
- I **left home** early but I was still late to the movie.

2 **school, church, prison/jail** 앞에는 **the**를 쓰지 않을 수도 있고, 쓸 수도 있다. 이때, 다음과 같은 차이가 있다.

school, church, prison/jail을 '공부, 예배, 수감' 등과 같이 장소들의 본래 목적으로 사용한 경우에는 **the**를 쓰지 않는다.

- John is at **school**. His class hasn't finished yet.
  (공부하기 위해 학교에 있음)
- My family attends **church** every Sunday.
  (예배하러 교회에 감)
- The police caught the thief and now he is in **prison**.

school, church, prison/jail을 이 장소들의 본래 목적이 아닌 다른 목적으로 사용한 경우에는 **the**를 쓴다.

- We went to **the school** to see Jack's graduation.
  (졸업식에 참석하기 위해 학교에 감)
- Lucy attended a wedding at **the church** last Friday. (결혼식에 참석하기 위해 교회에 감)
- The journalist visited **the prison** to interview prisoners about their lives.

3 다음과 같은 표현 앞에도 보통 **the**를 쓰지 않는다.

요일, 월, 연도	Sunday	Monday	March	November	1987	2020
공휴일	Thanksgiving	Easter	Christmas	New Year's Day		
식사	breakfast	lunch	dinner			

- "Do you have plans on **Sunday?**" 일요일에 계획이 있니? "No, not yet."
- In the US, **Thanksgiving** is in **November**. In Canada, it's in **October**.
- "What's in that bag?" "Just some food I brought for **lunch**."
- In **1987**, we started our business. Thankfully, it has been a success.

계절 앞에는 **the**를 쓰지 않을 수도 있고, 쓸 수도 있다. 이때, 의미 차이가 없다.

- We don't travel in **summer**. We always take a vacation in **winter**.
  또는 We don't travel in **the summer**. We always take a vacation in **the winter**.
  우리는 여름에 여행하지 않는다. 항상 겨울에 휴가를 간다.

4 사람 이름이나 호칭 앞에는 **the**를 쓰지 않는다.
- "Who wrote this story?" "I think it was **Marsha Cole**." Marsha Cole인 것 같아. (the Marsha Cole로 쓸 수 없음)
- "Have you met **Dr. Sanders** before?" "Yes, I have."

단, 가족 전체를 말할 때는 **the** 뒤에 사람의 성을 복수로 쓴다.
- "I'm looking for Jack Dawson. I have a package for him."
  "Oh, **the Dawsons** live next door." Dawson 가족은 옆집에 살아요.
- "How do you know **the Parkers?**" "Their son and my son go to the same school."

PRACTICE

A. 주어진 명사를 사용하여 문장을 완성하세요. 필요한 경우 the를 함께 쓰세요.

bed	bed	earth	home	home
sea	theater	universe	~~work~~	work

1. I don't have to go to _work_ today. I took the day off.
2. Most dolphins live in _____, but some are found in rivers.
3. Before you leave _____ today, please clean your bedroom.
4. "There's a new play at _____. I want to see it." "What's it called?"
5. Michelle brushed her teeth, put on her pajamas, and went to _____.
6. There are so many stars in _____. There are too many to count.
7. Elise is still at _____. She has a lot to do at the office today.
8. "How long does it take _____ to go around the sun?" "About 365 days."
9. Jason had to turn back and go _____. He forgot to lock his front door.
10. Your father is in _____. Keep the noise down so you don't wake him.

B. 그림을 보고 at school/at church/in jail을 사용하여 예시와 같이 문장을 완성하세요. 필요한 경우 the를 함께 쓰세요.

1. _Julia is at school_ .
2. _____ .
3. _____ .
4. _____
5. _____

C. 다음은 Linda가 Johnson 부부에게 보낸 이메일입니다. 괄호 안에 주어진 명사를 사용하여 문장을 완성하세요. 필요한 경우 the를 함께 쓰세요.

Subject	Christmas Party
To	georgesusan@fastmail.com
From	lindawilson@fastmail.com

Dear Susan and George,

1. We are having a party to celebrate _Christmas_ this year! (Christmas)
2. It will be on _____ night at 7 o'clock. (Saturday)
3. We will have _____ and drinks. (dinner)
4. Please call me at _____ and let me know if you can come. (home)
5. I know you don't like leaving your house in _____. (winter)
6. But you should come out! It'll be _____ of the year! (best party)
7. P.S. I've already invited _____. (Jacksons)
8. And I want to invite _____ too. (Mrs. Carson) Do you have her phone number?

Linda

LESSON 54

관사

Grammar Gateway Intermediate

She met him at the party. 사람 또는 사물을 가리키는 대명사

1 사람 또는 사물을 가리켜 말할 때 대명사 **I/me/you/they/them** 등을 쓸 수 있다.

주격	I	we	you	he	she	it	they
목적격	me	us	you	him	her	it	them

- "How does Janet know Sean?" "**She** met **him** at the party." 그녀는 그를 파티에서 만났어.
- "What do **you** think of these earrings?" "**They**'re beautiful. Where did **you** get **them**?"

전치사 뒤에는 항상 **me/you/them** 등과 같은 목적격을 쓰는 것에 주의한다.
- I might be late to dinner, so don't wait **for me**. (for I로 쓸 수 없음)
- "Look at this old picture **of us**!" "Wow! We were so young." (of we로 쓸 수 없음)

2 '～의'라는 의미로 소유를 나타낼 때는 **my/your/their** 등을 쓴다. 이때, 뒤에 항상 명사를 함께 쓴다.

주격	I	we	you	he	she	it	they
소유격	my	our	your	his	her	its	their

- "I can't find **my wallet**." 내 지갑을 못 찾겠어. "Have you checked in **your bag**?" 네 가방 안을 확인해봤니?
- "This is **our** new **office**." "It's nice! I like **its** big **windows**."

'～ 자신의'라는 의미로 소유의 의미를 강조하여 말하기 위해 **my/your/their** 등의 뒤에 **own**을 쓸 수 있다.
- For **your own safety**, you should always wear your seatbelt.
  너 자신의 안전을 위해 항상 안전벨트를 착용하는 게 좋겠다.
- "Does Tanya live in the dorm?" "No. She has **her own apartment**."

3 '～의 것'이라는 의미로 **mine/yours/theirs** 등을 쓸 수 있다.

소유격	my	our	your	his	her	its	their
소유대명사	mine	ours	yours	his	hers	-	theirs

- "Somebody's phone is ringing." "Oh, it's **mine**. I'll answer it." 내 것이야. (= my phone)
- "Does that scarf belong to Sarah?" "It might be **hers**. I think she left it here."

my/your/their 등의 뒤에는 항상 명사를 함께 쓰지만, **mine/yours/theirs** 등의 뒤에는 명사를 쓰지 않는 것에 주의한다.
- "I put **your ice cream** in the freezer." "Oh, OK. Thanks." (your 뒤에 명사 ice cream을 함께 썼음)
  "Did you buy ice cream?" "Yes. I put **yours** in the freezer." (yours ice cream으로 쓸 수 없음)

mine/yours/theirs 등을 주어로 쓰는 경우 **mine/yours/theirs** 등이 단수명사 또는 셀 수 없는 명사를 대신하면 단수동사를 쓰고, 복수명사를 대신하면 복수동사를 쓴다.
- Your room is so clean. **Mine is** always messy. (Mine이 단수명사인 my room을 대신하므로 단수동사 is를 썼음)
- "Are those your children?" "No. **Ours are** at home."
  (Ours가 복수명사인 Our children을 대신하므로 복수동사 are를 썼음)
- I think the chef put too much salt in my soup. How **does yours taste**?

4 **my/your** 등 + 명사 또는 **mine/yours** 등의 앞에는 **a/an/the**를 쓸 수 없는 것에 주의한다.
- **Your computer** is so fast! **Mine** is really slow. (A your computer 또는 The mine으로 쓸 수 없음)
- **Our company** is celebrating **its anniversary** this year. (an its anniversary 또는 the its anniversary로 쓸 수 없음)

PRACTICE

A. I/me/you/they/them 등을 써넣으세요.

1. This shirt fits me and _it_ is on sale. Should I buy _____?
2. Jim has my old bicycle. _____ told him to keep it.
3. "Do _____ know John and his brothers?" "No, I've never met _____."
4. "Can you return my dictionary?" "Of course. I'll bring it to _____ tonight."
5. Our teacher didn't give _____ any homework on Friday. Everyone was happy.
6. "Marie, these letters came for you." "Oh, are _____ for _____?"
7. "Does Tony like swimming?" "Yes. _____ really enjoys it."
8. I haven't spoken to Helen in weeks. Have you heard from _____ recently?

B. my/your/their 또는 mine/yours/theirs 등을 써넣으세요.

1. A: Are those Tommy's sunglasses?
   B: They aren't _his_. They belong to Ian.

2. A: Why isn't Sandra at work this morning?
   B: _____ son had to go to the hospital.

3. A: I have my ticket. Where's _____?
   B: I thought you had mine!

4. A: Rick and Tina sold _____ house.
   B: Why? Are they moving?

5. A: I'm so tired of riding the bus.
   B: Me too. We need _____ own car.

6. A: Is this your sweater?
   B: Yes, it's _____. I made it.

C. 다음 문장을 읽고 틀린 부분이 있으면 바르게 고치세요. 틀린 부분이 없으면 ○로 표시하세요.

1. "Is Ms. Morrison here today?" "Yes. She's at hers desk."   _hers → her_
2. The Millers built their own garage last year.   _____
3. "Are Debbie and Rob staying at that hotel?" "No. Their is the one next to it."   _____
4. "My parents are going on a trip this weekend." "Really? Mine is, too."   _____
5. "Someone left this briefcase in the meeting room." "Oh, that's mine briefcase."   _____
6. "How was a your date?" "I had a great time!"   _____
7. "Kevin gave a great presentation, didn't he?" "Yes. His were very interesting."   _____
8. We need a new soccer ball. The ours has a hole in it.   _____

D. 다음은 Chris가 Alberto에게 쓴 편지입니다. I/me/your/theirs 등을 사용하여 문장을 완성하세요.

Dear Alberto,

1. I'm going to Mexico City with _my_ sister for summer vacation.
2. _____ will arrive next Thursday and will be taking a tour together on Friday.
3. My sister is really excited because it will be _____ first time in Mexico.
4. Since your parents haven't met _____, we'd like to have dinner with _____ family on Friday.
5. Can you ask them if _____ are interested?
   By the way, I think I lost your phone number.
6. _____ is (810) 555-6477. 7. What's _____? Let me know.
8. I hope to talk to _____ soon!

AIR MAIL

From Chris

대명사와 소유격

LESSON 55

Grammar Gateway Intermediate

What is Mr. Elliott's address? 소유를 나타내는 -'s와 of

1 사람 또는 동물 뒤에 **-'s**를 써서 소유를 나타낼 수 있다. 이때, 뒤에 명사를 함께 쓴다.

- "What is **Mr. Elliott's address**?" "I'm not sure." (Elliott 씨의 주소)
- **Sheep's wool** is often used in clothing. (양의 털)
- "I like your car!" "Oh, this is **my brother's car**. I just borrowed it."

다음과 같은 시간 표현 뒤에도 **-'s**를 쓸 수 있다.

명사의 형태 변화: 부록 p.281 참고

today	yesterday	tomorrow	this/next/last + week/month/year 등

- "Have you read **today's newspaper**?" 오늘 신문 읽어봤어? "Not yet."
- **Tomorrow's weather** is going to be cold.
- Professor Nash will not speak at **this year's forum**. We'll have a different speaker.

2 무엇을 가리키는지 명확히 알 수 있는 경우에는 뒤에 명사를 쓰지 않고 **-'s**만 쓸 수 있다.

- "Is this your watch?" "No, it's **Colin's**." (Colin의 '시계'를 가리키는 것이 명확함)
- "Whose magazine is this?" "It's **Emily's**. She bought it earlier." (Emily의 '잡지'를 가리키는 것이 명확함)

누군가의 집에 대해 말할 때도 **-'s**만 쓸 수 있다.

- We went to **Alison's** last night to study. We have a test today. (= Alison's house)
- "What are you doing tonight?" "I'm going to a party at **Jimmy's**." (= Jimmy's house)

다음과 같은 경우에도 **-'s**만 쓸 수 있다.

the dentist's/doctor's (office) the hairdresser's (shop)	• I went to **the dentist's** because I had a toothache. 이가 아파서 치과에 갔다. • Sue has an appointment **at the hairdresser's** later today.

3 사물의 소유를 나타낼 때는 **of**를 주로 쓴다.

- Look at **the color of the sky**. It's beautiful. (하늘의 색깔)
- I don't remember **the title of this song**. (이 노래의 제목)
- "Who's **the author of that book**?" "Dale Addams."

4 국가, 도시, 기관 등의 소유를 나타낼 때는 **-'s**와 **of** 둘 다 쓸 수 있다.

- **Egypt's pyramids** are famous. 또는 **The pyramids of Egypt** are famous. (이집트의 피라미드)
- **The UN's main office** is in New York City. 또는 **The main office of the UN** is in New York City. (UN의 본부)

5 '~들 중 하나/몇몇'이라는 의미로 소유한 대상의 일부를 가리켜 말할 때 다음과 같이 쓸 수 있다.

a/an some	명사	of	mine/yours/theirs 등 Laura's/my father's 등	또는	one some	of	my/your/their 등 Jake's/my father's 등	명사

- **A friend of mine** went to the same high school as Brad.
  또는 **One of my friends** went to the same high school as Brad. 내 친구들 중 한 명이 Brad와 같은 고등학교에 다녔다.
- These are **some paintings of Laura's**.
  또는 These are **some of Laura's paintings**. They will be sold at the auction.
- We are preparing a nice meal because **a client of my father's** is coming to dinner.
  또는 We are preparing a nice meal because **one of my father's clients** is coming to dinner.

PRACTICE

A. 괄호 안에 주어진 표현들과 -'s 또는 of를 적절히 배열하여 문장을 완성하세요.

1. (sister / Jack) _Jack's sister_ is a waitress at a steakhouse nearby.
2. (the owner / this truck) Who is _____? It's blocking the street.
3. (that movie / the director) "I met _____." "Really? What is he like?"
4. (concert / last night) We had a great time at _____. It was amazing.
5. (the food / the ingredients) My friend always asks about _____ when she eats out.
6. (a turtle / shell) _____ protects it from other animals.
7. (election / next month) "Who will win _____?"
   "I'm not sure. Maybe Nate Lewis."
8. (the building / the roof) When the tree fell, it damaged _____.

B. 괄호 안에 주어진 표현들과 -'s를 사용하여 문장을 완성하세요. 가능한 경우 괄호 안의 두 표현 중 하나만 사용하세요.

1. (the doctor, office) "Is Max coming with us?" "No. He's at _the doctor's_ right now."
2. (Angela, suitcase) "Whose suitcase is this?" "I think it's _____."
3. (yesterday, picnic) We met a lot of people at _____. It was fun.
4. (Brazil, president) "Who is _____?" "I don't know."
5. (Ron, house) "Where are we going to watch the football game?" "How about at _____?"
6. (the hairdresser, shop) I saw Michelle at _____ last week. She was getting a haircut.
7. (rabbit, hair) This paintbrush is made from _____.
8. (my neighbor, flowers) "I like the flowers beside your house!" "They're actually _____."

C. 괄호 안에 주어진 표현들과 of를 적절히 배열하여 문장을 완성하세요.

1. (coworker / a / his) Mr. Lim went out for lunch with _a coworker of his_.
2. (his / one / coworkers) Mr. Lim went out for lunch with _____.
3. (some / my brother's / toys) _____ are missing. He's upset.
4. (goals / my / one) Losing weight is _____ for this year.
5. (some / classmates / Rita's) Those people in the photo are _____.
6. (a / ours / tradition) Sam and I cook together every Christmas. It's _____.
7. (drinks / their / some) My friends just opened a café. _____ are great.
8. (hobby / Melinda's / a) _____ is playing cards. She always wins.

D. 괄호 안에 주어진 표현들과 -'s 또는 of를 적절히 배열하여 Amy와 Kate의 대화를 완성하세요.

AMY: 1. Have you read _today's newspaper_ ? (newspaper / today)
KATE: Not yet. Why?
AMY: A famous magician is performing this Friday.
   2. They say his magic trick at _____ is amazing.
   (the end / the show)
KATE: 3. What's _____? (the magician / name)
AMY: I forgot. But his show will be held at the theater downtown.
KATE: 4. Oh really? _____ works there! (mine / a friend)
   5. He's _____. (that theater / the manager)
AMY: Great! He can probably give us a discount.

AMY

KATE

대명사의 소유격

LESSON 56

Grammar Gateway Intermediate

LESSON 57

Let me introduce **myself.** myself/yourself 등

1 주어와 목적어가 같은 대상을 가리킬 때 '~ 자신을'이라는 의미로 **myself/yourself** 등을 목적어로 쓴다.

주격	I	you (단수)	he	she	it	we	you (복수)	they
재귀대명사	**myself**	**yourself**	**himself**	**herself**	**itself**	**ourselves**	**yourselves**	**themselves**

- Let me introduce **myself.** My name is Chris Wilson. 제 자신을 소개하겠습니다.
- Just try your best. You might surprise **yourself.** 네 자신을 놀라게 할지도 몰라.
- Chameleons hide **themselves** by changing their skin color.
- Todd is going to quit smoking. He promised **himself.**

Let me introduce **myself.**

주어와 목적어가 가리키는 대상이 다를 경우 목적어로 **myself/yourself** 등을 쓰지 않고 **me/you** 등을 쓰는 것에 주의한다.

- "Who taught Henry how to ride a bike?" "He taught **himself.**"
  (주어 He와 목적어 himself가 가리키는 대상이 모두 Henry이므로 himself를 목적어로 썼음)

  "Who taught Henry how to ride a bike?" "His cousin taught **him.**"
  (주어 His cousin과 목적어 him이 가리키는 대상이 다르므로 him을 목적어로 썼음)

2 '직접, ~ 자체'라는 강조의 의미를 나타낼 때도 **myself/yourself** 등을 쓸 수 있다. 이때, **myself/yourself** 등을 문장의 끝이나 강조하고자 하는 대상 바로 뒤에 쓴다.

- "I took those pictures **myself.**" "They're great. You're like a photographer!" (내가 직접)
- The resort **itself** is small, but the location is perfect. (리조트 자체)
- I went to a job interview yesterday. I met the CEO **himself.**

강조의 의미를 나타내는 **myself/yourself** 등은 생략할 수 있다. 단, **myself/yourself** 등이 목적어로 쓰인 경우에는 생략할 수 없는 것에 주의한다.

- When her parents aren't home, Joanne takes care of her sister (**herself**).
  부모님이 집에 계시지 않을 때, Joanne은 그녀의 여동생을 직접 돌본다. (herself가 강조의 의미를 나타내므로 생략할 수 있음)

  Joanne is old enough to take care of **herself.**
  Joanne은 자신을 돌볼 만큼 충분히 나이가 들었다. (herself가 take care of의 목적어로 쓰였으므로 생략할 수 없음)

3 by myself/yourself 등: 혼자, 스스로

- "Who went shopping with you?" "No one. I went **by myself.**" 혼자 갔어요.
- I heard Jill went on a trip to Vietnam **by herself.** That's pretty brave.

이때, 의미를 강조해서 말하기 위해서 **by** 앞에 **all**을 쓸 수 있다.

- "Did you clean up the whole house **all by yourself**?" 집 전체를 혼자 다 치웠어? "Yes, I did."

by myself/yourself 등과 같은 의미로 **on my own/on your own** 등도 쓸 수 있다.

- "Did Ed's mom make him apply to medical school?" "No. He decided **on his own.**" (= by himself)
- Nobody helped us with the project. We finished it **on our own.** (= by ourselves)

4 다음과 같은 표현에서도 **-self**를 쓴다.

enjoy -self 즐겁게 보내다, 즐기다	- The guests **enjoyed themselves** at the party. 손님들은 파티에서 즐겁게 보냈다.
behave -self 예의 바르게 행동하다	- My daughter didn't **behave herself** today. 딸이 오늘 예의 바르게 행동하지 않았다.
help -self (to) (~을) 마음껏 먹다	- There are some drinks on the table. Please **help yourselves.**
make -self at home 편히 있다	- "Come in and **make yourself at home.**" "Thanks!"

PRACTICE

A. myself/himself/themselves 또는 me/him/them 등을 써넣으세요.

1. I wasn't careful with the scissors, so I cut _myself_ .
2. Amanda's husband surprised _____ with a lovely dinner for her birthday.
3. "We failed our group project because of me." "Don't blame _____. We picked a hard topic."
4. Kim and I visited Kevin last night. He showed _____ his new apartment.
5. In some countries, women have to cover _____ when they're outside.
6. Can you please pay attention to _____? I'm trying to tell you a story.
7. My son is only a year old. He can't feed _____ yet.
8. You and Molly did a great job. You should be proud of _____.

B. 주어진 표현 뒤에 myself/himself/themselves 등을 함께 사용하여 예시와 같이 문장을 완성하세요. 과거 시제로 쓰세요.

book all of the tickets	fix the sink	make them	not bake this pie	pack everything	~~see it~~

1. "How does Bill know about the car crash?" "He _saw it himself_ ."
2. "_____ the Smiths _____?" "No. I helped them get ready to move."
3. We _____. We got it at the bakery.
4. "Where did you buy these baby clothes?" "Actually, I _____."
5. Karen didn't use a travel agency. She _____ on the Internet.
6. "_____ you _____?" "No. Bob repaired it for me."

C. 주어진 표현과 myself/himself/themselves 등을 사용하여 문장을 완성하세요.

behave	~~enjoy~~	help	make	see	trust	turn

1. I always _enjoy myself_ in Tahiti. It is such a beautiful island.
2. "Was Jim excited to _____ on TV?" "Yes. It was his first TV interview."
3. "Welcome, Sue! Please _____ at home." "Thank you! Your home is very nice."
4. We are a good team and we can win this game! We just have to _____!
5. Boys, don't run in the hallway. _____, please.
6. Hotel guests may _____ to breakfast from 6 a.m. to 9 a.m.
7. That lamp is automatic. It will _____ off.

D. 다음은 Bio-Tech 사의 신입사원들을 위한 조언들입니다. yourself 또는 by yourself를 써넣으세요.

Guidelines for New Bio-Tech Employees

1. Familiarize _yourself_ with office policies.
2. If you are in the office _____, turn off some lights. Save energy!
3. Introduce _____ to other employees. It's a great way to make friends.
4. Keep asking _____ how you can help the company.
5. Don't eat lunch _____. Go out with others for lunch.
6. Always give _____ enough time to check your reports before you hand them in.

대명사와 소유격

LESSON 57

Grammar Gateway Intermediate

1 one과 ones는 앞에 나온 명사를 반복해서 말하지 않기 위해 쓴다. 앞에 나온 명사 하나를 말할 때는 **one**을 쓰고, 둘 이상을 말할 때는 **ones**를 쓴다.

- My brother has a car, but I don't have **one.** (= a car)
- "Which types of flowers do you like best?" "Roses and tulips are the **ones** I like." (= flowers)

  단, 셀 수 없는 명사는 **one** 또는 **ones**로 대신해서 쓸 수 없고, **some** 또는 **any**로 대신해서 쓰는 것에 주의한다.

  - "I forgot to bring money." "I can lend you **some.**" (money는 셀 수 없는 명사이므로 I can lend you one으로 쓸 수 없음)
  - "Was there more salad in the kitchen?" "I didn't see **any,** so maybe not."
    (salad는 셀 수 없는 명사이므로 I didn't see one으로 쓸 수 없음)

2 one/ones와 it/they/them은 다음과 같은 차이가 있다.

- My printer stopped working, so I bought a new **one.**
  (고장 난 프린터가 아닌 다른 프린터)
- These aren't my keys. The **ones** on the table are mine.
  (이 열쇠가 아닌 탁자 위에 있는 열쇠)

- My printer stopped working, so I took **it** to a repair shop. (고장 난 그 프린터)
- "Are these keys yours?" "Yes. **They** are mine."
  (그 열쇠)

3 one과 ones는 다음과 같이 쓸 수 있다.

a/an/the/소유격 + 형용사 + one

- "Did you answer the last question on the test?" "No. That was **a hard one.**" 어려운 것이었어.
- "Which desk is yours?" "**The tidy one,** of course. I never make a mess."
- I enjoy Mark Twain's books. **My favorite one** is *The Adventures of Tom Sawyer.*

some/the/소유격/two 등 + 형용사 + ones

- The movie had some exciting moments and **some boring ones.** 영화에 몇몇 신나는 순간도 있었고 몇몇 지루한 순간도 있었다.
- "Which forks do you need?" "Pass me **the silver ones.**"
- "How many milkshakes would you like? And what flavor?" "**Two chocolate ones,** please."

4 one/ones는 this/that, these/those와도 함께 쓸 수 있다.

this/that (+ 형용사) + one

- Which report should be done first, **this one** or **that one**? 이것과 저것 중에 어떤 보고서가 더 먼저 끝나야 하나요?
- "Can I open my Christmas present?" "Sure! **That big one** is for you."

these/those + 형용사 + ones

- "My drawer is full of socks." "Why don't you throw away **these old ones**?" 이 오래된 것들은 버리는 것이 어때?
- Let's put these red candles in the living room, and **those yellow ones** in the kitchen.

  단, **these ones/those ones**는 잘 쓰지 않고, **these/those**로 주로 쓴다.

  - "These chopsticks are broken." "Here, use **these.**" 자, 이것들을 사용해.
  - "The show's about to start. Do you see any seats?" "**Those** over there are empty."

5 the (+ 형용사) + one/ones 뒤에 in/on 등과 같은 전치사를 쓸 수 있다.

- "Who's that woman?" "Do you mean **the one in the photo**? That's my aunt." 사진에 있는 사람 말이야?
- I already washed my dishes. **The dirty ones on the table** are Susan's.

PRACTICE

A. one/ones 또는 it/they/them을 써넣으세요.

1. "Do you want a hot drink?" "No. I want a cold *one*_____. Maybe I'll have an iced tea."
2. "Are Mike and Julie in the office today?" "I don't think so. I haven't seen _____."
3. "These boots don't feel very nice." "How about these leather _____?"
4. Here, wear my sunglasses. _____ look good on you.
5. We stayed at a famous hotel in Las Vegas, but _____ wasn't very nice.
6. This puzzle is too difficult. Let's do the easier _____.
7. "Which cookies are the most delicious?" "The _____ with coconut."

B. 주어진 단어들과 one 또는 ones를 함께 사용하여 문장을 완성하세요.

best	blue	dry	~~short~~	wild	wrong

1. (the) "Is Gary the tall boy?" "No. He's *the short one*_____."
2. (my) "What color suit will you wear?" "_____. What do you think?"
3. (some) I've only seen elephants in zoos. I hope to see _____ one day.
4. (a) "This towel is still wet. Can you get me _____?" "Sure."
5. (his) All of Evan's artwork is good, and these two statues are _____. Aren't they nice?
6. (the) These aren't the books I ordered! They sent me _____!

C. 그림을 보고 this/that 또는 these/those를 사용하여 문장을 완성하세요. 가능한 경우 one/ones를 함께 쓰고, 괄호 안에 형용사가 주어진 경우 형용사를 함께 쓰세요.

1. (little) I know. *Those little ones*_____ are cute.
2. (expensive) I don't like _____.

3. Are you looking for _____?
4. (brown) _____ is mine.

D. 괄호 안에 주어진 표현들과 one 또는 ones를 사용하여 문장을 완성하세요. the를 함께 쓰세요.

1. (in my neighborhood) "Which gym do you go to?" "*The one in my neighborhood*_____."
2. (gold) Don't wear those earrings. You look better in _____.
3. (cozy, on the hill) "Did you find a house?" "Yes. I rented _____."
4. (big) "Are all of those suitcases yours?" "Just _____. I brought only two."
5. (spicy, with chicken) I'll order the pasta I had here before. It was _____.
6. (near the entrance) "Which oranges are on sale?" "_____."

대명사와 소유격

LESSON 58

Grammar Gateway Intermediate

LESSON 59

I have **some** tickets for a play. some과 any

1 '몇몇, 약간'이라는 의미로 대략적인 수나 양에 대해 말할 때 **some** 또는 **any**를 쓴다. **some**과 **any**는 뒤에 복수명사 또는 셀 수 없는 명사를 쓸 수 있고, 명사 없이 단독으로 쓸 수도 있다.

> I have **some tickets**.

- I have **some tickets** for a play. Do you have **any plans** for tonight?
  연극 티켓이 몇 장 있어. 오늘 밤에 계획이 있니?
- Our new cereal is made with natural ingredients. Try **some** today!
- I'm thirsty. I haven't drunk **any water** today.

2 긍정문에는 **some**을 주로 쓰고, 부정문과 의문문에는 **any**를 주로 쓴다.

- **Some snacks** will be provided on the flight. 비행 중에 약간의 간식이 제공될 것입니다.
- "Does Amanda own **any pets**?" "No. She doesn't own **any**."
- The running shoes at that store are 60 percent off. You should get **some**!

단, 요청이나 권유를 하는 의문문에는 **some**을 주로 쓴다.

- Can I ask you for **some advice** on this project? 이 프로젝트에 대해 약간의 조언을 요청해도 될까요?

3 hardly(거의 ~않다), without(~없이) 등과 같이 부정의 의미를 나타내는 단어는 주로 **any**와 함께 쓴다.

- There's **hardly any room** in the drawer. It's almost full. 서랍에 공간이 거의 없다.
- The interview was quite easy. I finished it **without any difficulty**.

if도 주로 **any**와 함께 쓴다.

- **If** Ben has **any time** tomorrow, he'll help us with the research. 만약 Ben이 내일 시간이 있다면, 우리 조사를 도와줄 거야.
- Let me know **if** there are **any changes** to the schedule.

4 someone/anything 등

someone/somebody 어떤 사람, 누구	**something** 어떤 것, 무엇	**somewhere** 어딘가에
anyone/anybody 어떤 사람, 누구	**anything** 어떤 것, 무엇	**anywhere** 어딘가에

- **Someone** is waving at you. Do you know that person? 누군가 너한테 손을 흔들고 있어.
- Tommy didn't like the clothes at that store. He didn't buy **anything**.
- "Did you go **anywhere** last weekend?" "Yes. I went to the mountains."

someone/anything 등의 뒤에 **형용사** 또는 **to + 동사원형**을 쓸 수 있다.

- You look beautiful! Are you going out with **someone special** tonight? (특별한 누군가)
- I don't have **anything to hide**. I've always told you everything. (숨기는 어떤 것)

5 **any**를 '어느 ~든지'라는 의미로도 쓸 수 있다. 이때, **any**는 긍정문에 쓴다.

- You can park your car in **any space** on this street. 이 도로의 어느 공간에든지 주차할 수 있어.
- "What do you want to do today?" "**Anything** is OK with me."

이때, **any** 뒤에 셀 수 있는 명사를 쓰는 경우에는 단수명사와 복수명사를 모두 쓸 수 있다.

- I'll treat you to dinner tonight. You may order **any dish** you want.
  또는 I'll treat you to dinner tonight. You may order **any dishes** you want. 어느 요리든지 주문할 수 있다.
- I can answer **any question** you have. 또는 I can answer **any questions** you have.

PRACTICE

A. 주어진 명사와 some 또는 any를 사용하여 문장을 완성하세요. 필요한 경우 명사를 복수로 쓰세요.

child	form	pill	time	~~towel~~	wind

1. I need to do laundry because I don't have _any towels_ to use.
2. You have to fill out _____ to apply for health insurance.
3. The air was so calm after the storm. There wasn't _____ at all.
4. The doctor gave me _____. I hope they make me feel better.
5. "When are you free to meet with us?" "I have _____ on Tuesday."
6. "Do you have _____?" "Yes. We have a son and a daughter."

B. 괄호 안에 주어진 명사와 some 또는 any를 사용하여 문장을 완성하세요. 필요한 경우 명사를 복수로 쓰세요.

1. (news) "Have you heard _any news_ from Jennifer?" "Not yet."
2. (apple juice) "Would you like _____?" "No, thank you."
3. (drugstore) "Are there _____ nearby?" "Yes. Pemberton Drugs is across the street."
4. (candle) The electricity is out. Do we have _____ at home?
5. (salt) "Can you get me _____ for my potatoes?" "Sure. Just a moment."
6. (suggestion) Professor Nelson gave me _____ for improving my writing.

C. some/someone 등 또는 any/anyone 등을 써넣으세요.

1. Luke wanted to plant some seeds, so he bought _some_.
2. "I need _____ to wear to the interview." "You can borrow my blue suit."
3. "Did Jack make that desk by himself?" "Yes. He did it without _____ help."
4. Do we have any butter? I need _____ for my toast.
5. This is a public library. It's open to _____.
6. "I can't find my stapler." "Maybe _____ took it."
7. Let's stop here. I want to take _____ pictures.
8. "What did you do last night?" "I just stayed at home. I didn't go _____."
9. Rosa likes _____ activity that she can do outdoors. She enjoys being outside.
10. Have you heard? Treasure is hidden _____ on this island!
11. I could hardly hear _____ on the phone. The people beside me were so loud.
12. "Are you hungry?" "Yes, I am. Is there _____ food?"

D. 다음은 Frank's Outlet의 라디오 광고입니다. 괄호 안에 주어진 표현과 some 또는 any를 사용하여 문장을 완성하세요.

> Do you need a new sofa? Or a bed?
> 1. (new furniture) Come and buy _some new furniture_!
> Frank's Outlet is having a one-day sale this Sunday!
> 2. (customer) _____ visiting us that day will receive a gift.
> We are offering a lot of great products at low prices.
> 3. (item) If you wait, there won't be _____ left!
> 4. (sofa) _____ will even be sold at half price!
> So make sure to tell all of your friends.
> 5. (trouble) Take Highway 78 and you'll get here without _____.
> 6. (question) Call us today, and we'll answer _____ you have!

There's no milk.

1 '~이 없다, 어떤 ~도 …않다'라는 의미로 말할 때 **no** + 명사를 쓴다.

- "There's **no milk**." 우유가 없네요. "I'll go to the store later today."
- **No visitors** may enter the building on the weekends.
- "Did you send Carrie an e-mail?" "Yes, but I got **no reply**."

   no 뒤에는 셀 수 있는 명사와 셀 수 없는 명사를 모두 쓸 수 있다. 단, 셀 수 있는 명사의 경우 단수명사보다 복수명사를 더 자주 쓴다.

   - **No seats** were empty at Mr. Thompson's speech. It was very popular. Thompson 씨의 강연에 빈 자리가 없었다.
   - "Is your company hiring?" "I don't know. There's **no information** about open jobs right now."

   no는 명사 없이 단독으로 쓸 수 없는 것에 주의한다.

   - That hair salon is never busy, so there's **no need** to make a reservation. (there's no to make로 쓸 수 없음)

2 no one/nobody/nothing/nowhere

no one/nobody 아무도 ~ 않다	**nothing** 아무것도 ~ 않다	**nowhere** 아무 데도 ~ 않다

- **Nobody** knows where Louise went. She didn't tell anyone. Louise가 어디에 갔는지 아무도 모른다.
- You'll do fine on the test. You have **nothing** to worry about.
- There's **nowhere** quiet in this town. It's full of bars and shops.

3 **no** + 명사와 같은 의미로 **not ~ any** + 명사를 쓸 수 있다.

- I don't have **any trees** in my yard. 또는 I have **no trees** in my yard. 마당에 나무가 없다.
- After Sally took the medicine, she didn't feel **any pain**. 또는 After Sally took the medicine, she felt **no pain**.

   nothing/nowhere 등과 같은 의미로 **not ~ anything/anywhere** 등도 쓸 수 있다.

   - We don't have **anything** to do this Saturday. 또는 We have **nothing** to do this Saturday.
     이번 토요일에 할 일이 없어요.
   - This road doesn't lead **anywhere**. 또는 This road leads **nowhere**.

   no + 명사는 주어로 쓸 수 있지만 **not ~ any** + 명사는 주어로 쓸 수 없는 것에 주의한다.

   - **No rain** fell this summer. The river is completely dry. (Not any rain fell로 쓸 수 없음)
   - "Excuse me, sir. **No pets** are allowed inside our restaurant." "Sorry. I didn't know."
     (Not any pets are allowed로 쓸 수 없음)

4 **no** + 명사와 **nobody/nothing** 등은 **not**과 함께 쓰지 않는 것에 주의한다.

- Shelly couldn't listen to the radio on the bus because she had **no earphones**.
  (She didn't have no earphones로 쓸 수 없음)
- We chose Bill for the position because there was **nobody** better. (there wasn't nobody로 쓸 수 없음)

5 **no** + 명사 대신 **none**을 쓸 수 있다.

- I did some experiments but **none** supported my ideas. (= no experiments)
- "Has any mail been delivered today?" "No. **None** has arrived yet." (= no mail)

   none 뒤에는 명사를 쓰지 않는 것에 주의한다.

   - "How many foreign countries have you been to?"
     "**None**. I've never been overseas." (None foreign countries로 쓸 수 없음)

PRACTICE

A. 주어진 명사와 no 또는 any를 사용하여 문장을 완성하세요.

advice	alcohol	energy	mistakes	~~patients~~	problem	secrets	snow

1. The doctor isn't seeing _any patients_____ this week. He's on vacation.
2. "Thanks for helping me yesterday." "Don't mention it. It wasn't _____ at all."
3. Max made _____ in his presentation. It was perfect.
4. I asked my teacher which college to choose, but she didn't offer me _____.
5. There was _____ last December. We didn't have a White Christmas.
6. My wife and I tell each other everything. There are _____ between us.
7. "I am so tired. I have _____ today." "You should get some rest."
8. "May I have a glass of red wine?" "Sorry. We don't serve _____ here."

B. 주어진 문장을 보고 no/nobody 등 또는 not ~ any/anybody 등을 사용하여 예시와 같이 다시 말해보세요.

1. The library contains no comic books. → _The library doesn't contain any comic books_____.
2. This highway doesn't have any gas stations.
   → _____.
3. I planned nothing for today. I'm totally free.
   → _____. I'm totally free.
4. Aaron did no homework all afternoon.
   → _____.
5. There wasn't anybody at the gym this morning.
   → _____.
6. I didn't go anywhere last night. I was at home.
   → _____. I was at home.

C. 다음 문장을 읽고 틀린 부분이 있으면 바르게 고치세요. 틀린 부분이 없으면 ○로 표시하세요.

1. The ballet school has none boys in it.   _none boys → no boys_
2. There's nowhere to stay. All of the hotels are full.   _____
3. Not any flights were available, so we took the train.   _____
4. There isn't nothing to eat in the fridge. Let's eat out. _____
5. Beth has to work this weekend. She has no choice.   _____
6. I wanted to watch some movies, but no seemed interesting. _____
7. We don't know nobody in the neighborhood. We just moved here. _____

D. some/any/no/none을 사용하여 Linda와 James의 대화를 완성하세요.

LINDA

LINDA: What are you looking for?
JAMES: I want something to drink.
　　　1. Maybe _some_____ milk, but there isn't _____.
LINDA: 2. I'm sure we have _____ in the refrigerator.
JAMES: I already looked. 3. We have _____. I think Chris drank all of it.
LINDA: Well, let me check just in case. Oh, you're right.
　　　4. We have _____ milk left. 5. But we have _____ orange juice.
JAMES: 6. Is there _____ grape juice?
LINDA: No. 7. There are _____ other juices in the refrigerator.

JAMES

정답 **p. 318** / Check-Up Test 12 **p. 256**
본 교재 동영상강의 www.ChampStudy.com | 131

61 All people need exercise. all/every/each

1 '모든 ~'이라는 의미로 사람 또는 사물 전체에 대해 말할 때 **all/every** + 명사를 쓴다.

all + 복수명사/셀 수 없는 명사

- **All people** need exercise.
  모든 사람은 운동이 필요하다.
- **All music** is interesting to me. I listen to **all types**.
- Laws should protect **all citizens**.

every + 단수명사

- **Every person** needs exercise.
  모든 사람은 운동이 필요하다.
- **Every song** on this album is amazing.
- Jane is the fastest runner. She wins **every race**.

2 '각각의 ~'라는 의미로 하나의 집단을 구성하는 사람 또는 사물 각각에 대해 말할 때는 **each** + 단수명사를 쓴다.

- **Each student** will choose a different essay topic. 각각의 학생들은 다른 에세이 주제를 선택할 것이다.
- There is a computer at **each desk** in this room. Any library visitor can use them.

each는 명사 없이 단독으로 쓸 수 있다.

- "How much were these shirts?" "They were $14 **each**." 각각 14달러였어요.
- This show consists of 10 episodes. **Each** is 30 minutes long.

3 **all/every/each**를 주어로 쓸 때 동사에 주의한다.

all 뒤에 복수명사를 쓸 때는 복수동사를 쓰고, 셀 수 없는 명사를 쓸 때는 단수동사를 쓴다.

- **All countries have** their own unique cultures. (countries는 복수명사이므로 복수동사 have를 썼음)
- **All bread** at Major Bakery **is** made from fresh ingredients. (bread는 셀 수 없는 명사이므로 단수동사 is를 썼음)

every + 단수명사, **each** (+ 단수명사) 뒤에는 항상 단수동사를 쓴다.

- **Every building** in Rome **is** interesting. The city is lovely. (Every building 뒤에 단수동사 is를 썼음)
- There are two ways to get to the museum. **Each takes** about 10 minutes. (Each 뒤에 단수동사 takes를 썼음)

4 everyone/everybody/everything/everywhere

everyone/everybody 모든 사람	everything 모든 것	everywhere 모든 곳

- They are at the beach. **Everyone** is having fun.
  모든 사람이 즐거운 시간을 보내고 있다.
- I like **everything** about this cell phone. It has many useful functions.
- These mountains are beautiful in April. There are flowers **everywhere**.

not + **everyone/everything** 등은 '모두 ~인 것은 아니다 (일부만 ~하다)'라는 의미이다.

- **Not everyone** enjoys cooking, but some people love it. 모든 사람이 요리를 즐기지는 않는다. (일부만 좋아한다)
- Our new store is opening soon. **Not everything** is ready yet, though.

not + **everyone/everything** 등과 **no one/nothing** 등의 의미 차이에 주의한다. **no one/nothing** 등은 '아무 ~도 …않다 (모두 … 않다)'라는 의미이다.

- We bought some soda for the dinner party because **not everyone** drinks wine.
  모든 사람들이 와인을 마시지는 않아서 탄산음료를 조금 샀다. (일부만 와인을 마신다)

  We didn't buy wine because **no one** in my family drinks it. 가족 중 아무도 와인을 마시지 않아서 사지 않았다.
- **Not everything** in our living room is mine. Some things are Ruth's.

  Nothing in our living room is mine. Everything is Ruth's.

PRACTICE

A. 괄호 안에 주어진 명사와 **all** 또는 **every**를 사용하여 문장을 완성하세요.

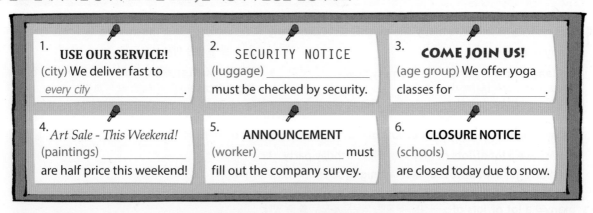

1. **USE OUR SERVICE!**
(city) We deliver fast to
every city .

2. SECURITY NOTICE
(luggage) _____
must be checked by security.

3. **COME JOIN US!**
(age group) We offer yoga
classes for _____.

4. *Art Sale - This Weekend!*
(paintings) _____
are half price this weekend!

5. **ANNOUNCEMENT**
(worker) _____ must
fill out the company survey.

6. **CLOSURE NOTICE**
(schools) _____
are closed today due to snow.

B. 그림을 보고 주어진 표현들과 **each**를 사용하여 문장을 완성하세요. 현재 시제로 쓰세요.

~~ball~~   band member   can   chapter   piece of chocolate

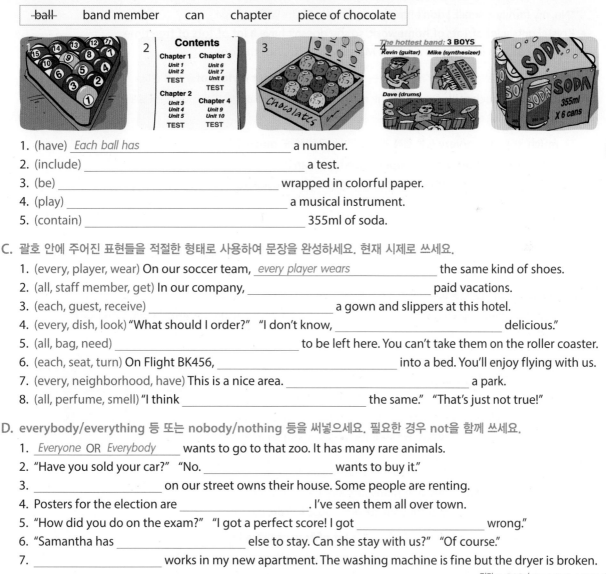

1. (have) _Each ball has_ _____ a number.
2. (include) _____ a test.
3. (be) _____ wrapped in colorful paper.
4. (play) _____ a musical instrument.
5. (contain) _____ 355ml of soda.

C. 괄호 안에 주어진 표현들을 적절한 형태로 사용하여 문장을 완성하세요. 현재 시제로 쓰세요.

1. (every, player, wear) On our soccer team, _every player wears_ _____ the same kind of shoes.
2. (all, staff member, get) In our company, _____ paid vacations.
3. (each, guest, receive) _____ a gown and slippers at this hotel.
4. (every, dish, look) "What should I order?" "I don't know, _____ delicious."
5. (all, bag, need) _____ to be left here. You can't take them on the roller coaster.
6. (each, seat, turn) On Flight BK456, _____ into a bed. You'll enjoy flying with us.
7. (every, neighborhood, have) This is a nice area. _____ a park.
8. (all, perfume, smell) "I think _____ the same." "That's just not true!"

D. everybody/everything 등 또는 nobody/nothing 등을 써넣으세요. 필요한 경우 not을 함께 쓰세요.

1. _Everyone_ OR _Everybody_ wants to go to that zoo. It has many rare animals.
2. "Have you sold your car?" "No. _____ wants to buy it."
3. _____ on our street owns their house. Some people are renting.
4. Posters for the election are _____. I've seen them all over town.
5. "How did you do on the exam?" "I got a perfect score! I got _____ wrong."
6. "Samantha has _____ else to stay. Can she stay with us?" "Of course."
7. _____ works in my new apartment. The washing machine is fine but the dryer is broken.

수학 표현

LESSON
61

Grammar Gateway Intermediate

Many rooms in our dorm are empty now.
many/much, a lot of/lots of, (a) few/(a) little

1 '많은 ~'이라는 의미로 말할 때 **many** 또는 **much**를 쓸 수 있다. **many** 뒤에는 복수명사를 쓰고, **much** 뒤에는 셀 수 없는 명사를 쓴다.

many + 복수명사

- **Many rooms** in our dorm are empty now.
  우리 기숙사의 많은 방들이 지금 비어 있다.
- People don't send **many postcards** these days.

much + 셀 수 없는 명사

- Is there **much space** in your car? I need to bring a big suitcase. 너의 차에 많은 공간이 있니?
- The pasta didn't take **much time** to cook.

many/much와 같은 의미로 **a lot of/lots of**를 쓸 수 있다. **a lot of/lots of** 뒤에는 복수명사와 셀 수 없는 명사를 모두 쓸 수 있다.

- We have **a lot of/lots of ideas** for Jill's birthday party. (= many ideas)
- I didn't get **a lot of/lots of rest** last night, so I'm tired. (= much rest)

2 **many**와 **a lot of/lots of**는 긍정문, 부정문, 의문문에 모두 쓸 수 있다.

- "I have **many cousins**. Do you have **many cousins?**" 나는 사촌들이 많아. 너도 사촌들이 많니?
  "No, my family is small. I don't have **many cousins**." 나는 사촌들이 많지 않아.
- Krystal gets **a lot of/lots of homework**, so she doesn't have **a lot of/lots of free time**.
- "Do **a lot of/lots of theaters** close on Mondays?" "No. Just this one."

much는 부정문과 의문문에 주로 쓴다. 긍정문에는 **much**를 쓰지 않고 **a lot of/lots of**를 주로 쓴다.

- "I don't drink **much milk**. Do you drink **much milk?**" 나는 우유를 많이 마시지 않아. 너는 우유를 많이 마시니?
  "Yes. I drink **a lot of/lots of milk**." 응. 나는 우유를 많이 마셔.

  단, **much** 앞에 **so/too/very** 등을 함께 쓰는 경우에는 긍정문에도 **much**를 쓸 수 있다.

  - There's **so much dirt** on the carpet. I need to clean it. 카펫에 너무 많은 먼지가 있다.
  - Ms. Jenson wears **too much perfume**. It gives me a headache.

3 '~이 조금 있는'이라는 의미로 말할 때 **a few** 또는 **a little**을 쓸 수 있다. **a few** 뒤에는 복수명사를 쓰고, **a little** 뒤에는 셀 수 없는 명사를 쓴다.

- I have **a few things** to do before I leave.
  떠나기 전에 해야 할 일이 조금 있다.

- "I put **a little butter** on your toast for you."
  "Thanks!" 네 토스트에 버터를 조금 발랐어.

few와 **little**은 '~이 거의 없는'이라는 부정의 의미로 쓴다.

- **Few places** allow smoking these days.
  요즘 흡연을 허용하는 장소는 거의 없다.

- I have **little patience** when I am busy.
  나는 바쁠 때 참을성이 거의 없다.

  a few/a little과 **few/little**의 의미 차이에 주의한다.

  - I found **a few errors** in your essay. Please check my comments. (오류가 조금 있음)
    I found **few errors** in your essay. You did a good job. (오류가 거의 없음)
  - Edgar had **a little** money left. He didn't spend too much.
    Edgar had **little** money left. He shouldn't have spent so much.

a few errors   few errors

4 **many/much**와 **(a) few/(a) little**은 명사 없이 단독으로 쓸 수 있다.

- Hawaii has a lot of beaches, and **many** are very nice. 하와이에는 많은 해변이 있고, 다수가 매우 멋있다.
- "Do you want some pepper for your steak?" "Just **a little**, please."

a lot of/lots of는 명사 없이 단독으로 쓸 수 없다. **a lot of/lots of** 대신 **a lot**을 단독으로 쓸 수 있다.

- "Did you buy any clothes at the mall?" "Yes, **a lot**." 응. 많이 샀어. (a lot of 또는 lots of로 쓸 수 없음)

PRACTICE

A. 주어진 명사와 **many** 또는 **much**를 사용하여 문장을 완성하세요.

advice	birds	clients	magazines	~~sugar~~	work

1. I didn't put _much sugar_ in your iced tea. You can add more if you want.
2. "Did you do _____ today?" "No. I wasn't very busy."
3. "Have _____ requested refunds?" "Just a few."
4. _____ live in this park. You can hear them sing in the morning.
5. "How was your meeting with your counselor?" "I didn't get _____. It was too short."
6. This bookstore doesn't have _____. Let's go to a different one.

B. **much** 또는 **a lot (of)**를 써넣으세요.

1. There hasn't been _much OR a lot of_ snow this winter. I hope there's more next winter.
2. I had _____ time today, so I read a whole book.
3. "How many people came to the conference?" "_____. The hall was full of people."
4. Too _____ food was left after the party, so we gave some to our neighbor.
5. Does this job require _____ experience in marketing?
6. Doctors say it's important to drink _____ water every day.
7. "How often do you go to the gym?" "I go _____. Maybe 5 or 6 times a week."

C. 괄호 안에 주어진 명사와 **(a) few/(a) little**을 사용하여 문장을 완성하세요. 필요한 경우 명사를 복수로 쓰세요.

1. (damage) Henry was in a car accident. Luckily there was _little damage_ to his vehicle.
2. (item) _____ will be left by tomorrow. The sale has been a huge success.
3. (friend) Greg has _____ in Germany. He is going to see them this summer.
4. (salad) "Would you like _____?" "Sure."
5. (noise) My apartment building is extremely quiet. There is _____.
6. (block) "Excuse me. Where is the bank?" "It's _____ away from here."
7. (soup) "What did you have for lunch?" "I had a sandwich with _____."
8. (train) There are _____ from here to Boston. In fact, on some days there are none.

D. 다음은 Amy가 Kate에게 보낸 이메일입니다. 둘 중 맞는 것을 고르세요.

Subject	Chicago trip?
To	kate77@gotmail.com
From	amy318@gotmail.com

Hi Kate,

1. I was thinking of going to Chicago for (**a few** / few) days. Do you want to come with me?

2. There are (so many / so much) things to do there, like shopping or sightseeing.

3. I have (much / a lot of) good friends there, so we can stay with them.

4. I found a flight that doesn't cost very (much / many).

5. But there is (few / little) time to buy the tickets, so please let me know soon.

6. P.S. I can help if you need (a little / little) money for the ticket. It's no problem.

Amy

LESSON
62

수팔표에

Grammar Gateway Intermediate

1 **Some of the flowers** are yellow.
그 꽃들 중 몇몇은 노란색이다.

'그 꽃들 중 몇몇'이라는 의미로 특정한 대상(그 꽃들)의 일부에 대해 말하기 위해
Some of the flowers를 썼다.

2 특정한 대상의 일부나 전체에 대해 말할 때 다음과 같이 쓸 수 있다.

some/any/none many/much (a) few/(a) little all/most/half/each	of	the my/your 등 this/that these/those	명사

- I invited **some of my neighbors** to the barbecue on Saturday. (나의 이웃들 중 몇몇)
- **Many of these cars** use electricity instead of gas. (이 자동차들 중 여럿)
- Tom showed me **a few of the poems** his students wrote. They were very funny.
- **All of our luggage** was lost during the trip, but **most of the bags** were found later.

이때, **all**과 **half** 뒤의 **of**는 생략할 수 있다.
- "Did you complete **all (of) your projects**?" "Yes, I just finished them today." (너의 프로젝트들 모두)
- "Your new coat looks nice." "Thanks. I got it for **half (of) the regular price**." (정가의 절반)

3 **some/any/(a) few/all of** 등의 뒤에 **it/us/you/them**도 쓸 수 있다.
- We still have some pizza left. Do you want **any of it**? (그것 중 조금이라도)
- **Each of us** is responsible for saving the Earth. (우리들 각각)

이때, **all**과 **half**를 썼을지라도 **of**는 생략할 수 없다.
- Kyle opened a bottle of soda and drank **all of it** by himself. (all it으로 쓸 수 없음)
- Please be careful when you deliver the eggs. **Half of them** were broken last time. (half them으로 쓸 수 없음)

4 **some of** ~와 **some + 명사**

some/many of ~ 등은 특정한 대상에 대해 말할 때 쓴다.
- I've been to **many of the museums** in Paris.
  (파리의 박물관들 중 여러 곳)
- **Some of those trees** don't have flowers.
  (저 나무들 중 몇몇)

some/many 등 + 명사는 일반적인 대상에 대해 말할 때 쓴다.
- **Many museums** won't allow you to take pictures.
  (일반적인 박물관 여러 곳)
- I want to plant **some trees** in my backyard.
  (일반적인 나무 몇 그루)

5 **some/many of** ~ 등을 주어로 쓰는 경우, **of** 뒤에 단수명사 또는 셀 수 없는 명사를 쓸 때는 단수동사를 쓰고, 복수명사를 쓸 때는 복수동사를 쓴다.
- The storm was terrible. **Half of the city was** flooded. (the city는 단수명사이므로 단수동사 was를 썼음)
- **Most of the countries** in Asia **have** long histories. (the countries는 복수명사이므로 복수동사 have를 썼음)

단, **each of** ~을 주어로 쓰는 경우에는 항상 단수동사를 쓰는 것에 주의한다.
- **Each of these mugs belongs** to a different person. (Each of these mugs를 주어로 썼으므로 단수동사 belongs를 썼음)

P R A C T I C E

A. 그림을 보고 괄호 안에 주어진 명사와 **all/most/some/none of**를 사용하여 예시와 같이 문장을 완성하세요.

1. (boys) *All of the boys* _____ are wearing caps.
2. (girls) _____ have glasses on.
3. (players) _____ are boys.

4. (main dishes) _____ are not available.
5. (appetizers) _____ are over $8.
6. (desserts) _____ come with coffee.

B. 괄호 안에 주어진 단어와 **it/us/you/them**을 사용하여 예시와 같이 대화를 완성하세요.

1. A: Did you receive many gifts for your birthday?
   B: (all) Yes. *All of them* _____ were very nice.

2. A: Is everyone in your family tall?
   B: (some) No. Only _____ are.

3. A: (a little) Is that fried rice? It looks delicious.
   Can I try _____ ?
   B: Yes, but it's not very good.

4. A: (any) Are _____ going out tonight?
   B: Bruce and Kim are, but I can't.

5. A: How was your trip?
   B: (half) Not great. I was sick for _____ .

6. A: Did your friends enjoy the movie?
   B: (most) _____ enjoyed it, but a few
   didn't.

C. 괄호 안에 주어진 표현들을 적절히 배열하여 문장을 완성하세요. 필요한 경우 **of**를 함께 쓰세요.

1. (my classmates / none / Spanish / speak) *None of my classmates speak Spanish* _____ .
2. (fish / all / in water / live) _____ .
3. (a little / with my pie / ice cream) I want _____ .
4. (most / us / Jenny / don't know) _____ .
5. (don't have / people / some / a mobile phone) _____ .
6. (them / made / a few / mistakes)
   Most dancers were perfect, but _____ .
7. (the cup / half / is filled)
   Your drink will stay cold for a while. _____ with ice.

D. 주어진 표현들을 적절한 형태로 사용하여 문장을 완성하세요. 필요한 경우 **of**를 함께 쓰고, 현재 시제로 쓰세요.

(his fridge, be)	(my friends, own)	(the bedrooms, have)
(the snow, melt)	(their earrings, cost)	~~(these trees, appear)~~

1. Many *of these trees* _____ *appear* _____ to be burned. Was there a fire at this park?
2. All _____ _____ in March here, so we can't go skiing in April.
3. Each _____ in this house _____ its own bathroom.
4. Some _____ _____ cars. But most of them use public transportation.
5. That new shop sells some cheap jewelry. Most _____ _____ only $5.
6. Charlie likes to drink beer. Half _____ _____ filled with it.

Both houses are downtown. both, either, neither

1 두 사람 또는 사물에 대해 말할 때, **both/either/neither** (+ 명사)를 쓴다.

> **both** (+ 복수명사) 두 ~ 모두   **either** (+ 단수명사) 두 ~ 중 아무 것이나 하나   **neither** (+ 단수명사) 두 ~ 모두 아닌

- Scott owns two houses. **Both houses** are downtown. (두 집 모두)
- "Who do you think will win the game?" "I'm not sure. **Either team** could win." (두 팀 중 아무 팀이나 하나)
- "Have you seen these movies?" "Yes, but **neither** was very good." (두 영화 모두 아닌)

both와 **either**는 다음과 같은 차이가 있다.

- I want to visit Tahiti and Guam. Let's go to **both islands** when we are retired. (두 섬 모두 갈 것임)
  "Should we go to Tahiti or Guam?" "**Either island** would be great." (두 섬 어느 것이든 상관없지만 하나만 갈 것임)

2 **neither**와 같은 의미로 **not ~ either**를 쓸 수 있다.

- I tried a swim class and a dance class at my gym, but I liked **neither**.
  또는 I tried a swim class and a dance class at my gym, but I did**n't** like **either**. 두 수업 모두 마음에 안 들었다.
- We called you twice, but you answered **neither time**.
  또는 We called you twice, but you did**n't** answer **either time**.

neither는 **not**과 함께 쓰지 않는 것에 주의한다.

- My sister likes reading mystery and science fiction, but I like **neither**. (I don't like neither로 쓸 수 없음)

3 **both** (+ 복수명사)를 주어로 쓸 때는 항상 복수동사를 쓰고, **either/neither** (+ 단수명사)를 주어로 쓸 때는 항상 단수동사를 쓴다.

- "**Both shirts look** good on you!" "Thanks. But **neither shirt is** my style."
  (Both shirts를 주어로 썼으므로 복수동사 look을 썼고, neither shirt를 주어로 썼으므로 단수동사 is를 썼음)
- "Do you want this table or that one?" "**Either seems** all right." (Either를 주어로 썼으므로 단수동사 seems를 썼음)

4 **both/either/neither of ~**

both/either/neither	of	the/my/these 등 + 복수명사
		us/you/them

- **Both of my brothers** have blue eyes. 나의 두 형제 모두 파란 눈을 가졌다.
- I can't open the door with **either of these keys**.
- "Which of those hats is yours?" "**Neither of them** is mine."

both와 **the/my/these** 등 사이의 **of**는 생략할 수 있다. 단, **both**와 **us/you/them** 사이의 **of**는 생략할 수 없는 것에 주의한다.

- Pam wrote to **both (of) her best friends** last weekend. **Both of them** live abroad. (Both them으로 쓸 수 없음)

5 **both of ~**을 주어로 쓸 때는 항상 복수동사를 쓰고, **either/neither of ~**을 주어로 쓸 때는 단수동사와 복수동사를 모두 쓸 수 있다.

- **Both of Mila's roommates are** away this weekend, so she invited some friends to watch a movie.
  (Both of Mila's roommates를 주어로 썼으므로 복수동사 are를 썼음)
- "Which do you prefer, jazz or classical music?"
  "**Neither of them interests** me." 또는 "**Neither of them interest** me."
  (Neither of them을 주어로 썼으므로 단수동사 interests와 복수동사 interest를 둘 다 쓸 수 있음)

PRACTICE

A. both, either, 또는 neither를 써넣으세요.

1. "Who brought these chairs?" "I'm not sure. _Both_ were here when I arrived."
2. "Should we turn left or right here?" "You can go _____ way. They'll both get you to the beach."
3. I think _____ bakeries are closed. Let's come back tomorrow.
4. "Do you want a black or a blue pen?" "It doesn't matter. _____ is fine."
5. Jenny suggested running in the park or going swimming. _____ sounded fun, so I stayed home.
6. "Which necklace is cheaper?" "_____ are the same price."
7. "Let's buy some roses or lilies." "But I like _____ flower. How about some daisies?"
8. "Where shall we meet, at the bus stop or at the mall?" "_____ place works for me, so you choose."
9. I complained to _____ managers. I still didn't get a refund, though.
10. We invited John and his sister to my exhibit, but _____ came. I was disappointed.

B. 그림을 보고 주어진 명사와 both/either/neither를 사용하여 문장을 완성하세요. 필요한 경우 명사를 복수로 쓰세요.

| camera | drawing | girl | house | jacket | test | toy | ~~woman~~ |

1. _Both women_ _____ are riding horses.
2. He didn't pass _____ .
3. _____ has buttons.
4. She hasn't started coloring _____ yet.
5. _____ are on sale.
6. _____ is wearing pants.
7. He doesn't like _____ .
8. He wants _____ .

Can I have these?

No. Oh, no.

C. 괄호 안에 주어진 표현들을 적절한 형태로 사용하여 문장을 완성하세요. 필요한 경우 of를 함께 쓰고, 현재 시제로 쓰세요.

1. (both, TVs, be) _Both TVs_ _are_ expensive. Let's look at the cheaper ones.
2. (neither, the subway lines, go) _____ _____ to city hall. We have to take a taxi.
3. (both, us, look) I have a twin sister. _____ _____ like our mother.
4. (either, them, be) "Do you want to watch the comedy or the drama?"
   "_____ _____ OK with me."
5. (neither, suit, fit) _____ _____ me well. They are too small.
6. (both, these flashlights, need) _____ _____ a new battery.
7. (either, event, sound) "Should we go to the art exhibit or the concert?"
   "_____ _____ good to me!"
8. (neither, us, play) Rita and I love music, but _____ _____ an instrument.

1

She got a new camera.
그녀는 새로운 카메라를 샀다.

It's small and light.
그것은 작고 가볍다.

'새로운, 작은, 가벼운'이라는 의미로 카메라의 상태와 특징에 대해 말하기 위해
형용사 new, small, light를 썼다.

2

사람이나 사물의 상태 또는 특징에 대해 말할 때 형용사를 쓴다. 형용사는 명사 앞에 자주 쓴다.

- Tom is my neighbor. He's a **nice** person. 그는 좋은 사람이다.
- "Would you like some **hot** tea?" 따뜻한 차 좀 드시겠어요? "Sure. Thanks."
- That **old** couple looks so happy together.
- I watched a **sad** movie last night. I cried at the end.

형용사는 다음과 같은 동사 뒤에도 자주 쓴다.

be/get/become/seem	look/feel/sound/taste/smell

- The weather is **getting cold**. It'll be winter soon. 날씨가 추워지고 있다.
- Skydiving **looks dangerous**, but it's quite **safe**. 스카이다이빙은 위험해 보이지만 꽤 안전하다.
- "Angela **seems tired**." "She just got back from a business trip."
- What did you put in this pasta sauce? It **tastes spicy**.

3

다음과 같은 형용사는 항상 명사 앞에만 쓴다.

former	indoor/outdoor	inner/outer	main	only	upper

- Abraham Lincoln is a **former president** of the United States. (The president is former 등으로 쓸 수 없음)
- "Can you meet me at the **main gate**?" "Sure. I'll see you then." (The gate is main 등으로 쓸 수 없음)
- "Does Pete have any brothers or sisters?" "No. He's the **only child**."

다음과 같은 형용사는 **be/get/look/feel** 등의 동사 뒤에만 쓰고, 명사 앞에는 쓸 수 없는 것에 주의한다.

afraid	alive	alone	asleep	glad	ill	sorry

- Sally heard a strange noise and **became afraid**. (an afraid girl 등으로 쓸 수 없음)
- Look! The lion **is asleep** in his cage. (an asleep lion 등으로 쓸 수 없음)
- I **feel ill**. I think I'm going to leave work early.

4

명사 앞에 두 개 이상의 형용사를 함께 쓸 수도 있다. 이때, 주로 다음과 같은 순서로 쓴다.

의견	길이, 크기	나이, 오래된 정도	색깔
beautiful, great, nice	short, big, large	young, old, new	black, blue, red

- I met a **beautiful young** woman on my trip to France. 프랑스 여행에서 아름답고 젊은 여자를 만났다.
- "Which boy is Evan?" "He's the boy in the **short black** jacket."
- My grandfather drives a **big old blue** truck. He has had it for 30 years.

P R A C T I C E

A. 주어진 단어들을 사용하여 문장을 완성하세요.

dirty	~~happy~~	large	sweet	wrong

1. (seems) "Is your son enjoying college?" "I think so. He _seems happy_____."
2. (tastes) I ordered this coffee without sugar, but it _____.
3. (families) _____ aren't common these days. People aren't having many children.
4. (answer) Matt thought he got a perfect score on his test, but he had one _____.
5. (got) My skirt _____. I need to wash it.

familiar	fresh	long	strong	true

6. (is) I'm not telling you a lie. It _____.
7. (hair) Jenny has always had _____. I can't imagine her cutting it.
8. (sounds) "Have you heard this song?" "I think so. It _____"
9. (looks) "This bread _____." "It is. We just baked it."
10. (wind) During the storm, the _____ blew down a lot of trees.

B. 괄호 안에 주어진 표현들을 적절히 배열하여 문장을 완성하세요.

1. (floor / the bedroom / the upper / on / is) _The bedroom is on the upper floor_____.
2. (was / I / alone / not) _____ at home last night. I was with my mom.
3. (this / the / train / only / is) "_____ to Portland?" "Yes, it is."
4. (feel / sorry / I) _____ about not going to your party.
5. (became / The Beatles / famous) _____ in the 1960s.
6. (pool / doesn't / have / outdoor / an / the hotel) _____.
7. (the snake / alive / is) _____ ! I thought it was dead.
8. (moved / the company's / office / main) _____ to New Zealand.
9. (glad / to meet / I / you / am) "This is my friend Eric." "_____, Eric."
10. (important / is / day / tomorrow / an)
    _____ for me. I have several interviews.

C. 그림을 보고 주어진 단어들을 적절히 배열하여 문장을 완성하세요.

(nice / suit / gray / new)	~~(old / building / tall)~~	(puppies / cute / little)
(roses / pink / beautiful)	(table / large / white)	

1. There is a _tall old building_____ next to the post office.
2. She's holding some _____.
3. There is a _____ in the yard.
4. Three _____ are sitting on the sofa.
5. He is wearing a _____.

1   The **crying** baby is Justin.
울고 있는 아기는 Justin이다.

He is crying because of the **broken** toy.
그는 망가진 장난감 때문에 울고 있다.

'울고 있는'이라는 의미로 아기의 상태에 대해 말하기 위해 crying을 썼고,
'망가진'이라는 의미로 장난감의 상태에 대해 말하기 위해 broken을 썼다.

2   사람이나 사물의 상태 또는 특징에 대해 말할 때 명사 앞에 **-ing** 또는 **과거분사**도 쓸 수 있다. 이때, **-ing**와 **과거분사**는 형용사와 같은 역할을 한다.

-ing는 사람이나 사물이 직접 하는 일이나 지금 하고 있는 일에 대해 말할 때 쓴다. **-ing**는 '~하는, ~하고 있는'이라는 의미이다.

- The **departing passengers** are boarding the plane now. (출발하는 승객들)
- "Do you see that **shining star** in the sky?"   "Wow! It's so bright." (빛나고 있는 별)
- Be careful of **passing cars** when you cross the street.
- Our town is getting crowded because of the **growing population**.

과거분사는 사람이나 사물에 일어나는 일에 대해 말할 때 쓴다. **과거분사**는 '~된, ~해진'이라는 의미이다.

- Only **invited guests** may attend the party. (초대된 손님)
- The accident was caught on a **hidden camera**. The video provided good evidence. (숨겨진 카메라)
- If you have any questions, please ask our **trained staff**.
- "I'd like to request a refund for the **damaged goods**."   "OK. Just a moment, please."

동사의 형태 변화: 부록 p. 280 참고

3   다음과 같이 **-ing** 또는 **과거분사** 뒤에 여러 단어를 함께 쓸 수 있다. 이때, **-ing** 또는 **과거분사**를 명사 앞이 아니라 명사 뒤에 쓴다.

	명사	-ing	
•	The man	carrying the suitcase	looks like Mr. Jones. (여행 가방을 들고 있는 남자)
•	The river	flowing through Paris	is the Seine.
• "Do you know	those girls	sitting over there?"	"No. Do you?" (저기에 앉아 있는 소녀들)
• "Who owns	the cat	playing in the street?"	"She's mine."

	명사	과거분사	
•	The articles	published in that newspaper	are usually interesting. (그 신문에 실린 기사)
•	The seats	reserved for us	are near the windows.
• Your present is	the box	wrapped in blue paper.	(파란색 종이로 포장된 상자)
• "Did you read	the information	provided in the website?"	"Yes. It was very helpful."

PRACTICE

A. 주어진 동사를 적절한 형태로 사용하여 문장을 완성하세요.

bark	~~fall~~	renovate	sign	sleep	steal

1. "I like to watch the _falling_ snow." "Me too. It's so peaceful."
2. The police arrested the man because he was carrying a _____ passport.
3. Please be quiet in the hospital. Try not to disturb the _____ patients.
4. That _____ dog is so annoying. Make it stop.
5. We must receive your _____ application by August 31.
6. The _____ lobby is beautiful. I like it better now.

B. 주어진 표현들을 하나씩 사용하여 대화를 완성하세요. 필요한 경우 단어를 적절한 형태로 바꾸어 쓰세요.

all the songs	the boy		climb the tree	~~display in that store~~
~~the dress~~	the flowers	**+**	grow in your garden	park over there
the motorbike	the woman		perform by the band	speak right now

1. A: _The dress displayed in that store_ is pretty.
   B: Why don't you try it on?

2. A: What are you looking at?
   B: _____.
   I hope he doesn't fall.

3. A: _____
   were great.
   B: I agree. The concert was fantastic.

4. A: Is _____ Jake's?
   B: Yes. He rides it to work every day.

5. A: Who is your boss?
   B: _____.
   She's practicing her speech.

6. A: What are _____?
   They're getting so tall.
   B: Most of them are lilies.

C. 괄호 안에 주어진 단어들을 적절히 배열하여 문장을 완성하세요. 필요한 경우 단어를 적절한 형태로 바꾸어 쓰세요.

1. (stand / man) "Is that your husband over there?" "No. He's the _man standing_ near the window."
2. (use / computer) Jack bought a _____ because he couldn't afford a new one.
3. (stare / woman) "There's a _____ at us. Do you know her?" "I don't think so."
4. (tour / guide) We went to Beijing on a _____. We really enjoyed it.
5. (crowd / cheer) As the players entered the stadium, they waved at the _____.
6. (characters / describe) The _____ in the book weren't very interesting.

D. 괄호 안에 주어진 단어들을 적절히 배열하여 Paul과 Amy의 대화를 완성하세요. 필요한 경우 단어를 적절한 형태로 바꾸어 쓰세요.

PAUL

PAUL: 1. What's that _picture hanging_ on the wall? (hang / picture)
AMY: 2. Oh, that's a _____ by my grandmother. (take / photo)
PAUL: 3. Who's the _____? (cry / baby)
AMY: That's Justin! 4. Can you see the _____? (toy / break)
Ginger broke it! That's why he was crying.
PAUL: Oh, poor Justin! He looks so sad!
5. So who's the _____ at Justin? (laugh / girl)
AMY: Ha ha, that's me!

AMY

정답 p. 319 / Check-Up Test 13 p. 258

LESSON
66

Grammar Gateway Intermediate

형용사 역할을 하는 분사

1 Chris is telling a story.

The story is interesting. 그 이야기는 흥미롭다.

They are interested in the story. 그들은 그 이야기에 흥미를 느낀다.

Guess who he loves!

'흥미로운'이라는 의미로 이야기가 일으키는 감정에 대해 말하기 위해 형용사 interesting을 썼고,
'흥미를 느끼는'이라는 의미로 그들이 느낀 감정에 대해 말하기 위해 형용사 interested를 썼다.

2 감정이나 느낌에 대해 말할 때 -ing와 -ed로 끝나는 형용사를 쓸 수 있다. 이때, -ing와 -ed는 다음과 같은 의미 차이가 있다.

'(사람 또는 사물이) ~한 감정을 일으키는'이라는 의미로 말할 때는 -ing로 끝나는 형용사를 주로 쓴다.

amazing (감탄스럽도록) 놀라운, 굉장한
exciting 신이 나게 하는, 흥분시키는
interesting 흥미를 일으키는, 흥미로운
satisfying 만족스러운
relaxing 마음을 편하게 해주는

- "John played really well at the music festival."
  "He was **amazing**." (그가 놀라게 함)
- The breakfast at the hotel wasn't **satisfying**.
- I had a very **relaxing** weekend.

boring 지루하게 하는
tiring 피곤하게 하는
annoying 짜증나게 하는
depressing 우울하게 하는
disappointing 실망시키는
frustrating 좌절감을 주는

- "Is that book good?" "No, it's **boring**."
  (책이 지루하게 함)
- Those people are **annoying**. They're too loud.
- Heavy traffic can be **frustrating**.

frightening 무섭게 하는
shocking 충격을 주는, 충격적인
surprising 놀라게 하는, 놀라운
confusing 혼란스러운
puzzling 어리둥절하게 하는
embarrassing 당황하게 하는

- That rollercoaster was **frightening**.
  (롤러코스터가 무섭게 함)
- The test results were **surprising** to scientists.
- Dancing in front of people was **embarrassing**.

'(사람이) ~한 감정을 느끼는'이라는 의미로 말할 때는 -ed로 끝나는 형용사를 주로 쓴다.

amazed (감탄스러울 정도로 대단히) 놀란
excited 신이 난, 흥분한
interested 흥미를 느끼는
satisfied 만족한
relaxed 마음이 편안한

- I was **amazed** by John. He played the guitar so
  well. (내가 놀라움을 느낌)
- "Are you **satisfied** with your new car?" "Yes!"
- I feel **relaxed** when I'm lying on the beach.

bored 지루해하는
tired 피곤한, 지친
annoyed 짜증난
depressed 우울한
disappointed 실망한
frustrated 좌절한

- If you're **bored**, let's go out somewhere.
  (상대방이 지루함을 느낌)
- We were **annoyed** because Tim was late again.
- My computer isn't working. I'm so **frustrated**.

frightened 무서워하는, 겁먹은
shocked 충격받은
surprised 놀란
confused 혼란스러워하는
puzzled 어리둥절해하는
embarrassed 당황한

- I was **frightened** by a bat. It flew right at me.
  (내가 무서움을 느낌)
- We were **surprised** by the price of the apartment.
- Max was **embarrassed** after he fell on the stairs.

PRACTICE

A. 그림을 보고 괄호 안에 주어진 단어들 중 하나를 적절한 형태로 사용하여 문장을 완성하세요.

MR. and MRS. MILLER

1. (relax / (amaze))
   Mr. and Mrs. Miller are _amazed_____.
   The magic trick is _____.

2. (satisfy / disappoint)
   The Falcons' performance was _____.
   The players are _____.

3. (confuse / surprise)
   The map is _____.
   He is _____.

4. (depress / frighten)
   The kids are _____.
   The man is _____.

B. 괄호 안에 주어진 단어를 적절한 형태로 사용하여 대화를 완성하세요.

1. A: (tire) Hiking was so _tiring_____.
   B: Yes, but we got to the top of the mountain!

2. A: (tire) I'm really _____.
   B: (relax) Get a massage. It will be _____.

3. A: Bill made several mistakes in his speech.
   B: (embarrass) I heard. He seemed _____.

4. A: (bore) I think Bobby is _____.
   B: Not at all. He's actually a very fun person.

5. A: (puzzle) Many questions on the test were
      _____.
   B: (puzzle) I was _____ by them too.
      I couldn't answer many of them.

6. A: (depress) That was a _____ song!
   B: I agree. Now I feel sad.

7. A: Did you see that girl's jacket?
   B: (shock) Yes! The design was _____.

8. A: (interest) Is your roommate _____?
   B: (bore) Yes. I'm never _____ with her.

9. A: (depress) Mandy looks _____ today.
   B: I know. Let's go and cheer her up.

10. A: (excite) Are you _____ about moving
       abroad?
    B: (interest) Yes, I am. I've always been
       _____ in other cultures.

C. 괄호 안에 주어진 단어를 적절한 형태로 사용하여 문장을 완성하세요.

A Night at the Opera

By Chris Wilson

Last night, I saw an opera with my girlfriend. It was called *The Quest for a Queen*.
1. (interest) The story was _interesting_____. It was about a king who lived alone in a castle.
2. (excite) The opera was _____ from the opening scene.
The king traveled around the country to look for a beautiful woman to be his queen.
3. (surprise) But his final choice was _____.
4. (shock) In fact, I was _____ by it. The king fell in love with the ugliest girl in the country!
5. (disappoint) Although we enjoyed the opera, the acting was a little _____.
6. (satisfy) However, we were mostly _____ with it.

LESSON

68 The car is moving **slowly.** 부사

1 The car is moving **slowly.** 차가 느리게 움직이고 있다.
They are **really** worried. 그들은 매우 걱정스럽다.

We might be late. I'm worried.

'느리게'라는 의미로 차가 어떻게 움직이는지를 말하기 위해 부사 slowly를 썼고,
'매우'라는 의미로 그들이 얼마나 걱정하는지를 말하기 위해 부사 really를 썼다.

2 일이나 행동이 '어떻게' 일어나는지에 대해 말할 때 부사를 쓴다. 부사는 주로 형용사 끝에 **-ly**를 붙인다.

clear → **clearly**	easy → **easily**	terrible → **terribly**
excited → **excitedly**	automatic → **automatically**	

형용사/부사의 형태 변화: 부록 p. 282 참고

- There's so much fog this morning. I can't see **clearly.** 또렷하게 볼 수가 없다.
- Kim always tries her best. She never gives up **easily.** 그녀는 절대 쉽게 포기하지 않는다.
- Our team played **terribly** at the game yesterday. We lost.
- The children talked **excitedly** about their field trip.

3 일이나 행동이 어떻게 일어나는지 나타내는 부사는 주로 동사 뒤에 쓴다.

- The students **sat quietly** and listened to the teacher. 학생들은 조용히 앉아서 선생님 말씀을 들었다.
- "What time is it?" "I don't **know exactly,** but it's around noon."

단, 동사 뒤에 목적어가 있을 때는 부사를 목적어 뒤에 쓴다. 이때, 부사를 동사와 목적어 사이에 쓰지 않는 것에 주의한다.

- Larry needs to **spend his money wisely.** He buys too much stuff. (spend wisely his money로 쓸 수 없음)
- I think the mayor **answered the questions honestly.** (answered honestly the questions로 쓸 수 없음)

4 형용사나 다른 부사가 나타내는 의미의 정도가 얼마나 되는지를 말할 때도 부사를 쓸 수 있다. 이때, 부사를 주로 형용사나 다른 부사의 앞에 쓴다.

- These pants seem **slightly long.** Do you have shorter ones? (약간 긴)
- "Have you ever been to London?" "Actually, I was there **fairly recently.**" (상당히 최근에)
- "Your apartment looks **completely different.**" "I replaced all the furniture."
- My presentation went **really badly.** I should have prepared more.

어떤 일에 대한 의견을 말할 때도 부사를 쓸 수 있다. 이때, 부사를 주로 문장의 맨 앞에 쓴다.

- We hurried to the post office. **Luckily,** it was still open. (운 좋게도)
- **Hopefully,** I'll get a job soon. I've applied to several companies. (바라건대)
- I thought John couldn't ski. **Surprisingly,** he was very good at it!

5 다음과 같은 단어는 **-ly**로 끝나지만 부사가 아니라 형용사인 것에 주의한다.

friendly 다정한	**lovely** 예쁜, 사랑스러운	**lively** 생기 넘치는	**elderly** 연로한
likely 가능성 있는, 그럴듯한	**lonely** 외로운	**silly** 어리석은	**ugly** 못생긴

- Your family is so **friendly.** It was great to meet them. 너희 가족은 매우 다정하다.
- I saw some **lovely** curtains at the store today. I might go back and buy them. 오늘 상점에서 예쁜 커튼을 보았다.
- Helen works with **elderly** people at a local hospital.
- "Will you be here before 10:30?" "It's not **likely.**"

P R A C T I C E

A. 주어진 형용사를 적절한 형태로 사용하여 문장을 완성하세요.

careful	dramatic	~~fluent~~	kind	lazy	responsible

1. "Is Dave's German good?" "Yes. He speaks it _fluently_____."
2. "The temperature has fallen _____ since yesterday." "I know. It's freezing now!"
3. Marco hasn't moved all day! He's been sitting _____ on the sofa and watching TV.
4. Mr. Jones always treats people _____. He's never rude to anyone.
5. "Could you show me how to use this photocopier?" "Sure. Watch _____."
6. Don't throw garbage on the street. You should always act _____.

B. 괄호 안에 주어진 표현들을 적절히 배열하여 문장을 완성하세요. 필요한 경우 형용사를 부사로 바꾸어 쓰세요.

1. (perfect / the fish) The chef cooked _the fish perfectly_____. It was delicious.
2. (normal / complete) Babies usually wake up a lot during the night. It's _____.
3. (church / regular) When I was a child, I attended _____.
4. (total / different) Rob and I rarely agree. We think _____.
5. (loud / real) "I just heard a _____ noise. Did you hear it?" "Yes. What was it?"
6. (tight / the window) Close _____. It's cold outside.
7. (the new mall / rapid / surprising) The workers built _____.
8. (amazing / cheap) "How much was your flight?"
   "It was _____. It was only $200."

C. 다음 문장을 읽고 틀린 부분이 있으면 바르게 고치세요. 틀린 부분이 없으면 ○로 표시하세요.

1. You should think serious before moving abroad. It's a big decision. _serious → seriously_
2. Read closely the instructions and answer the questions. _____
3. Our honeymoon was incredible. It was absolute wonderful. _____
4. "Did you catch the train?" "Yes. Luckily, it was delayed." _____
5. "Was the workshop successful?" "Yes. It went smoothly relatively." _____
6. What's wrong with Kevin? He shut the door angry and left the room. _____
7. We moved gently the furniture because we didn't want to damage it. _____
8. This town is lively on weekends. A lot of tourists come here. _____

LESSON 68

Grammar Gateway Intermediate

D. 주어진 형용사를 적절한 형태로 사용하여 Amy와 Kate의 대화를 완성하세요.

~~complete~~	hopeful	immediate	patient	slight

AMY: Hurry up Kate! We're going to be late for the wedding!
   1. The roads are _completely_____ crowded on the weekends.
   2. We need to leave _____.
KATE: OK. I'm almost ready. Is it cold outside? Do I need a coat?
AMY: 3. It's _____ chilly, but not too bad.
   Anyway, I can't wait to see Nancy in her wedding dress. She's going to
   look so lovely in it.
KATE: I think so too. I'm ready now.
   4. Thank you for waiting _____.
AMY: Good, let's go. 5. _____, we'll arrive on time.

AMY

KATE

1

The sun is bright. 태양이 밝다.	**The sun is shining brightly.** 태양이 밝게 빛나고 있다.

형용사는 사람이나 사물의 상태 또는 특징에 대해 말할 때 쓴다.

- Ron and Betty look like a **happy couple**.
  (행복한 커플)
- "This singer has a **wonderful voice**." "I agree."
  (멋진 목소리)
- My **alarm clock** was **loud**. It woke up everyone in the house.

부사는 일이나 행동이 '어떻게' 일어나는지에 대해 말할 때 쓴다.

- Ron and Betty are **smiling happily** in that photo.
  (행복하게 웃고 있음)
- Sara is an excellent pianist. She **plays wonderfully**.
  (멋지게 연주함)
- Tom **snores loudly** when he sleeps. It's really hard to share a room with him.

2 형용사는 주로 다음과 같은 위치에 쓴다.

명사 앞

- "I hope you have a **safe flight**." "Thank you."
  안전한 비행 되시길 바랍니다.
- Simon is looking for a **new roommate**.
- Why don't you take a **warm bath**? It'll make you relax.

be/get/look/feel 등의 동사 뒤

- That diamond is huge! **Is it real?** 진짜인가요?
- We should **get ready**. It's already 8:30.
- "I'm going bungee jumping this weekend."
  "That **sounds scary**!"

부사는 주로 다음과 같은 위치에 쓴다.

동사 (+ 목적어) 뒤

- "I'm leaving for Toronto now."
  "OK. **Drive safely**." 조심히 운전해.
- If there's a fire, **leave the building quickly**.
- Larry **takes his job seriously**. It's the most important thing to him.

형용사/다른 부사 앞

- This soup is **really salty**. 이 수프는 매우 짜다.
- Elizabeth goes jogging **fairly regularly**.
- "Are you sure this is the right way?"
  "Yes. I'm **absolutely certain**."

3 look은 '~해 보이다'라는 의미로 사람이나 사물의 상태 또는 특징에 대해 말할 때 뒤에 형용사를 쓴다. 그러나 look을 '보다'라는 의미로 쓸 때는 뒤에 부사를 쓸 수 있다.

look + 형용사

- "Greg **looks great** in his new suit."
  "I helped him pick it out."
  Greg은 새 정장을 입으니 멋져 보여.
- I think I'll get some of these grapes. They **look fresh**.

look + 부사

- "I can't find my wallet."
  "**Look carefully**. It must be here somewhere."
  주의 깊게 봐.
- In some cultures, it's rude to **look directly** into other people's eyes.

PRACTICE

A. 괄호 안에 주어진 단어들을 적절히 배열하여 문장을 완성하세요. 필요한 경우 형용사를 부사로 바꾸어 쓰세요.

1. (skirt / colorful) "Which woman is Ms. Dawson?" "The lady in the *colorful skirt*_____."
2. (surprising / strong) Sean is a small boy, but he's _____.
3. (getting / hungry) Let's find a place to eat. I'm _____.
4. (speakers / famous) Were there any _____ at the conference?
5. (extreme / rapid) My hometown is growing _____. It will be a big city soon.
6. (busy / normal) "When can we meet?" "I'm _____ on weekdays. How about Saturday?"
7. (popular / became) This TV show _____ last year. Now all of my friends watch it.
8. (automatic / open) You don't have to open the garage door. It will _____.

B. 주어진 단어들을 적절한 형태로 사용하여 문장을 완성하세요. 현재 시제 또는 과거 시제로 쓰세요.

anxious	brave	close	~~dizzy~~	sharp	sweet

1. (feel) "I *feel dizzy*_____." "You should sit down and rest."
2. (act) The man jumped into the river and saved the boy. He _____.
3. (smell) Your perfume _____. The scent reminds me of honey.
4. (look) You should be careful with those scissors. They _____.
5. (wait) We _____ for our exam results. We were so nervous.
6. (look) The doctor _____ at my eyes and said there was nothing wrong.

C. 다음은 Brian이 고객에게 보낸 이메일입니다. 괄호 안에 주어진 형용사를 적절한 형태로 사용하여 문장을 완성하세요.

To	taylor77@fastmailco.com
From	bsmith@buildahouse.com

Dear Mr. Taylor,

I am writing to you about your order with our company.

1. (recent) It seems that you've decided to build a house *recently*_____.

You have asked for two different design ideas for your new house.

2. (accurate) I hope this is _____. We'll start the designs once you confirm your order.
3. (incorrect, immediate) If this is _____, please contact us _____.
4. (glad) We will be _____ to change your order.
5. (short) Anyway, the designs will be sent to you _____.
6. (careful) Please review them _____ when you receive them.

Thank you,
Brian Smith

D. 다음 문장을 읽고 틀린 부분이 있으면 바르게 고치세요. 틀린 부분이 없으면 ○로 표시하세요.

1. When you're doing this exercise, you should bend your knees slight.   *slight → slightly*
2. "Dinner tasted deliciously. Thank you." "You're welcome."   _____
3. Something's wrong with my phone. It's not working proper.   _____
4. This is an easily video game. Anyone can play it.   _____
5. When I become angrily, I take a deep breath and count to 10.   _____
6. My kids are extreme excited about going back to school after vacation.   _____
7. You're eating too fast. You should chew your food slowly.   _____

Nick is a **fast** learner. Nick learns **fast**. 형용사와 부사 (2)

1 **fast, long, early**는 형용사와 부사로 모두 쓸 수 있다. 이 단어들의 끝에 **-ly**를 붙이지 않도록 주의한다.

| fast | (형용사) 빠른 |
| | (부사) 빠르게, 빨리 |

- Nick is a **fast** learner. Nick은 빠른 학습자이다.
- Nick learns **fast**. He's easy to teach. Nick은 빨리 배운다.

| long | (형용사) 긴, 오랜 |
| | (부사) 길게, 오래 |

- I haven't been camping for a **long** time.
- Sorry I'm late. Have you been waiting **long**?

| early | (형용사) 이른 |
| | (부사) 일찍 |

- Diane's flight lands in the **early** morning.
- If we leave **early**, we can avoid the traffic.

2 **late, high, near, hard**도 형용사와 부사로 모두 쓸 수 있다. 이 단어들의 끝에 **-ly**를 붙일 경우 다른 의미의 부사가 되므로 주의한다.

late	(형용사) 늦은
	(부사) 늦게
lately	(부사) 최근에

- "Are you hungry?" "No. I had a **late** lunch." 늦은 점심을 먹었어.
- We arrived at the seminar **late**. 우리는 세미나에 늦게 도착했다.
- I've gained a lot of weight **lately**. 최근에 체중이 많이 늘었다.

high	(형용사) 높은
	(부사) 높이
highly	(부사) 매우

- That mountain is really **high**. It must have a great view at the top.
- Bob hung the picture **high** on the wall.
- Ms. Thomas is **highly** successful. She owns several businesses.

near	(형용사) 가까운
	(부사) 가까이, 근처에
nearly	(부사) 거의

- I hope to see you again in the **near** future.
- Summer vacation is drawing **near**. I can't wait!
- Frank **nearly** fell when he was on the ladder.

hard	(형용사) 열심히 (일/공부)하는
	(부사) 열심히
hardly	(부사) 거의 ~하지 않는

- Richard is a **hard** worker. He always does a good job.
- Marcia studies **hard** every day.
- Tom is my classmate, but I **hardly** know him.

3 **free**도 형용사와 부사로 모두 쓸 수 있다.

free	(형용사) 자유로운
	무료의
	한가한
	(부사) 무료로

- This is a **free** country. We can express our opinions openly. 자유로운 국가이다.
- I have two **free** tickets to tomorrow's exhibition. 내일 전시회 무료 티켓이 두 장 있다.
- "Are you busy this weekend?" "No, I'm **free**. Why?" 아니. 한가해.
- Children under five may travel **free** on the train. 5살 이하 어린이는 무료로 기차에 탈 수 있습니다.

'자유롭게'라는 의미로 말할 때는 부사 **freely**를 주로 쓴다.

- Don't be shy. Please talk **freely** and share your ideas with us. 자유롭게 이야기하며 생각을 공유해 주세요.

4 **good**(좋은)의 부사는 **well**(잘)이다.

- Jack is a **good** athlete. He plays every sport **well**. Jack은 좋은 운동선수이다. 그는 모든 스포츠를 잘 한다.

well은 '건강한'이라는 의미의 형용사로도 쓸 수 있다.

- "I heard you were sick last week. But you look **well** now." 지금은 건강해 보여. "Yes. I feel much better."

PRACTICE

A. 주어진 단어를 적절한 형태로 사용하여 문장을 완성하세요.

comfortable	early	~~fast~~	hard	high	long	near	silent

1. The cheetah is a _fast_ animal. It can run 100 meters in six seconds.
2. "Can you help me with something? It won't take _____." "Sure. What is it?"
3. I thought the jeans would be too small, but they fit _____.
4. You're too far away. Come _____ so I can hear you better.
5. "Why are you going to bed so soon?" "I've got an _____ meeting tomorrow morning."
6. Steve didn't say a word during dinner. He was _____ the whole time.
7. We've _____ had any rain this month. It has been so dry.
8. Bob hit the ball and it flew _____ over the fence.

B. 괄호 안에 주어진 단어들을 적절한 형태로 사용하여 문장을 완성하세요.

1. (long, late) Janice has been working _long_ hours _____, so she has been very tired.
2. (late) This morning she woke up _____.
3. (near) When she opened her eyes, it was _____ noon.
4. (high) The sun was already _____ in the sky.
5. (immediate) She jumped out of bed and called the office _____.
6. (surprising) _____, nobody answered the phone. Then she remembered it was a holiday!
7. (happy) So she went back to sleep _____.

C. free/freely 또는 good/well을 써넣으세요.

1. You don't have to pay to get into the museum. Everyone can enter _free_.
2. The swimming pool closes at night, but you're _____ to use it during the day.
3. "This is a _____ book." "Yes. I enjoyed it too."
4. Marsha has been in the hospital for a while. I hope she gets _____ soon.
5. Our university provides many language courses, so you can choose _____.
6. My grandmother has bad eyesight. She can't read _____ without her glasses.
7. I can't go out tonight, but I am _____ tomorrow.

D. 다음 문장을 읽고 틀린 부분이 있으면 바르게 고치세요. 틀린 부분이 없으면 ○로 표시하세요.

1. I need a copy of this article fastly.   _fastly → fast_
2. Lisa tried hard, but she failed to win the gold medal.   _____
3. Mr. Collins is high intelligent. He's the smartest man I know. _____
4. "Have you been teaching longly?" "Yes, for over 10 years."   _____
5. "Let's dance!" "I don't want to. I can't dance good."   _____
6. We should go to the stadium early. I want to find good seats. _____
7. Fred paid the bill lately, so he had to pay an extra fee.   _____
8. Buy one of our T-shirts and get the second one freely.   _____

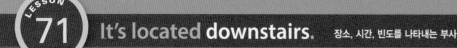

1 어떤 일이 일어나는 장소나 시간에 대해 말할 때 다음과 같은 부사를 쓸 수 있다. 이때, 부사를 주로 문장 맨 뒤에 쓴다.

장소	**here/there** 여기에/거기에	**upstairs/downstairs** 위층에/아래층에	**inside/outside** 안에/밖에
시간	**now/then** 지금/그때	**soon** 곧, 빨리	**yesterday/today/tomorrow** 어제/오늘/내일

- "Where's the restroom?" "It's located **downstairs.**" 아래층에 있어요.
- The weather is beautiful **today.** We should do something **outside.**
- "Let's meet at 6." "I'll still be working **then.** How about 7?"

    시간을 나타내는 부사는 문장의 맨 앞에 쓸 수도 있다.

    - **Yesterday**, I had a date with Matthew. We saw a musical. 어제 Matthew와 데이트했다.
    - John is saving money for a bike. **Soon**, he'll be able to buy it.

장소를 나타내는 부사와 시간을 나타내는 부사를 함께 쓸 수도 있다. 이때, 장소를 나타내는 부사를 먼저 쓴다.

- "Is Sally coming?" "Yes. She'll arrive **here tomorrow.**" 그녀는 여기에 내일 도착할 거야.
- It's getting dark. We should go **inside now.**

2 다음과 같은 부사들은 어떤 일이 얼마나 자주 일어나는지(빈도)를 말할 때 쓴다.

100% ◄─────────────────────────────────────── 0%					
always	**usually**	**often**	**sometimes**	**rarely/seldom**	**never**
항상	보통	자주	때때로	거의 ~ 않는	전혀 ~ 않는

- I **always** wake up late, so I **never** have enough time for breakfast. 항상 늦게 일어나서, 아침을 먹을 충분한 시간이 전혀 없다.
- We **sometimes** do our grocery shopping online.
- Our children **usually** play outside on weekends. They're **rarely** inside.

빈도를 나타내는 부사는 주로 다음과 같은 위치에 쓴다.

일반동사 앞	• I **sometimes forget** people's names. 나는 때때로 사람들의 이름을 잊어버린다.
	• Ted doesn't **usually drive.** He **usually rides** the bus.
be동사 뒤	• This park **is seldom** crowded. 이 공원은 거의 붐비지 않는다.
	• Ms. Walker **isn't usually** in town. She**'s often** away on business.
will/can/may 등과 동사원형 사이	• Too much exercise **can sometimes cause** injury. 너무 심한 운동은 때때로 부상을 일으킬 수 있다.
	• You **won't often see** many stars at night in the city.
have/has/had와 과거분사 사이	• I've **never been** to Asia before. 전에 아시아에 가본 적이 전혀 없다.
	• Gina **hasn't always lived** in LA. She lived in Dallas when she was young.
have to와 used to 앞	• Do you **always have to** wear a suit to work? 직장에 항상 정장을 입고 가야 하니?
	• My sister and I **rarely used to** do anything together.

3 **just, really, hardly, already**도 빈도를 나타내는 부사와 같은 위치에 주로 쓴다.

- "Have you seen Katie?" "Yes. She **just left.**" 그녀는 방금 떠났어.
- "I'm **really** sorry about not attending your wedding." 결혼식에 참석 못 해서 정말 미안해. "Don't worry about it."
- We **could hardly see** the stage because our seats were so far away.
- "I need to wash the dishes." "Oh, I**'ve already done** them."

PRACTICE

A. 괄호 안에 주어진 표현들을 적절히 배열하여 문장을 완성하세요.

1. (to leave / need / soon) Hurry up, Mitchell. We _need to leave soon_ .
2. (there / it / left / yesterday) The file isn't on my desk, but I _____.
3. (you / waiting for / downstairs) "Someone is _____." "Oh, it's my cousin."
4. (have / tomorrow / a doctor's appointment) I _____.
5. (you / then / can meet) I have some free time at noon, so I _____.
6. (now / upstairs / move / this sofa) We want to _____. Can you help us?
7. (outside / sit / today) Let's _____. The weather is so nice.

B. 주어진 표현과 always/often/never 등을 사용하여 자신에 대해 말해보세요.

1. drink coffee at night	1. _I often drink coffee at night_ OR _I never drink coffee at night_ .
2. use public transportation	2. _____.
3. brush my teeth after meals	3. _____.
4. go jogging in the morning	4. _____.
5. travel to foreign countries	5. _____.
6. watch TV on weekends	6. _____. You

C. 괄호 안에 주어진 부사를 사용하여 예시와 같이 대화를 완성하세요. 필요한 경우 부정문으로 쓰세요.

1. Are Mr. Brown's tests easy? — (seldom) No. His tests _are seldom easy_ .
2. Did Terry's flight arrive? — (just) Yes. It _____.
3. Is Mary friendly? — (usually) No. She _____.
4. Has Beth gone to work yet? — (already) Yes. She _____.
5. Can a hot shower help a cold? — (sometimes) Yes. It _____.
6. Have you seen Peter lately? — (hardly) No. We _____.
7. Do you go skiing in the winter? — (often) No. I _____.
8. Did you have to study a lot in college? — (always) Yes. I _____.

D. 괄호 안에 주어진 단어들을 적절히 배열하여 Sandy와 Justin의 대화를 완성하세요.

SANDY: 1. I _went hiking yesterday_ . (yesterday / hiking / went)
2. I _____, but I enjoy it now. (go / never / used to)
How about you? Do you like hiking?

JUSTIN: No. 3. I don't like _____. (anything / doing / outside)
4. Also, I _____ taking long walks. (hate / really)

SANDY: But hiking is good for you.
5. You _____ for your health. (often / exercise / should)
6. By the way, I'm _____. (going to / tomorrow / the mall)
I need to buy hiking boots. Do you want to go together?

JUSTIN: Well . . . OK. How about tomorrow around 7?

SANDY: 7. Sure! Let's _____. (meet / then / there)

SANDY   JUSTIN

LESSON 72

The water is **too** cold! too와 enough

1 **too** + 형용사/부사: (필요 이상으로) 너무 ~한/~하게

'(필요 이상으로) 너무'라는 의미로 형용사 또는 부사의 의미를 강조할 때 형용사와 부사 앞에 **too**를 쓸 수 있다.

The water is **too cold**!

- The water is **too cold**! I don't want to go in. 물이 너무 차갑다!
- Don't take Jimmy's words **too seriously**. He was just joking.
- How much do you earn? Or is that question **too personal**?

형용사 또는 부사의 의미를 강조할 때 **very**도 쓸 수 있다. 단, **very**는 상황에 관계없이 쓸 수 있는 반면 **too**는 그 정도가 지나쳐서 문제가 되는 상황에 주로 쓴다.

- The exam questions were **very difficult**, but I answered all of them. 시험 문제가 매우 어려웠다.
  The exam questions were **too difficult**. I wasn't able to answer all of them. (시험 문제가 너무 어려워서 다 풀 수 없었음)

2 **too many/much** + 명사: 너무 많은 ~

- There are **too many people** on the bus. Let's wait for the next one. 버스에 너무 많은 사람들이 있다.
- I need a vacation. I've been under **too much stress** lately.

3 **too**의 의미를 강조하기 위해 **too** 앞에 **way/far** 등을 쓸 수 있다.

- I can't wear this dress. It's **way too tight**. 그것은 너무 꽉 조인다.
- This school is strict. There are **far too many rules**.

4 형용사/부사 + **enough**: 충분히 ~한/~하게

'충분히'라는 의미로 형용사 또는 부사의 의미를 강조할 때 형용사와 부사 뒤에 **enough**를 쓸 수 있다.

It's **cold enough**.

- "Do you need more ice in your drink?"
  "No, thanks. It's **cold enough**." 충분히 차가워요.
- I can't usually understand Mr. Johns. He doesn't speak **clearly enough**.

'충분한'이라는 의미로 **enough**를 명사 앞에 쓸 수도 있다.

- I didn't get **enough sleep** last night, so I took a nap. 어젯밤에 충분한 잠을 자지 못했다.
- "Does your bike have **enough air** in the tires?" "No. I think I need to add some."

enough를 단독으로 쓸 수도 있다.

- I don't want any more pizza. I've had **enough**. 충분히 먹었어요.

5 **too/enough** 뒤에 **for** + 사람/사물 또는 **to** + 동사원형을 쓸 수 있다.

- I can't accept this money. It's **too much** **for me**. 내겐 너무 많다.
- You're never **too old** **to learn**. 배우기에 전혀 나이가 너무 많지 않다.
- There is **enough space** **for 120 cars** in this parking lot.
- I'm not **strong enough** **to carry** this box. Could you help me?

'~가 … 하기에'라는 의미로 **for** + 사람/사물과 **to** + 동사원형을 함께 쓸 수도 있다. 이때, **for** + 사람/사물을 **to** + 동사원형 앞에 쓴다.

- "Is it **too late for me to buy** tickets for the show?" 제가 티켓을 사기에 너무 늦었나요? "No. Tickets are still available."
- Don't worry. There's **enough gas for us to get** to a gas station.

PRACTICE

A. 그림을 보고 주어진 단어와 **too** 또는 **enough**를 사용하여 문장을 완성하세요.

| beds | dirty | high | ~~large~~ | long | milk | slowly | small |

1. The box isn't _large enough_ .
2. The towels are _____.
3. She doesn't have _____.
4. She can jump _____.
5. He's eating _____.
6. The sleeves aren't _____.
7. The writing is _____.
8. There are not _____.

B. 괄호 안에 주어진 표현들과 **too** 또는 **enough**를 사용하여 문장을 완성하세요.

1. (far, young) "Do you remember your childhood in Canada?" "No. I was _far too young_ ."
2. (comfortable) "Why didn't you buy those shoes?" "They weren't _____."
3. (many mistakes) There were _____ in Troy's article, so he had to write it again.
4. (carefully) "What did the boss say?" "I don't know. I wasn't listening _____."
5. (much homework) Professor Edwards gives _____. It's hard to finish all of it.
6. (cash) I don't have _____. Could you lend me some?
7. (suddenly) The musical ended _____. It seemed like the story hadn't finished.
8. (way, short) I cut my hair yesterday, and now it's _____!
9. (games) I think you've played _____ today. Please put them away.
10. (far, early) We arrived at the airport _____. We waited for the flight for three hours.

C. 주어진 표현들과 **too** 또는 **enough**를 사용하여 문장을 완성하세요. 필요한 경우 **for**나 **to**를 함께 쓰세요.

| (big, our living room) | (dark, read) | ~~(expensive, me)~~ | (loudly, us, have) |
| (safe, you, walk) | (sunlight, survive) | (time, me, go) | (well, you) |

1. That car is _too expensive for me_ . I can't afford it.
2. "Is the steak cooked _____?" "Yes. It's good."
3. "Is there _____ to the bathroom?" "Sure. We'll wait for you."
4. It's _____ the newspaper. Could you turn on the light?
5. My plant died. It didn't receive _____.
6. The band is playing _____ a conversation. It's impossible to hear.
7. I'll go with you. That street isn't _____ alone.
8. That sofa is _____. Let's find a smaller one.

1 **so + 형용사/부사: 매우 ~한/~하게**

'매우'라는 의미로 형용사 또는 부사의 의미를 강조할 때 형용사와 부사 앞에 **so**를 쓸 수 있다.

Your dog is **so cute!**

- Your dog is **so cute!** What's her name? 당신의 개는 매우 귀엽네요!
- Brian is very smart. He solves these math problems **so easily.**
- "This mall is always **so crowded** on weekends."
  "Yes. There are too many people!"
- "Why did Jennifer go home **so early?**" "Oh, she had a headache."

2 **so + 형용사** 바로 다음에 명사를 쓰지 않는 것에 주의한다.

- "Have you met Leo's family?" "Yes. They're **so friendly.**" (so friendly people로 쓸 수 없음)
- The lecture lasted for three hours. It was **so boring.** (so boring lecture로 쓸 수 없음)

  단, **so many/much** 뒤에는 명사를 쓸 수 있다.

  - Robert travels a lot. He has been to **so many places.** 그는 매우 많은 곳에 가보았다.
  - This article has **so much information** about health. You should read it.

3 **such (+ a/an) + 형용사 + 명사: 매우 ~한 …**

'매우'라는 의미로 **형용사 + 명사** 앞에 **such**를 쓸 수 있다.

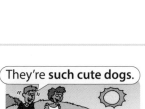

They're **such cute dogs.**

- They're **such cute dogs.** 매우 귀여운 개들이다.
- Getting married on a boat was **such an amazing experience.**
  배 위에서 결혼한 것은 매우 멋진 경험이었다.
- This area has **such clean air.** I'd like to live here.
- "Cheer up. Everybody makes mistakes." "Thanks. You're **such a good friend.**"

'그러한 ~'이라는 의미로 형용사 없이 **such (+ a/an) + 명사**도 쓸 수 있다.

- Mandy is an excellent skater. **Such talent** is rare. 그러한 재능은 드물다.
- "Why are you in **such a hurry?**" "I have a presentation in 30 minutes."
- I can't believe Mike said that. **Such words** can be hurtful.

4 '매우 ~해서 …하다'라는 의미로 **so/such** 뒤에 **that + 주어 + 동사**를 쓸 수 있다.

	so + 형용사/부사	that + 주어 + 동사	
The book was	**so funny**	**that I read**	it three times. 책이 매우 재미있어서 세 번 읽었다.
I slept	**so deeply**	**that I didn't hear**	you come in. 매우 깊이 자서 네가 들어오는 것을 듣지 못했다.
My son plays	**so loudly**	**that I can't rest**	at home.
David is	**so tall**	**that it's**	hard to find clothes in his size.

	such (+ a/an) + 형용사 + 명사	that + 주어 + 동사	
It was	**such a funny book**	**that I read**	it three times. 책이 매우 재미있어서 세 번 읽었다.
It's	**such an important meeting**	**that I shouldn't be**	late. 매우 중요한 회의여서 늦으면 안 된다.
Mia works	**such long hours**	**that she has**	little free time.
We live in	**such a small town**	**that everyone knows**	one another.

PRACTICE

A. 주어진 단어와 so를 사용하여 문장을 완성하세요. 필요한 경우 many/much를 함께 쓰세요.

animals	different	funny	~~long~~	often	pain

1. There were a lot of people at the ticket office. We had to wait in line *so long*_____.
2. Fred had _____ in his tooth. He had to see a dentist.
3. "You look _____. I hardly recognized you." "Well, I've lost a lot of weight."
4. Harry must like Natalie. He talks about her _____.
5. "Mom, we saw _____ at the zoo!" "Which one was your favorite?"
6. Michael is _____! His jokes make everyone laugh.

B. 괄호 안에 주어진 단어들과 so 또는 such를 사용하여 문장을 완성하세요. 필요한 경우 a/an을 함께 쓰세요.

1. (beautiful, flowers) I've never received *such beautiful flowers*_____ before. They're lovely!
2. (old, song) This is _____. I rarely hear it these days.
3. (excited) "I'm _____ to meet your cousins!" "They can't wait either."
4. (polite, children) "You have _____." "Thank you."
5. (strange, dream) "I had _____ last night." "Oh? Tell me about it."
6. (well) Wendy could have been a chef. She cooks _____.
7. (great, news) I have _____! Tommy got promoted!
8. (heavily) We could hardly see the car in front of us. It was raining _____!

C. 주어진 단어와 such를 사용하여 문장을 완성하세요. 필요한 경우 a/an을 함께 쓰세요.

accidents	age	hobby	knowledge	~~places~~

1. "Stan went to a nightclub." "Why do people go to *such places*_____? I don't get it."
2. I'm going to try scuba diving. Having _____ must be fun.
3. Knowing how to fix a car is useful. _____ can be very helpful in an emergency.
4. Babies sometimes swallow small objects. Watch them carefully to avoid _____.
5. Joe became a CEO when he was 25. It's not easy to achieve success at _____.

D. 주어진 문장을 보고 so/such ~ that을 사용하여 다시 말해보세요.

1. Willy quit soccer because he had a very busy schedule.
   → *Willy had such a busy schedule that he quit soccer*_____.
2. Because I was sick, I couldn't go to work.
   → _____
3. We left the café because the service was slow.
   → _____
4. People clapped at the end because it was an impressive movie.
   → _____
5. Because Michelle left quickly, I didn't have a chance to say goodbye.
   → _____
6. Because Rudy has really great style, people dress like him.
   → _____

The backpack is **smaller** and **more expensive.** 비교급 (1)

1 The backpack is **smaller** and **more expensive.**

배낭은 더 작고 더 비싸다.

'더 작은', '더 비싼'이라는 의미로 배낭의 특징을 다른 대상과 비교해서 말하기 위해 비교급 smaller와 more expensive를 썼다.

2 '더 ~한/하게'라는 의미로 둘 이상의 대상을 비교할 때 비교급을 쓴다. 비교급은 형용사/부사 끝에 **(e)r**을 붙이거나, **more + 형용사/부사**로 쓴다.

형용사/부사 + **(e)r**	1음절 형용사/부사	fast → **faster**	nice → **nicer**	big → **bigger**
	-y로 끝나는 2음절 형용사/부사	heavy → **heavier**	early → **earlier**	funny → **funnier**
more + 형용사/부사	2음절 이상 형용사/부사	quickly → **more quickly**	comfortable → **more comfortable**	
	-ing/-ed로 끝나는 형용사	interesting → **more interesting**	crowded → **more crowded**	
-(e)r과 **more**	quiet → **quieter** 또는 **more quiet**	simple → **simpler** 또는 **more simple**	
둘 다 가능한 형용사	lively → **livelier** 또는 **more lively**	polite → **politer** 또는 **more polite**	
예외) good/well → **better**	bad/badly → **worse**	far → **farther/further**		

형용사/부사의 형태 변화: 부록 p. 282 참고

- Take a taxi instead of the bus. It's **faster**, so you'll get home **more quickly**. 더 빨라서 집에 더 빨리 갈 수 있을 거야.
- We like our new sofa. It's **bigger** and **more comfortable**. 더 크고 더 편안하다.
- The snow is getting **heavier** and the roads are becoming **worse**.
- "The park seems **livelier/more lively** today." "Yes, it's **more crowded** too."

3 '~보다'라는 의미로 비교하는 대상을 말할 때 비교급 뒤에 **than**을 쓴다.

- "You're early today." "Yes. I finished work **earlier than** usual." (평소보다 더 일찍)
- Julie sang **more beautifully** in this concert **than** in the last concert. (지난 콘서트에서보다 더 아름답게)
- "Is Dan **older than** you?" "I think he's **younger than** me."
- That book was **more interesting than** I expected.

4 '덜 ~한/하게'라는 의미로 말할 때 **less + 형용사/부사**를 쓴다.

- CD players are **less common** now. Not many people use them these days. CD 플레이어는 이제 덜 흔하다.
- I've been exercising **less often** lately. I haven't been feeling well. 요즘 운동을 덜 해오고 있다.
- "How is your new job?" "Good. It's **less stressful** than my old one."
- Ben seems **less lonely** since he got a puppy.

5 **more**는 **many/much**의 비교급으로 쓸 수 있고, **less**는 **little**의 비교급으로 쓸 수 있다. 이때, 뒤에 형용사/부사 없이 단독으로 쓰거나 뒤에 명사를 함께 쓴다.

many/much → **more** 더 많은/더 많이	little → **less** 더 적은/더 적게

- I have many pairs of earrings, but Sarah has **more**. 나는 많은 귀걸이를 가지고 있지만, Sarah는 더 많이 가지고 있다.
- We always buy this soda because it contains **less sugar**. 더 적은 설탕이 들어있기 때문에 항상 이 탄산음료를 산다.
- Our company is hiring **more people** this month. You should apply.
- My grandmother used to go swimming a lot. Now she goes **less**.

PRACTICE

A. 주어진 형용사/부사를 비교급으로 사용하여 문장을 완성하세요. 필요한 경우 less를 함께 쓰세요.

carefully	~~close~~	difficult	hungry	painful	quiet	regularly	surprised

1. My cousins moved _closer_____ to our house. I see them every week now.
2. Finding a nice apartment was _____ than I thought. I found one quite quickly.
3. Mike used to talk a lot, but he's _____ these days.
4. I often have a big breakfast because I feel _____ in the morning than at night.
5. "Do you still write in your diary every day?" "No. I write in it _____ than before."
6. You need to use that knife _____ or you might hurt yourself.
7. "How is your leg?" "Better. It's _____ than it was before."
8. "I was shocked by Jenny's strange haircut." "I was _____ by the color! It was so shocking."

B. 괄호 안에 주어진 표현과 than을 사용하여 예시와 같이 문장을 완성하세요.

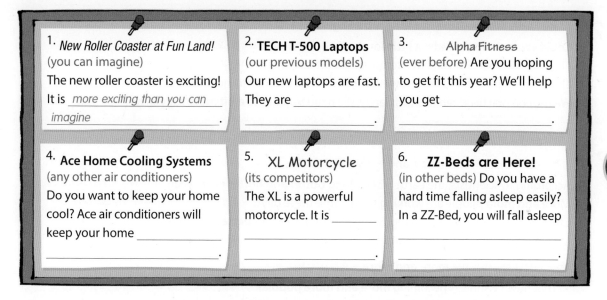

1. *New Roller Coaster at Fun Land!*
(you can imagine)
The new roller coaster is exciting!
It is _more exciting than you can imagine_ .

2. **TECH T-500 Laptops**
(our previous models)
Our new laptops are fast.
They are _____ .

3. _Alpha Fitness_
(ever before) Are you hoping
to get fit this year? We'll help
you get _____ .

4. **Ace Home Cooling Systems**
(any other air conditioners)
Do you want to keep your home
cool? Ace air conditioners will
keep your home _____
_____ .

5. **XL Motorcycle**
(its competitors)
The XL is a powerful
motorcycle. It is _____
_____
_____ .

6. **ZZ-Beds are Here!**
(in other beds) Do you have a
hard time falling asleep easily?
In a ZZ-Bed, you will fall asleep
_____
_____ .

C. 괄호 안에 주어진 명사와 than을 사용하여 문장을 완성하세요. more 또는 less를 함께 쓰세요.

1. (housework) My mom had me do _less housework than_____ yesterday, so I'm free tonight!
2. (customers) Our store's grand opening was a success! There were _____ we expected.
3. (clothes) I'm buying _____ I used to these days. I'm trying to save money.
4. (traffic) There is _____ last weekend. I've never seen this many cars!
5. (children) I have four kids but Jo has _____ me. She has three sons and two daughters.
6. (wine) Daniel had _____ usual, but he still had a bad headache the next day.

D. 다음 문장을 읽고 틀린 부분이 있으면 바르게 고치세요. 틀린 부분이 없으면 ○로 표시하세요.

1. People live more long than in the past because of modern medicine.   _more long → longer_
2. "Can we meet tomorrow? I'll be less busier then." "Sounds good."   _____
3. The train station was farther than it looked on the map.   _____
4. "This puzzle is simple than that one." "OK. Let's do that one."   _____
5. I made many mistakes on my biology exam than my chemistry exam.   _____
6. Mike and I both smoke, but I smoke less.   _____

비교급과 최상급

LESSON
74

Grammar Gateway Intermediate

LESSON 75 — The water is **much deeper** than it looks! 비교급 (2)

1 '훨씬'이라는 의미로 비교급의 의미를 강조할 때 비교급 앞에 **much/even/far/a lot** 등을 쓸 수 있다.

- Be careful! The water is **much deeper** than it looks! 물이 보이는 것보다 훨씬 더 깊어!
- "My new project is **even more difficult** than the last one." 새 프로젝트는 지난 프로젝트보다 훨씬 더 어려워.
  "Really? It must be really hard."
- Both Mr. and Mrs. Mills can speak French. Mr. Mills speaks it **far more fluently**, though.
- The line at the bank was **a lot longer** than usual.

  이때, 비교급 앞에 **very**를 쓸 수 없는 것에 주의한다.

  - I live close to downtown, but Shawn lives **even closer**. (very closer로 쓸 수 없음)
  - Jack has more time these days, so he goes out with his friends **far more often** than before.
    (very more often으로 쓸 수 없음)

2 '조금, 약간'이라는 의미로 비교급 앞에 **a little/a bit/slightly** 등을 쓸 수 있다.

- Could you turn up the radio **a little louder**? 라디오 소리를 조금 더 크게 틀어줄래?
- "This shirt is small. Do you have something **a bit larger**?" 약간 더 큰 게 있나요? "Yes, we do."
- The price of gas in this part of town is **slightly lower** than in my neighborhood.
- We haven't practiced tennis much lately. We need to practice **a bit more regularly**.

3 비교급 + **and** + 비교급

'점점 더 ~한/하게'라는 의미로 비교급 + **and** + 비교급을 쓸 수 있다.

- According to scientists, the earth is becoming **hotter and hotter** every year. 지구가 매년 점점 더 더워지고 있다.
- **More and more** people are working from home these days. 요즘 점점 더 많은 사람들이 재택근무를 하고 있다.
- Cheryl's piano skills are improving. She's getting **better and better** every day.
- My heart began beating **faster and faster** before my presentation. I was so nervous.

  2음절 이상의 형용사/부사는 **more and more** + 형용사/부사로 쓴다.

  - That new TV show is becoming **more and more popular**. 저 새로운 TV 쇼는 점점 더 인기가 많아지고 있다.
  - A storm must be coming. The wind is blowing **more and more strongly**.

4 **the** + 비교급 ~, **the** + 비교급 …

'~할수록 더 …하다'라는 의미로 **the** + 비교급 ~, **the** + 비교급 …을 쓸 수 있다.

the + 비교급		the + 비교급	
The bigger	the apartment is,	**the more costly**	rent is. 아파트가 클수록 임대료가 더 비싸다.
The more crowded	the café became,	**the slower**	the service got. 카페가 북적일수록 서비스가 더 느려졌다.
The busier	we are,	**the less**	we see each other.
The more frequently	I exercised,	**the healthier**	I became.

'~할수록 더 좋다'라는 의미로 **the** + 비교급 + **the better**를 쓸 수 있다.

- "When do you want to eat?" "**The sooner the better**. I'm really hungry." 빠를수록 더 좋아.
- I'm looking for a cheap bicycle. In fact, **the cheaper the better**. 쌀수록 더 좋아요.
- "This sauce has hot pepper in it." "Good. **The spicier the better**."
- "How many balloons do we need for the event?" "**The more the better**."

PRACTICE

A. 그림을 보고 주어진 표현들을 사용하여 예시와 같이 문장을 완성하세요.

| big   far   high   light   long   old   ~~small~~   young |

1. (slightly, much) The chocolate bar is *slightly smaller*_____, but its calorie count is _____.
2. (a bit, even) The Super S200 laptop is _____, but it's _____ than the Super S100.
3. (far, much) John is _____ than Tom, but he looks _____.
4. (a little, a lot) Greenville is _____ away, but it takes _____ to get there.

B. 주어진 형용사/부사를 비교급 + and + 비교급 형태로 사용하여 문장을 완성하세요.

| afraid   ~~clearly~~   close   quickly   tall |

1. As the fog disappeared, we could see the road *more and more clearly*_____.
2. Those sunflowers in my garden are getting _____. They used to be so short.
3. I'm scared of heights. I became _____ as the plane rose into the air.
4. My wedding is drawing _____. It's only a week away now.
5. The ice in the Arctic is melting _____ because of global warming.

C. the + 비교급, the + 비교급을 사용하여 예시와 같이 문장을 완성하세요.

1. When bread is fresh, it is tasty.
   → The fresher bread is, *the tastier it is*_____.
2. We will be more successful if we work hard.
   → The harder we work, _____.
3. When a coin is rare, it becomes valuable.
   → The rarer a coin is, _____.
4. When kids are tired, they fall asleep fast.
   → The more tired kids are, _____.
5. People invest carefully if the economy is bad.
   → The worse the economy is, _____.

D. 주어진 형용사/부사와 the + 비교급 + the better를 사용하여 예시와 같이 대화를 완성하세요.

| easy   many   scary   ~~soon~~   sweet |

1. When do you want the report? Do you need it quickly?   Yes. *The sooner the better*_____.
2. Do you like sugar in your coffee?   Yes. _____.
3. It's a horror movie. Are you sure you want to see it?   Sure. _____.
4. I want to bring a lot of friends to the party. Is that OK?   Sure. _____.
5. Take Professor White's class. It isn't hard.   OK. _____.

비교급과 최상급

LESSON
75

Grammar Gateway Intermediate

The wallet is the smallest and the most expensive. 최상급 (1)

1 The wallet is **the smallest** and **the most expensive**.
지갑이 가장 작고 가장 비싸다.

'가장 작은, 가장 비싼'이라는 의미로 지갑의 특징을 다른 여러 대상과 비교해서 말하기
위해 최상급 the smallest와 the most expensive를 썼다.

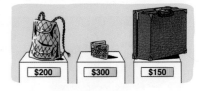

2 '가장 ~한/하게'라는 의미로 말할 때 최상급을 쓴다. 최상급은 형용사/부사 끝에 **(e)st**를 붙이거나, **most + 형용사/부사**로 쓴다.
최상급 앞에는 보통 **the**를 함께 쓴다.

형용사/부사 + **(e)st**	1음절 형용사/부사	hard → **the hardest**	fast → **the fastest**
		big → **the biggest**	nice → **the nicest**
	-y로 끝나는 2음절 형용사/부사	busy → **the busiest**	funny → **the funniest**
most + 형용사/부사	2음절 이상 형용사/부사	popular → **the most popular**	recently → **the most recently**
	-ing/-ed로 끝나는 형용사	amazing → **the most amazing**	crowded → **the most crowded**
-(e)st와 most	quiet → **the quietest** 또는 **the most quiet**		simple → **the simplest** 또는 **the most simple**
둘 다 가능한 형용사	lively → **the liveliest** 또는 **the most lively**		polite → **the politest** 또는 **the most polite**
예외) good/well → **the best**	bad/badly → **the worst**		far → **the farthest/the furthest**

형용사/부사의 형태 변화: 부록 p. 282 참고

- Emily is **the busiest** person in our office. She also works **the hardest**.
  Emily는 우리 사무실에서 가장 바쁜 사람이다. 그녀는 일도 가장 열심히 한다.
- **The biggest** building in town was built **the most recently**. 마을에서 가장 큰 빌딩은 가장 최근에 지어졌다.
- "Nancy can run **the fastest**." "Can she run **the farthest** too?"
- Our hotel has **the liveliest/most lively** bar and **the most amazing** view of the ocean.

단, 형용사의 최상급을 뒤에 명사 없이 단독으로 쓰거나 부사의 최상급을 쓸 때는 **the**를 생략할 수 있다.

- I think this dress is **(the) prettiest**. What do you think?
  (형용사의 최상급 prettiest를 명사 없이 단독으로 썼으므로 the를 생략할 수 있음)
- We love this golf course, so we come here **(the) most often**.
  (부사의 최상급 most often을 썼으므로 the를 생략할 수 있음)

3 '가장 덜 ~한/하게'라는 의미로 말할 때 **the least + 형용사/부사**를 쓴다.

- **The least crowded** park is Green Hills Park. Let's go there. 가장 덜 붐비는 공원은 Green Hills Park이다.
- There are a lot of buses that come by my house, but this one comes **the least frequently**.
- That report is **the least important**. We can do it last.

4 **the most**는 **many/much**의 최상급으로 쓸 수 있고, **the least**는 **little**의 최상급으로 쓸 수 있다. 이때, 뒤에 형용사/부사 없이
단독으로 쓰거나 뒤에 명사를 함께 쓴다.

| many/much → **the most** 가장 많은/가장 많이 | little → **the least** 가장 적은/가장 적게 |

- "Which café do you go to **the most**?" 어느 카페에 가장 많이 가니? "City Café."
- In a band, the drummer usually gets **the least attention**. 밴드에서는 드럼 연주자가 보통 가장 적은 관심을 받는다.
- I caught **the most fish** of all of us. You should have come and watched.
- Let's just get the toothpaste that costs **the least**. I'm sure there's no difference.

P R A C T I C E

A. 그림을 보고 주어진 단어들을 하나씩 사용하여 문장을 완성하세요. 최상급으로 쓰세요.

| high | ~~long~~ | many | popular | warm | **+** | ~~coat~~ | day | people | score | song |

1. Jen is wearing _the longest coat_____ .
2. _____ is "A Lonely Heart."
3. Wednesday will be _____ of the week.
4. There are _____ in front of Pizza World.
5. Todd got _____ .

B. 주어진 단어를 사용하여 문장을 완성하세요. 형용사/부사를 비교급 또는 최상급으로 쓰고, 가능한 경우 the를 생략하고 쓰세요.

| comfortably | dark | early | little | ~~much~~ | old | polluted | sad |

1. "Do you miss your family much?" "Yes. I miss my mom _(the) most_____ . I really want to see her."
2. These shoes fit _____ than the other pair. I think I'll buy these.
3. "What is _____ time you can meet?" "Around 7:30. I won't be free until then."
4. It was sunny in the morning, but the sky has gotten _____ . There are a lot of clouds now.
5. "Does Mitchell have any younger sisters?" "No. He just has an _____ one."
6. "This area of the river is _____ of all." "I know. It smells really bad."
7. "I thought Mel's poetry was the best." "I disagree. I liked it _____ ."
8. "I cried at the end of the documentary." "I did too. It was _____ part."

C. 괄호 안에 주어진 형용사/부사를 최상급으로 사용하여 문장을 완성하세요. 필요한 경우 the least를 함께 쓰세요.

1. (interesting) We really enjoyed our trip to Ireland. They have _the most interesting_____ culture there.
2. (short) "Do you know _____ way to the town center?" "Yes. That way is the quickest."
3. (close) Jeff is the one sitting _____ to the exit. He's right next to the door.
4. (frequently) I see all of my friends often, but I see Julie _____ . We are best friends.
5. (polite) Nathan is _____ boy in the neighborhood. He always says "thank you."
6. (common) _____ blood type is AB. Only about 4 percent of people have it.
7. (often) I recommend Sun Airlines. Their flights are delayed _____ .
8. (heavy) "I'm looking for a light camera." "Here. This is _____ one."

D. 주어진 명사와 the most 또는 the least를 사용하여 문장을 완성하세요.

| experience | ~~fans~~ | interest | money | damage | votes |

1. Of all our basketball players, Scott has _the most fans_____ . He's loved by so many people.
2. "Who has _____ in this school?" "Tom. He has taught here the longest."
3. My son shows _____ in physics. He thinks it's the most boring subject.
4. I went shopping with my friends and spent _____ . I only bought a hairband.
5. Jenny became the class president because she received _____ .
6. The house that faced _____ from the storm was built of bricks.

비교급과 최상급

LESSON 76

Grammar Gateway Intermediate

77 What's the tallest building in the world? 최상급 (2)

1 최상급 뒤에 다음과 같은 표현을 자주 함께 쓴다.

in + 장소/집단

- "What's **the tallest building in the world?**" 세계에서 가장 높은 건물이 무엇이니? "I'm not sure."
- I'm not **the oldest in my family**. I have two older sisters.
- Marie dances **the most wonderfully in our ballet class.**

of + 기간

- "How was your vacation?" "Great. I had **the best time of my life.**" 내 인생에서 가장 좋은 시간을 보냈어.
- Getting out of bed is **the hardest part of the morning**.
- "Wow. That was **the most exciting game of the year!**" "I agree! Both teams played well."

of all (+ 복수 명사)

- The blue whale is **the largest of all animals**. It is nearly 30 meters long. 흰긴수염고래는 모든 동물 중 가장 크다.
- I think roses are **the most beautiful flowers of all**.
- "Could you recommend a salad?" "Greek salad is **the tastiest of all our salads.**"

I know

- Brian won the lottery twice! He's **the luckiest man I know**. 그는 내가 아는 가장 운이 좋은 사람이다.
- This beach is **the most peaceful place I know**. I often come here to think.

I've (ever) + 과거분사

- Roy and Jane are **the smartest people I've met**. Roy와 Jane은 내가 만나본 가장 똑똑한 사람들이다.
- "How was your test?" "It was **the most difficult exam I've ever taken.**"

2 '단연코, 분명히'라는 의미로 최상급의 의미를 강조할 때 the + 최상급 앞에 by far/easily 등을 쓸 수 있다.

- *War and Peace* is **by far the longest** book I've ever read. '전쟁과 평화'는 내가 읽어본 단연코 가장 긴 책이다.
- "College was **easily the most memorable** time of my life." 대학은 내 삶에서 분명히 가장 기억에 남는 시간이야. "Me too."
- Our country's economy grew **by far the most rapidly** during the 1970s.
- The Hyde Hotel is **easily the nicest** hotel I've been to. I want to go there again one day.

3 '~ 번째로 가장 …한/하게'라는 의미로 the second/third 등 + 최상급을 쓸 수 있다.

- On the history exam, I scored **the second highest** in the class! 역사 시험에서 나는 반에서 두 번째로 가장 높게 점수를 받았어!
- Manchester Airport is **the third busiest** airport in Britain. Manchester 공항은 영국에서 세 번째로 가장 분주한 공항이다.
- Olivia was **the fifth most common** name for baby girls in 2005.
- There was a big earthquake in the Atlantic yesterday. It was **the second strongest** in 20 years.

4 **one of the** + 최상급 + 복수명사: 가장 ~한 … 중 하나

- The New Year's party is **one of the biggest events** in our company. 신년 파티는 우리 회사에서 가장 큰 행사 중 하나이다.
- **One of the most famous astronauts** in America was Neil Armstrong.
  미국에서 가장 유명한 우주비행사 중 하나는 Neil Armstrong이었다.
- The Internet is **one of the greatest inventions** in history.
- "That was **one of the most interesting** movies I've ever seen." "I thought so too."

PRACTICE

A. 괄호 안에 주어진 표현들을 적절히 배열하여 문장을 완성하세요. 형용사/부사를 최상급으로 쓰고, 필요한 경우 in 또는 of 를 함께 쓰세요.

1. (month / the year / short) _The shortest month of the year_ _____ is February.
2. (quiet / town / street) This is _____. There's rarely any traffic.
3. (I've ever had / relaxing / holiday) My trip to Hawaii was _____.
4. (all materials / hard) People thought diamonds were _____ until recently.
5. (person / I know / honest) Tim is _____. You can trust him.
6. (composer / the 18th century / famous) Mozart was _____.
7. (our class / healthy / student) Rick is _____. He's never sick.
8. (all / slow) There are a few slow runners on our football team, but I'm _____.
9. (our museum / ancient / paintings) Those are _____.
10. (I've ever received / expensive / gift) _____ was this necklace.

B. 괄호 안에 주어진 표현들을 사용하여 예시와 같이 문장을 완성하세요.

1. (by far, popular) "How about this model? It's _by far the most popular_ _____ car we sell." "It looks nice."
2. (by far, loudly) Jo sings _____ of all our chorus singers. I can't hear the others.
3. (easily, big) "This park is huge!" "Yes. It's _____ park in the city."
4. (by far, funny) I never feel bored around Jimmy. He's _____ person I know.
5. (easily, dangerous) Hockey is _____ sport I've ever played.

C. Jesse의 가족은 새로 이사할 집을 정하기 위해 여러 집들을 비교하고 있습니다. 표를 보고 괄호 안에 주어진 형용사를 최상급으로 사용하여 문장을 완성하세요. 필요한 경우 second/third를 함께 쓰세요.

	House on Fifth Avenue	House on Acton Road	House in Lakeview Heights	House in Colton Village
Area (m²)	175	140	240	200
Number of Rooms	6	4	8	7
Price ($)	550,000	390,000	470,000	890,000
Built	in 1988	in 2006	in 1990	in 2010

1. (small) _The third smallest_ _____ house is the one in Colton Village.
2. (large) The house with _____ area is the one in Lakeview Heights.
3. (expensive) The house on Fifth Avenue is _____.
4. (new) _____ house is the one in Colton Village.
5. (old) The house on Acton Road is _____.
6. (many) The house in Colton Village has _____ rooms.

D. one of the + 최상급을 사용하여 예시와 같이 문장을 완성하세요.

1. This cake is very sweet. It's _one of the sweetest cakes_ _____ we offer.
2. I have a noisy neighbor. He's _____ I've ever had.
3. Yesterday's meeting was so boring. It was _____ I've attended.
4. Picasso was a great artist. He was _____ of the 20th century.
5. Greg's job is extremely important. It's _____ at our company.

비교급과 최상급

LESSON **77**

Grammar Gateway Intermediate

The backpack is **as expensive as** the belt. as ~ as (1)

1 The backpack is 150 dollars. The belt is 150 dollars.

The backpack is **as expensive as** the belt.

'벨트만큼 비싼'이라는 의미로 말하기 위해 as expensive as를 썼다.

2 '…만큼 ∼한/하게'라는 의미로 말할 때 **as** + 형용사/부사 + **as**를 쓴다.

- "Your dog is **as friendly as** mine." 네 개는 내 개만큼이나 친근하구나. "Yes. He likes people."
- Our new printer model is selling **as well as** the old one. 우리의 새 프린터 모델은 이전 것만큼 잘 팔리고 있습니다.
- Some of these statues look **as real as** people.
- I reviewed your essay **as carefully as** I could. I didn't see any mistakes.

'…만큼 ∼하지 않은/않게'라는 의미로 말할 때는 **not as** + 형용사/부사 + **as**를 쓴다.

- The strawberries were **not as fresh as** last week, so I didn't get any.
  딸기가 지난주만큼 신선하지 않아서, 하나도 사지 않았다.
- William doesn't jog **as regularly as** he used to. William은 예전에 했던 것만큼 규칙적으로 조깅하지 않는다.
- "Was the video game fun?" "Yes, but it was**n't as exciting as** I expected."
- Don't close the jar **as tightly as** you did last time. It was hard to open.

3 **not as ∼ as**와 비슷한 의미로 **비교급 + than**도 쓸 수 있다.

- My sofa is **not as comfortable as** yours. 내 소파는 네 것만큼 편안하지 않다.
  또는 Your sofa is **more comfortable than** mine. 네 소파가 내 것보다 더 편안하다.
- Yesterday's interview **didn't go as smoothly as** today's.
  또는 Today's interview **went more smoothly than** yesterday's.
- Ms. Grace's lecture was **not as easy as** Mr. Mann's lecture.
  또는 Mr. Mann's lecture was **easier than** Ms. Grace's lecture.

4 **as many/much** + 명사 + **as**: …만큼 많은 ∼

- We invited **as many guests as** last time. It's going to be another big party! 우리는 지난번만큼 많은 손님들을 초대했다.
- Tara doesn't have **as much time as** in the past. She's very busy these days.
- I got to the train station early because there weren't **as many cars as** usual.

5 **the same as**: …과 같은

- That suitcase is **the same as** mine. Where did you get it? 그 여행가방은 내 것과 같아.
- "Are there any new movies?" "No, they're **the same as** last week."
- "How was school today?" "It was **the same as** always."

'…과 같은 ∼'이라는 의미로 **the same** + 명사 + **as**도 쓸 수 있다.

- I'm **the same size as** my sister. We share our clothes. 나는 내 여동생과 같은 사이즈이다.
- "We are staying at the Plaza Hotel." "Really? We are staying at **the same hotel as** you!"
- Tomorrow will be **the same temperature as** today.

PRACTICE

A. 주어진 표현들과 as ~ as를 사용하여 예시와 같이 문장을 완성하세요.

badly	~~busy~~	calmly	famous	heavy	often

1. (usual) We just finished our exams, so we're not *as busy as usual* _____ .
2. (Kevin) I practice football _____ , but he plays far better than I do.
3. (they look) "Do you need help with those grocery bags?" "No. They're not _____ ."
4. (the others in the city) Only a few people visit this museum because it isn't _____ .
5. (I could) I was angry at Laura, but I spoke _____ .
6. (we had feared) Jeremy was in a car accident. Fortunately, he wasn't injured _____ .

B. 괄호 안에 주어진 형용사를 사용하여 예시와 같이 문장을 완성하세요. 1–3번은 not as ~ as를 함께 쓰고, 4–6번은 비교급 + than을 사용하여 1–3번 문장을 다시 말해보세요.

The Brooklyn Bridge
- built in 1883
- 1,825 meters long
- 26 meters wide

The Golden Gate Bridge
- built in 1937
- 2,737 meters long
- 27 meters wide

1. (long) *The Brooklyn Bridge isn't as long as the Golden Gate Bridge* .
2. (old) _____ .
3. (wide) _____ .

4. (long) _____ .
5. (old) _____ .
6. (wide) _____ .

C. 주어진 문장을 보고 괄호 안에 주어진 명사와 as many/much ~ as를 사용하여 예시와 같이 문장을 완성하세요.

1. I drank two cups of tea. So did Mr. Hall.
   → (tea) I drank *as much tea as Mr. Hall* .
2. There are six men and two women on my team.
   → (women) There aren't _____ on my team.
3. Ted has $50 in his wallet. I have the same amount.
   → (cash) I have _____ .
4. My brother's room gets a lot of light, but my room doesn't.
   → (light) My room doesn't get _____ .
5. This theater has 150 seats. The new theater has 300 seats.
   → (seats) This theater doesn't have _____ .

D. 주어진 명사와 the same ~ as를 사용하여 예시와 같이 대화를 완성하세요.

~~age~~	city	day	height	school	time

1. A: Fred is 10 years old.
   B: Really? My son is *the same age as him* .

2. A: I go to St. Mary's High School.
   B: My sister goes to _____ .

3. A: Stacy finishes work at 5 o'clock. What about you?
   B: I finish work at _____ .

4. A: I'm 6 feet tall.
   B: I'm _____ .

5. A: My checkup is on Monday. When is yours?
   B: Mine is on _____ .

6. A: Did you know that Henry and Jill were from Texas?
   B: Yes. We lived in _____ .

비교급과 최상급

LESSON 78

Grammar Gateway Intermediate

1 **as** + 형용사/부사 + **as** 앞에 **just/nearly/almost**를 함께 쓸 수 있다.

just as ~ as: 꼭 …만큼 ~한/하게

- Sarah's cooking is **just as good as** her mother's. Sarah의 요리는 꼭 그녀의 어머니 것만큼 괜찮다.
- "Did you fail the driving test again?" "Yes. I did **just as badly as** last time." 꼭 지난번만큼 못했다.
- The author's newest novel is **just as exciting as** her other books. I finished it in two days.
- I can use a typewriter **just as easily as** I can use a computer.

nearly/almost as ~ as: 거의 …만큼 ~한/하게

- Brian is **nearly as old as** me. Brian은 거의 나만큼 나이가 많다.
- "Is it still raining?" "Yes. It's raining **almost as heavily as** it did yesterday." 거의 어제 온 것만큼 많이 내리고 있어.
- This book is **nearly as thick as** a dictionary.
- My math class is **almost as hard as** my history class.

2 '~ 배만큼'이라는 의미로 **as** + 형용사/부사 + **as** 앞에 **twice/three times** 등을 쓸 수 있다.

- Vegetables are **twice as expensive as** last year because of the flood. 홍수 때문에 채소가 작년보다 두 배만큼 비싸다.
- The new train travels **three times as fast as** the old one. 새 기차는 옛날 것의 세 배만큼 빠르다.
- The Pacific Ocean is **12 times as large as** the Arctic Ocean.
- Cleaning the house took **twice as long as** I expected.

3 **as** + 형용사/부사 + **as possible**: 가능한 ~한/하게

- Our resort offers excellent service. We want our guests to feel **as comfortable as possible**.
  우리는 손님들이 가능한 편안하게 느끼기를 원합니다.
- If you can't attend the meeting, please let me know **as soon as possible**.
  회의에 참석하지 못한다면, 가능한 빨리 저에게 알려주세요.
- We parked **as close as possible** to the mall so we didn't have to walk far.
- The baby is sleeping, so we should talk **as quietly as possible**.

  이때, **possible** 대신 주어 + **can**도 쓸 수 있다.

  - I'm on a diet, so I try to eat **as little as I can**. 또는 I'm on a diet, so I try to eat **as little as possible**.
    다이어트를 하고 있어서 가능한 적게 먹으려고 한다.
  - "Could you describe the thief **as clearly as you can**?"
    또는 "Could you describe the thief **as clearly as possible**?" "Well, he was tall and thin."

4 **as far as**

as far as I'm concerned 내 생각에는	- **As far as I'm concerned**, the best baseball team is the Knights. 내 생각에는 최고의 야구팀은 Knights이다.
as far as I know 내가 알기로는	- "Did Shirley graduate?" "**As far as I know**, she's still a student."
as far as I remember 내가 기억하기로는	- "Do people leave tips in China?" "**As far as I remember**, they don't."

PRACTICE

A. 주어진 단어들과 **as ~ as**를 사용하여 문장을 완성하세요.

confused	hungry	important	~~quickly~~	terribly	well

1. (almost) This tornado won't last long. It'll disappear _almost as quickly as_ _____ the last one.
2. (just) Getting enough exercise is _____ eating healthy food.
3. (nearly) "Brandon's writing is awful." "I know. He writes _____ I do!"
4. (almost) The breakfast at the hotel was too small. I'm _____ before breakfast.
5. (nearly) Carl is still a good basketball player. He plays _____ he did in college.
6. (just) "Do you understand the directions?" "No. I'm _____ you."

B. 그림을 보고 주어진 형용사와 **twice / three times / four times as ~ as**를 사용하여 문장을 완성하세요.

1-3

Area	4.5km^2	9km^2
Tuition Fee	$30,000	$10,000

100 years of tradition   25 years of tradition

4-6

Weight	40 tons	120 tons
Speed	3,200km/h	800km/h

1. (old) Hill College is _four times as old as_ _____ Valley College.
2. (big) Valley College's campus is _____ Hill College's campus.
3. (expensive) Hill College's tuition fee is _____ Valley College's.
4. (long) The A360 is _____ the F71.
5. (fast) The F71 is _____ the A360.
6. (heavy) The A360 is _____ the F71.

C. 주어진 형용사/부사와 **as ~ as**를 사용하여 예시와 같이 문장을 완성하세요. 1–3번은 **possible**을 함께 쓰고, 4–6번은 주어 + **can**을 함께 쓰세요.

loudly	often	soon	~~straight~~	truthfully	unique

1. Always try to sit _as straight as possible_ _____. It's better for your back.
2. Tammy's art is very different. She tries to be _____.
3. I answered all of your questions _____. I was really honest.
4. Please reply to this e-mail _____. I need your opinion right away.
5. "I can't hear you." "I'm talking _____. Maybe something's wrong with your phone."
6. Stephen lives overseas, but he visits us _____.

D. 주어진 상황을 보고 괄호 안에 주어진 표현과 **as far as**를 사용하여 예시와 같이 문장을 완성하세요.

1. Someone asks you where the bank is. You think it's on 22nd Avenue.
   YOU: (I know) _As far as I know, it's on 22nd Avenue_ _____.
2. Your roommate asks you when Donna is coming back from her trip. You think it's tomorrow.
   YOU: (I remember) _____.
3. Your friend wants some advice on which dress to wear. You think the red dress looks best.
   YOU: (I'm concerned) _____.
4. Your coworker wants to know where Mr. Brown is. You think he is in his office.
   YOU: (I know) _____.

비교급과 최상급

LESSON 79

Grammar Gateway Intermediate

He's watching the birds **at the window.** 장소를 나타내는 전치사 at, in, on (1)

1 어떤 지점, 공간, 표면 등 특정한 장소에 대해 말할 때 **at, in, on**을 쓴다.

at: ～(지점)에
He's at the window.

in: ～(공간 안)에
He's in the box.

on: ～(표면 위)에
He's on the roof.

at the window/door	in the box	on the roof
at the bus stop	in the living room	on the table/sofa
at the intersection	in the building	on the floor/ground/wall
at the traffic light	in the town/city/country	on my face/cheek

- "Rachel, what's your cat doing?" "He's watching the bird **at the window.**" 창가에서 새를 보고 있어.
- I saw you **at the bus stop**. Where were you going?
- There is a new shopping mall **at the intersection** of Main Street and Maple Road.

- "Where's your cat?" "He's sleeping **in the box** over there." 저기 있는 상자 안에서 자고 있어.
- "Did the children come home?" "Yes. They're playing **in the living room.**"
- Hana Grill is one of the most popular restaurants **in New York City**.

- "Look! Your cat is **on the roof.**" 네 고양이가 지붕 위에 있어. "Yes. He likes high places."
- After cleaning her house all afternoon, Rita sat down **on her sofa** to relax.
- Why are you staring at me like that? Is there something **on my face**?

2 **at**과 **in**은 다음과 같은 의미 차이가 있다.
- Can you drop me off **at the bank**? I need to get some cash. 은행에 내려주시겠어요? (은행이라는 지점)
  I waited for a long time **in the bank**. Many people were trying to pay their bills.
  은행에서 오래 기다렸다. (은행이라는 공간 안)
- We're meeting Eric **at the station**. He's meeting us outside Exit 3.
  "Is the café outside the station?" "No. It's **in the station.**"

3 **at**과 **on**은 다음과 같은 의미 차이가 있다.
- I went to talk to Ms. Jones, but she wasn't **at her desk**. Jones 씨와 이야기하러 갔지만, 책상에 없었어요. (책상이라는 지점)
  "Did you give the report to Ms. Jones?" "I put it **on her desk.**" 책상 위에 놓았어요. (책상 표면 위)
- Someone left a package **at the door**. It's for you.
  The store's business hours are posted **on the door**.

4 **in**과 **on**은 다음과 같은 의미 차이가 있다.
- "What's **in the envelope**?" "It's a card from Kelly." 봉투 안에 무엇이 들었니? (봉투 안)
  Please write your address **on the envelope**. 봉투 위에 주소를 쓰세요. (봉투 표면 위)
- When I was crossing the bridge, I could see fish **in the river**.
  There were a lot of ducks **on the river** this morning.

PRACTICE

A. at/in/on을 써넣으세요.

1. This car key was _on_ the table. Is it yours?
2. "Which way should I turn _____ the traffic light?" "Left."
3. Let's take a picture _____ that gate. It's a famous place for tourists.
4. Every night, Charlotte says good night to her son with a kiss _____ the cheek.
5. Paco was born and raised _____ village _____ India.
6. "There are many schools _____ this town." "There are a lot of children, too!"
7. The spider was _____ the ceiling, and then it fell _____ my shoulder. It was scary!
8. "Dan's house is _____ the next intersection." "That's very close to my house."

B. 그림을 보고 주어진 표현과 at/in/on을 사용하여 문장을 완성하세요.

the bus stop	the car	the car	the crosswalk	the desk	the desk
the door	the door	~~the lake~~	the tent	their bags	their faces

1. There is a boat _on the lake_ .
2. Two people are _____ .
3. There is a bicycle _____ .

4. There is a poster _____ .
5. A man is sitting _____ .
6. He's looking at a picture _____ .

7. A man is getting off the bus _____ .
8. A dog is _____ .
9. Two girls are standing _____ .

10. Three children are _____ .
11. They have paint _____ .
12. They have candy _____ .

C. 괄호 안에 주어진 표현과 at/in/on을 사용하여 대화를 완성하세요.

1. A: (the window) Henry, why are you standing _at the window_ ?
   B: (the door) I'm looking outside. There's someone _____ .

2. A: (the carpet) What did you drop _____ ?
   B: (the sofa) Jam. It's _____ too. Sorry.

3. A: How do I get to the museum?
   B: (the mall) After you drive past the church, turn left _____ .

4. A: (the library) Excuse me, sir. Food isn't allowed _____ .
   B: (the grass) Sorry. I didn't know. Then, can I eat _____ outside?

5. A: (the floor) The dog made a mess _____ .
   B: (the yard) We should keep him _____ .

6. A: (his office) Is Jim _____ ?
   B: Yes. He's working on a report right now.

We heard some wonderful music **at** the concert. 장소를 나타내는 전치사 at, in, on (2)

1 다음과 같은 표현에 **at**을 쓴다.

행사/공연	at a concert	at a party	at a football game	
집/직장	at home	at work	at Tom's (house)	at the dentist's/doctor's

- We heard some wonderful music **at the concert**. 콘서트에서 멋진 음악을 들었어.
- "What are you going to do this weekend?" "I'll probably just stay **at home**." 아마 집에 있을 거야.
- "I didn't see Betty **at the party**. Did you?" "Yes. She left early."
- Helen and I are having dinner **at Tom's** tonight.

2 다음과 같은 표현에 **in**을 쓴다.

자연/환경	in the rain	in the sky	in the sea	in the ocean	in the woods	in the world
줄/열	in (a) line	in a row	in a circle			
인쇄물	in a book	in a newspaper	in a magazine	in a picture		
	예외) on a map	on a menu	on a page	on a list		

- When I was young, I liked playing outside **in the rain**. 어렸을 때, 밖에서 비를 맞으며 노는 것을 좋아했다.
- A lot of students were waiting **in (a) line** at the cafeteria. 많은 학생들이 구내식당에서 줄을 서서 기다리고 있었다.
- "Can pigs swim?" "Yes. I think I read that **in a book**."
- I'm trying to find the museum. Where is it **on this map**?

3 다음과 같은 표현에 **on**을 쓴다.

거리/층	on the street	on the road	on the first/second/third floor	
교통수단	on a bus	on a train	on a plane	on a bicycle/bike
	예외) in a car	in a taxi		
기타	on the screen	on the platform	on the railway	

- There were musicians singing and playing guitars **on the street**. 노래하고 기타를 치는 음악가들이 길에 있었다.
- Joe left his gloves **in the taxi**. He realized it when he was **on the plane**.
  Joe는 택시 안에 장갑을 놓고 내렸다. 그는 비행기에 탔을 때 그것을 깨달았다.
- "The error message keeps appearing **on the screen**." "Try restarting the computer."
- "Do you know where Sophie's Closet is?" "It's **on the third floor**."

4 다음과 같이 위치를 나타내는 표현에 **at/in/on**을 쓴다.

at the top/bottom of ~의 상단/하단에	**in the middle of** ~의 가운데에

- A man is sitting **at the top of** the stairs. 한 남자가 계단의 상단에 앉아 있다.
- **At the bottom of** the chart, you can see our sales records from last year.
- The fountain **in the middle of** the garden is beautiful.

at the top of

on the left/right (side of) (~의) 왼쪽/오른쪽에, 왼쪽/오른쪽 부분에

- Are you looking for the bathroom? Walk that way and it'll be **on the left**.
  저 길로 걸어가면 왼쪽에 있을 거예요.
- Many countries in the world drive **on the right side of** the road.
- There's a plant **on the left side of** my desk. Please give it water while I'm gone.

on the left

P R A C T I C E

A. at/in/on을 써넣으세요.

1. Dr. Kim's article was printed _in_ the newspaper.
2. "Why are there so many cars _____ the road?"
   "It's probably because of the holiday."
3. We had fun _____ the football game last night.
4. Jack went to the store _____ his bicycle.

5. The Amazon is the widest river _____ the world.
6. "Where were you earlier?"
   "I was _____ the dentist's. I had a toothache."
7. We sat _____ a circle and listened to a story.
8. Never walk _____ the railway. It's too dangerous.

B. 주어진 표현과 at/in/on을 사용하여 문장을 완성하세요.

| Carrie's house   rows   the bus   the car   the eye doctor's   the menu   the ocean   ~~the street~~ |

1. Don't throw your trash _on the street_____. There's a garbage can around the corner.
2. "Why were you _____ today?" "I needed glasses."
3. When I drive to work, I usually listen to music _____.
4. "I don't see my favorite pasta dish _____ anymore." "Let's ask about it."
5. The chairs in the conference room were arranged _____ for the meeting.
6. We're going to be _____ tonight for her graduation party. Can you come?
7. I fell asleep _____ this morning. I almost missed my stop.
8. Sea turtles lay their eggs on land, but they live _____.

C. 그림을 보고 주어진 표현과 the top/middle 등을 사용하여 문장을 완성하세요. at/in/on을 함께 쓰세요.

| the door   the ladder   ~~the letter~~   the poster   the table |

1. Janet signed _at the bottom of the letter_____ .
2. A bowl of fruit is _____ .
3. A man is standing _____ .

4. There's a doorbell _____ .
5. The date of the concert is _____ .

D. 다음은 Paul이 여행 중에 Amy에게 보낸 편지입니다. 문장을 읽고 틀린 부분을 바르게 고치세요.

Dear Amy,

I am in Rome! ¹·I am staying at a hotel ~~on~~ _in_ the middle of the city.

²·My room is at the 15th floor. It has a great view.

³·In the plane, I met a girl named Giana. She invited me to a party last night.

⁴·I met so many people in the party and had a lot of fun.

⁵·The party was in her home. There was a big garden and I loved it.

⁶·Tomorrow, I'm going to pick out a few places in a map for sightseeing.

⁷·I think Rome is the most amazing city on the world.

I hope you can visit Rome someday.

From Paul

전치사와 구동사

LESSON
81

Grammar Gateway Intermediate

1 다음과 같이 시간이나 식사시간 앞에는 **at**을 쓴다.

> at 8:30/6 o'clock 등　　at breakfast/lunch/dinner

- Let's meet **at 8:30**. Don't be late. 8시 30분에 보자.
- I didn't eat anything **at lunch**, so I'm really hungry.
- We're going to watch our favorite TV show **at 6 o'clock**.

2 다음과 같이 날짜, 요일, 기념일 등 앞에는 **on**을 쓴다.

> on September 27/March 15 등　　on Saturday/Wednesday 등
> on weekdays/weekends/weeknights 등　　on your birthday/anniversary 등

- **On September 27**, we are having a huge sale. Visit our store! 9월 27일에 큰 세일을 합니다.
- I go to bed early **on weeknights**. But **on Saturdays**, I stay up late.
- "What are we doing **on our anniversary**?" "We can do anything you want."

일상 대화에서 날짜와 요일 앞의 **on**은 생략할 수 있다.

- "When did you meet your boyfriend?" "I met him **(on) July 14**, two years ago." 2년 전 7월 14일에 그를 만났어.
- Sam didn't come to school **(on) Wednesday**. He wasn't feeling well.

yesterday/today/tomorrow 앞에는 **on**을 쓰지 않는 것에 주의한다.

- "What are your plans tonight?" "I have to prepare for a meeting **tomorrow**." (on tomorrow로 쓸 수 없음)
- I saw Cindy **yesterday**. She was talking to someone in the hallway. (on yesterday로 쓸 수 없음)

3 다음과 같이 오전/오후/저녁, 월/계절, 연도/세기, 과거/미래 앞에는 **in**을 쓴다.

> in the morning/afternoon/evening　　in April/the summer 등
> in 2012/the 19th century 등　　in the past/the future

- "Did you go to Hawaii **in the summer**?" 여름에 하와이에 갔니? "No, we went **in April**." 아니. 4월에 갔어.
- **In 2012**, Janice was very busy. She worked **in the afternoon** and attended classes **in the evening**.
- Our company only sold phones **in the past**, but we will offer other products **in the future**.

the morning/the afternoon/the evening 앞에는 **in**을 쓰지만, **night** 앞에는 **at**을 쓰는 것에 주의한다.

- This street is usually very quiet **in the morning**, but it's always crowded **at night**.
  이 거리는 아침에는 보통 매우 조용하지만, 밤에는 항상 붐빈다. (in night으로 쓸 수 없음)

4 요일과 **morning/afternoon** 등을 함께 쓰는 경우에는 앞에 **on**을 쓴다. 일상 대화에서는 **on**을 생략할 수 있다.

- My flight to London leaves **(on) Tuesday afternoon**. 런던으로 가는 내 비행기는 화요일 오후에 떠난다.
- "When is the next soccer game?" "**(on) Monday evening**."
- I'm going to the movies **(on) Thursday night** with Jack. Do you want to join us?

5 **last/next/every/this/that** 등 + 시간 표현 앞에는 **at/on/in**을 쓰지 않는 것에 주의한다.

- "What did you do **last weekend**?" "I went camping." (on last weekend로 쓸 수 없음)
- Gabriel is retiring **next year**. He and his wife are moving to the country. (in next year로 쓸 수 없음)
- Let's visit Joey **this Saturday**. We haven't seen him in a while.

P R A C T I C E

A. at/on/in을 써넣으세요.

1 **PARTY INVITATION!**
My party will be held _on_
May 20 _____ 6:00 p.m.
There will be a singing
competition _____ the
party. I hope you can come!

2 *New Restaurant Opening!*
Casa Restaurant will have
its grand opening _____
October 2 _____ 4:30 p.m.
It's a great place for dinner
_____ your anniversary.

3 *Concert Schedule: July*
A concert series will be
held _____ July.
_____ weekends, Jay
Samson will perform each
night _____ 8:00 p.m.

4 **Car for Sale:**
Dodger GT for sale. I bought
it _____ 2008. For more
information, call _____ the
evening after 5:00 or come
see it _____ a weekday.

5 **Memo:**
There will be a staff meeting
_____ Thursday. We will
meet in the conference room.
Please be there _____ 1:30
_____ the afternoon.

6 **Swimming Pool Open!**
Escape the heat at Eaton
Swimming Pool! It opens
_____ 8:00 _____
the morning and closes
_____ 9:00 _____ night.

B. 주어진 표현과 at/on/in을 사용하여 대화를 완성하세요.

lunch	March 8	night	the 19th century	the future	the winter	~~weekends~~

1. _On weekends_____, there aren't many trains. There are two on Saturdays, and none on Sundays.
2. "Did Lincoln live _____?" "Yes. He was born in 1809."
3. "When can you call me today?" "Probably _____, right after my morning classes."
4. Derek's birthday is _____. He was born in the spring.
5. Tommy wants to be a pilot _____. His dream is to have his own airplane.
6. I love cold weather. I especially enjoy ice fishing _____.
7. "I have trouble sleeping _____." "You should drink some hot tea."

C. 다음은 Amy가 Paul에게 보낸 답장입니다. at/on/in을 써넣거나, 필요하지 않은 경우는 −로 표시하세요.

Dear Paul,
1. I got your letter ___−___ yesterday! I am happy you are enjoying Rome.
2. Actually, I was there _____ 1997 with my family.
Anyway, I'm doing well. 3. I went to the beach with Justin _____ last weekend.
4. We went _____ Sunday morning, but it was so crowded.
5. So _____ lunch we left and went for some burgers downtown.
6. By the way, my family and I are going to visit my grandmother _____ Saturday.
7. We are all going to see a play _____ 2 o'clock _____ the afternoon.
It will be a fun day!

From Amy

AIR MAIL

전치사와 구동사

LESSON **82**

Grammar Gateway Intermediate

1 다음과 같은 시간 표현에 **at**을 쓴다.

at first 처음에	**at last** 마침내	**at that time** 그때	**at the moment** 지금	**at the end of** ~의 마지막에

- **At first**, I didn't like living in the city. But now I enjoy it. 처음에 도시에 사는 것이 좋지 않았지만 지금은 좋아한다.
- You're here **at last**! I've been waiting for over an hour. 마침내 오셨군요!
- "Why didn't you answer my call last night?" "Sorry. I was already in bed **at that time**."
- Carla is very interested in learning yoga **at the moment**.
- We finally solved the problem **at the end of** the discussion.

at the earliest (아무리) 빨라도	**at the latest** (아무리) 늦어도	**at the same time** 동시에	**at once** 동시에, 즉시

- I have to work late tonight. I'll be home around 10 **at the earliest**. (아무리) 빨라도 10시쯤 집에 올 거야.
- The show starts at 10:00. You should be here by 9:30 **at the latest**. (아무리) 늦어도 9시 30분까지 여기 오는 게 좋겠어.
- Don't try to do too many things **at the same time**. It's better to focus on one thing.
- "In college, I had three part-time jobs **at once**." "Wow! You must have been busy."
- We'd better finish the report **at once**. Mr. Kim has been waiting for it.

2 다음과 같은 시간 표현에 **in**을 쓴다.

in advance 미리, 사전에	**in the meantime** 그 동안에, 그 사이에	**in the end** 결국에는	**in years** 몇 년 동안이나, 수년간

- We should make a reservation **in advance**. That hotel is very popular. 미리 예약을 하는 것이 좋겠어.
- "Is dinner ready yet?" "No, but you can have a snack **in the meantime**." 아니, 하지만 그 동안에 간식을 먹어도 돼.
- Finding a good job took a long time, but Travis got one **in the end**.
- "I haven't been on a vacation **in years**." "You need a break!"

in the end와 **at the end of**의 의미 차이에 주의한다.

- In action movies, the hero always wins **in the end**. 액션 영화에서 영웅이 항상 결국에는 이긴다.
  I cried **at the end of** the movie. 영화의 마지막에 울었다.
- Julie and Claire argued for a long time. **In the end**, they decided not to talk.
  At the end of the argument, Juile and Claire apologized to each other.

3 **in time**과 **on time**

'시간 안에 여유 있게'라는 의미로 말할 때는 **in time**을 쓴다.

'정해진 시간에, 정각에'라는 의미로 말할 때는 **on time**을 쓴다.

- They arrived **in time** for the biology exam.
  (시험 시작 전 여유 있게 도착했음)
- Cindy got home **in time** to cook for her guests.
  (손님들을 위해 요리하기 위해 여유있게 귀가했음)
- I didn't register for the class **in time**. Now it's full and I can't take it.

- The biology exam started **on time**.
  (시험이 정해진 시간에 시작되었음)
- Cindy's guests arrived **on time** for her dinner party.
  (손님들이 정해진 시간에 도착했음)
- "Timothy isn't **on time**."
  "He never is. We'll have to wait again."

PRACTICE

A. 주어진 표현과 **at** 또는 **in**을 사용하여 문장을 완성하세요.

once	~~the earliest~~	the latest	the meantime	the moment	years

1. "When can you call me?" "Around 2 p.m. *at the earliest*_____. I'll be in a meeting until then."
2. I did the laundry in the morning. My husband cleaned our car _____.
3. "We ate a lot." "I know. I'm feeling very full _____."
4. I haven't heard from Laura _____. I wonder how she is doing.
5. Thomas has to give his speech in 10 minutes. Tell him to come _____.
6. Please hand in your homework by Friday _____. After that, I won't accept it.

B. 다음은 에펠탑에 관한 글입니다. 주어진 표현과 **at** 또는 **in**을 사용하여 문장을 완성하세요.

advance	first	the end	~~the end of~~	the same time

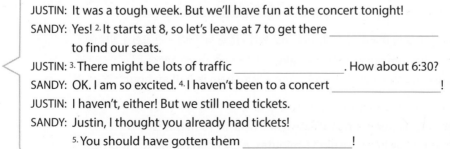

1. *At the end of*_____ the 1880s, Paris was preparing to host the World's Fair.
2. _____, architects were building the Eiffel Tower to celebrate the event.
3. To complete the construction on time, workers had started building it several years _____.
4. _____, the tower opened to the public in March of 1889.
5. _____, people thought it was ugly.
However, it quickly became a symbol of Paris.

C. at the end of/in the end 또는 in time/on time을 써넣으세요.

1. I couldn't understand the assignment at first. But *in the end*_____, I finished it and got an A.
2. We couldn't begin the play _____. An actor showed up late, so it started 30 minutes later.
3. There was a chance to ask questions _____ the presentation.
4. Nancy tried on several dresses. _____, she chose none of them.
5. Some people aren't here yet, but we need to start _____. There's a lot to discuss.
6. I got to the violin contest _____. I had a chance to practice before it began.

D. 주어진 표현과 **at/on/in**을 사용하여 Sandy와 Justin의 대화를 완성하세요.

advance	~~last~~	that time	time	years

MP3

SANDY: 1. *At last*_____, the exams are over!
JUSTIN: It was a tough week. But we'll have fun at the concert tonight!
SANDY: Yes! 2. It starts at 8, so let's leave at 7 to get there _____ to find our seats.
JUSTIN: 3. There might be lots of traffic _____. How about 6:30?
SANDY: OK. I am so excited. 4. I haven't been to a concert _____!
JUSTIN: I haven't, either! But we still need tickets.
SANDY: Justin, I thought you already had tickets!
5. You should have gotten them _____!

SANDY

JUSTIN

정답 **p. 323** / Check-Up Test 15 **p. 262**
본 교재 동영상강의 www.ChampStudy.com | 177

LESSON 84

She has been abroad **for** five years.

시간을 나타내는 전치사
for, during 등

1 **for**와 **during**은 '~ 동안'이라는 비슷한 의미를 나타내지만 다음과 같은 차이가 있다.

for는 '~ 동안 (내내)'라는 의미로 어떤 일이 얼마나 오랫동안 계속 되는지(기간)에 대해 말할 때 쓴다.

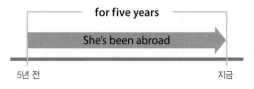

during은 '~ 동안에'라는 의미로 어떤 일이 언제 일어나는지 (시점)에 대해 말할 때 쓴다.

- "How long has Rebecca lived overseas?"
  "She has been abroad **for five years**." (5년 동안 내내)
- The baby cried **for 20 minutes**. I don't know why. (20분 동안 내내)
- I've been cleaning the house **for an hour**. I'm still not done.

- "What did you do **during vacation**?"
  "I visited my friend Dave in San Diego." (휴가 동안에)
- We do most of our shopping **during the weekend**. (주말 동안에)
- The doorbell kept ringing **during my phone conversation**.

2 **until/till**과 **by**는 '~까지'라는 비슷한 의미를 나타내지만 다음과 같은 차이가 있다.

until/till은 '~까지 계속'이라는 의미로 특정 시점까지 어떤 일이 계속되는 것을 말할 때 쓴다. 일상 대화에서는 **till**을 더 자주 쓴다.

- "Can I borrow your car **until/till Friday**?"
  "Sure. I don't need it." (금요일까지 계속)
- The sale will last **until/till the end of the week**. (이번 주말까지 계속)
- Joe exercises **until/till 10 p.m.** on weekdays.

by는 '늦어도 ~까지'라는 의미로 늦어도 특정 시점까지 어떤 일이 완료되는 것을 말할 때 쓴다.

- "You have to return this book **by Friday**."
  "OK. I won't forget." (늦어도 금요일까지)
- We must complete the project **by the end of the month**. (늦어도 이번 달 말까지)
- "Come home **by 7 p.m.**" "I'll try."

not ~ until … 은 '…에서야 비로소 ~하다'라는 의미로 말할 때 쓴다.

- Yesterday, I did**n't** go to sleep **until midnight** . I'll go to bed earlier today.
  어제 자정에서야 비로소 잠자리에 들었다.
- "When does the workshop begin?" "It wo**n't** start **until 4 o'clock**."
- "Are you moving to Florida soon?" "No, **not until** next month."

3 '~ 후에'라는 의미로 말할 때는 **after**를 쓴다.

- "What are you doing **after soccer practice**?" 축구 연습 후에 무엇을 할 거니? "I'm going to go for a swim."
- **After six years** of studying, Morgan finally graduated from college.

'~ 후에'라는 의미로 말할 때 **in**도 쓸 수 있다. 이때, **in**은 항상 기간을 나타내는 시간 표현과 함께 쓴다.

- The new art museum opens **in two weeks**. 새로운 미술관이 2주 후에 개장한다.
- "I invited Julie to come over for drinks. She will be here **in half an hour**." "Great!"

  '~ 이내에'라는 의미로 말할 때는 **in**이 아닌 **within**을 쓴다. **in**과 **within**의 의미 차이에 주의한다.

  - Our lunch break is until 1 p.m. Please come back **in 10 minutes**. (10분 후에)
    I have to finish my lunch **within 10 minutes**. A client is coming to my office. (10분 이내에)

PRACTICE

A. for 또는 during을 써넣으세요.

1. "I called you earlier, but you didn't answer." "Sorry, but you called _during_ a meeting."
2. We have been taking dance classes _____ two months. We enjoy them a lot.
3. Julia fell asleep _____ the movie. She must have been so tired.
4. It snowed _____ about three hours this morning. Then it stopped around noon.
5. "Mike has been sick _____ five whole days." "I hope he feels better soon."
6. "Could you understand the speaker _____ the lecture?" "Only a little bit. He had a strange accent."
7. Please do not take pictures _____ the performance. There will be time for photos after the show.

B. 괄호 안에 주어진 시간 표현과 until 또는 by를 사용하여 문장을 완성하세요.

1. (2 o'clock) To avoid extra fees, you must check out of the hotel _by 2 o'clock_.
2. (9 o'clock) I have to work _____ today. I still haven't finished my report.
3. (dinnertime) I should be there _____, but there is a lot of traffic on the road.
4. (next Saturday) I'm staying at a friend's house _____. My apartment is being renovated.
5. (the beginning of July) "How long will you be in Florida?" "We'll be there _____."
6. (August) The design for the new building will be decided _____.
7. (the end of the week) You must register for the seminar _____. Next week will be late.

C. 주어진 문장을 보고 괄호 안에 주어진 표현과 not ~ until을 사용하여 예시와 같이 다시 말해보세요.

1. Leo will move to England next year. → (move to England) Leo _won't move to England until next year_.
2. I will hand in my essay this Friday.
   → (be submitted) My essay _____
3. The company pays the staff the last day of every month.
   → (pay the staff) The company _____
4. We picked the winner of the contest at 5 o'clock.
   → (be chosen) The winner of the contest _____
5. Ms. Cruz gave the students the test results yesterday.
   → (receive the test results) The students _____

D. 다음은 James의 식당에 대한 기사입니다. 셋 중 맞는 것을 고르세요.

James's Restaurant Grand Opening!

By Sam Davis of *Restaurant Reviews*

1. James Wilson worked at a bank (by / during /(for)) 30 years.
2. (After / Until / In) his retirement last month, he opened a restaurant.
3. (For / During / In) my visit last night, I was very surprised because my food came out so quickly.
4. It was served (for / until / within) 15 minutes of ordering, and the food tasted excellent.
5. If James keeps serving delicious meals like last night, I'm sure his restaurant will be famous (by / in / for) a few months!
6. To celebrate the grand opening, all noodle dishes will be half price (by / in / until) the end of this month.

Please visit James's Restaurant! You will have an unforgettable experience.

1 by

(교통 수단)을 타고	by plane	by subway	by car/taxi	by bus
	by train	예외) on foot 걸어서		
(통신 수단)으로	by phone	by e-mail	by mail	by fax
(지불 수단)으로	by credit card	by check	예외) in cash	
기타	by mistake 실수로	by accident 우연히	by chance 우연히	

- We're going to Italy **by train**! I sent you the schedule **by e-mail**. 우린 기차를 타고 이탈리아에 갈 거야. 너에게 이메일로 일정을 보냈어.
- I wanted to pay the deliveryman **by credit card**, but he asked me to pay **in cash**.
- "Why is Jerry's phone in the fridge?" "He must have left it there **by mistake**."

2 with

(사람/동물)과 함께	with my dog	with a friend	with my parents	with me
(도구)를 가지고/사용하여	with a knife	with a pen	with a stick	
외모	with blond hair 금발 머리의	with blue eyes 파란 눈의	with glasses 안경을 쓴	
감정	with excitement 신이 나서	with joy 기뻐서	with fear 무서워하며	with anger 분노하여

- When I go to the park **with my dog**, he always jumps **with excitement**. 개와 함께 공원에 가면 신이 나서 뛰어오른다.
- Julia prefers writing **with a pen**. She doesn't like to type on a keyboard.
- "Which child is your son?" "The boy **with blond hair**."

3 in

(옷, 신발 등)을 입고/신고	in a suit/dress	in shorts/jeans	in sneakers/boots	in glasses
(문자, 숫자 등)으로	in writing 글로, 서면으로	in words 말로	in capital letters 대문자로	in numbers 숫자로
기타	in a hurry 바쁜, 급한	in general 보통	in use 사용 중인	
	in danger 위험에 처한	in love 사랑에 빠진	in my opinion 내 생각에는	

- "Brent was **in a suit** and **in a hurry** when I saw him." "Oh, he had an interview today."
  Brent를 보았을 때 그는 정장을 입었고 바빠 보였어.
- All refund requests must be made **in writing**.

4 for

(식사)로	for breakfast	for lunch	for dinner
판매/대여	for sale 판매 중인	for rent 임대 가능한	

- Jim and I had Thai food **for lunch**. It was so good. Jim과 나는 점심 식사로 태국 음식을 먹었다.
- Our neighbors must be moving. Their house is **for sale**.

5 on

~ 중인	on holiday/vacation 휴가 중인	on a trip/a tour 여행 중인	on sale 판매/할인 중인	on (the) air 방송 중인
	on the phone 통화 중인	on a diet 다이어트 중인	on (a) strike 파업 중인	
기타	on business 업무차, 볼일이 있어서	on purpose 의도적으로	on the whole 대체로	

- "Is Bob **on vacation**?" Bob은 휴가 중인가요? "No. He's away **on business**." 아니요. 업무차 자리를 비우셨어요.
- Ms. Wallace is **on the phone** right now. She's talking to a client.

P R A C T I C E

A. 그림을 보고 주어진 표현과 **by/with/in**을 사용하여 문장을 완성하세요.

| a tour guide   boots   ~~bus~~   capital letters   chopsticks   glasses   love   phone   shorts   taxi |

1. They are traveling to Sydney _by bus_____.
2. The man _____ is riding a motorcycle.
3. He went to the airport _____.
4. The woman _____ is the manager.
5. The children are walking _____.

6. The warning is written _____.
7. She is making a reservation _____.
8. The boy _____ is very tall.
9. She is _____ with him.
10. He is eating _____.

B. 적절한 전치사를 써넣으세요.

1. Ann didn't have dessert because she was _on_____ a diet.
2. Jenny's Wedding Shop has dresses and tuxedos _____ rent.
3. Sometimes I have trouble expressing my thoughts _____ words.
4. I saw an old friend _____ chance on the street this morning.
5. That girl _____ the dark brown eyes is really pretty. She looks like a model.
6. "Peter didn't invite me to his party." "He's so forgetful. I'm sure it was not _____ purpose."

C. 주어진 문장을 보고 주어진 표현과 적절한 전치사를 사용하여 문장을 완성하세요.

| air   anger   fax   ~~my opinion~~   use |

1. I think Julie should win the essay contest. → _In my opinion_____, Julie should win the essay contest.
2. Chuck's face was red. He was angry. → Chuck's face was red _____.
3. That meeting room is being used. → That meeting room is _____.
4. I sent my application with a fax machine. → I sent my application _____.
5. You can listen to the radio program every morning. → The radio program is _____ every morning.

D. 다음은 **Schwann** 자전거 광고입니다. 주어진 표현과 적절한 전치사를 함께 사용하여 문장을 완성하세요.

1. (car) Traveling _by car_____ costs a lot of money.
2. (a hurry) But you don't have time to walk because you're always _____.
So what will you do? Come and get a Schwann bicycle!
3. (sale) Our bicycles are now _____. They're 20 percent off the regular price!
Don't wait! Buy today! 4. (check) You can pay _____ or credit card.
5. (e-mail) For further details, contact us _____ at info@schwann.com.

전치사와 구동사

LESSON
85

Grammar Gateway Intermediate

Tara chose the bag **because of** its color. 두 단어 이상으로 된 전치사

1 because of

because of는 '~ 때문에'라는 의미로 이유에 대해 말할 때 쓴다.

- Tara chose the bag **because of its color**. She loves pink. Tara는 색깔 때문에 그 가방을 골랐어.
- "They play some good songs at this bar!" "I know! I come here **because of the music**."
- Gina couldn't go to the movies **because of her younger sister**. She had to take care of her.

because of와 같은 의미로 **due to**나 **owing to**도 쓸 수 있다.

- **Due to the traffic jam**, I was late for my appointment.
  또는 **Because of the traffic jam**, I was late for my appointment. (교통 체증 때문에)
- Oranges grow well in Florida **owing to its warm climate**.
  또는 Oranges grow well in Florida **because of its warm climate**. (따뜻한 기후 때문에)

2 thanks to

thanks to는 '~ 덕분에'라는 의미로 긍정적인 상황에 주로 쓴다.

- **Thanks to our customers**, our business has improved every year. 고객분들 덕분에, 우리 사업이 매년 성장해왔습니다.
- "**Thanks to your help**, the presentation was a success." "Thank you for saying that."
- I can easily communicate with my family from abroad **thanks to the Internet**.

3 instead of

instead of는 '~ 대신에'라는 의미로 말할 때 쓴다.

- Let's get fish **instead of chicken**. I had chicken for lunch. 닭고기 대신 생선을 사자.
- Why don't we walk **instead of driving**? It's not that far.
- "Can we record the lecture **instead of taking** notes?" "We should ask."

다음과 같이 '대신'이라는 의미로 **instead**만 쓸 수도 있다. 이때, 뒤에 **of**를 쓰지 않는 것에 주의한다.

- Jack didn't want to go shopping, so we went to a coffee shop **instead**.
  Jack이 쇼핑하러 가기를 원하지 않아서, 대신 커피숍에 갔다. (we went to a coffee shop instead of로 쓸 수 없음)
- "Will your brother go to college after graduation?" "I think he'll get a job **instead**."

4 in spite of

in spite of는 '~에도 불구하고'라는 의미로 말할 때 쓴다.

- **In spite of his efforts**, the repairman couldn't fix the dishwasher.
  그의 노력에도 불구하고 수리공은 식기세척기를 고칠 수 없었다.
- Karen hurt her ankle. **In spite of the injury**, she finished the race.
- **In spite of arguing** a lot, Brad and Mark are still best friends.

in spite of와 같은 의미로 **despite**도 쓸 수 있다. **despite** 뒤에는 **of**를 쓰지 않는 것에 주의한다.

- **Despite living** in China for years, Susan speaks very little Chinese.
  또는 **In spite of living** in China for years, Susan speaks very little Chinese. (오랫동안 중국에 살았음에도 불구하고)
- Jerry is a fantastic basketball player **despite his small size**.
  또는 Jerry is a fantastic basketball player **in spite of his small size**. (그의 작은 체구에도 불구하고)

PRACTICE

A. 주어진 문장을 보고 괄호 안에 주어진 표현을 사용하여 예시와 같이 다시 말해보세요. 1–3번은 **because of**를, 4–6번은 **thanks to**를 함께 쓰세요.

1. Ben had to attend a friend's wedding, so he couldn't go to the concert.
   → (his friend's wedding) *Because of his friend's wedding, Ben couldn't go to the concert* _____ .
2. Maria had a headache, so she had to go home early.
   → (her headache) _____ .
3. My grandparents have bad hearing, so they rarely hear the phone ring.
   → (their bad hearing) _____ .
4. Betty took a computer class, so she knows computers better than I do.
   → (her computer class) _____ .
5. Helen and Ryan had made a reservation, so they didn't have to wait.
   → (their reservation) _____ .
6. Jim had a map, so he was able to find his hotel without any problem.
   → (the map) _____ .

B. instead of 또는 instead를 써넣으세요.

1. "Did you go to the beach?" "No. We went to the mountains *instead* _____ ."
2. _____ paper cups, use mugs. It's better for the environment.
3. "This credit card doesn't work." "Why don't you try this one _____ ?"
4. We should ask Mom for her pasta recipe _____ looking for one on the Internet.
5. Let's move closer to the intersection _____ standing here. It'll be easier to get a taxi there.
6. You don't need to call me. _____ , just send a text message!

C. 주어진 표현과 in spite of를 사용하여 문장을 완성하세요.

being nervous	her busy schedule	taking vitamins
the darkness	~~the icy roads~~	washing my shirt

1. "The car didn't slow down *in spite of the icy roads* _____ ." "That sounds dangerous!"
2. _____ three times, I couldn't get the ink out.
3. Lucy has two jobs. She also volunteers at a hospital _____ .
4. It was getting late at night. _____ , the police kept searching for the child.
5. Don tried to look confident during his speech _____ .
6. _____ , Jamie often gets a cold.

D. 다음은 모차르트에 관한 글입니다. because of/instead (of)/despite를 써넣으세요.

Mozart was a great musician from a very young age.
1. *Because of* _____ his talents, he was often asked to perform in front of the king.
2. He became popular in Salzburg, especially _____ his young age.
But Mozart did not want to stay there. 3. He moved to Vienna _____ .
4. In Vienna, he focused on creative music _____ traditional styles and became even more famous.
5. _____ his fame, he did not become wealthy during his lifetime.
However, he was one of the best musicians that has ever lived.

Let's **talk about** it later. 동사 + 전치사

1 다음과 같이 동사와 전치사를 함께 쓸 수 있다.

about

talk about ~에 대해 말하다	**think about** ~에 대해 생각하다	**complain about** ~에 대해 불평하다
worry about ~에 대해 걱정하다	**forget about** ~에 대해 잊다	**learn about** ~에 대해 배우다

- I don't have time to chat now. Let's **talk about** it later. 나중에 그것에 대해 이야기하자.
- "I hope I pass my test!" "I'm sure you will. Don't **worry about** it so much."

at

stare at ~을 빤히 쳐다보다	**point at** ~을 가리키다	**shout at** ~에게 소리치다
smile at ~를 보고 미소 짓다	**laugh at** ~를 비웃다, ~를 보고 웃다	**wave at** ~에게 손을 흔들다

- "What are you **staring at**?" 무엇을 빤히 쳐다보고 있니? "Those flowers. They are so colorful."
- My baby **smiled at** me for the first time today. I feel so happy.

for

wait for ~를 기다리다	**leave for** ~로 떠나다	**pay for** ~의 비용을 지불하다
care for ~를 돌보다	**apply for** ~에 지원하다, ~을 신청하다	**apologize for** ~에 대해 사과하다

- Gary had to **wait for** his wife while she shopped for clothes. Gary는 아내가 옷을 살 동안 그녀를 기다려야 했다.
- "Is Adam the oldest child?" "Yes. He often **cares for** his younger sisters."

to

object to ~에 반대하다	**lead to** ~으로 이어지다	**reply to** ~에 답하다
stick to ~을 계속하다, 고집하다	**belong to** ~의 것이다, ~에 속하다	**happen to** ~에 일어나다

- Most citizens **object to** the tax increase. 대부분의 시민이 세금 인상에 반대한다.
- If we want to meet the deadline, we must **stick to** the schedule.

2 다음과 같이 동사 뒤에 어떤 전치사를 쓰는지에 따라 의미가 달라지는 경우에 주의한다.

look	**at** ~을 보다	- **Look at** this menu! Everything looks delicious. (메뉴를 보다)
	for ~을 찾다	- Kevin is **looking for** a roommate. (룸메이트를 찾다)
	after ~를 돌보다	- David is going to **look after** our dog while we're traveling. (개를 돌보다)

ask	**for** ~을 요청하다	- Brian **asked for** a ride, so I drove him home. (태워줄 것을 요청하다)
	about ~에 대해 묻다	- Gina **asked about** your brother. I think she wants to meet him. (네 남동생에 대해 묻다)

익혀두면 유용한 동사 표현: 부록 p. 291 참고

3 다음과 같은 동사는 뒤에 **to, about, with** 등의 전치사를 쓰지 않는 것에 주의한다.

answer ~에 대답하다	**call** ~에게 전화 걸다	**enter** ~에 들어가다
discuss ~에 대해 논의하다	**marry** ~와 결혼하다	**resemble** ~와 닮다

- Someone is ringing the doorbell. Could you **answer** it, please? (answer to it 등으로 쓸 수 없음)
- Let's **discuss** our travel plans at dinner. (discuss about our travel plans 등으로 쓸 수 없음)
- Jim **resembles** his father. They look exactly alike.

PRACTICE

A. 그림을 보고 주어진 표현들과 적절한 전치사를 함께 사용하여 예시와 같이 문장을 완성하세요. 현재진행 시제로 쓰세요.

learn	pay	point	think	~~wait~~	wave

1   2 GEOGRAPHY   3   4 (Here.)   5   6

NEWS STAND

1. (the elevator) He _'s waiting for the elevator_ .
2. (geography) They _____ .
3. (a sign) He _____ .
4. (the newspaper) She _____ .
5. (chocolate cake) She _____ .
6. (the cameras) They _____ .

B. 주어진 표현들을 사용하여 문장을 완성하세요. 현재 시제 또는 과거 시제로 쓰세요.

(apologize, losing)	~~(apply, a job)~~	(belong, Monica)
(forget, appointments)	(lead, many health problems)	(shout, each other)

1. Two hundred people _applied for a job_ at our company last week.
2. A lot of research shows that smoking _____ .
3. Angela and Gabby _____ loudly. Lisa told them to stop.
4. Ted _____ my umbrella, but he didn't offer to buy me a new one.
5. "Whose shoes are those?" "They _____ ."
6. Ron _____ easily. You should remind him.

C. look 또는 ask와 적절한 전치사를 함께 사용하여 문장을 완성하세요.

1. Mary will _look for_ a new apartment before she moves to Manchester.
2. I'm trying to take a picture of you! Please _____ me.
3. I called the gym to _____ their weekend hours.
4. "Did you _____ another bottle of wine?" "Yes. The waiter is going to bring it."
5. Susan's job is to _____ patients. She works as a nurse.
6. "I can't find my cell phone." "Let's _____ it together."

D. 다음 문장을 읽고 틀린 부분이 있으면 바르게 고치세요. 틀린 부분이 없으면 ○로 표시하세요.

1. The air conditioner wasn't working, so we complained at it.   _complained at → complained about_
2. Please answer to my question. I'm still waiting. _____
3. "What's so funny?" "I'm laughing at this magazine article." _____
4. Aaron married with his wife at a beautiful church. _____
5. "When do the speeches begin?" "Look after the schedule." _____
6. The crowd cheered when the boxer entered the stadium. _____
7. "Did you hear from Jill?" "No. She hasn't replied for my message." _____
8. Let's call to Taco Factory and order dinner. _____

1 Chris is working.

Paul is **working out.**
Paul은 운동하고 있다.

'운동하다'라는 의미로 말하기 위해 동사 work와 out을 함께 썼다.
이때, work out은 구동사이다.

2 다음과 같이 동사 뒤에 **out, along** 등을 함께 써서 하나의 의미를 나타내는 구동사들이 있다.

work out 운동하다. (일이) 잘 풀리다	**get along** 사이 좋게 지내다	**hang out** 많은 시간을 보내다
hold on 기다리다	**calm down** 진정하다	**run away** 달아나다
show up 나타나다	**break up** 헤어지다	**look around** 둘러보다

- "Do your children **get along?**" 아이들이 사이 좋게 지내나요? "Yes. They rarely argue."
- "Bob, hurry up! We're late." "**Hold on!** I'm coming." 기다려!
- I **showed up** on time for our meeting, but my counselor was late.
- Please **calm down** and listen to me. I can explain everything.
- "That shop seems interesting." "Well, do you want to **look around?**"

3 구동사 뒤에 전치사를 함께 쓸 수도 있다.

- "Do you **hang out with** Rob much?" 너는 Rob과 많은 시간을 함께 보내니? "Not really. He's always busy."
- In my dream, I was in a jungle. I was **running away from** a tiger. 호랑이로부터 도망치고 있었다.
- Ashley **broke up with** her boyfriend. She regrets it.
- I **get along with** my roommates very well. They're nice people.

다음과 같은 구동사 + 전치사 표현도 있다.

get out of ~에서 나가다	• "I want to go home." "Me too. Let's **get out of** here." 여기에서 나가자.
run out of ~을 다 써버리다	• We **ran out of** paper for the fax machine. 팩스의 종이를 다 써버렸다.
sign up for ~에 등록하다	• Brian is going to **sign up for** tennis classes.

4 구동사와 목적어를 함께 쓸 때, 목적어는 구동사의 가운데 또는 뒤에 쓸 수 있다.

turn on/off ~을 켜다/끄다	**put off** ~을 미루다/연기하다	**pick up** ~을 집다/들어 올리다	**throw away** ~을 버리다
put on ~을 입다	**take off** ~을 벗다	**clean up** ~을 치우다	**take away** ~을 가져가다/치우다
try on ~을 입어보다	**turn down** ~을 거절하다	**make up** ~을 지어내다	**point out** ~을 지적하다

	목적어				목적어	
• We **put**	the deadline	off.		We **put off**	the deadline.	마감 기한을 미뤘다.
• Please **take**	our dishes	away.	또는	Please **take away**	our dishes.	접시를 치워주세요.
• Susie **turned**	my proposal	down.		Susie **turned down**	my proposal.	
• Mr. Lee **pointed**	some errors	out.		Mr. Lee **pointed out**	some errors.	

단, 구동사의 목적어로 **it, them** 등의 대명사를 쓰는 경우에는 항상 구동사의 가운데에 쓰고 뒤에 쓰지 않는 것에 주의한다.

- If you like the shirt, you should **try it on.** (try on it으로 쓸 수 없음)
- "Why are the lights on?" "Sorry, I forgot to **turn them off.**" (turn off them으로 쓸 수 없음)

익혀두면 유용한 동사 표현: 부록 p. 291 참고

PRACTICE

A. 주어진 단어들을 사용하여 문장을 완성하세요.

calm down	hold on	~~look around~~	show up	work out

1. "I don't know where I put my wallet!" "Let's _look around_ the house."
2. Brenda drank some hot tea to _____ after a hard day at work.
3. Julia is always really popular. So many people _____ to her parties.
4. Let's _____ for a bit before we start. Not everyone is here.
5. My plan to go to Europe didn't _____. Maybe I can go next year.

B. 그림을 보고 주어진 단어들을 하나씩 사용하여 문장을 완성하세요. 현재진행 시제로 쓰세요.

clean	~~pick~~	run	take	turn	+	away	down	off	~~up~~	up

1. She _'s picking up_ a puzzle piece.   4. He _____ .
2. He _____ his socks.   5. She _____ the invitation.
3. They _____ the garage.

C. 주어진 구동사와 적절한 전치사를 함께 사용하여 문장을 완성하세요. 필요한 경우 동사를 적절한 형태로 바꾸세요.

break up	get along	get out	~~hang out~~	run out	sign up

1. Karen usually _hangs out with_ her friends on Friday nights.
2. I've tried everything to stop the baby from crying. I have_____ ideas!
3. My sister and I used to fight a lot when we were young. Now, we _____ each other.
4. "Did Stella _____ John?" "No. They just had an argument. They'll be OK soon."
5. I _____ the crowded bar because I needed some fresh air.
6. Marshall _____ a class at the art gallery. He is excited to learn about modern art.

D. 괄호 안에 주어진 표현들을 적절히 배열하여 문장을 완성하세요.

1. (going to / your coat / are / on / you / put)
   " _Are you going to put your coat on_ OR _Are you going to put on your coat_ ?" "No. I'm not cold."
2. (turn / the TV / why / on / you / did) _____ ? I'm trying to sleep.
3. (made / it / she / up) "Do you believe Lauren's story?" "Yes. I don't think _____ ."
4. (these shoes / on / have to / try / you)_____ . They're perfect for the dance!
5. (want to / I / it / away / throw) I hate that lamp. _____ , but my husband likes it.
6. (can't just / you / take / away / them)
   Jimmy, these are your little brother's toys. _____ !
7. (the mistake / out / pointed / Susan)
   _____ in your charts.

LESSON 88

Grammar Gateway Intermediate

I'm curious about this book. 형용사 + 전치사

1 다음과 같이 형용사와 전치사를 함께 쓸 수 있다.

about

curious about ~에 대해 궁금해하는	concerned about ~에 대해 걱정하는	crazy about ~에 (대해) 열광하는

- I'm **curious about** this book. The title sounds interesting. 이 책에 대해 궁금해.
- George watches a lot of soccer and baseball on TV. He's **crazy about** sports.

at

shocked at ~에 놀란	excellent at ~에 뛰어난	terrible at ~을 못하는

- Carry was **shocked at** the price of the purse. It was really expensive. Carry는 지갑의 가격에 놀랐다.
- In high school, I was **terrible at** science.

for

sorry for ~에 대해 미안한/유감스러운	responsible for ~에 책임이 있는	late for ~에 늦은
ready for ~에 대한 준비가 된	eager for ~을 열망하는	suitable for ~에 적합한

- I feel **sorry for** shouting at Thomas. I think I should apologize. Thomas에게 소리지른 것에 대해 미안하게 느낀다.
- I'm **ready for** the interview tomorrow. I'm really **eager for** this job.
- Jane was **late for** class on the first day because she couldn't find the classroom.

of

scared of ~을 무서워하는	fond of ~을 좋아하는	full of ~으로 가득 찬
short of ~이 부족한	aware of ~을 알고 있는	capable of ~을 할 수 있는

- Nina used to be **scared of** birds. But now she is **fond of** them. Nina는 새를 무서워했다. 그러나 지금은 새를 좋아한다.
- We're **short of** toilet paper. We need to go to the store soon.
- Max dove into the sea to save the boy even though he was **aware of** the danger.

to

similar to ~와 비슷한	related to ~와 관련된/친척 관계인	close to ~에 가까운
rude to ~에게 무례한	polite to ~에게 예의 바른	kind to ~에게 친절한

- "Andrea looks **similar to** Jill." Andrea는 Jill과 비슷해 보여.
  "I think so too. Maybe they're **related to** each other." 어쩌면 서로 친척 관계일지도 몰라.
- "Sometimes Frank is **rude to** people." "Really? He's always **polite to** me."
- England is really **close to** Germany. I'll show you on a map.

2 다음과 같이 형용사 뒤에 어떤 전치사를 쓰는지에 따라 의미가 달라지는 경우에 주의한다.

good	at ~에 능숙한	• "Are you **good at** yoga?" "Not really. I just like it." (요가에 능숙한)
	for (건강 등)에 좋은	• Eating vegetables is **good for** you. (너의 건강에 좋은)
	to ~에게 친절한	• Roy is so **good to** his friends. He always helps them. (친구들에게 친절한)

familiar	to (사람)에게 익숙한	• The *Mona Lisa* is **familiar to** everyone. (모든 사람에게 익숙한)
	with (사물, 상황)에 익숙한	• Carl just moved here, so he isn't **familiar with** the area. (그 지역에 익숙하지 않은)

익혀두면 유용한 형용사 + 전치사 표현: 부록 p. 300 참고

PRACTICE

A. 주어진 형용사와 적절한 전치사를 함께 사용하여 문장을 완성하세요.

| ~~aware~~ | close | curious | eager | fond | related | suitable | terrible |

1. "Andy is selling his house." "Really? I wasn't _aware of_ that. When did he decide to sell it?"
2. "Are you staying at a hotel?" "Yes. It's very _____ the city center."
3. Many bees are dying these days. The problem might be _____ global warming.
4. Could you tell me your name again? I'm _____ remembering names.
5. I need to change my shoes. These aren't _____ wearing in the rain.
6. Rita isn't _____ yogurt. She has never liked its flavor.
7. My sister is so _____ good grades. She's always studying.
8. "I don't want to watch the rest of this movie." "Aren't you _____ the ending?"

B. 괄호 안에 주어진 단어들과 about/at/for 등을 적절히 배열하여 문장을 완성하세요.

1. (crazy / fashion) Melissa is _crazy about fashion_. She is always buying new clothes.
2. (shocked / the news) "Phil got into law school." "I heard. I was _____!"
3. (sales / responsible) "What does John do at your company?" "He's _____."
4. (similar / limes) Lemons are _____. You can use them instead.
5. (Sue's performance / concerned) I'm _____ at work lately.
6. (the noise / scared) When there's a thunderstorm, my dog gets _____.
7. (people / full) The elevator is _____. Let's take the stairs.

C. good 또는 familiar와 적절한 전치사를 함께 사용하여 문장을 완성하세요.

1. I'm quite _good at_ cooking. All of my friends think my food is delicious.
2. We should go outside. Taking a break will be _____ us.
3. "Do you know Harry Parsons?" "No. I'm not _____ that name."
4. Be _____ strangers. You might need someone's help one day.
5. "Have you been to that museum before?" "I think so. It seems _____ me."

D. 다음은 교수님이 Amy를 위해 써준 추천서입니다. 괄호 안에 주어진 형용사와 적절한 전치사를 함께 사용하여 문장을 완성하세요.

> Dear Sir or Madam,
>
> I'd like to recommend Amy Wilson for the Future Leaders Scholarship.
> 1. (suitable) I am confident that she is definitely _suitable for_ it.
> 2. (excellent) She is _____ her studies and has strong leadership skills.
> 3. (capable) Last summer, she showed that she is _____ organizing large social events.
> 4. (kind) She is also _____ her classmates. She has helped them study for exams.
> 5. (late) Furthermore, Amy has never been _____ class.
> She has been a great student of mine, and I strongly believe that she should get this scholarship.
>
> Yours sincerely,
> Professor Carol Yang
> Department of Law

전치사와 구동사

LESSON
89

Grammar Gateway Intermediate

1 다음과 같이 명사와 전치사를 함께 쓸 수 있다.

between

difference between ~의 차이	relationship between ~의 관계	conversation between ~(간)의 대화

- Can you find the **difference between** these two pictures? 이 두 그림의 차이를 찾을 수 있나요?
- This article talks about the **relationship between** regular exercise and good health.
- "What were you talking to Eric about?" "Nothing much. It was just a **conversation between** friends."

for

need for ~의 필요	demand for ~에 대한 수요	search for ~에 대한 탐색/수색
reason for ~의 이유	responsibility for ~에 대한 책임	respect for ~에 대한 존경
room for ~을 위한 공간/여지	desire for ~에 대한 열망	request for ~에 대한 요청

- Don't throw away the receipt. There might be a **need for** it later. 나중에 그것이 필요할지도 몰라.
- One **reason for** water pollution is the use of chemicals. 수질오염의 한 이유는 화학 약품의 사용이다.
- "Is there **room for** my luggage in your car?" "I think so."
- Kevin has a lot of **respect for** Thomas Edison, because he never gave up until he succeeded.

in

interest in ~에 대한 흥미	success in ~에서의 성공	belief in ~에 대한 믿음
increase in ~의 증가	decrease in ~의 감소	change in ~의 변화

- My son has a strong **interest in** music. He wants to be a professional musician. 내 아들은 음악에 대한 강한 흥미가 있다.
- "We had an **increase in** sales last month." 지난달 판매량의 증가가 있었어요. "That's good news!"
- Professor Reynolds has achieved great **success in** his research.
- There has been a **change in** the schedule. The meeting will be at 1:30, not 1 o'clock.

of

cause of ~의 원인	example of ~의 예시	cost of ~의 비용	lack of ~의 부족
idea of ~에 대한 생각	advantage of ~의 장점	knowledge of ~에 대한 지식	way of ~하는 방식/방법

- Stress is one **cause of** illnesses. 스트레스는 질병의 한 원인이다.
- "What's your **idea of** the perfect date?" 완벽한 데이트에 대한 네 생각은 무엇이니? "A romantic dinner and a movie."
- The big swimming pool is the main **advantage of** this gym.
- Every culture has a different **way of** greeting people.

to

answer to ~에 대한 답	key to ~의 방법/비결	solution to ~의 해결 방법
reply to ~에 대한 대답/답장	reaction to ~에 대한 반응	damage to ~의 피해

- Henry probably knows the **answer to** the math problem. You should ask him for help.
  Henry는 아마 그 수학 문제에 대한 답을 알 거야.
- "Have you sent a **reply to** Sue's e-mail?" Sue의 이메일에 대한 답장을 보냈니? "Yes, I sent it yesterday."
- The **key to** success is hard work.
- "What was Simon's **reaction to** the news?" "He wasn't even surprised."

익혀두면 유용한 명사 + 전치사 표현: 부록 p. 302 참고

PRACTICE

A. 적절한 전치사를 써넣으세요.

1. The bookshelf is full. I have no room _for_ more books.
2. Steve has a lot of success _____ his toy car business. Nobody expected it.
3. The cause _____ your skin condition is simple. It's a reaction _____ peanuts.
4. The storm did a lot of damage _____ the crops. We have to find a solution _____ this.
5. The relationship _____ language and culture has been studied for many years.
6. "Your idea _____ going fishing next weekend sounds like fun." "Great. Let's do it."
7. Our store needs more customers. Last month, we had a decrease _____ sale by 20 percent.

B. 주어진 단어들을 하나씩 사용하여 문장을 완성하세요.

change	cost	difference	example		between	~~for~~	for	in
key	~~respect~~	responsibility		+	of		of	to

1. Many people have _respect for_ that movie director. He has made some meaningful films.
2. "How much is the _____ delivery?" "It's already included in your payment."
3. My grandmother says that the _____ a happy life is to make lots of friends.
4. "Mr. Watson got fired. I feel bad." "Yes, but everyone has to take _____ their mistakes."
5. Notre Dame is a good _____ a European church.
6. The biggest _____ the twins is their hair. One has short hair and the other has long hair.
7. It was sunny in the morning, but there was a _____ the weather. It's raining now.

C. 괄호 안에 주어진 표현들과 between/for/in 등을 적절히 배열하여 문장을 완성하세요.

1. (seeing that movie / any interest) "Do you have _any interest in seeing that movie_ ?" "Not really."
2. (thanking people / a good way) _____ is to write them letters.
3. (belief / Santa Claus) _____ is common among children.
4. (a desire / wealth) Many people have _____ .
5. (your suggestion / Mary's reply) "What was _____ ?" "She said yes."
6. (the conversation / Chuck and Arnold) I heard _____ . They seemed upset.
7. (a vegetarian meal / a request) Tim made _____ on his flight.

D. 다음은 Stanley City 지역 신문입니다. 괄호 안에 주어진 표현들과 적절한 전치사를 함께 사용하여 문장을 완성하세요.

THE STANLEY DAILY

July 02, 2018

1. (an advantage, a great need)
An advantage of an engineering degree is that there's always _____ it. Research shows that employers want more engineers.

2. (an answer)
The concerned people of Stanley City requested safer parks for children. The mayor still hasn't given _____ this request.

3. (the search, knowledge)
_____ the robber has continued since last night, but the police say they have no _____ where he is now.

4. (the demand, an increase)
_____ houses has gone up recently because there's been _____ the city population.

5. (the lack, the reason)
_____ public transportation is surely _____ the bad traffic on 5th Avenue.

정답 **p. 324** / Check-Up Test 15 **p. 262**

전치사와 구동사

LESSON
90

Grammar Gateway Intermediate

1 while

'~하는 동안에'라는 의미로 어떤 일이 일어나는 시점에 진행되고 있는 일에 대해 말할 때
while + 주어 + 동사를 쓴다.

- **While he was playing outside,** he broke the window. 그는 밖에서 노는 동안에 창문을 깼다.
- "Are you going to visit the Great Wall **while you are in China?**" "Yes."

  이때, **while** 대신 **when**도 쓸 수 있다.
  - **When I wasn't looking,** the baby spilled his milk. (= While I wasn't looking)

while은 어떤 일과 동시에 진행되는 일에 대해 말할 때도 쓴다.

- I listen to the radio **while I'm cooking.** 요리하는 동안에 라디오를 듣는다.
- **While Harry was waiting in the lobby,** he read a magazine.

  while과 비슷한 의미로 **during**도 쓸 수 있다. 단, **during** 뒤에는 명사를 쓰는 것에 주의한다.
  - We slept on the plane **during our flight** to Phoenix. (비행 동안)
    We slept on the plane **while we were flying** to Phoenix. (비행하는 동안)

2 until

'~할 때까지'라는 의미로 어떤 일이 어느 시점까지 계속되는지 말할 때 **until + 주어 + 동사**를 쓴다.

- **Until everyone left,** he stayed in the room. 모두가 떠날 때까지 그는 방 안에 있었다.
- Andrea is taking care of our plants **until we come back from our trip.**

  until 뒤에 명사도 쓸 수 있다.
  - The store will be closed **until next week.** They are renovating the store. (다음 주까지)
    The store will be closed **until the renovations are completed.** (수리가 완료될 때까지)

3 by the time

'~할 때쯤'이라는 의미로 어떤 일이 어느 시점에 완료되는지 말할 때 **by the time + 주어 + 동사**를 쓴다.

- **By the time he finished his work,** it was dark outside.
  그가 일을 끝냈을 때쯤 밖이 어두워져 있었다.
- (전화상에서) I'm on my way. Will you still be at the mall **by the time I get there?**

  by the time과 비슷한 의미로 **by**를 쓸 수도 있다. 단, **by** 뒤에는 명사를 쓰는 것에 주의한다.
  - **By winter,** all of the leaves will have fallen off the trees. (겨울쯤에는)
    By the time winter comes, all of the leaves will have fallen off the trees. (겨울이 올 때쯤에는)

Good night!

4 while, when, until, by the time 다음에 미래의 일을 말할 때는 현재 시제를 쓴다. 이때, **will**이나 **am/is/are going to** 등을 쓰지 않는 것에 주의한다.

- (전화상에서) "May I speak to Mr. Jones?" "Sure. Please wait **while I connect** you." (while I will connect you로 쓸 수 없음)
- Sally isn't allowed to go out **until she apologizes** to her brother. (until she's going to apologize 로 쓸 수 없음)
- **By the time we're** home, the babysitter will have fed the kids.

시간을 나타내는 문장에서의 미래에 대한 더 자세한 내용은 Lesson 21 참고

P R A C T I C E

A. 그림을 보고 주어진 문장들과 while을 사용하여 문장을 완성하세요. A → B의 순서로 주어진 문장을 하나씩 사용하세요.

A

he brushed his teeth	he fell
she played the guitar	~~the phone rang~~
they were walking in the forest	

B

he was snowboarding	he watched the news
she sang	they saw a deer
~~they were having coffee~~	

1. *The phone rang while they were having coffee* .
2. _____ .
3. _____ .
4. _____ .
5. _____ .

B. until 또는 by the time을 적절한 위치에 사용하여 주어진 두 문장을 예시와 같이 한 문장으로 바꾸어 쓰세요. 두 문장을 순서대로 사용하세요.

1. Travelers searched for an oasis. They found one. → *Travelers searched for an oasis until they found one* .
2. Frank called Julie back. She was already asleep. → _____ .
3. Max applied for jobs. He finally got one. → _____ .
4. Hans kept studying Russian. He became fluent. → _____ .
5. We were already back in the hotel. It began to rain. → _____ .
6. Our seminar ended. Everyone was pleased with it. → _____ .

C. 다음은 Mike의 음성 사서함에 남겨진 메시지입니다. 괄호 안에 주어진 표현들을 사용하여 문장을 완성하세요. 현재 시제로 쓰거나 will을 함께 쓰세요.

1. TIM: There's a party on Friday. When I _find_____ out the time, I _____ you know. (find, let)
2. KEVIN: We _____ anything until you _____ at the restaurant. (not order, arrive)
3. TINA: By the time you _____ this message, I _____ on my way to London. (hear, be)
4. JOHN: _____ you _____ my dog while I _____ away? (feed, be)
5. MICHELLE: I had fun tonight. Take care of yourself until we _____ again. (meet)
6. BRAD: When your brother _____ from school, _____ you _____ him to call me? (return, tell)

D. 다음 문장을 읽고 틀린 부분이 있으면 바르게 고치세요. 틀린 부분이 없으면 ○로 표시하세요.

1. When I will go to France, I will visit the Louvre Museum. — *When I will go → when I go*
2. In just one day, Steve read the long book until the end. — _____
3. By Selena got to the platform, the train had left. — _____
4. You can't vote until you are going to be 18. — _____
5. Ben checked the weather during he was getting ready. — _____
6. By the time Helen finished all of her laundry, she was very tired. — _____

1 **as**는 **while**과 같이 '~하는 동안에'라는 의미로 어떤 일이 일어나는 시점에 진행 중인 일에 대해 말할 때 쓴다.

- **As I was surfing the Internet,** I read an interesting article. 인터넷 서핑을 하는 동안에, 흥미로운 기사를 읽었다.
- Bella followed the recipe really carefully **as she was cooking**. Her chicken was perfect.
- Jimmy fell off the bed **as he was sleeping**. He woke up right away.

'~할 때'라는 의미로 동시에 일어나는 두 가지 일에 대해 말할 때도 **as**를 쓴다.

- **As the thief entered the house,** the dog started barking. 도둑이 집에 들어왔을 때, 개가 짖기 시작했다.
- Everyone clapped **as the pianist bowed to the audience**.
- We got excited **as we discussed starting a business together**. We're going to be great partners.

'~함에 따라'라는 의미로 비교적 긴 시간에 걸쳐 동시에 진행되는 두 가지 변화에 대해 말할 때도 **as**를 쓴다.

- **As Stan grew older,** he looked more and more like his father. Stan은 나이가 들어감에 따라, 점점 더 그의 아버지처럼 보였다.
- "You seem happy these days." "I am! I get more excited **as the holidays get closer**."
- **As the seasons changed,** our friendship became stronger.

  as 다음에 미래의 일을 말할 때는 현재 시제를 쓴다. 이때, **will**이나 **am/is/are going to** 등을 쓰지 않는 것에 주의한다.

  - You will see the mall **as you drive** through the next intersection. (as you will drive로 쓸 수 없음)
  - **As you leave** the plane, please remember to take all of your belongings. (As you're going to leave로 쓸 수 없음)

2 **as**는 '~처럼, ~대로'라는 의미로 말할 때도 쓸 수 있다.

- **As I mentioned during our last class,** we will have a test next Friday.
  지난 수업 동안 언급했던 것처럼 다음 주 금요일에 시험을 볼 거예요.
- "Here's your steak, **as you requested**." "Thank you."
- **As we agreed,** the time of the meeting will be changed to 1:30.

as I said 내가 말했던 것처럼, 말했다시피	• "I don't know what to order." "**As I said,** all the food here is good." 내가 말했던 것처럼, 여기 음식은 다 맛있어. • "Are you sure you can give me a ride?" "**As I said** before, it's no trouble."
as you know 너도 알고 있는 것처럼, 알다시피	• **As you know,** wasting water has become a serious issue. 알다시피, 물 낭비는 심각한 문제가 되었다. • **As you know,** life is full of challenges. We should learn to enjoy them.

3 **as**는 '~ 때문에'라는 의미로 이유에 대해 말할 때도 쓸 수 있다. 단, 일상 대화보다는 격식을 갖춰서 말할 때 주로 쓴다.

- **As sales have decreased sharply,** the company plans to advertise more.
  매출이 급격하게 줄었기 때문에, 회사는 광고를 더 많이 하려고 합니다.
- You'll have to wait **as we are still preparing to open our store**.
- Please keep the restroom clean, **as it is used by other customers too**.

  as와 비슷한 의미로 이유에 대해 말할 때 **because**와 **since**도 쓸 수 있다.

  - "Did you find the office building?"
    "No. I couldn't find it **because the roads were too confusing**." 길이 너무 혼란스러웠기 때문에 찾을 수 없었어.
  - **Since you love jazz music,** I'll take you to a jazz club tonight.

P R A C T I C E

A. 그림을 보고 주어진 문장과 **as**를 사용하여 문장을 완성하세요.

he crossed the finish line	~~he was using a hammer~~	she was looking through her bag
she was pouring it	they introduced themselves	

1. He hurt himself _as he was using a hammer_ .
2. She dropped some money on the ground _____ .
3. He raised his arms _____ .
4. She spilled the coffee _____ .
5. They shook hands _____ .

B. 주어진 문장과 **as**를 사용하여 문장을 완성하세요.

gas becomes more expensive	Melissa drank more water	the population grows
~~the sun came out~~	we went up the mountain	

1. _As the sun came out_ , it started to get hot. By the afternoon, the temperature had reached 36°C.
2. People drive less _____ . They use public transportation more.
3. _____ , she noticed that her skin felt smoother.
4. _____ , the city will build more schools and parks.
5. We had great view _____ . From the top, we could see everything.

C. 괄호 안에 주어진 표현들과 **as**를 적절히 배열하여 예시와 같이 문장을 완성하세요.

1. (told you / be late / I / am going to / I) _As I told you, I'm going to be late_ for dinner tonight.
2. (can't park / says / your car / the sign / you) _____ here.
3. (promised / I / bought / my wife / I) _____ a diamond ring.
4. (is giving / mentioned / Sandra / I / on the phone)

   _____ a speech at the science academy.
5. (in the e-mail / explained / I / has / Mr. Jennings)

   _____ the day off tomorrow.

D. 주어진 문장을 보고 괄호 안에 주어진 주어와 **as**를 사용하여 예시와 같이 다시 말해보세요.

1. Nobody answered the door. So I left a note. → (nobody) _As nobody answered the door_ , I left a note.
2. A lot of fruit is grown in this area. That's because it has a warm climate.

   → (this area) _____ , a lot of fruit is grown here.
3. Because the elevator was broken, I had to take the stairs.

   → (the elevator) _____ , I had to take the stairs.
4. Claire asked for help. That's because she didn't understand the instructions.

   → (Claire) _____ , she asked for help.
5. Our products are high quality. That's the reason people trust our brand.

   → (our products) _____ , people trust our brand.

접속사와 절

LESSON 92

Grammar Gateway Intermediate

1   She studies law **so that she can become a lawyer**.

그녀는 변호사가 되기 위해 법학을 공부한다.

'변호사가 되기 위해'라는 의미로 법학을 공부하는 목적에 대해 말하기 위해
so that she can become a lawyer를 썼다.

2 **so that**은 '~하기 위해서'라는 의미로 어떤 일을 하는 목적에 대해 말할 때 쓴다. 이때, **so that** 뒤에 **can/could/will/would** 등의 조동사를 자주 함께 쓴다.

- We rented a car **so that we could travel more comfortably during our trip**.
  여행 중에 더 편하게 이동하기 위해서 차를 빌렸다.
- I woke John up **so that he wouldn't miss his flight**.
- "Can you take my suit to the cleaners **so that it will be ready tonight**?" "No problem."

  so that 다음에 미래의 일을 말할 때 현재 시제도 쓸 수 있다.

- Keep your passport in a safe place **so that you don't lose it**.
  여권을 잃어버리지 않기 위해서 안전한 장소에 보관하세요. (= so that you won't lose it)
- Let's all introduce ourselves **so that everyone knows each other's names**.
  모두가 서로의 이름을 알기 위해서 자기소개를 합시다. (= so that everyone will know each other's names)

  일상 대화에서는 **that**을 자주 생략하고 쓴다.

- "Should we meet **so (that) we can go to the exhibit together**?" 전시회에 같이 가기 위해서 만날까? "OK."
- It's getting late. Let's call Mom and Dad **so (that) they don't worry about us**.

3 **so that**과 비슷한 의미로 목적에 대해 말할 때 **to + 동사원형** 또는 **for + 명사/-ing**도 쓸 수 있다.

- "We need to turn here **to go** to the beach!" "Are you sure? I think it's the next street." (= so that we can go)
- Mr. Barry will be in Vancouver tomorrow **for a seminar**. (= so that he can attend a seminar)
- I bought a pan **for frying**. It's big but not heavy.

  so that/to/for의 다음과 같은 형태 차이에 주의한다.

  so that + 주어 + 동사 • Can we use that closet **so that we can store** our luggage?
  우리 짐을 보관하기 위해 저 벽장을 써도 될까?

  to + 동사원형 • Can we use that closet **to store** our luggage?

  for + 명사/-ing • Can we use that closet **for (storing)** our luggage?

4 **so that**과 **so + 형용사/부사 + that**의 의미 차이에 주의한다. **so + 형용사/부사 + that**은 '매우 ~해서 …하다'라는 의미이다.

so that	**so + 형용사/부사 + that**
• Andy stayed up all night **so that** he could read the book. (책을 읽기 위해서)	• The book was **so long that** Andy had to stay up all night to read it. (책이 매우 길어서 밤을 새웠음)
• I wrapped the baby in a blanket **so that** she wouldn't feel cold. (추워하지 않게 하기 위해서)	• This package is **so heavy that** I can't carry it. (소포가 매우 무거워서 옮길 수 없음)
• Anthony has been practicing the song **so that** he will be able to sing it at Jim's wedding.	• The speaker spoke **so quietly that** few people could hear her.
	so + 형용사/부사 + that에 대한 더 자세한 내용은 Lesson 73 참고

P R A C T I C E

A. 사람들의 새해 계획을 보고 괄호 안에 주어진 조동사와 **so that**을 함께 사용하여 예시와 같이 문장을 완성하세요. 필요한 경우 부정문으로 쓰세요.

1	I plan to visit my family more often. I want to spend more time with them.	4	I'm going to work hard. I hope to get a promotion.
2	I'm going to exercise every day. I don't want to gain any more weight.	5	I plan to get a bigger apartment. I want to have more space for my children.
3	I plan to study Spanish. I want to speak it fluently.	6	I'm going to get up early. I don't want to be late for school again.

1. (can) He plans to visit his family more often *so that he can spend more time with them* .
2. (will) She is going to exercise every day _____ .
3. (can) She plans to study Spanish _____ .
4. (will) He is going to work hard _____ .
5. (can) She plans to get a bigger apartment _____ .
6. (will) He is going to get up early _____ .

B. 주어진 표현과 **so that/to/for**를 함께 사용하여 문장을 완성하세요.

drinks	I won't forget	make some extra money	running
send Mom's birthday card	~~we could go camping~~		your hands don't get cold

1. "Did you buy a tent *so that we could go camping* ?" "Yes, I'm so excited for our trip."
2. Marcia got a part-time job _____ . Her rent has increased.
3. These shoes are _____ . I wear them to jog every morning.
4. Wear your gloves today _____ .
5. "Do you want to go out _____ tonight at the bar?"
   "Sorry, but I have to wake up early tomorrow."
6. I need to go to the post office _____ .
7. I'm going to take notes _____ the important parts of the lecture.

C. 괄호 안에 주어진 표현들을 적절히 배열하여 문장을 완성하세요.
1. (could / so / help / that / I) I became a doctor *so that I could help* sick people.
2. (loud / I / couldn't / that / so / concentrate)
   The music was _____ on my homework.
3. (get / can / so / he / that)
   Alex eats an orange every morning _____ some vitamin C.
4. (bright / that / so / need / I)
   It's _____ sunglasses.
5. (that / skate / so / couldn't / we / thin)
   The ice on the lake was _____ .
6. (so / be / that / we / won't)
   We should leave soon _____ stuck in traffic.

LESSON
93

Grammar Gateway Intermediate

1   **Although the food was spicy,** she liked it.
음식이 매웠지만, 그녀는 좋아했다.

It's spicy, but I like it.

'음식이 매웠지만'이라는 의미로 말하기 위해 Although the food was spicy를 썼다.

2   **although**는 '~하지만, ~함에도 불구하고'라는 의미로 말할 때 쓴다.

- **Although the bus was crowded,** we were able to get on it. 버스가 붐볐지만, 탈 수 있었다.
- Janice enjoys living overseas, **although she sometimes misses her family.**
  때때로 가족이 그립지만, Janice는 해외에 사는 것을 즐긴다.
- **Although I went to bed early last night,** I woke up late this morning.
- The documentary was good, **although it was a bit too long.**

3   **although**와 같은 의미로 **though**도 쓸 수 있다.

- **Though the resort is expensive,** it isn't very nice. (= Although the resort is expensive)
- I love the style of that dress **though I don't like the color.** (= although I don't like the color)
- **Though I didn't win a prize,** I think the contest was a good experience.

though는 '그렇지만, 하지만'이라는 의미로 문장 맨 뒤에도 쓸 수 있다.

- "How was the exam?" "It was really hard. I think I passed, **though.**" 그렇지만 합격한 것 같아.
- "Did you go to the Metropolitan Museum of Art?" "Yes. It wasn't open, **though.**"

4   **although/though**보다 더 강한 의미로 말할 때 **even though**를 쓸 수 있다.

- **Even though I want to stay longer,** I can't. I have an appointment. 더 오래 있고 싶지만, 그럴 수 없다.
- I had fun at the party **even though I didn't know anyone there.**
- **Even though Johnny is a chef,** he doesn't cook at home.

5   **although**와 비슷한 의미로 **in spite of** 또는 **despite**도 쓸 수 있다. **in spite of**와 **despite** 뒤에는 명사 또는 **-ing**를 쓴다.

- Zoe arrived at work on time **in spite of the traffic jam.** (= although there was traffic jam)
- **Despite being** a terrible singer, Jillian sang for Tim on his birthday. (= Although she is a terrible singer)
- **In spite of playing** for hours, the children weren't tired.
- The mayor did not try to explain **despite all of the rumors.**

although/in spite of/despite의 다음과 같은 형태 차이에 주의한다.

although + 주어 + 동사	• **Although Cassie had** a cold, she went to school. Cassie는 감기에 걸렸지만, 학교에 갔다.
in spite of/despite + 명사/-ing	• **In spite of/Despite (having) a cold,** Cassie went to school. 감기에도 불구하고 학교에 갔다.

in spite of나 **despite** 뒤에 **the fact (that)** + 주어 + 동사도 쓸 수 있다.

- **In spite of the fact (that) the weather was** bad, we went camping. 날씨가 나빴음에도 불구하고 우리는 캠핑을 갔다.
- Karen's necklace looks great **despite the fact (that) it didn't cost** much.

PRACTICE

A. 두 문장을 적절히 연결하여 예시와 같이 문장을 완성하세요. **although**를 함께 쓰세요.

1. Carla lives in the United States. •   • It works perfectly.
2. My computer is old. •   • He plays golf really well.
3. I washed my sneakers twice. •   • They're still very active.
4. I didn't put much salt on the food. •   • The smell didn't disappear.
5. Greg is just a beginner. •   • Sam said it was too salty.
6. My grandparents are over 70 years old. •   • She has never been to Washington, DC.

1. *Although Carla lives in the United States, she has never been to Washington, DC* .
2. _____ .
3. _____ .
4. _____ .
5. _____ .
6. _____ .

B. 주어진 표현들을 사용하여 예시와 같이 문장을 완성하세요.

failing the test	I've been on a diet for a month
she isn't famous	Terry practiced his speech many times
the flight's delayed departure	~~Tom is interested in winter sports~~

1. (though) *Though Tom is interested in winter sports* , he's never learned to ski.
2. (in spite of) Some passengers still missed the plane _____ .
3. (although) _____ , he forgot what he was going to say.
4. (despite) I feel good _____ . I tried my best.
5. (even though) The singer's song is quite popular _____ .
6. (in spite of the fact that) _____ , I haven't lost any weight.

C. 다음은 Nancy가 식당 매니저에게 보낸 이메일입니다. **although/though/in spite of**를 써넣으세요.

Subject	Unhappy with my recent visit
To	customerservice@therosegarden.com
From	nancy@gomail.com

✉ Dear Manager,

I recently went to your restaurant with a friend for dinner.

1. *In spite of* _____ having a reservation for 6:30, we had to wait 30 minutes to be seated.
2. Also, we were served the chicken pasta, even _____ we had ordered the seafood pasta.
3. _____ the fact that the waiter had made a mistake, he did not apologize.
4. So _____ the food was very good, we were very unhappy with the service.

Since the service was so bad, we were expecting a discount.

5. We had to pay our entire bill, _____ .
6. We really enjoy your food, but _____ that, we might not return.

You should train your staff better, or you could lose more customers.

Nancy Lewis

정답 **p. 325** / Check-Up Test 16 **p. 264**
본 교재 동영상강의 www.ChampStudy.com

Cleaning his room, he found some money. -ing 구문

1 **Cleaning his room,** he found some money.
방을 청소하는 동안에, 그는 돈을 찾았다.

'방을 청소하는 동안에'라는 의미로 언제 돈을 찾았는지에 대해 말하기 위해
Cleaning his room을 썼다.

2 '～하는 동안에, ～할 때, ～하면서' 등의 의미로 어떤 일이 언제 일어나는지에 대해 말할 때 **-ing**를 쓸 수 있다.

- **Walking to the supermarket,** Rebecca realized she'd forgotten her wallet.
  슈퍼마켓으로 걸어가는 동안에, Rebecca는 지갑을 안 가져온 것을 깨달았다. (= While she was walking to the supermarket)

- **Running to catch the taxi,** I heard someone yell my name.

- **Reaching the top of the mountain,** we could see the whole city.

- John always listens to music **packing his bag in the morning.**
  John은 아침에 가방을 쌀 때 항상 음악을 듣는다. (= when he packs his bag in the morning.)

- I hurt my back **picking up a heavy box.**

- Melanie got a flat tire **driving down the road.**

  이때, **-ing** 앞에 **when**이나 **while** 등을 함께 쓸 수도 있다.

  - **While living** in Malaysia, Pam traveled around Asia a lot.
    말레이시아에 사는 동안 Pam은 아시아를 많이 여행했다.

  - Make sure to wear a mask **when entering** the factory.

3 '～해서, ～ 때문에' 등의 의미로 어떤 일의 원인이나 이유에 대해 말할 때도 **-ing**를 쓸 수 있다.

- **Feeling hungry,** Daniel went to the café to buy a bagel.
  배가 고파서, Daniel은 베이글을 사러 카페에 갔다. (= Because he felt hungry)

- Becky usually comes home late **working as a bartender.**
  바텐더로 일하기 때문에, Becky는 보통 늦게 귀가한다. (= because she works as a bartender)

- **Being retired,** my grandparents have a lot of free time.

- We saved a lot of money **traveling by train.**

- **Being injured,** Ben couldn't play soccer for six months.

4 부정으로 말할 때는 **-ing** 앞에 **not**을 쓴다.

- **Not having** her glasses on, Jane wasn't able to read the road sign.
  안경을 쓰지 않아서, Jane은 도로 표지판을 읽을 수 없었다. (= Because she didn't have her glasses on)

- My house was a mess when my friends arrived. I hadn't cleaned up **not expecting guests.**
  손님을 기대하고 있지 않았기 때문에, 청소를 하지 않았다. (= because I didn't expect guests)

- The directions were very confusing. **Not understanding** them, I asked the teacher to explain.

- Phil went outside with no umbrella **not thinking** it was going to rain.

- **Not knowing** where to stay, we searched the Internet for a hotel recommendation.

PRACTICE

A. 그림을 보고 주어진 표현을 사용하여 예시와 같이 문장을 완성하세요.

> look at himself in the mirror   open the window   put pepper in her soup
> receive the award   ~~shop at the mall~~

1. *Shopping at the mall* _____, she saw her friend Terry.
2. She sneezed _____.
3. _____, he noticed it was raining.
4. _____, she said "thank you."
5. He put on his necktie, _____.

B. 주어진 문장을 보고 -ing를 사용하여 예시와 같이 다시 말해보세요.

1. While she waited for Peter, Lisa checked her text messages.
   → *Waiting for Peter, Lisa checked her text messages* _____.
2. Because Shelly needed to borrow a blouse for an interview, she asked her sister.
   → _____.
3. Because we noticed the smoke from the building, we called 911.
   → _____.
4. When Max ate his burger, he dropped some ketchup on his pants.
   → _____.
5. As I'm married to a pilot, I don't see my husband every day.
   → _____.
6. When I rode my bicycle around the neighborhood, I saw many of my friends.
   → _____.

C. 주어진 표현을 사용하여 문장을 완성하세요. 필요한 경우 not을 함께 쓰세요.

> be old enough   be stuck   feel refreshed after our vacation   own my house
> ~~remember his doctor's appointment~~   ride on the boat   want to argue anymore

1. Bob said goodbye and left suddenly, *remembering his doctor's appointment* _____.
2. I have to pay rent every month, _____.
3. _____, we were ready to go back to work.
4. Chad hung up the phone _____.
5. _____, Laura could smell the sea.
6. I was late for work, _____ in traffic.
7. _____, Mandy wasn't allowed to watch that movie.

1

If Chris is busy, **she'll be** at home.
Chris가 바쁘면, 그녀는 집에 있을 것이다.

If Chris isn't busy, **she'll have** dinner with him.
Chris가 바쁘지 않으면, 그녀는 그와 함께 저녁을 먹을 것이다.

'(그럴 수도 있고 아닐 수도 있지만) 바쁘면', '바쁘지 않으면'이라는 의미로 말하기 위해
If 뒤에 현재 시제 is와 isn't를 썼다.

2 '(그럴 수도 있고 아닐 수도 있지만) ~하면'이라는 의미로 말할 때 **if** 뒤에 현재 시제를 쓴다. 이때, 다음과 같이 쓴다.

If + 주어 + 현재 시제 ~, 주어 + will/can 등 + 동사원형 ··· ~하면 ···할 것이다

- **If you stay** up longer, **you'll be** tired tomorrow. 더 늦게까지 깨어 있으면, 내일 피곤할 것이다.
- **If Maggie doesn't have** time to finish the assignment, **I can help** her.
  Maggie가 과제를 끝낼 시간이 없다면, 내가 도와줄 수 있을 것이다.
- **Jack and Paula might not take** a trip to Italy **if they don't save** enough money.
- "**Can we make** a snowman **if it snows** a lot?" "Yes, of course!"

  if 다음에 미래의 일에 대해 말할지라도 현재 시제를 쓴다. 이때, **will**이나 **am/is/are going to** 등을 쓰지 않는 것에 주의한다.

  - **If you go** near that dog, it might bite you. (If you will go로 쓸 수 없음)
  - Roger's team won't play in the final match **if it doesn't win** the next game. (if it isn't going to win으로 쓸 수 없음)

    조건을 나타내는 문장에서의 미래에 대한 더 자세한 내용은 Lesson 21 참고

3 **if** + 주어 + 현재 시제와 **명령문**을 함께 쓸 수도 있다.

- (전화상에서) **If you want** to speak to customer service, please **press** 2. 고객센터와 통화를 원하시면, 2번을 눌러주세요.
- **Take off** your coat **if you are** hot.
- **If you don't understand** the instructions, **don't hesitate** to ask me.

4 어떤 일이 일어나면 그 결과로 항상 다른 일이 일어난다고 말할 때는 다음과 같이 쓴다.

If + 주어 + 현재 시제 ~, 주어 + 현재 시제 ··· ~하면 ···한다

- **If water reaches** 100°C, **it boils**. 물은 100도가 되면 끓는다.
- **If lightning strikes, thunder follows**. That's because light travels faster than sound. 번개가 치면 천둥이 뒤따른다.
- Dan has allergies. **He sneezes if he is** near flowers.
- **Cindy does not have** breakfast **if she wakes up** late.

5 **if ~ not**과 같은 의미로 **unless**를 쓸 수 있다.

- **Unless you come** home soon, I will fall asleep. 집에 빨리 오지 않으면, 나는 잠들 거야. (= If you don't come)
- We might get lost **unless we ask** for directions. 길을 물어보지 않으면, 길을 잃을 거야. (= if we don't ask)
- Staff can't use the conference room **unless they reserve** it.

  unless는 '~하지 않는다면'이라는 의미이다. 따라서 뒤에 **not**을 쓰지 않는 것에 주의한다.

  - **Unless that shirt is** on sale, I **won't buy** it. (Unless that shirt isn't on sale로 쓸 수 없음)
  - I won't date you **unless you shave** that beard. (unless you don't shave that beard로 쓸 수 없음)

PRACTICE

A. 주어진 표현들과 **if**를 사용하여 문장을 완성하세요. 필요한 경우 동사를 적절한 형태로 바꾸어 쓰세요.

~~be not too cloudy~~	be nothing interesting on TV	get a scholarship
hurry to the theater	not reply	not pay the electricity bill

1. (the sky) The full moon will be visible tonight _if the sky isn't too cloudy_____.
2. (he) I really need Don to answer my e-mail. I'll call him _____ soon.
3. (Emma) _____, she can quit her part-time job.
4. (there) I might just go to sleep _____.
5. (I) The lights might go out _____ by next week.
6. (we) _____, we can see the movie from the beginning.

B. Tina는 장래에 하고 싶은 일들이 많습니다. 예시와 같이 문장을 완성하세요.

buy a sports car ← get my driver's license 1 →   3 → move to France 4 → learn to paint →
                                                                              have an exhibit

open a children's hospital ← become a doctor 2 ↙   5 ↙ graduate college → work at the UN

TINA

1. _If I get my driver's license, I'll buy a sports car_____.
2. _____.
3. _____.
4. _____.
5. _____.

C. 괄호 안에 주어진 표현들을 적절한 형태로 사용하여 문장을 완성하세요. 필요한 경우 **will**을 함께 쓰세요.

1. (not be, not take) If the traffic _isn't_____ heavy, it _____ long to get to the mall.
2. (send, travel) I love postcards. _____ me one if you _____ somewhere this summer.
3. (open, eat) You're such a good cook! If you _____ a restaurant, I _____ there every day.
4. (lock, leave) Please _____ the door if you _____ before I come back.
5. (mix, not get) If you _____ red and blue, you _____ green. The result would be purple.
6. (not order, not be) If we _____ these swimsuits today, they _____ here until next week.
7. (take, hurt) _____ a break from the computer if your eyes _____.
8. (pour, sink) If you _____ water into oil, the water _____.

D. 주어진 문장을 보고 **unless**를 사용하여 예시와 같이 다시 말해보세요.

1. We can't go into the museum if we don't pay a fee.
   → _We can't go into the museum unless we pay a fee_____.
2. If Sarah doesn't have an important appointment, she doesn't wear makeup.
   → _____.
3. You can't borrow new DVDs if you don't return the old ones first.
   → _____.
4. If Rick doesn't call his mom back, she will keep worrying.
   → _____.
5. If you're not interested, I'm not going to ask you again.
   → _____.

If she felt well, she'd visit her friend. if (2) if + 주어 + 과거 시제

1 She wants to visit her friend, but she doesn't feel well.

If she felt well, **she'd visit** her friend.
만약 그녀의 몸 상태가 좋다면, 친구를 방문할 것이다.

'(실제로는 아니지만) 만약 몸 상태가 좋다면'이라는 의미로 현재 상황을 반대로 가정하여 말하기
위해 If 뒤에 과거 시제 **felt**를 썼다.

2 '(실제로는 아니지만) 만약 ~한다면'이라는 의미로 현재 상황을 반대로 가정하여 말할 때 **if** 뒤에 **과거 시제**를 쓴다. 이때, 다음과 같이 쓴다.

> **If + 주어 + 과거 시제 ~, 주어 + would/could 등 + 동사원형** ··· 만약 ~한다면 ···할 것이다

- Laura is such a nice person. **If you knew** Laura, **you would like** her.
  (실제로는 아니지만) 만약 네가 Laura를 안다면, 그녀를 좋아할 거야.

- **If Bob worked** in a team, **he wouldn't be** so stressed. He has to do everything by himself.
  (실제로는 아니지만) 만약 Bob이 팀에서 일한다면 이렇게 스트레스 받지 않을 것이다.

- **Charlotte would enjoy** African music **if she listened** to it.

- I never have time for the gym. **I would exercise** every day **if I wasn't** so busy.

  이때, **if** 뒤에 현재 시제를 쓰지 않고 과거 시제를 쓴다. **if + 주어 + 과거 시제**는 과거의 의미가 아닌 것에 주의한다.

  - **If I understood** Chinese, I could translate this document for you.
    만약 내가 중국어를 이해한다면, 이 문서를 번역해 줄 수 있을 것이다. (If I understand로 쓸 수 없음)

  - Fiona is a vegetarian. We would take her to a steakhouse **if she ate** meat.
    만약 그녀가 고기를 먹는다면, 우리는 그녀를 스테이크 식당에 데려갈 거예요. (if she eats로 쓸 수 없음)

  if 뒤에 **be**동사를 쓰는 경우에는 주어가 I/he/she/it 등일지라도 **were**를 쓴다. 단, 일상 대화에서는 **was**를 쓸 수도 있다.

  - **If I were/was** an actress, I'd be rich and famous. 만약 내가 여배우라면, 부유하고 유명할 것이다.

  - We could go to the park **if the weather weren't/wasn't** rainy.

3 앞으로 일어날 가능성이 매우 적은 일이 일어날 것을 가정하여 말할 때도 **if** 뒤에 과거 시제를 쓸 수 있다.

- "**If you had** only one more day to live, how **would you spend** it?" "I'd go skydiving."
  (가능성이 매우 적지만) 단 하루만 살 수 있다면, 어떻게 보낼 것인가요?

- **If I won** the lottery, **I wouldn't work** anymore. (가능성이 매우 적지만) 복권에 당첨된다면, 더 이상 일하지 않을 것이다.

- What would you do **if there were/was** a fire in the building?

- I would climb up a tree **if I met** a wolf in the forest.

4 **if + 주어 + 과거 시제**와 **if + 주어 + 현재 시제**는 다음과 같은 의미 차이가 있다.

현재 상황을 반대로 가정하거나, 일어날 가능성이 매우 적은 일이 일어나는 것을 가정하여 말할 때는 **if** 뒤에 **과거 시제**를 쓴다.	실제로 일어날 가능성이 있는 일에 대해 말할 때는 **if** 뒤에 **현재 시제**를 쓴다.
- **If my boyfriend drove**, we would go on road trips. (실제로는 운전을 하지 않음)	- **If my boyfriend drives**, we can go on road trips. (실제로 운전을 할 가능성이 있음)
- I would end poverty in our country **if I became** president. (실제로는 대통령이 될 가능성이 매우 적음)	- I'll hire more staff **if I become** manager. (실제로 관리자가 될 수도 있음)

PRACTICE

A. if를 사용하여 예시와 같이 문장을 완성하세요.

1. Howard doesn't have hair. _If he had hair_____, he'd look younger.
2. You live near me. I couldn't visit you often _____.
3. I'm so shy. I'd ask Sally on a date _____.
4. I don't draw well. _____, I could draw your portrait.
5. My brother owns a garden. _____, he wouldn't grow all these vegetables.
6. Sharon doesn't have glasses. She could read the menu _____.

B. 주어진 문장을 보고 예시와 같이 문장을 완성하세요.

1. The company doesn't sell a lot of products because it doesn't advertise.
   → If _the company advertised_____, _it would sell a lot of products_____.
2. Daniel doesn't read many books because he plays so many video games.
   → _____ if _____.
3. Eric will not attend the wedding because he's on a business trip.
   → If _____, _____.
4. We have to call the repairman because our heater doesn't turn on.
   → If _____, _____.
5. Cindy won't go dancing tonight because she doesn't have a partner.
   → _____ if _____.

C. 괄호 안에 주어진 표현들을 적절한 형태로 사용하여 문장을 완성하세요. 필요한 경우 will 또는 would를 함께 쓰세요.

1. (pay, do) Jen doesn't focus in class. If she _paid_____ attention, she _____ better on her exam.
2. (take, not be) If you _____ a taxi to the airport right now, you _____ late for your flight.
3. (arrive, mail) _____ this package _____ tomorrow if I _____ it today?
4. (not ask, not be) I really need your help on my homework. I _____ if it _____ difficult.
5. (have, go) It's too bad you're not going camping. We _____ more fun if you _____ with us.
6. (get, give) "Could you call me later?"
   "I'll try. If I _____ home before midnight, I _____ you a call."

D. 괄호 안에 주어진 동사들을 적절한 형태로 사용하여 Sara와 James의 대화를 완성하세요. 필요한 경우 will 또는 would 를 함께 쓰세요.

SARA: Thanks for coming, James. Where's Linda? Isn't she coming?
JAMES: She's sick. 1. If she _felt_____ well, she _____ here. (feel, be)
SARA: Oh. I hope she gets better soon. It's too bad she can't eat with us.
JAMES: I know.
   2. She _____ your food if she _____ it. (love, taste)
SARA: Thanks. 3. I think I _____ see her tomorrow if I _____ time. (go, have)
JAMES: Good idea. 4. She'll appreciate it if you _____ her. (visit)
SARA: Anyway, I'm glad you came. 5. If you _____ here,
   I _____ very disappointed. (not be, feel)

SARA

JAMES

If she had had a camera, she would've taken a photo. if (3) if + 주어 + 과거완료 시제

1 She wanted to take a photo, but she didn't have a camera.

If she had had a camera, **she would've taken** a photo.
그녀가 카메라를 가지고 있다면, 사진을 찍었을 것이다.

어제

'(실제로는 아니었지만) 만약 카메라를 가지고 있다면'이라는 의미로 과거의 상황을 반대로 가정하여 말하기 위해 If 뒤에 과거완료 시제 had had를 썼다.

2 '(실제로는 아니었지만) 만약 ~했다면'이라는 의미로 과거의 상황을 반대로 가정하여 말할 때 if 뒤에 **과거완료 시제**를 쓴다. 이때, 다음과 같이 쓴다.

> **If + 주어 + had + 과거분사 ~, 주어 + would/could 등 + have + 과거분사** ··· 만약 ~했다면 ···했을 것이다

- **If Anna had worn** a coat, **she would have been** warm. (실제로는 아니었지만) 만약 Anna가 외투를 입었다면, 따뜻했을 것이다.
- **If I hadn't attended** that seminar, **I couldn't have met** professor Jones.
  (실제로는 아니었지만) 만약 그 세미나에 참석하지 않았다면, Jones 교수님을 만날 수 없었을 거야.
- **You would have enjoyed** the show **if you had gone** with me.
- **Luke might have paid** less for the stereo **if he had ordered** it online.

  이때, **if** 뒤에 과거 시제를 쓰지 않고 과거완료 시제를 쓰는 것에 주의한다.
  - **If Sandra had told** me she had plans, I would have understood. (If Sandra told me로 쓸 수 없음)
  - I would have missed the meeting **if Jamie hadn't reminded** me about it. (if Jamie didn't remind로 쓸 수 없음)

3 **if** + 주어 + 과거완료 시제와 **if** + 주어 + 과거 시제는 다음과 같은 의미 차이가 있다.

과거의 상황을 반대로 가정하여 말할 때는 **if** 뒤에 **과거완료 시제**를 쓴다.	현재의 상황을 반대로 가정하거나, 일어날 가능성이 매우 적은 일이 일어나는 것을 가정하여 말할 때는 **if** 뒤에 **과거 시제**를 쓴다.
- I had roommates when I was in college. **If I had lived** alone, I would have been very lonely. (실제로는 대학에 다닐 때 혼자 살지 않았음)	- **If I lived** alone, I'd be very lonely. I'm glad I have roommates. (실제로는 현재 혼자 살지 않음)
- The car appeared suddenly! **If Peter hadn't stopped** so quickly, he could have hit it. (실제로는 과거에 빨리 차를 멈추었음)	- **If we bought our own airplane**, we could travel around the world. (실제로는 현재 비행기를 사지 않음)

4 과거의 상황을 반대로 가정해보면 현재의 결과가 다를 것이라고 말할 때도 **if** 뒤에 과거완료 시제를 쓴다. 이때, 다음과 같이 쓴다.

> **If + 주어 + had + 과거분사 ~, 주어 + would/could 등 + 동사원형** ··· (과거에) 만약 ~했다면 (지금) ···할 것이다

- **If Valerie had saved** John's phone number, **she could call** him.
  (과거에) Valerie가 John의 전화번호를 저장했다면, (지금) 전화할 수 있을 거야.
- I'm angry that Tim took my bike. **If he had asked** me first, **I wouldn't feel** upset.
- **We would be** at the gallery by now **if we had left** before rush hour.

  would/could 등의 뒤에 **have** + 과거분사를 썼을 때와는 다음과 같은 의미 차이가 있다.
  - **If I had cleaned** my room this morning, **it wouldn't look** so messy now.
    (과거에) 만약 방 청소를 했다면 (지금) 이렇게 지저분해 보이지 않을 거야.

    If I had cleaned my room this morning, **it would have looked** clean when I came home from work.
    (과거에) 만약 방 청소를 했다면 (과거에) 내가 퇴근해서 집에 왔을 때 방이 깨끗했을 거야.

PRACTICE

A. if를 사용하여 예시와 같이 문장을 완성하세요.

1. Sally didn't review the article. *If Sally had reviewed the article*_____, she could've fixed the errors.

2. Ben studied business in college. He would have studied math _____.

3. We didn't work hard. _____, we could have finished the project by now.

4. Tom scored three goals. _____, we would have lost.

5. I had a bad dream. I wouldn't have woken up at night _____.

6. We didn't return the book on time. _____, we could've avoided the late fee.

B. 문장을 보고 예시와 같이 문장을 완성하세요.

1. I was late for work because I didn't hear the alarm.
   → *If I had heard the alarm, I wouldn't have been late for work*_____.

2. Lucy didn't practice enough, so she didn't do well in her speech.
   → _____.

3. Greg drank too much wine, so he got a headache.
   → _____.

4. Mike and Jenny fell because they ran on the icy sidewalk.
   → _____.

5. We didn't know about Claire's birthday, so we didn't send her a present.
   → _____.

6. I didn't complete my report because my computer broke.
   → _____.

C. 괄호 안에 주어진 표현들을 적절한 형태로 사용하여 문장을 완성하세요. 필요한 경우 would를 함께 쓰세요.

1. (ask, give) We gave our sofa to Jill. If you *had asked* about it earlier, we _____ it to you.

2. (lock, not get) If Max _____ his office, his wallet _____ stolen.

3. (know, tell) "Who's that girl?" "I don't know. If I _____ her name, I _____ you."

4. (not be, come) I'm sorry I missed your graduation. If I _____ out of town, I _____.

5. (have, buy) I don't like the color. If the store _____ these shoes in black, _____ them.

6. (not use, be) I _____ that cup if I _____ you. It looks dirty.

D. Jay가 한 말을 보고 예시와 같이 문장을 완성하세요.

JAY

1. I can't listen to music because I gave my earphones to Joe.
2. I didn't go to the bank, so I don't have cash.
3. I can cook Spanish food well because I grew up in Spain.
4. I don't feel hungry because I had a big lunch.
5. I can't get in my car because I forgot my keys.

1. If *he hadn't given his earphones to Joe, he could listen to music*_____.
2. If _____.
3. If _____.
4. If _____.
5. If _____.

98
LESSON

if와 가정법

Grammar Gateway Intermediate

LESSON 99

I wish I had blue eyes like Caroline. I wish

1 I wish + 주어 + 과거 시제: (사실 지금은 그렇지 않지만) ~하면 좋을 텐데

상황이 현재와 다르기를 바란다고 말할 때 **I wish + 주어 + 과거 시제**를 쓴다.

- **I wish I had** blue eyes like Caroline. I think her eyes are really pretty. Caroline처럼 파란 눈을 가지고 있다면 좋을 텐데.
- "**I wish Steve wasn't** so angry with me." Steve가 내게 화난게 아니면 좋을 텐데. "Don't worry. Just give him some time."
- I like these suits, but they're too expensive. **I wish they didn't cost** so much.
- **I wish we knew** the answer to this math question. It's so hard.

   이때, **I wish** 뒤에 **be동사**를 쓰는 경우에는 주어가 **I/he/she/it** 등일지라도 **were**를 쓴다. 단, 일상 대화에서는 **was**를 쓸 수도 있다.
   - I'm too lazy. **I wish I were/was** more active. 좀 더 활동적이라면 좋을 텐데.
   - **I wish my interview weren't/wasn't** tomorrow. I'm not ready for it.

2 I wish + 주어 + 과거완료 시제: (사실 과거에 그렇지 않았지만) ~했다면 좋았을 텐데

상황이 과거와 달랐기를 바란다고 말할 때는 **I wish + 주어 + 과거완료 시제**를 쓴다.

- **I wish I had gone** on the trip with my friends last weekend. They said they had a lot of fun.
  지난 주말에 친구들과 같이 여행을 갔다면 좋았을 텐데.
- I think this road takes longer. **I wish I had taken** the other road.
  다른 길을 택했다면 좋았을 텐데.
- "There's still so much to do!" "I know. **I wish we had started** earlier."
- **I wish you had come** to class today. We had an excellent guest speaker.

   I wish + 주어 + 과거 시제와는 다음과 같은 의미 차이가 있다.
   - It was raining when I got off the bus. **I wish I had had** an umbrella! (실제로는 과거에 우산을 가지고 있지 않았음)
     It's raining! **I wish I had an umbrella** right now! (실제로는 현재 우산을 가지고 있지 않음)

3 I hope 역시 어떤 일이 일어나기를 바란다고 말할 때 쓴다. 단, I wish와 I hope는 다음과 같은 차이가 있다.

I wish는 사실이 아니거나 일어날 가능성이 거의 없는 일이 일어나기를 바란다고 말할 때 쓴다.	**I hope**는 일어날 가능성이 있는 일이 일어나기를 바란다고 말할 때 쓴다.
• **I wish** she liked my gift. I shouldn't have picked it myself. (실제로는 선물을 좋아하지 않음)	• **I hope** she likes my gift. I picked it myself. (선물을 좋아할 가능성이 있음)
• **I wish** we had seen Andy when we were in LA. But we ran out of time. (실제로는 Andy를 보지 못했음)	• **I hope** we will see Andy when we go to LA. Let's call him when we arrive. (Andy를 볼 가능성이 있음)
• **I wish** I played the violin. It sounds so beautiful.	• **I hope** I win. I prepared a lot for this competition.

4 If only

상황이 현재 또는 과거와 다르기를 바란다고 말할 때 **If only**도 쓸 수 있다. **If only**는 **I wish**보다 더 강한 바람을 나타낸다.

- Jennifer could show me how to use this program. **If only she were** here. (실제로는 지금 Jennifer가 여기에 없음)
- My favorite band is performing at 7 p.m. **If only I didn't** have to work late tonight.

- **If only I had done** laundry yesterday! I have nothing to wear today. (실제로는 어제 빨래를 하지 않았음)
- College wasn't fun for me. **If only I had chosen** a different major.

PRACTICE

A. 그림을 보고 주어진 문장과 I wish를 사용하여 예시와 같이 문장을 완성하세요. 필요한 경우 부정문으로 쓰세요.

he is so busy	I am alone	I am stronger
I can ski like him	~~my kids eat more vegetables~~	we have more space

1. *I wish my kids ate more* *vegetables* .

2. _____ .

3. _____ .

4. _____ .

5. _____ .

6. _____ .

B. 괄호 안에 주어진 동사를 과거 시제 또는 과거완료 시제로 사용하여 문장을 완성하세요.

1. (not order) I wish I *hadn't ordered* the fish at the restaurant. It wasn't good.
2. (visit) I rarely see my aunt. I wish she _____ us more often.
3. (go) Strawberries were sold out at the market. I wish we _____ earlier.
4. (live) I wish I _____ near the ocean. I would go to the beach every day.
5. (not be) I wish this café _____ so loud. I can't have a conversation here.
6. (not read) I wish I _____ the book before I saw the movie. I already knew the ending.

C. I wish 또는 I hope를 써넣으세요.

1. A: *I hope* you'll write me often while you're overseas.
   B: Don't worry. I will.

2. A: Thanks for the cake. It looks delicious.
   B: _____ you enjoy it.

3. A: _____ my husband didn't snore.
   B: I understand. My husband snores too.

4. A: The dry cleaner closes at 5 p.m.
   B: _____ you had told me sooner. It's 5:30 now.

5. A: I hear you're going to take an art class.
   B: Yes. _____ it's interesting.

6. A: _____ I had worn a suit.
   B: I know. It seemed like a formal event.

D. If only를 사용하여 예시와 같이 문장을 완성하세요.

1. Jill can't go to the bar with us because she is not old enough. *If only she was/were old enough* .
2. Andrew wasn't nice to Judy, and now she's crying. _____ .
3. I left the cookies in the oven too long and they burned. _____ .
4. Mike is so scared that he can't go on the roller coaster. _____ .
5. Sandra is mad at us because we didn't visit her in the hospital. _____ .
6. I have a stomachache so I can't go to my yoga class tonight. _____ .

She met a man **who had a beard.** 관계대명사 (1) 주격 관계대명사 who/which/that

1 She met a man. He had a beard.

She met a man **who had a beard**.
그녀는 턱수염이 있는 남자를 만났다.

'턱수염이 있는'이라는 의미로 a man이 어떤 사람인지 설명하기 위해 a man 뒤에 관계대명사 who를 썼다.

2 말하고 있는 대상이 어떤 사람 또는 사물인지 설명할 때 명사 뒤에 관계대명사 who/which/that을 쓸 수 있다.

	명사	who/which/that	
Do you know	the person	who didn't sign this form?	(이 서류에 서명하지 않은 사람)
I'm looking forward to	the picnic	which will be on June 5th.	(6월 5일에 있을 소풍)
	The dancers	that aren't performing right now	can take pictures with you.
	The flight	which goes to Madrid	departs from Gate 6.

who는 사람, which는 사물에 대해 설명할 때 쓴다. that은 사람과 사물에 모두 쓸 수 있다.

- Gandhi is **a person who/that fought for peace in India.** 간디는 인도의 평화를 위해 싸운 사람이다.
- "Is that **the road which/that leads to Paradise Resort?**" "Yes, it is."

3 관계대명사 who/which/that은 뒤에 오는 동사의 주어로 쓸 수 있다.

Ben knows a girl. She is from France.
주어 동사

Ben knows a girl **who** is from France. Ben은 프랑스 출신의 소녀를 안다.

	명사	who/which/that	
Ms. Walker is	the nurse	who took care of my grandmother.	(동사 took의 주어로 who를 썼음)
I prefer	desserts	which aren't too sweet.	(동사 aren't의 주어로 which를 썼음)
	The guest	that hasn't checked in yet	is Mr. Thompson.
	The mail	which must be sent today	is on your desk.

이때, **who/which/that**이 설명하는 명사가 단수명사 또는 셀 수 없는 명사이면 **who/which/that** 뒤에 단수동사를 쓰고, 복수명사이면 복수동사를 쓴다.

- **A secretary who doesn't speak** Japanese won't be very helpful. We do a lot of business in Japan.
  (who가 설명하는 명사 a secretary가 단수이므로 단수동사 doesn't speak을 썼음)
- Are there any **restaurants that are** open on Thanksgiving Day?
  (that이 설명하는 명사 restaurants가 복수이므로 복수동사 are를 썼음)
- That advertisement had a lot of **information which wasn't** correct.

4 who/which/that을 주어로 쓸 때 뒤에 **he/it** 등의 다른 주어를 함께 쓰지 않는 것에 주의한다.
- **The boy who is riding** a bicycle is my cousin. (The boy who he is로 쓸 수 없음)
- I see **a sign which says** "Chicago 21 miles." We are getting close. (a sign which it says로 쓸 수 없음)
- "Were there **any items that were** damaged during your move?" "Luckily, no."

PRACTICE

A. 그림을 보고 who 또는 which를 사용하여 예시와 같이 문장을 완성하세요.

> I don't like roller coasters. — MOLLY
> My car might not get fixed. — ALAN
> I own two dogs. — HARRIET
> I bought some shoes. They cost $500. — PAULA
> This is my brother. He was born in 1992. — BOB

1. Harriet is a woman _who owns two dogs_____.
2. Paula bought some shoes _____.
3. Bob has a brother _____.
4. Molly is a girl _____.
5. Alan has a car _____.

B. 괄호 안에 주어진 동사와 who 또는 which를 사용하여 문장을 완성하세요. 현재 시제로 쓰세요.

1. (grow) Plants _which grow_____ in the desert don't need much water.
2. (not want) Visitors _____ beer can have wine or soda.
3. (play) I'm looking for someone _____ badminton because I need a partner.
4. (be) Regina writes poems _____ difficult to understand.
5. (go) The subway line _____ to the city center is the blue line.
6. (not lie) Ted is a person _____. He always tells the truth.
7. (not have) The rings _____ a sale tag are regular price.
8. (understand) Our team needs a new coach _____ soccer better.

C. that을 사용하여 주어진 두 문장을 한 문장으로 바꾸어 쓰세요. 2~4번은 1번 예시와 같이, 6~8번은 5번 예시와 같이 쓰세요.

1. Mr. White is the mailman. He delivers our mail.
   → Mr. White _is the mailman that delivers our mail_____.
2. I have a leather bag. It doesn't get dirty easily.
   → I _____.
3. This is the music album. It has sold over one million copies.
   → This _____.
4. The clerk brought Samantha a shirt. It wasn't her size.
   → The clerk _____.
5. The artist is famous. He created this painting.
   → The artist _that created this painting is famous_____.
6. The room is on the top floor. It provides the best view.
   → The room _____.
7. The actress has only been in two movies. She won the big award.
   → The actress _____.
8. Our friends invited us to dinner on Friday. They are chefs.
   → Our friends _____.

관계절

LESSON
100

Grammar Gateway Intermediate

He is the man **who she saw in the newspaper.** 관계대명사 (2) 목적격 관계대명사 who/which/that

1 관계대명사 **who/which/that**은 뒤에 오는 동사의 목적어로도 쓸 수 있다. 이때, **who/which/that**을 생략할 수 있다.

> He is the man. She saw <u>him</u> in the newspaper.
> 　　　　　　　　동사　목적어
>
> He is the man **(who)** <u>she saw</u> in the newspaper.
> 그는 그녀가 신문에서 본 남자이다.

	명사	who/which/that	
• Is there	anyone	**(who) I can help**?	(동사 help의 목적어로 who를 썼음)
• Summer is	the season	**(which) Elise likes best.**	(동사 likes의 목적어로 which를 썼음)
•	The letters	**(that) you wrote**	were very long.
•	The person	**(that) Steve has interviewed**	got hired.

단, **who/which/that**을 주어로 쓸 때는 생략할 수 없는 것에 주의한다.

- **People who don't exercise** every day may feel more tired. (People don't exercise ~으로 쓸 수 없음)
- The museum has **a statue which is** more than 500 years old. (a statue is ~으로 쓸 수 없음)

who를 목적어로 쓸 때 **who** 대신 **whom**도 쓸 수 있다. 일상 대화에서는 **who**를 더 자주 쓴다.

- Isn't that **the boy (who/whom) we met at the park earlier**? 쟤는 아까 우리가 공원에서 만났던 소년 아니니?

2 **who(m)/which/that**은 뒤에 오는 전치사의 목적어로도 쓸 수 있다. 이때, **who(m)/which/that**을 생략할 수 있다.

> Ms. Brown is the boss. Paul works for <u>her</u>.
> 　　　　　　　　　　　　전치사 목적어
>
> Ms. Brown is **the boss (who/whom)** <u>Paul works for</u>.
> Brown씨는 Paul이 밑에서 일하는 상사이다.

	명사	who/which/that	
• Science is	a subject	**(which) I'm not interested in.**	(전치사 in의 목적어로 which를 썼음)
• Did you buy	the house	**(that) you looked at?**	(전치사 at의 목적어로 that을 썼음)
•	The travelers	**(that) we rode the train with**	told us funny stories.
•	The man	**(who) Anna has talked about all week**	is a famous poet.

전치사를 관계대명사 앞에 쓸 수도 있다. 이때, **who/that**은 쓸 수 없고 **whom/which**만 쓴다.

- Nora is **the friend with whom I took dance lessons.** (with who 또는 with that으로 쓸 수 없음)
- **The land on which we stand** used to be a golf course. (on that으로 쓸 수 없음)

전치사를 관계대명사 앞에 쓰는 경우, 전치사 뒤의 **whom/which**는 생략할 수 없는 것에 주의한다.

- Ms. Nelson is **the neighbor to whom I gave some of my tomatoes.** (the neighbor to I gave로 쓸 수 없음)
- Everyone must follow the rules of **the society in which they live.** (the society in they live로 쓸 수 없음)

3 **who/which/that**을 목적어로 쓸 때 뒤에 **it/her** 등의 다른 목적어를 함께 쓰지 않는 것에 주의한다.

- **The woman who I voted for** didn't win the election. (The woman who I voted for her로 쓸 수 없음)
- "Do you have **a pen that I can borrow**?" "Sure." (a pen that I can borrow it으로 쓸 수 없음)

PRACTICE

A. 주어진 표현과 that을 사용하여 문장을 완성하세요.

I've ever seen	you might wear	~~my younger brother read~~
she hasn't met before	we attended today	William can cook

1. A book _that my younger brother read_____ recently is *Jungle Jim*. He really enjoyed it.
2. The only dish _____ is spaghetti. He's never made anything else.
3. Tina doesn't go to many parties. She doesn't like talking to people _____.
4. This is a nice dress. Is this the one _____ to the opera?
5. The lecture _____ was very popular. There were no empty seats.
6. This is the best movie _____. I really love the story.

B. 그림을 보고 주어진 표현들을 하나씩 사용하여 예시와 같이 문장을 완성하세요.

~~a box~~	a person	a place		you can get medicine from	you can make beer with
a plant	a tool		+	you can open a wine bottle with	~~you can store valuable things in~~
				you can wash your clothes at	

1 **a safe** 2 **a pharmacist** 3 **barley** 4 **a laundromat** 5 **a corkscrew**

1. A safe is _a box you can store valuable things in_____ . 4. _____ is a laundromat.
2. _____ is a pharmacist. 5. A corkscrew is _____ .
3. Barley is _____ .

C. who 또는 which를 사용하여 예시와 같이 주어진 두 문장을 한 문장으로 바꾸어 쓰세요. 가능한 경우 who 또는 which 를 생략하고 쓰세요.

1. The bowl broke. I dropped it. → The bowl _I dropped broke_____ .
2. These are photos. They were taken last week. → These _____ .
3. Sarah has two sisters. She shares a bedroom with them. → Sarah _____ .
4. Fred's cousins are traveling abroad. They write to him. → Fred's cousins _____ .
5. Mark is a VIP member of the gym. He exercises at it. → Mark _____ .
6. The bus was crowded. Christina got on it. → The bus _____ .

D. 다음 문장을 읽고 틀린 부분이 있으면 바르게 고치세요. 틀린 부분이 없으면 ○로 표시하세요.

1. The boy from who I received this chocolate is Greek.   _from who → from whom_
2. The song you sang at the concert was perfect.   _____
3. The building in I am living was constructed last year.   _____
4. I always love the cookies that Antonio makes them.   _____
5. Taylor High School is the school I go to.   _____
6. Claire is the girl with that I went hunting.   _____
7. I visited a park had the biggest lake in Canada.   _____

Amy is the girl **whose hair is blond.** 관계대명사 (3) whose와 what

1 앞에서 말한 사람 또는 사물의 소유를 나타낼 때 **whose**를 쓸 수 있다. 이때, **whose**는 **his/her/its** 등을 대신하며, 뒤에 명사를 항상 함께 쓴다.

Hi, Amy.

> Amy is the girl. Her hair is blond.
>   소유격 명사
>
> Amy is the girl **whose hair is blond.**
> Amy는 머리가 금발인 여자아이이다.

                            명사   whose + 명사

- Charles owns **a dog**   **whose name is Charlie.** (이름이 Charlie인 개)
- I have **friends**   **whose lockers are messy.** (사물함이 지저분한 친구들)
- **The player**   **whose nose Harry broke** is in the hospital.

2 **whose + 명사**는 뒤에 오는 동사의 주어 또는 목적어로 쓸 수 있다.

- **The author whose novel sold the most this year** is Ian Riley. (동사 sold의 주어로 whose novel을 썼음)
- Is there **any language whose grammar is similar to English**?
- **The woman whose bag I found** thanked me. (동사 found의 목적어로 whose bag을 썼음)
- Switzerland **is a country whose scenery you must see**. It's amazing.

whose + 명사를 뒤에 오는 동사의 주어로 쓰는 경우, **whose** 뒤에 단수명사 또는 셀 수 없는 명사를 쓸 때는 단수동사를 쓰고, 복수명사를 쓸 때는 복수동사를 쓴다.

- I have **a friend whose brother works** at City Hall. (whose 뒤의 명사 brother가 단수이므로 단수동사 works를 썼음)
- **The yoga teacher whose classes are** the most popular is Helen. (whose 뒤의 명사 classes가 복수이므로 복수동사 are를 썼음)
- Fiona lives in **a city whose public transportation is** very convenient. I want to move there.

3 '~하는 것'이라는 의미로 **what**을 쓸 수 있다. 이때, **what**은 **the thing(s) that**과 같은 의미이다.

- I'm enjoying our new project, but **what worries me** is the deadline.
  새 프로젝트를 즐기고 있지만, 나를 걱정하게 하는 것은 마감 기한이다. (= the thing that worries me)
- I can't remember **what I wore yesterday**. I am so forgetful these days!
  어제 입은 것을 기억하지 못한다. (= the things I wore yesterday)
- **What Sam brought** was doughnuts. I was expecting something else.

what은 뒤에 오는 동사의 주어 또는 목적어로 쓸 수 있다.

- **What confused me** about the movie was the ending. Can you explain it? (동사 confused의 주어로 what을 썼음)
- Selena didn't do very well, but **what impressed us** was her effort.
- Did you find **what you needed** at the mall? (동사 needed의 목적어로 what을 썼음)
- "What are the children talking about?" "Oh, they're talking about **what they learned** at school today."

4 관계대명사 **who/which/that**은 주로 명사 뒤에 쓰지만, **what**은 명사 뒤에 쓰지 않는 것에 주의한다.

- **The dinner that you prepared** was delicious. 네가 준비한 저녁은 맛있었다. (명사 The dinner 뒤에 that을 썼음)
  What you prepared was delicious. 네가 준비한 것은 맛있었다. (The dinner what으로 쓸 수 없음)
- "This is **the ring which I got** from Pete." "Wow. It's nice!"
  "This is **what I got** from Pete." "That's a nice ring!"

PRACTICE

A. 다음은 영화 *Space Battle*의 등장인물들입니다. **whose**를 사용하여 예시와 같이 문장을 완성하세요.

 MALACHI - *King*
His dream is to control all of the planets.

 DORN - *Teacher*
His school trained all of the fighters!

 JAKE - *Pilot*
Malachi killed his parents.

 DAN VIVO - *Warrior*
His leg was injured during battle.

 LULU - *Princess*
Malachi attacked her planet.

1. Malachi is _the king_ _whose dream is to control all of the planets_.
2. Dorn is _____ _____.
3. Jake is _____ _____.
4. Dan Vivo is _____ _____.
5. Lulu is _____ _____.

B. 괄호 안에 주어진 표현들과 **whose**를 적절히 배열하여 문장을 완성하세요. 현재 시제로 쓰세요.

1. (score / be / the team) _The team whose score is_ _____ the highest will get a $500 prize.
2. (a garden / look / flowers) Jessica has _____ really pretty.
3. (seeds / have / a vegetable) A pumpkin is _____ many vitamins.
4. (a country / be / oil industry) Saudi Arabia is _____ famous.
5. (not be / a company / employees) _____ satisfied won't succeed.
6. (a store / not cost / furniture) Jim's Home Design is _____ a lot.

C. 주어진 표현과 **what**을 사용하여 문장을 완성하세요.

attracts me to Jenny	caused Kevin's illness	scares Patrick
she learned	~~you said~~	you wear

1. Could you repeat that? I couldn't hear _what you said_.
2. _____ is her smile. It's the most beautiful smile I've seen in my life.
3. _____ to the interview is important. You should dress nicely.
4. Erica attended a boxing class last week, and she's been practicing _____.
5. The doctors aren't sure _____. They need to do more tests.
6. _____ about flying is the height. He's afraid that he might fall.

D. whose/what/that을 써넣으세요.

1. A vacuum is a machine _that_ helps people clean floors.
2. The building _____ roof is damaged is the bookstore.
3. Ms. Lawrence is the woman _____ called 911. She saw the accident first.
4. _____ made Amanda so angry was the way her husband talked to her while they were fighting.
5. Everything on the menu looks great. I can't decide _____ I want.
6. The museum _____ we visited was built in 1820.
7. I bought another balloon for the little girl _____ balloon flew away.
8. Tim wants to know _____ happened at the party after he left.

정답 **p. 327** / Check-Up Test 18 **p. 268**

LESSON
103
Joe, who drives a bus, is his favorite uncle.
관계대명사 (4)
부가 정보를 제공하는 who/which

1 Joe, **who drives a bus,** is his favorite uncle.
버스를 운전하는 Joe는 그가 가장 좋아하는 삼촌이다.

Joe is my favorite uncle.
He drives a bus.

'버스를 운전하는'이라는 의미로 말하고 있는 대상인 Joe에 대한 부가 정보를 말하기 위해
콤마(,) 뒤에 who drives a bus를 썼다. 이때, who drives a bus가 없어도 말하고 있는
대상이 Joe라는 것이 명확하다.

2 말하고 있는 대상이 누구 또는 무엇인지 명확한 경우, 이 대상에 대한 부가 정보를 말할 때 **who/which**를 쓸 수 있다. 이때, **who/which** 앞에 항상 콤마(,)를 함께 쓴다.

- **Tom, who married my cousin,** seems nice. 내 사촌과 결혼한 Tom은 친절해 보인다.
- **My old house, which was on Easton Street,** didn't have a balcony.
- Gina bought that new phone, **which she broke in two days.** Gina는 그 휴대폰을 새로 샀는데 이틀 만에 망가뜨렸다.
- Mr. Johnson introduced me to his two sons, **who he always talks about.**

   who/which 대신 **that**을 쓸 수 없는 것에 주의한다.

   - I'll connect you to **Hilary, who can answer your questions.** (Hilary, that can answer ~로 쓸 수 없음)
   - **These chairs, which I designed,** are now sold at furniture stores. (These chairs, that I designed ~로 쓸 수 없음)

말하고 있는 대상이 누구인지 또는 무엇인지를 설명하는 필수적인 정보를 말할 때도 **who/which/that**을 쓴다. 단, 이때는
앞에 콤마를 쓰지 않는 것에 주의한다.

- The doctor **who/that performed my surgery** is Dr. Kim.
  내 수술을 한 의사는 Kim 박사님이야. (who/that performed ~가 없으면 말하고 있는 대상이 누구인지 알 수 없음)

  Dr. Kim, **who performed my surgery,** was great.
  내 수술을 한 Kim 박사님은 정말 훌륭했어. (, who performed ~가 없어도 말하고 있는 대상이 Dr. Kim이라는 것이 명확함)
- We stayed at the resort **which/that you recommended.**
  Aloha Resort, **which you recommended,** was a great place to stay.

3 **which**는 앞에서 말한 문장의 내용 전체에 대한 부가 정보를 말할 때도 쓸 수 있다. 이때, **which** 앞에 항상 콤마를 함께 쓴다.

> George closed the door loudly. That woke up the baby.
>
> George closed the door loudly, **which woke up the baby.** George가 문을 시끄럽게 닫았는데, 이것이 아기를 깨웠다.

- I was up very late the day before the test, **which wasn't a smart idea.**
  시험 전날 매우 늦게까지 깨어 있었는데, 이는 영리한 생각이 아니었다.
- We went skiing in Colorado last winter, **which was a fun experience.**
- The team's best player got hurt, **which made the team lose.**

   which 대신 **that**을 쓸 수 없는 것에 주의한다.

   - I couldn't remember if I locked my door, **which made me nervous.** (~, that made me nervous로 쓸 수 없음)

   which가 앞에서 말한 문장의 내용 전체에 대한 부가 정보를 나타낼 때, 뒤에 항상 단수동사를 쓴다.

   - Our office recycles all paper products, **which is** good for the environment. (which 뒤에 단수동사 is를 썼음)
   - Amber wanted to surprise Jim, **which explains** her strange behavior. (which 뒤에 단수동사 explains를 썼음)

PRACTICE

A. who/which와 콤마를 함께 사용하여 예시와 같이 주어진 두 문장을 한 문장으로 바꾸어 쓰세요.

1. Lyon is a beautiful city. It is in France.
   → _Lyon, which is in France, is a beautiful city_____.

2. My English professor is very intelligent and friendly. I won't ever forget her.
   → _____.

3. Tracey had already decorated a room for her twins. They weren't born yet.
   → _____.

4. Everyone enjoyed Annie's chocolate cookies. She baked them yesterday.
   → _____.

5. Matt owns that small car. His friends always joke about it.
   → _____.

6. Kevin's parents will retire soon. They've been working as lawyers.
   → _____.

B. 두 문장을 적절히 연결하여 예시와 같이 문장을 완성하세요. which를 함께 쓰세요.

1. Ms. Marsh prepares a lot for her class.   •   • That worried her whole family.
2. My neighbors painted their fence yellow.   •   • That wasn't good news for the fans.
3. Lisa didn't eat anything at the family dinner. •   • That made their garden look bright.
4. Kevin showed up late for the meeting.   •   • That isn't normal for him.
5. The final match was canceled due to rain.   •   • That helps her students learn better.
6. I took a vacation last week.   •   • That was very relaxing.

1. _Ms. Marsh prepares a lot for her class, which helps her students learn better_____.
2. _____.
3. _____.
4. _____.
5. _____.
6. _____.

C. who/which/that을 써넣으세요. 필요한 경우 콤마를 함께 쓰세요.

1. **Two People** _Who_ OR _That_ **Are Important to Me**

   By Justin Wilson

2. Joe _____ is a bus driver, is my favorite uncle.
3. And his wife Betty _____ is my mom's sister, is always very kind to me.
4. Since I was young, I've often visited their house _____ is close to mine.
5. The memories _____ we have created together are very special.
   They both have taught me many things.
6. Betty _____ is a great advisor, solved many of my problems while I was growing up.
7. She taught me how to be confident _____ is still very valuable.
8. Joe and I have discussed a lot of topics _____ has helped me to become an excellent
   speaker.
9. Joe and Betty are two of the people _____ I love most. I hope I grow up to be like them.

1 시간, 장소, 이유에 대해 설명할 때 관계부사 **when/where/why**를 쓸 수 있다.

the time/day 등 (시간) + **when**: ~하는 때/날 등

- I'm thinking about **the time when I first met you.** (내가 널 처음 만났던 때)
- Next Monday is **the day when we vote for a new president.** (우리가 새로운 대통령을 뽑기 위해 투표하는 날)
- 1988 was **the year when the Seoul Olympics were held.**
- **The summer when I worked as a lifeguard** was many years ago.

the place/zoo 등 (장소) + **where**: ~하는 장소/동물원 등

- I'd like to visit **the place where Jerry took these pictures.** It looks amazing. (Jerry가 이 사진들을 찍었던 장소)
- **The zoo where we saw polar bears** has closed down. (우리가 북극곰을 봤던 동물원)
- Do you know **a store where I can get rain boots?**
- "Is this **the church where you got married?**" "Yes, it is."

the reason + **why**: ~하는 이유

- Melanie told me **the reason why she couldn't meet Josh.** (그녀가 Josh를 만나지 못한 이유)
- "Are you on a diet?" "Yes. That's **the reason why I've been eating less.**" (내가 더 적게 먹는 이유)

2 일상 대화에서는 다음과 같은 명사 뒤에 **when/where/why**를 자주 생략하고 쓴다.

the time/day/year	the place	the reason

- "Do you remember **the time (when) we went scuba diving?**" 우리가 스쿠버다이빙하러 갔던 때를 기억하니?
  "Yes. It was so much fun!"
- "Is this **the place (where) you lost your wallet?**" "Actually, I'm not sure."
- **The reason (why) Carrie moved out** was that her roommate was so messy.

  이때, **when/where/why** 대신 **that**을 쓸 수 있고, **that**도 생략할 수 있다.

  - **The year (that) Kevin started working for the airline** was 2001.
    Kevin이 항공사에서 일하기 시작한 해는 2001년이다. (= The year (when) Kevin started working for the airline.)
  - Last weekend, Morris and I visited **the place (that) he grew up.**
    지난주에 Morris와 나는 그가 태어났던 장소를 방문했다. (= the place (where) he grew up.)
  - Dr. Clark is **the reason (that) I chose this college.** He is a famous biology professor.

3 '~하는 방식/방법'이라는 의미로 말할 때는 **the way (that)**을 쓴다. 일상 대화에서는 주로 **that**을 생략한다.

- **The way (that) you're holding your chopsticks** isn't correct. 네가 젓가락을 잡는 방법은 옳지 않아.
- I think **the way (that) this café makes coffee** is great. It smells good and it's strong.

  the way (that)과 비슷한 의미로 **how**를 쓸 수도 있다. 이때, **the way**와 **how**를 함께 쓰지 않는 것에 주의한다.

  - Celia isn't happy about **the way (that) her haircut looks,** but I think it's cute.
    또는 Celia isn't happy about **how her haircut looks,** but I think it's cute.
    (the way how her haircut looks로 쓸 수 없음)
  - **The way (that) Kim sings** is unique. 또는 **How Kim sings** is unique. She has her own style.
    (The way how Kim sings로 쓸 수 없음)

PRACTICE

A. 주어진 문장과 when/where/why를 사용하여 문장을 완성하세요.

a lot of accidents happen	Andy didn't take	I buy my groceries
I had to speak	my daughter was born	she's so tired all the time

1. I was so nervous that morning *when I had to speak* in front of the whole school.
2. The reason _____ that job was the company's location. It was too far.
3. This intersection is dangerous. It's a place _____.
4. Flora is taking too many classes. That's the reason _____.
5. The day _____ was the happiest moment of my life. I love being a dad.
6. The prices are usually lower at the store _____. That's why I shop there.

B. 괄호 안에 주어진 표현과 when/where/why를 사용하여 예시와 같이 문장을 완성하세요. 가능한 경우 when/where/why를 생략하고 쓰세요.

1 **Construction Ahead** The bridge will be closed for repair work.	2 **Best Pizza in Town!** Sophia's Pizzeria! You can get the city's best pizza here!	3 *Summer Vacation!* Summer vacation begins on Wednesday!
4 **Concert Canceled** The concert is canceled because of the singer's illness.	5 **Warning!** Swimming at Glory Coast is not allowed.	6 *Wild Animal Safari* Some animals start to hunt after sunset.

1. (the reason) Repair work is *the reason (why) the bridge will be closed* .
2. (the restaurant) Sophia's Pizzeria is _____.
3. (the day) Wednesday is _____.
4. (the reason) The singer's illness is _____.
5. (the beach) Glory Coast is _____.
6. (the time) After sunset is _____.

C. 주어진 문장을 보고 틀린 부분이 있으면 바르게 고치세요. 틀린 부분이 없으면 ○로 표시하세요.

1. The library I got these books is closed on Sundays. *The library → The library where*
2. I'm looking forward to the day which I can travel more. _____
3. I'm proud of the way my children behaved today. _____
4. This is the stadium the basketball game will be held. _____
5. I like the way how Ralph talks. He has an interesting accent. _____
6. The reason Matt went to the hospital was his broken leg. _____

D. when/where/why/who/which를 사용하여 Amy와 Chris의 대화를 완성하세요.

AMY: 1. Do you remember the time *when* we went to London?
CHRIS: Oh yes! 2. The week _____ we were there is my favorite memory.
3. Do you remember the boy _____ we met there?
AMY: I do. 4. He showed us all of the pictures _____ he had taken.
CHRIS: Right. 5. I also liked the hotel _____ we stayed.
AMY: Me too. 6. The reason _____ it was so nice was the garden.
CHRIS: That's right! I'd like to go back to London one day.

AMY

CHRIS

LESSON 104

Grammar Gateway Intermediate

Kim **said that** Gina's house was huge. 다른 사람의 말을 전달하기 (1)

1 다른 사람의 말을 전달할 때 **said that**을 쓸 수 있다. 다른 사람의 말이 현재/현재진행/현재완료 시제이면 각각 과거/과거진행/과거완료 시제를 써서 전달한다.

현재
Kim: "Gina's house is huge!" → • Kim **said that** Gina's house **was** huge. Kim은 Gina의 집이 크다고 말했다.
Nick: "I don't read mystery books." → • Nick **said that** he **didn't read** mystery books.

현재진행
Molly: "Tim and Ann are taking a walk." → • Molly **said that** Tim and Ann **were taking** a walk.
Jason: "I'm not sleeping." → • Jason **said that** he **wasn't sleeping**.

현재완료
The reporter: "The government has made a new law about education." → • The reporter **said that** the government **had made** a new law about education.
Rita: "I haven't heard from Jeff in weeks." → • Rita **said that** she **hadn't heard** from Jeff in weeks.

이때, **that**을 생략할 수 있다.
• "Where is Ms. Brown?" "She **said (that)** she was almost here." 거의 다 왔다고 말했어요.

2 조동사 **will/can**은 각각 **would/could**를 써서 전달한다.

Jake: "I will see you at the party." → • Jake **said (that)** he **would see** us at the party.
   Jake는 파티에서 보자고 말했다.

Mr. Jones: "You can borrow my car." → • Mr. Jones **said** I **could borrow** his car.
Kelly: "I won't be home until 8 o'clock." → • Kelly **said** she **wouldn't be** home until 8 o'clock.

3 다른 사람의 말이 지금도 사실이면, 전달하는 말의 동사는 과거 시제 대신 현재 시제로도 쓸 수 있다.

Denise: "I exercise every day."
→ • Denise **said (that)** she **exercised** every day. 또는 Denise **said (that)** she **exercises** every day.
   Denise는 매일 운동한다고 말했다. (지금도 매일 운동함)

Mr. and Mrs. Smith: "We travel somewhere new every summer."
→ • Mr. and Mrs. Smith **said** they **traveled** somewhere new every summer.
   또는 Mr. and Mrs. Smith **said** they **travel** somewhere new every summer.
   Smith 씨 부부는 여름마다 새로운 곳을 여행한다고 말했다. (지금도 여름마다 여행을 함)

단, 다른 사람의 말이 지금 사실이 아니면 과거 시제로 쓰는 것에 주의한다.

Sam: "It's cold." → • Sam **said** it **was** cold yesterday, but it has gotten warmer today.
   Sam이 어제 날씨가 춥다고 말했지만 오늘은 더 따뜻해졌다. (오늘은 춥지 않으므로 과거 시제 was를 썼음)

4 다른 사람의 말이 과거 시제이면, 전달하는 말의 동사는 과거 시제와 과거완료 시제를 모두 쓸 수 있다.

Ray and Jacob: "We washed the carpet."
→ • Ray and Jacob **said (that)** they **washed** the carpet.
   또는 Ray and Jacob **said (that)** they **had washed** the carpet. Ray와 Jacob은 그들이 카펫을 청소했다고 말했다.
Liz: "I didn't have anything for dinner."
→ • Liz **said** she **didn't have** anything for dinner. 또는 Liz **said** she **hadn't had** anything for dinner.

PRACTICE

A. Jack이 하는 말을 보고 **said that**을 사용하여 예시와 같이 Jack의 말을 전달해보세요.

> 1. I've met a famous actress before.
> 2. I'm trying to lose weight.
> 3. My parents haven't been to Europe.

JACK

> 4. I don't like the food at that restaurant.
> 5. My neighbor's dogs bark too much.
> 6. Cindy and Julie aren't paying their rent.

1. *He said that he had met a famous actress before* .
2. _____ .
3. _____ .
4. _____ .
5. _____ .
6. _____ .

B. 그림을 보고 **said**를 사용하여 예시와 같이 각 사람들이 한 말을 전달해보세요.

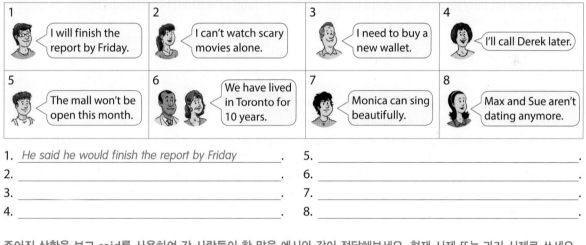

1	2	3	4
I will finish the report by Friday.	I can't watch scary movies alone.	I need to buy a new wallet.	I'll call Derek later.

5	6	7	8
The mall won't be open this month.	We have lived in Toronto for 10 years.	Monica can sing beautifully.	Max and Sue aren't dating anymore.

1. *He said he would finish the report by Friday* .
2. _____ .
3. _____ .
4. _____ .

5. _____ .
6. _____ .
7. _____ .
8. _____ .

C. 주어진 상황을 보고 **said**를 사용하여 각 사람들이 한 말을 예시와 같이 전달해보세요. 현재 시제 또는 과거 시제로 쓰세요.

1. SEAN: "I feel great." (But he feels tired now.)
   YOU: *Sean said he felt great* .

2. JANE: "Robert doesn't like jazz music." (And he still doesn't like jazz music.)
   YOU: _____ .

3. DANA: "I studied English literature in college."
   YOU: _____ .

4. BILL: "I won't be attending Joel's presentation." (But later he attended.)
   YOU: _____ .

5. SYLVIA: "My office is too small." (And it is still too small.)
   YOU: _____ .

6. TED: "Roger can draw portraits well." (And he can still draw portraits well.)
   YOU: _____ .

7. MR. PHILLIPS: "The clock wasn't broken when I left."
   YOU: _____ .

LESSON
105

Grammar Gateway Intermediate

The doctor **told** Tim **that** he was very healthy. 다른 사람의 말을 전달하기 (2)

1 다른 사람의 말을 전달할 때 **said** 대신 **told**도 쓸 수 있다. **told** 뒤에는 **사람 + that**을 쓴다.

- The doctor **told Tim that** he was very healthy. 의사는 Tim에게 그가 매우 건강하다고 말했다.
- "Did you leave some cake for Dorothy?" "No. She **told us that** she didn't want any."
- Mr. Potter **told his students that** the assignments had been uploaded on his website.

  이때, **that**을 생략할 수 있다.

  - The mechanic **told me (that)** my car would be ready in a week. 정비공은 나에게 차가 일주일 후에 준비될 것이라고 말했다.

2 **told**와 **said**는 다음과 같은 차이가 있다.

told + 사람 + (that)

told 뒤에 사람을 빠뜨리지 않는 것에 주의한다.

- John **told his boss (that)** he needed a break.
  (John told that he needed로 쓸 수 없음)
- "Is Tina coming to the meeting?"
  "No. She **told me** she couldn't come."
  (She told she couldn't come으로 쓸 수 없음)

said + (that)

said와 **that** 사이에 사람을 쓰지 않는 것에 주의한다.

- John **said (that)** he needed a break.
  (John said his boss that he needed로 쓸 수 없음)
- Rebecca **said** she couldn't go out with us this weekend. She has a bad cold.
  (Rebecca said us she couldn't go로 쓸 수 없음)

said 뒤에 사람을 쓰는 경우도 있다. 단, 이때는 **said ~ to + 사람**으로 쓴다.

- Has Matt **said anything to you** about last night? Matt이 어젯밤에 대해 너에게 무언가를 말했니?
- You should **say** "thank you" **to people** when they help you.

3 다른 사람이 명령하거나 요청한 내용을 전달할 때는 **tell/ask + 사람 + to + 동사원형**을 쓴다.

Mike: "Billy, put on your seat belt." → • Mike **told Billy to put** on his seat belt.
　　　　　　　　　　　　　　　　　　　　　Mike는 Billy에게 안전벨트를 하라고 말했다.

Sally: "Could you give me a ride, Phil?" → • Sally **asked Phil to give** her a ride.

'~하지 말라'고 명령하거나 요청한 내용을 전달할 때는 **to + 동사원형** 앞에 **not**을 쓴다.

Ellen: "Don't talk so loudly, Jim." → • Ellen **told Jim not to talk** so loudly.
　　　　　　　　　　　　　　　　　　　　Ellen은 Jim에게 너무 크게 말하지 말라고 말했다.

George: "Tara, please don't bother me." → • George **asked Tara not to bother** him.

4 다른 사람이 질문한 내용을 전달할 때는 **ask/wonder/want to know** 등을 사용하여 다음과 같이 쓴다.

의문사가 있는 질문을 전달할 때는 **의문사 + 주어 + 동사**를 쓴다.

Hugh: "Where is the post office?" → • Hugh **asked where the post office was**.
　　　　　　　　　　　　　　　　　　　　Hugh가 우체국이 어디인지 물었다.

Sue: "When does the library close?" → • Sue **wondered when the library closed**.

의문사가 없는 질문을 전달할 때는 **if/whether + 주어 + 동사**를 쓴다.

Ms. Tyler: "Has Gary called me?" → • Ms. Tyler **wondered if/whether Gary had called** her.
　　　　　　　　　　　　　　　　　　　　Tyler 씨는 Gary가 그녀에게 전화를 걸었는지 궁금해했다.

Bob: "Are those pants on sale?" → • Bob **wanted to know if/whether those pants were** on sale.

간접의문문에 대한 더 자세한 내용은 Lesson 31 참고

PRACTICE

A. 그림을 보고 **told**를 사용하여 예시와 같이 각 사람들이 한 말을 전달해보세요.

1 I don't drive to the office.	2 You look like twins.	3 You can't smoke in the building.	4 We haven't cleaned the bathroom yet.	5 I'm learning to cook Thai food.

1. *He told her he didn't drive to the office* .   4. _____ .
2. _____ .   5. _____ .
3. _____ .

B. 괄호 안에 주어진 표현들을 적절히 배열하여 문장을 완성하세요. 필요한 경우 **to**를 함께 쓰세요.

1. (her friends / got / told / she) Wendy *told her friends she got* _____ a scholarship.
2. (his brother / said / goodbye) Jeremy _____ on the platform.
3. (Joey / he / told / wait / should) Cassie _____ for her after school.
4. (said / me / nothing) Lucy _____ because she was angry with me.
5. (Nate / it / told / that / was snowing) Frank _____ outside.
6. (the concert / had been canceled / that / said)
   Last week, the band _____ .

C. **Janet**이 사람들에게 여러 가지 일을 요청, 명령하고 있습니다. 괄호 안에 주어진 동사를 사용하여 예시와 같이 문장을 완성하세요. 필요한 경우 **not**을 함께 쓰세요.

JANET

1. Barbara, could you close the door?
2. Don't turn on the radio, Harry.
3. Would you take out the garbage, Laura?
4. Beth, get some rest.
5. Christine, don't open the present yet.
6. Roy, please don't leave too early.

(ask) *She asked Barbara to close the door* .
(tell) _____ .
(ask) _____ .
(tell) _____ .
(tell) _____ .
(ask) _____ .

D. **Karen**은 친구에게 어제 **Martin**이 한 말을 전달하고 있습니다. 괄호 안에 주어진 표현을 사용하여 예시와 같이 문장을 완성하세요. 필요한 경우 **if**를 함께 쓰세요.

1. Do you like spicy food?
2. Who's your favorite actor?
3. Do you have any hobbies?
4. Where are you from?
5. Are you interested in sports?

어제

MARTIN

KAREN

오늘

1. (ask) He *asked if I liked spicy food* .
2. (want to know) He _____ .
3. (ask) He _____ .
4. (want to know) He _____ .
5. (wonder) He _____ .

간접화법

LESSON
106

Grammar Gateway Intermediate

LESSON
107 **It is said that** elephants have good memories. It is said that ~

1 특정한 사람이 아니라 여러 사람들 사이에서 일반적으로 말해지는 사실에 대해 말할 때 **It is said** 뒤에 **that** + 주어 + 동사를 쓸 수 있다.

> People say that elephants have good memories.
>
> **It is said that elephants have** good memories. 코끼리는 기억력이 좋다고 한다.

People say that women live longer than men. → • **It is said that women live** longer than men.
여자가 남자보다 오래 산다고 한다.

People say that money can't buy happiness. → • **It is said that money can't buy** happiness.
돈으로 행복을 살 수 없다고 한다.

• **It is said that children learn** languages faster than adults.
• **It is said that chocolate gives** you energy right away.

다음과 같은 표현도 사람들 사이에서 일반적으로 말해지는 사실에 대해 말할 때 쓸 수 있다.

It is	believed/thought/known/expected	that + 주어 + 동사

• **It is** | **believed** | **that the earth is** | over four billion years old. 지구는 사십억 년 이상 되었다고 믿어진다.
• **It is** | **thought** | **that fireworks were** | invented in China. 폭죽은 중국에서 발명되었다고 여겨진다.
• **It is** | **known** | **that air pollution causes** | some types of cancer.
• **It is** | **expected** | **that you don't wear** | shoes inside the house in some countries.

2 사람들 사이에서 일반적으로 말해지는 사실에 대해 말할 때 **주어 + is/are said to** + 동사원형도 쓸 수 있다.

> People say that elephants have good memories.
>
> **Elephants are said to** have good memories. 코끼리는 좋은 기억력을 가지고 있다고 한다.

People say that warm milk helps you sleep. → • **Warm milk is said to help** you sleep.
따뜻한 우유가 잠 자는 것을 도와준다고 한다.

People say that almonds are the healthiest nut. → • **Almonds are said to be** the healthiest nut.
아몬드는 가장 건강한 견과류라고 한다.

• **Colors are said to** greatly **influence** people's feelings.
• **The president is said to be** a big basketball fan.

believed/thought/known/expected도 같은 형태로 쓸 수 있다.

주어	is/are believed/thought/known/expected to	동사원형

• **The number 13** | **is believed to** | **bring** | bad luck. 숫자 13은 불운을 가져온다고 믿어진다.
• **Some plants** | **are thought to** | **grow** | well in the shade. 어떤 식물들은 그늘에서 잘 자란다고 여겨진다.
• **New Zealand** | **is known to** | **have** | beautiful mountains.
• **Thousands of people** | **are expected to** | **attend** | the music festival.

PRACTICE

A. 다음은 세계 여러 나라에서 말해지는 내용들입니다. 그림을 보고 괄호 안에 주어진 단어와 that을 사용하여 예시와 같이 문장을 완성하세요.

> 4. Whistling inside a building will cause you to lose money.
>
> **UK**
>
> **RUSSIA**
>
> 1. Knocking on wood makes your wish come true.
>
> **THE NETHERLANDS**
>
> 2. A broken dish brings good fortune.
>
> 5. People with big ears live longer.
>
> **MEXICO**
>
> **THE PHILIPPINES**
>
> 3. Brides wearing pearls will have bad marriages.

1. (said) In the UK, *it is said that knocking on wood makes your wish come true* .
2. (believed) In the Netherlands, _____ .
3. (said) In Mexico, _____ .
4. (thought) In Russia, _____ .
5. (believed) In the Philippines, _____ .

B. 그림을 보고 괄호 안에 주어진 단어와 to를 사용하여 예시와 같이 문장을 완성하세요.

> 1. Lander Hotel has good service.
> 2. Dogs feel emotions.
> 3. Exercise reduces stress levels.

> 4. Carrots are good for eyesight.
> 5. That house on the hill belongs to a famous singer.
> 6. The rose is the flower of love.

1. (known) *Lander Hotel is known to have good service* .
2. (believed) _____ .
3. (known) _____ .
4. (thought) _____ .
5. (said) _____ .
6. (thought) _____ .

C. 다음은 Justin이 쓴 학교 신문 기사입니다. 괄호 안에 주어진 표현들과 that 또는 to를 적절히 배열하여 문장을 완성하세요.

> ### *Choose Us, Harry!*
>
> *By Justin Wilson*
>
> Big news this week!
>
> 1. The famous CEO Harry Crow is *known to visit* high schools often. (visit / known)
> 2. It is _____ to meet young people and listen to their stories. (he / said / likes)
> 3. Mr. Crow is _____ a good example to students because he does a lot of charity work. (be / thought)
> 4. It is _____ which high school to visit. (will soon decide / believed / Mr. Crow)
> 5. On Thursday, it is _____ everyone his decision. (expected / will tell / he)
>
> Hopefully, we will get a chance to meet him.
>
> 6. Mr. Crow is _____ in our town, so I hope that means he'll come! (said / have lived)

There are a lot of people watching the fashion show. there + be동사

1 '~이 있다'라는 의미로 말할 때 **there + be동사**를 쓴다.

(현재 시제)	there	is/are	(not)
(과거 시제)		was/were	

FASHION SHOW

- **There are** a lot of people watching the fashion show. 패션쇼를 보는 사람이 많이 있다.
- The game is about to start. **There isn't** time to get snacks. 간식 살 시간이 없어.
- "**Was there** anyone in the office when you left?" "No. I was the last person to leave."
- We had to use the stairs because **there weren't** any elevators in the building.

(현재완료 시제)	there	have/has	(not)	been

- **There have been** three accidents this month at that intersection. 저 교차로에서 이번 달에 사고가 세 번 있었다.
- Recently, **there hasn't been** enough snow to ski on the slopes.
- "It has been colder than usual lately." "I know. **There's been** so much damage to the crops."

2 there + be동사 뒤에 단수명사 또는 셀 수 없는 명사를 쓸 때는 be동사를 단수동사로 쓰고, 복수명사를 쓸 때는 복수동사로 쓴다.

- Look! **There's a dolphin** near that boat. (a dolphin이 단수명사이므로 단수동사 is를 썼음)
- Our store just opened. **There haven't been any visitors** so far. (visitors가 복수명사이므로 복수동사 haven't been을 썼음)
- **There is not enough oil** in the pan. We need to add some more.

3 will/may/must 등 또는 used to와 함께 쓸 때는 다음과 같이 쓴다.

there	will/may/must 등	(not)	be

- **There'll be** a cocktail party on Friday at 7 o'clock. 금요일 7시에 칵테일 파티가 있을 것이다.
- A staff member said that **there may be** a delay in tonight's show.
- This soup is not spicy at all. **There must not be** any pepper in it.

there	used to	be

- **There used to be** nothing here. But now, there are many tall buildings. (과거에는) 여기에 아무것도 없다.
- "I think **there used to be** more dishes on the menu." "I think so too."

4 there seem/appear to be: ~이 있는 것 같다, ~이 있는 것처럼 보이다

there seem/appear to be 뒤에 단수명사 또는 셀 수 없는 명사를 쓸 때는 동사 **seem/appear**를 단수로 쓰는 것에 주의한다.

- **There seems to be** an error with this program. Can you check? (an error는 단수명사이므로 There seems to be로 썼음)
- I can't find anything useful in this book. **There doesn't appear to be** any information about the war.
  (information은 셀 수 없는 명사이므로 단수동사 doesn't appear로 썼음)
- Which resort do you want to stay at? **There seem to be** many resorts on that island.

5 there + be동사는 다음과 같이 수량을 나타내는 표현과 자주 함께 쓴다.

some/any/no	many/much/a lot of	two/three 등	(명사)

- **There were some empty seats** near the window, so we sat there. 창가에 몇몇 빈 자리가 있었다.
- I'm trying to decide between these two phones. **Is there much difference**?
- "**Were there any people** at the park?" "Yes, but **there were** only **two**."

PRACTICE

A. there + be동사를 적절한 시제로 사용하여 문장을 완성하세요. 필요한 경우 부정문으로 쓰세요.

1. _There is_   some orange juice in the fridge. Have some.
2. _____ any job openings at the company since 2005, but there might be some this year.
3. "Do we have any shampoo?"   "I'm looking now. No, _____ any."
4. "_____ any scary movies at the theater?"   "Yes. There's one I really want to see."
5. We were relieved because _____ any problems with our grandmother's health.
6. Since the road construction started, _____ so much noise. It's horrible.
7. Our office isn't usually busy, but _____ a lot of calls from customers yesterday.
8. "_____ a delivery for me last week? I was on vacation."   "No, nothing came."

B. 주어진 표현들과 there + be동사를 사용하여 문장을 완성하세요. 필요한 경우 부정문으로 쓰세요.

a fire	~~a lot of traffic~~	any live music	cheap clothes
enough copies	many fish	much snow	

1. (could) "Why is Dad late?"   " _There could be a lot of traffic_ . I think he'll be home soon."
2. (may) _____ of the poster. Maybe we should make some more.
3. (will) "_____ at the dinner?"   "Yes. There'll be a band."
4. (used to) "The prices at this store have increased!"   "I know._____ here."
5. (could) _____ on the street. It snowed only for a few minutes.
6. (must) "Look at all that smoke!"   "_____ somewhere."
7. (used to) _____ in this lake. Now, it's too polluted.

C. 주어진 문장을 보고 괄호 안에 주어진 동사를 사용하여 예시와 같이 다시 말해보세요.

1. I think you cooked enough food for everyone. → (seem) _There seems to be enough food for everyone_ .
2. I think we have some problems with the project. → (seem) _____ .
3. I guess there is a concert at city hall. → (appear) _____ .
4. I think someone put flowers on your desk. → (seem) _____ .
5. I guess there is no mail today. → (appear) _____ .

D. 괄호 안에 주어진 표현들과 there + be동사를 적절한 형태로 사용하여 Linda와 Amy의 대화를 완성하세요. 필요한 경우 부정문으로 쓰세요.

LINDA: Why did you come home so late?
AMY: I went to see a fashion show.
   1. And when it was over, _there were no_ buses. (no)
   2. So _____ people trying to get taxis. (a lot of)
LINDA: 3. Well, you know _____ buses after 11 p.m. (any)
     Why didn't you leave sooner?
AMY: There was a party after the show!
   4. You know, _____ time for fun activities next week. (any)
LINDA: Oh, that's right. You'll have final exams. Well, did you eat dinner?
AMY: 5. No. _____ food there. (no) They just had drinks.
LINDA: You should eat something!
   6. _____ snacks in the cabinet. (might, some)

LINDA

AMY

정답 **p. 328** / Check-Up Test 20 **p. 272**

LESSON 109

So do I, I think not   so, neither, not

1 '~도 그렇다'라는 의미로 말할 때 **so/neither + 동사 + 주어**를 쓸 수 있다. '~도 역시 …하다'라는 의미로 말할 때는 **so**를 쓰고, '~도 역시 …하지 않다'라는 의미로 말할 때는 **neither**를 쓴다.

	동사	주어
so neither	am/is/are 등 do/does/did have/has/had will/can 등	I/we/you/they he/she/it my mom/Jacob 등

- "I'm ready to leave." **"So am I."** 나도 그래. (나도 준비됐어)
- "My parents don't like dogs." "Really? **Neither do my parents.**" 우리 부모님도 그래. (우리 부모님도 개를 싫어하셔)
- "I have been taking the subway to school." **"So has Jacob.** He said it's very convenient."
- "I couldn't believe Stacy won the contest." **"Neither could she.** It was a big surprise for everyone."

2 앞에서 말한 내용을 반복하는 대신 다음과 같은 표현을 쓸 수 있다. 긍정의 의미로 말할 때는 **so**를, 부정의 의미로 말할 때는 **not**을 쓴다.

I	think/hope/guess/suppose/believe/am afraid	so

- "I forgot where Tom lives. Was it 7th Avenue?" **"I think so."** 그런 것 같아. (= I think it was 7th Avenue.)
- "Do you think we'll do well in this match?" **"I hope so."** 그러길 바라. (= I hope we'll do well in this match.)
- "I was going to take the 7 o'clock shuttle. Did I miss it?" **"I believe so."**

I	think/hope/guess/suppose/believe/am afraid	not

- "I don't think Sam is coming." **"I guess not."** 안 오는 것 같아. (= I guess Sam isn't coming.)
- "Nobody will be on time. It won't matter if we're five minutes late." **"I suppose not."** 내 생각에도 그렇지 않을 것 같아. (= I suppose it won't matter if we're five minutes late.)
- "Is parking allowed here?" **"I'm afraid not.** It's only for fire trucks."

이때, **think/guess/suppose/believe**는 I don't ~ so로도 쓸 수 있다.

- "Is the post office still open?" **"I don't think so.** It's past 5 o'clock." 내 생각에는 아닌 것 같아. (= I think not.)
- "Will we get our exam results back today?" **"I don't believe so."** 그렇지 않은 것 같아. (= I believe not.)

단, **hope/am afraid**는 I hope not, I'm afraid not으로만 쓰는 것에 주의한다.

- "Do we have to work this weekend?" **"I hope not."** 그러지 않기를 바라. (I don't hope so로 쓸 수 없음)
- "Is there any more coffee?" **"I'm afraid not."** 유감스럽게도 아니야. (I'm not afraid so로 쓸 수 없음)

3 **if so/not**: 만약 그렇다면/그렇지 않다면
- "I might be free this afternoon." "Well, **if so**, let's watch a movie." (= If you are free this afternoon)
- Are there any questions? **If not**, we can end the meeting now. (= If there aren't any questions)

4 **why not?**
상대방이 말한 부정문에 대해 이유를 물을 때 앞에서 말한 내용을 반복하는 대신 **why not?**을 쓸 수 있다.
- "I don't want to stay at that hotel." **"Why not?** It looks OK." 왜 원하지 않아? (= Why don't you want to stay at that hotel?)

제안이나 요청에 대해 흔쾌히 수락할 때도 **why not?**을 쓸 수 있다.
- "Do you want to order a pizza?" "Sure. **Why not?**" 물론이지.

PRACTICE

A. Tina와 Alison이 대화하고 있습니다. 괄호 안에 주어진 주어와 so 또는 neither를 사용하여 대화를 완성하세요.

1. My family is from Italy.
2. We haven't lived here long.
3. My daughter plays tennis.
4. My son isn't taking art lessons now.
5. My mom has been a teacher for a long time.
6. My family didn't travel last summer.
7. I should call home.
8. I can't stay out much longer.

TINA

(my father) *So is my father* . He was born in Rome.
(we) _____. We moved here last year.
(my son) _____. He's really good at it.
(my kids) _____. They take ski classes instead.
(my husband) _____. He's been teaching since 1985.
(my family) _____. We were too busy.
(I) _____. My family might worry about me.
(I) _____. We should go home soon.

ALISON

B. Philip의 질문에 대해 괄호 안에 주어진 표현과 so 또는 not을 사용하여 예시와 같이 답하세요.

PHILIP

1. Is that man's name Thomas?
2. Are you coming home late again?
3. Will they serve pork for dinner?
4. Will Alice sell her car?
5. Are you attending the seminar?
6. Did you get some eggs from the store?
7. Will you get a new dress for the party?

1. I think that man's name is Thomas.
2. I have to work late again.
3. I hate pork.
4. Alice said she probably won't sell her car.
5. My boss told me I should attend it.
6. I didn't buy any groceries today.
7. I'll probably get a new dress for the party.

LYNN

1. (think) *I think so* .
2. (am afraid) _____.
3. (hope) _____.
4. (believe) _____.
5. (guess) _____.
6. (am afraid) _____.
7. (suppose) _____.

C. so/neither/not을 사용하여 Paul과 Chris의 대화를 완성하세요.

PAUL

MP3

PAUL: Are Amy and Kate coming on the fishing trip?
CHRIS: 1. I don't think _so_____. Amy said they're not coming.
      2. _____ are Justin and Sandy.
PAUL: 3. Why _____? I thought everybody liked fishing.
CHRIS: 4. _____ did I. But they all wanted to stay home.
      It'll still be a good trip, though.
PAUL: 5. I suppose _____. But I heard it might rain on Sunday.
CHRIS: Really? 6. If _____, we won't be able to catch a lot of fish.
PAUL: But it would be so much fun anyway. And maybe it won't rain!
CHRIS: 7. I hope _____!

CHRIS

He thinks **that she is** beautiful. 동사/형용사 + that + 주어 + 동사

1 He **thinks that she is** beautiful.

그는 그녀가 아름답다고 생각한다.

She's beautiful.

'그녀가 아름답다'라는 의미로 그가 어떤 생각을 하는지 말하기 위해 동사 thinks 뒤에
that she is를 썼다.

2 think와 같이 생각, 감정, 의견 등을 나타내는 다음과 같은 동사 뒤에 **that + 주어 + 동사**를 쓸 수 있다. 일상 대화에서는 주로 **that**을
생략한다.

think	believe	know	learn	feel	notice	suppose	hope

- That woman over there looks familiar. I **think (that) I've seen** her somewhere before.
  전에 어디에선가 그녀를 본 적이 있는 것 같아.
- "Did you **know (that) Ron moved** to Seattle?" Ron이 시애틀로 이사 간 것을 알았니? "No. When did he move?"
- "I **noticed you don't drive** to work." "No. I don't have a car."
- I didn't bring my socks. I don't **suppose you have** extra socks, do you?

다음과 같이 감정을 나타내는 형용사 뒤에도 **(that) + 주어 + 동사**를 쓸 수 있다. 이때, **(that) + 주어 + 동사**는 그 감정을 느끼는 이유
를 나타낸다.

happy	glad	proud	surprised	afraid	sorry	disappointed

- We weren't **happy (that) we had to wait** in line for so long. 우리는 오랫동안 줄을 서서 기다려야 해서 불쾌했다.
- Monica's parents were **proud (that) she received** a scholarship. Monica의 부모님은 그녀가 장학금을 받아서 자랑스러워하셨다.
- Tom and Doris seemed like a perfect couple. Everyone was **surprised they broke** up.
- I'm **afraid I can't come** to your birthday party. I'll be out of town.

3 다음과 같이 어떤 일을 할 것을 요구, 제안, 주장할 때 쓰는 동사 뒤에도 **(that) + 주어 + 동사**를 쓸 수 있다. 이때, **that** 뒤에 **동사원형**
을 쓴다.

demand	propose	suggest	recommend	insist	advise

- The teacher **demanded (that) everyone be** quiet during the test. 선생님은 시험 시간 동안 모두 조용히 하라고 요구했다.
- "Would you **recommend (that) I wear** the red tie or the blue tie?" "The red one."
- "We should leave now." "Please, I **insist you stay** a bit longer."

요구, 제안, 주장 등을 나타내는 **It's essential/important/necessary/vital** 등의 뒤에도 **that + 주어 + 동사**를 쓸 수 있다.
이때, **that** 뒤에 **동사원형**을 쓴다.

- If you don't do well in the interview, you won't get the job. **It's essential that you be** prepared.
  준비가 되어있는 것이 중요하다.
- "**Is it necessary that I read** all of the instructions?" "Well, it's probably a good idea."
- **It's vital that Jack take** his medicine at the same time every day. He'll feel better much sooner.

  이때, **that** 뒤에 부정문을 쓰는 경우에는 **동사원형** 앞에 **not**을 쓴다.

  - The lawyer **advised that his client not say** anything in court.
    변호사는 그의 의뢰인이 법정에서 아무 말도 하지 말아야 한다고 조언했다.

  - **It's important that you not forget** what you've learned. Keep practicing!

PRACTICE

A. 그림을 보고 괄호 안에 주어진 동사를 사용하여 예시와 같이 문장을 완성하세요.

1 Hannah is smart.	2 Jake will win the race.	3 The restaurant is too crowded.	4 The bookstore opens at 9 o'clock.	5 What Jen said isn't true.

1. (think) *She thinks (that) Hannah is smart* .
2. (suppose) _____ .
3. (feel) _____ .
4. (know) _____ .
5. (believe) _____ .

B. 그림을 보고 괄호 안에 주어진 동사를 사용하여 예시와 같이 문장을 완성하세요.

1 You should watch the movie.	4 Can I cook dinner tonight?
2 You should invite Sam and Liz.	5 Let's not go to the exhibit. You
3 Don't smoke in my car.	6 You shouldn't leave your bag there. You

1. (recommend) *He recommended (that) she watch the movie* .
2. (insist) _____ .
3. (demand) _____ .
4. (propose) _____ .
5. (suggest) _____ .
6. (advise) _____ .

C. 주어진 문장을 보고 that을 사용하여 예시와 같이 다시 말해보세요.

1. Denny can play the drums. We are surprised. → *We are surprised that Denny can play the drums* .
2. Lesley canceled our date. I'm disappointed. → _____ .
3. The music festival isn't sold out. Pam is glad. → _____ .
4. You should drink enough water. It's important. → _____ .
5. Schools must teach history. It's vital. → _____ .
6. People should exercise regularly. It's essential. → _____ .

D. 주어진 동사를 사용하여 문장을 완성하세요. 필요한 경우 not을 함께 쓰세요.

climb	learn	lower	miss	~~visit~~	wait

1. It's essential that you *visit* the doctor immediately if you have any more pain.
2. It is necessary that you _____ the deadline. Late applications will not be accepted.
3. I'd recommend that you _____ that tree. You might fall.
4. It's important that kids _____ manners. They need them to live with other people.
5. The citizens demanded that the city _____ taxes. They think they are paying too much.
6. Cindy advised that we _____ for her, so we left without her.

GRAMMAR
GATEWAY
INTERMEDIATE

www.Hackers.co.kr

Check-Up Test

지금까지 학습한 내용을 확실하게 점검할 수 있는 Check-Up Test입니다.
틀리거나 확실하지 않은 문제는 해당 Lesson으로 돌아가 복습하세요.

괄호 안에 주어진 표현들을 적절히 배열하여 문장을 완성하세요. 필요한 경우 부정문으로 쓰세요.

1. (is / far / Boston)
   _Boston isn't far_____ from New York. It's only a few hours by bus.

2. (socks / I / wear)
   _____ at home because they're uncomfortable.

3. (in the kitchen / they / are)
   "I made some sandwiches for you." "Thank you! _____?"

4. (Mike and Kim / preparing / are)
   _____ for their exams these days. They're studying very hard.

5. (always / breakfast / eat / you)
   "_____?" "Not every day."

6. (is / it / raining)
   You don't need an umbrella. _____ anymore.

 괄호 안에 주어진 표현들을 사용하여 대화를 완성하세요. 현재 시제 또는 현재진행 시제로 쓰세요.

7. Can I talk to Diane, please?	(she, take) _She's taking_____ a shower now.
8. I really enjoy my history class.	(you, learn) Really? What _____ these days?
9. I love the park next to the city hall.	(I, not go) Me too, but _____ there often.
10. Is Derek's house near yours?	(he, live) Yes. _____ across the street.
11. Jessica wants to live in France.	(she, speak) _____ French?
12. Are you on vacation?	(I, not work) Yes. _____ this week.

 괄호 안에 주어진 표현들을 사용하여 현재 시제 또는 현재진행 시제 문장을 완성하세요.

To	billnelson@fastmail.com
From	lisamoore@fastmail.com

✉ Hi Bill,

How is everything going? All is OK here.

13. (my sister, not stay) _My sister isn't staying_____ with me this week.

14. (she, visit) _____ our cousin, Jamie, in New York.

15. (Jamie and I, not see) _____ each other often.

16. (we, talk) However, _____ on the phone almost every day.

17. (I, listen) Anyway, _____ to Jim King's music at the moment.

18. (you, know) _____ him?

19. (his voice, sound) _____ so peaceful. Listen to him when you have the chance.

Well, I have to go now. I'll talk to you soon.

Lisa

20. "_____ cold?" "Yes. Could you turn on the heater, please?"
   a) Are you feeling   b) Are you feel   c) Does you feel   d) Do you feeling

21. "_____ a basketball player." "Is she tall?"
   a) Mary are   b) Mary does   c) Mary is   d) Is Mary

22. Mr. Thompson is a professor. He _____ math at a university.
   a) is teach   b) teaching   c) teaches   d) does teaches

23. My leg is hurt, so _____ at all this week.
   a) I don't jog   b) I'm not jogging   c) I'm jogging   d) I jog

24. _____ in the office at the moment. Please leave a message.
   a) I'm not   b) I am   c) I don't   d) I doesn't

25. Water _____ most of the earth. The rest is land.
   a) covers   b) is covering   c) cover   d) is cover

26. Jessica is in the garden. _____ the flowers now.
   a) She isn't smelling   b) She is smelling   c) She smells   d) She smell

보기 중 틀린 것을 고르세요.

27. "Is this your jacket?" "No, it doesn't mine. I think it's Jane's."
     a)   b)   c)   d)

28. This milk isn't tasting good. When did you buy it?
            a)   b)   c)   d)

29. My house is very old, so I am plan to move into a new house.
            a)   b)   c)   d)

30. "Are you and your brother like sports?" "Yes. We play hockey every Sunday."
     a)   b)   c)   d)

31. Jill is in Hawaii on vacation. She has a good time with her family there.
     a) b)   c)   d)

32. "Are you be honest right now?" "Yes. I'm not lying to you."
     a)   b)   c)   d)

정답 **p.330**

틀리거나 확실하지 않은 문제는 아래의 표를 확인하여 해당 Lesson으로 돌아가 복습하세요.

문제	1	2	3	4	5	6	7	8	9	10	11	12	13	14	15	16
Lesson	1	3	1	2	3	2	5	5	5	5	5	5	5	5	5	5
문제	17	18	19	20	21	22	23	24	25	26	27	28	29	30	31	32
Lesson	5	4	4	4	1	3	5	1	5	4	1	4	2	4	4	2

괄호 안에 주어진 표현들을 사용하여 대화를 완성하세요. 과거 시제 또는 과거진행 시제로 쓰세요.

1. A: (you, see) _Did you see_____ Christine
   at the party last Friday?
   B: (she, dance) Yes. _____
   with someone when I saw her.

2. A: (you, not work) _____
   when I got to the shop two hours ago.
   B: (I, have) I _____ dinner.

3. A: (you, get) I sent you an e-mail yesterday.
   _____ it?
   B: (I, not check) _____ my
   e-mail yesterday. Was it important?

4. A: (you, turn off) Why _____
   the radio?
   B: (you, listen) Sorry. _____
   to it?

5. A: (I, meet) _____ Tara at
   the mall by chance this morning.
   B: (she, shop) _____ again?

6. A: (Mark, not visit) _____
   me when I was at the hospital.
   B: (he, want) _____ to see
   you, but he was really busy that week.

 주어진 동사와 **used to** 또는 현재 시제를 사용하여 문장을 완성하세요. 필요한 경우 부정문으로 쓰세요.

drink	~~have~~	play	prepare	spend	wear

7. I _used to have_____ a lot of comic books, but I lost most of them.
8. Karen always _____ dinner for us, and I always wash the dishes.
9. Timothy_____ glasses, but now he can't see well without them.
10. "_____ Mr. Lopez _____ guitar in the band?"   "No. He's the drummer."
11. I _____ alcohol because it gives me a headache.
12. "_____ you and Julia _____ a lot of time together when you were little?"
    "Not really, but we do a lot of things together now.

 틀린 부분이 있으면 바르게 고치세요. 틀린 부분이 없으면 ○로 표시하세요.

Aaron's Diary   May 5, 2017

By Aaron Rogers

13. I ~~was waking~~ *woke* up at 6 o'clock this morning.

14. Helen did yoga when I went to the living room.

15. She's used to jogging every day, but now she practices yoga instead.

16. I was hungry, so I was making some breakfast in the kitchen.

17. While I was cooking eggs, Helen set the table.

18. After breakfast, I was wanting to go for a walk.

19. However, when I opened the door, it was raining. So I stayed inside with Helen.

---

20. "Jake _____ at Anna on the street last night." "Why? Did Anna do something wrong?"

    a) was shouting   b) were shouting   c) is shouting   d) shouts

21. "Why were you running this morning?" "_____ late for school."

    a) I did   b) I didn't   c) I wasn't   d) I was

22. I _____ anything when I went to the auction a week ago.

    a) didn't buy   b) bought   c) don't buy   d) wasn't buying

23. Maria _____ in Japan when she had her daughter. She was in Beijing.

    a) was living   b) lived   c) wasn't living   d) not living

24. When Joseph _____ up suddenly, everyone looked at him.

    a) stands   b) is standing   c) wasn't standing   d) stood

25. I _____ well yesterday, so I didn't go to work.

    a) was feeling   b) wasn't feeling   c) felt   d) don't feel

26. I tried to call you several times around 10 o'clock. What _____ then?

    a) do you do   b) did you do   c) are you doing   d) were you doing

27. "Were you in town last weekend?" "No, I traveled in Canada."

    a)   b)   c)   d)

28. I saw a bear while I was hiking. I told Daniel, but he wasn't believing me.

    a)   b)   c)   d)

29. Somebody called my name while Betty and I walked across the street this morning.

              a)   b)   c)   d)

30. "There were some difficult questions during my job interview." "What were they ask you?"

        a)   b)   c)   d)

31. "Did Sarah and Jason at the meeting this afternoon?" "No, they weren't."

    a)   b)   c)   d)

32. My wife and I moved to Atlanta in 2009, and we was buying this house in 2010.

        a)   b)   c)   d)

정답 p.330

틀리거나 확실하지 않은 문제는 아래의 표를 확인하여 해당 Lesson으로 돌아가 복습하세요.

문제	1	2	3	4	5	6	7	8	9	10	11	12	13	14	15	16
Lesson	7	7	7	7	7	7	9	9	9	9	9	9	7	8	9	7
문제	17	18	19	20	21	22	23	24	25	26	27	28	29	30	31	32
Lesson	8	7	8	7	6	7	7	8	7	7	7	7	8	6	6	7

 주어진 표현들을 사용하여 현재완료 시제 또는 과거 시제 문장을 완성하세요. 필요한 경우 부정문으로 쓰세요.

| eat | hurt | play | rain | read | ~~see~~ |

1. (we) _We didn't see_ _____ Tony at the office last night. He wasn't there.
2. (I) "_____ golf since I was 12 years old."
   "You must be really good."
3. (you) "_____ a lot of books when you were young?"
   "Yes. I loved books."
4. (it) _____ for months. It's very dry.
5. (Mr. Young) _____ his leg a week ago, but he's OK now.
6. (she) I'm making a hamburger for Jenny. _____ dinner yet.

 괄호 안에 주어진 표현들을 사용하여 현재완료 시제 또는 현재완료진행 시제 문장을 완성하세요.

7. (Allison, try) _Allison has tried_ _____ sushi twice. She liked it both times.
8. (Jack, work) _____ at the bank since 2012. He really enjoys it.
9. (you, stay) "How many times _____ at this hotel?" "This is my second time."
10. (I, not study) _____ Spanish very long, but I'm improving every day.
11. (you, live) "How long _____ in this apartment?" "About six months."
12. (I, not travel) "Let's go to Paris this summer."
    "That sounds like fun. _____ to Europe before."

괄호 안에 주어진 동사를 사용하여 과거완료 시제 또는 과거 시제 문장을 완성하세요.

My Trip to Denver

By Sam Carter

13. (go) I _went_ _____ to Denver in December for a ski trip.
14. (arrive) When I got there, my friend Tom _____ at the resort already.
    We skied together for three days.
15. (meet) On our last day there, we _____ some interesting people.
16. (move) They _____ to Denver two years before.
    They said they were really enjoying their lives there.
17. (take) They _____ us to the Cherry Tree Shopping Center that night.
18. (do, have) We _____ some shopping at the mall and _____ dinner together.
19. (return, leave) We _____ to the hotel by taxi because the last bus _____
    already.
    Anyway, Tom and I had a lot of fun in Denver. We are planning to go there again next year.

20. "I _____ to Jacob's house before. How about you?" "I've visited him a few times."

    a) haven't gone   (b) haven't been   c) don't go   d) hadn't go

21. Edison _____ the light bulb in 1879.

    a) invented   b) had invented   c) has invented   d) has been inventing

22. _____ the street already when Terry called my name. I didn't hear him.

    a) I have crossed   b) I haven't crossed   c) I have been crossing   d) I had crossed

23. "Where are our drinks?" "The waiter _____ them yet."

    a) has brought   b) had brought   c) hadn't brought   d) hasn't brought

24. Ian and Laura _____ the house when we got home. It was very neat.

    a) have cleaned   b) have been cleaning   c) had cleaned   d) are cleaning

25. "_____ well last night?" "Not at all. I had a nightmare."

    a) Did you sleep   b) Have you slept
    c) Have you been sleeping   d) Had you slept

26. "You look very fit. _____ out since I saw you last time?" "Yes. Every evening after work."

    a) Did you work   b) Have you been working
    c) Do you work   d) Had you worked

27. That film is very good. Maria and I had seen it several times.
              a)   (b))   c)   d)

28. I haven't climbed a mountain before I hiked Mt Fuji. It was my first time.
     a)   b)   c)   d)

29. Daniel didn't spend much money lately. He's saving to buy a new car.
              a)   b)   c)   d)

30. Have you talked to Professor Lim since you have graduated from college?
     a)   b)   c)   d)

31. "Is Mr. Jackson in his office?" "He has been to the bank. He'll be back in a few minutes."
     a)   b)   c)   d)

32. Ms. Green makes amazing pies! They are the best pies I ever taste.
              a)   b)   c)   d)

--------- 정답 **p.330**

틀리거나 확실하지 않은 문제는 아래의 표를 확인하여 해당 Lesson으로 돌아가 복습하세요.

문제	1	2	3	4	5	6	7	8	9	10	11	12	13	14	15	16
Lesson	12	12	12	12	12	12	14	14	14	14	14	14	15	15	15	15
문제	17	18	19	20	21	22	23	24	25	26	27	28	29	30	31	32
Lesson	15	15	15	11	12	15	12	15	12	13	11	15	14	10	11	11

괄호 안에 주어진 표현들을 적절히 배열하여 문장을 완성하세요. will을 함께 쓰거나 현재 시제로 쓰세요.

1. (with my parents / live / I)
   I'll live with my parents _____ until I get a job.

2. (the fashion show / after / watch / we)
   _____, we are going to shop at the mall.

3. (the children / I / take / not)
   _____ to the doctor if they feel better this afternoon.

4. (lose / he / 10 pounds / until)
   Jim will exercise every day _____.

5. (tell / you / me)
   "_____ when my package arrives?" "Of course."

6. (red wine / the restaurant / sell / if / not)
   _____, we'll go to a wine bar after dinner.

괄호 안에 주어진 표현들을 사용하여 미래 시제 또는 미래진행 시제 문장을 완성하세요. 필요한 경우 부정문으로 쓰세요.

7. A: I think I'll arrive around 5.
   B: (I, wait) OK. *I'll be waiting* for you in the lobby at that time.

8. A: I'm already full. I don't want these French fries.
   B: (I, eat) Are you sure? Then _____ them.

9. A: Can I call you at 6?
   B: (I, drive) _____ home then. Please call me at 7.

10. A: (you, swim) _____ already when I get to the hotel?
    B: Yes. Come and see me at the pool.

11. A: Did you win the competition?
    B: (we, know) I hope so, but _____ until next week.

12. A: (Mr. Perez, teach) _____ us in May.
    B: Is he quitting?

괄호 안에 주어진 표현들과 will을 사용하여 미래 시제 또는 미래완료 시제 문장을 완성하세요.

Hello Cindy,

How are you these days?

13. (I, finish) I'm busy doing my graduation work now, but *I'll have finished* it by next week.

14. (I, graduate) As you know, _____ from college next month.

15. (I, study) By the time I graduate, _____ in Korea for five years!

Anyway, I met a man here and his name is Eric.

16. (we, get) _____ married next year.

17. (we, date) _____ for six months by the end of this month.

He's always nice to me.

18. (Eric and I, leave) By the time you get this letter, _____ for a trip to Japan.

19. (I, send) _____ you a postcard there.

Catherine

20. _____ to this store again. The staff is so rude.
    a) I think I'll come
    b) I don't think I won't come
    c) I don't think I come
    d) I don't think I'll come

21. "Do you and Dan need a ride to the airport?" "No, thanks. _____ a taxi."
    a) We take   b) We'll take   c) We'll have taken   d) Will we take

22. You should fasten your seatbelt. The plane _____ land.
    a) will be about to   b) be about to   c) is about to   d) is to about

23. _____ for a walk tonight. I'm really tired.
    a) I'll go   b) I'll have gone   c) I won't go   d) I won't have gone

24. "When _____?" "At 9 a.m."
    a) does the bank open
    b) will the bank have opened
    c) is the bank be opening
    d) is the bank open

25. All of the leaves _____ by the time winter comes.
    a) will be falling   b) will have fallen   c) are going to fall   d) will fall

26. We _____ 10 songs at the concert, but we only did five.
    a) are going to perform   b) will perform   c) will be performing   d) were going to perform

보기 중 틀린 것을 고르세요.

27. "Jake and I are going to the cinema tonight." "Great. What movie do you watch?"
         a)   b)   c)   d)

28. Janice wasn't going to return to work until next Friday because she is on summer vacation.
          a)   b)   c)   d)

29. "Will you be believing me if I tell you a true story?" "Yes. I promise."
         a)   b)   c)   d)

30. "Sam went to medical school." "Really? I thought he will be going to become a lawyer."
              a)   b)   c)   d)

31. "While you are going to make the salad, I'll set the table." "Thanks. That will help a lot."
                    a)   b)   c)   d)

32. Brian has an appointment at noon today, so he won't have joined us for lunch.
          a)   b)   c)   d)

정답 p.330

틀리거나 확실하지 않은 문제는 아래의 표를 확인하여 해당 Lesson으로 돌아가 복습하세요.

문제	1	2	3	4	5	6	7	8	9	10	11	12	13	14	15	16
Lesson	21	21	21	21	21	21	19	19	19	19	19	19	20	20	20	20
문제	17	18	19	20	21	22	23	24	25	26	27	28	29	30	31	32
Lesson	20	20	20	16	16	18	16	18	20	17	18	17	19	17	21	19

 괄호 안에 주어진 표현들을 적절히 배열하여 문장을 완성하세요.

1. (right / may / you / be)
   "I think the movie starts at 7, not 8."
   " *You may be right* _____. Let me check."

2. (submit / have / do / my résumé / I / to)
   "_____ online?" "You can also send it by mail."

3. (a bike / be / to / I / able / ride / will)
   _____ soon. Sam promised to teach me.

4. (we / meet / should)
   "Where _____?" "Let's meet at the café downtown."

5. (much time / Tony / been / has / able / spend / to)
   _____ with you since he quit his job?

6. (open / not / the windows / better / had / we)
   _____. It's raining harder now.

 주어진 표현들 중 적절한 것을 사용하여 예시와 같이 문장을 완성하세요. 필요한 경우 부정문으로 쓰세요.

be	buy	~~drive~~	get up	pass	turn off

7. (had better/ have to) You *'d better not drive* _____ so fast or you might get a speeding ticket.
8. (could / was able to) The math test was very difficult, but I _____ it.
9. (had better / should) We _____ that sofa. It looks very comfortable.
10. (could / might) "Is this your key?" "It _____ mine. Mine's in my pocket."
11. (might / must) You _____ your cell phone. The plane is about to take off.
12. (must / have to) Jeff _____ now because he has only afternoon classes.

 주어진 표현들을 사용하여 문장을 완성하세요. 필요한 경우 동사를 **have + 과거분사**로 쓰세요.

ask	~~be~~	forget	get	make	read	start

Dear Dan,

Did you get your essay score?
13. (could not) My score is too low, so it
    couldn't be _____ right.
I made some good points.
14. (might) I think Professor Reed
    _____ a mistake when
    he graded my essay.
15. (should) _____ I _____
    him about it?
I've attached my essay. Please let me know
your opinion.

Dear Cindy,

16. (must not) You _____
    his comments carefully.
Your score was low because you did not have a
conclusion.
17. (should not) You _____
    to include a conclusion next time.
18. (might) Or you _____
    another low score.
19. (could) And you _____ with
    a better introduction before you mentioned
    the main point. I hope you do better next time.

보기 중 가장 적절한 것을 고르세요.

20. "_____ speak Chinese?" "Yes. They took classes when they were young."
    a) Can your children be able to   b) Can your children to
    c) Are your children able to   d) Are able your children to

21. This bag is very light. It _____ many things in it.
    a) must have   b) must not have   c) must have had   d) must not have had

22. Sam _____ an umbrella this morning. He got wet because he didn't have one.
    a) should have taken   b) shouldn't have taken   c) should take   d) shouldn't take

23. I _____ at the hospital for a few days last month because I got hurt in a car accident.
    a) have to stay   b) don't have to stay   c) had to stay   d) didn't have to stay

24. Our team didn't practice very much. We _____ the game.
    a) have to lose   b) were able to lose   c) could lose   d) had better lose

25. Sandra's boss is in an important meeting right now. She _____ disturb him.
    a) had better not   b) had better   c) should   d) doesn't have to

26. Melanie _____ here last week. She was in Canada.
    a) might not have been   b) may not have been   c) shouldn't have been   d) couldn't have been

보기 중 틀린 것을 고르세요.

27. "Laura <u>could find</u> her purse. It's gone." "She <u>must</u> <u>have been</u> very upset."
         (a)   b)   c)   d)

28. "Tanya <u>must</u> be very angry at Aaron." "I <u>think</u> so. He <u>may</u> not <u>have damaged</u> her car."
        a)   b)   c)   d)

29. Eric <u>might not</u> <u>clean</u> his room yesterday. He <u>had to</u> <u>do</u> his homework.
         a)   b)   c)   d)

30. "I just <u>heard</u> that Steve is sick, so I'll <u>must</u> visit him tonight." "<u>Can</u> I <u>come</u> with you?"
         a)   b)   c)   d)

31. "<u>Where's</u> Lynn?" "She could <u>leave</u> for lunch. <u>Do you have to</u> <u>see</u> her now?"
         a)   b)   c)   d)

32. You <u>don't have to</u> <u>run</u> around the swimming pool. You <u>may</u> fall down and <u>get</u> hurt.
            a)   b)   c)   d)

.... 정답 **p.331**

틀리거나 확실하지 않은 문제는 아래의 표를 확인하여 해당 Lesson으로 돌아가 복습하세요.

문제	1	2	3	4	5	6	7	8	9	10	11	12	13	14	15	16
Lesson	24	26	22	27	22	28	28	22	28	24	26	26	23	24	27	25
문제	17	18	19	20	21	22	23	24	25	26	27	28	29	30	31	32
Lesson	27	24	23	22	25	27	26	23	28	23	22	27	24	26	23	26

괄호 안에 주어진 표현들을 사용하여 대화를 완성하세요. 현재 시제 또는 과거 시제로 쓰세요.

1. (the bus, stop) *Does the bus stop* _____ near my house?
2. (what, you, study) _____ in college?
3. (you, come) _____ to this restaurant often?
4. (when, the bank, open) _____ ?
5. (I, call) _____ you too late?
6. (where, you, go) _____ shopping for clothes?

No. It goes the opposite direction.
I majored in politics.
Yes. I usually eat here.
At 9 o'clock on weekdays.
No. I was awake.
I often go to the department store.

 괄호 안에 주어진 표현들과 what/who/which를 적절히 배열하여 문장을 완성하세요.

7. (the flight / has / delayed)
" *What has delayed the flight* _____ ?" "There is a lot of fog outside."

8. (give / we / should)
" _____ a tip to?" "That waiter with glasses. He was so nice."

9. (is / computer / yours)
" _____ , this one or that one?" "This one."

10. (order / you / are / to / going)
" _____ for dinner?" "What about Chinese noodles?"

11. (you / helped)
" _____ with your assignment?" "Dan. He was very helpful."

12. (enjoy / sport / does / Tom)
_____ more, basketball or tennis?

괄호 안에 주어진 표현들을 적절히 배열하여 문장을 완성하세요.

To	dawncollins@fastmail.com
From	terryallen@fastmail.com

Hello. I have some questions about your dance classes. I hope you can help.
My main goal is to lose some weight.
13. (which / is / dance) So can you tell me *which dance is* _____ the best for losing weight?
14. (should / class / whose / I / take) Also, I wonder _____ .
I've heard good things about Ms. Wright.
15. (she / does / what / teach / kind of dance) _____ ?
16. (her class / be / will / if) I'm not sure _____ too difficult for me.
17. (I / must / when / register) And _____ for a class if I want to start in September?
18. (open / you / are) Oh, and one more question. _____ on Sundays?
Thank you in advance!

Terry Allen

19. "_____ your dress for the party?" "Yes. I'm going to wear the blue one."
    a) Have you choose   b) Have chosen you   c) Have you chosen   d) You chosen have

20. "_____ from here?" "It takes 20 minutes on foot."
    a) How your school is   b) How far is your school
    c) How far your school is   d) How your school is far

21. "_____ my wedding invitation?" "Yes. I just received it this morning."
    a) Did you get not   b) Don't you got   c) Didn't get you   d) Didn't you get

22. "_____ do you usually listen to?" "Bruno Dars's."
    a) Whose songs   b) What songs   c) Which songs   d) How songs

23. "I'd like to know _____ an ATM on this floor." "There's one near the elevator."
    a) if is there   b) if there is   c) where there be   d) where is there

24. "Gary and Louise were at the meeting, _____ they?" "I'm not sure."
    a) weren't   b) didn't   c) were   d) did

25. Can you tell me _____ improve my writing?
    a) how can I   b) what can I   c) how I can   d) what I can

26. "Why you did stay home last weekend?" "I wasn't feeling very well."
    a)   b)   c)   d)

27. "The cookies are ready. Who do you want one?" "I do!"
            a)   b)   c)   d)

28. "Charlie didn't wake up until late, does he?" "No. He got up after lunch time."
            a)   b)   c)   d)

29. "Aren't your parents in town this weekend?" "Yes, they aren't."
        a)   b)   c)   d)

30. "To where do I have to send this package to?" "To Jacob's office in New York."
        a)   b)   c)   d)

31. "How do you go to the movies?" "About once a week. How about you?"
    a) b)   c)   d)

32. "Is Kevin at school now?" "I'm not sure whether did he go to school today."
        a)   b)   c)   d)

정답 p.331

틀리거나 확실하지 않은 문제는 아래의 표를 확인하여 해당 Lesson으로 돌아가 복습하세요.

문제	1	2	3	4	5	6	7	8	9	10	11	12	13	14	15	16
Lesson	29	29	29	29	29	29	30	30	30	30	30	30	31	31	30	31
문제	17	18	19	20	21	22	23	24	25	26	27	28	29	30	31	32
Lesson	29	29	29	29	32	29	31	32	31	29	30	32	32	29	29	31

 괄호 안에 주어진 표현을 사용하여 능동태 또는 수동태 문장을 완성하세요. 현재 시제 또는 과거 시제로 쓰세요.

1. Whose hat is that?
2. Is Teresa single?
3. How was your job interview?
4. Your house is always tidy.
5. Those buildings look very old.
6. Is John at the airport now?

(find) I don't know. I _found_ it under the sofa.
(marry) No. She _____.
(not ask) It was OK. I _____ many questions.
(clean) Peter _____ it every day.
(build) They _____ 50 years ago.
(not arrive) No. His flight _____ until 8 o'clock.

 괄호 안에 주어진 표현들을 적절히 배열하여 수동태 문장을 완성하세요.

7. (chosen / not / Mr. Clark / be / might)
" _Mr. Clark might not be chosen_ as the mayor of this city." "Why do you say that?"

8. (being / the package / shipped / is)
"_____ by airmail?" "Yes. So you'll get it soon."

9. (the meeting / been / had / arranged)
_____ for 6 o'clock, but Dan didn't appear.

10. (will / the renovations / not / be / completed)
"_____ until next month." "It's taking longer than I expected."

11. (were / menus / being / handed)
_____ out by the waiters.

12. (have / postponed / all of today's games / been)
_____ due to bad weather?"
"Yes. They announced it about 10 minutes ago."

 괄호 안에 주어진 표현들을 사용하여 능동태 또는 수동태 문장을 완성하세요. 현재 시제로 쓰고, 필요한 경우 to를 함께 쓰세요.

Mr. Miller's Cooking School By Jacob Gardeners	13. (Mr. Miller, own) _Mr. Miller owns_ a cooking school.
	14. (various classes, offer) _____ the students there.
	15. (the students, teach) _____ both traditional and modern cooking styles.
	16. (some scholarships, give) _____ the top students.
	17. (the school, send) Also, _____ the top student to a famous restaurant for an internship after graduation!
	18. (the intern, not pay) _____ any money, but he or she gets valuable experience.
	19. (Mr. Miller, hope) Because of the school's success, _____ to open another cooking school within the next five years.

20. Those clothes are beautiful. _____ by a famous designer?
    a) Did they design   b) Did they designed   c) Were they design   d) Were they designed

21. The music festival _____ yet. It lasts until Sunday night.
    a) isn't finished   b) isn't finish   c) wasn't finished   d) doesn't finish

22. At the Christmas celebration, all of the children _____.
    a) were given to presents   b) were given presents
    c) were given by presents   d) were giving to presents

23. "I like this song, but it _____ at tonight's concert." "Why not?"
    a) won't be performed   b) won't perform   c) will be performed   d) will perform

24. "I heard you had an accident. Are you OK?" "I'm fine. I _____."
    a) didn't be injured   b) didn't injure   c) didn't get injured   d) didn't injured

25. _____ when nobody was inside?
    a) Did the robbery occurred   b) Did the robbery occur
    c) Was the robbery occurred   d) Was the robbery occur

26. That website is very popular. It _____ by millions of people.
    a) has visited   b) hasn't visited   c) has been visited   d) visited

27. "This food <u>tastes</u> really good." "All the dishes <u>were</u> <u>prepared</u> of my wife."
              a)   b)   c)   (d)

28. I <u>received</u> a letter but I <u>couldn't read</u> it. It <u>didn't write</u> <u>in English</u>.
       a)   b)   c)   d)

29. "<u>Are</u> <u>these</u> your pens?" "No. <u>They</u> <u>are belonged</u> to Peter."
    a) b)   c)   d)

30. "Did you <u>be</u> <u>invited</u> to <u>Tom's</u> birthday party?" "Yes. <u>Are you</u> going too?"
           a) b)   c)   d)

31. The actor <u>didn't know</u> by <u>a lot of people</u> <u>five years ago</u>, but now <u>he is</u> very famous.
             a)   b)   c)   d)

32. "<u>Are</u> you still <u>working</u>?" "No. I <u>did</u>. I'm <u>leaving</u> in a minute."
    a)   b)   c)   d)

정답 p.331

틀리거나 확실하지 않은 문제는 아래의 표를 확인하여 해당 Lesson으로 돌아가 복습하세요.

문제	1	2	3	4	5	6	7	8	9	10	11	12	13	14	15	16
Lesson	33	34	35	33	33	33	33	33	33	33	33	33	33	35	35	35
문제	17	18	19	20	21	22	23	24	25	26	27	28	29	30	31	32
Lesson	33	35	33	33	34	35	33	34	34	33	34	33	34	34	33	34

괄호 안에 주어진 표현들을 적절히 배열하여 문장을 완성하세요. 동사를 -ing 또는 to + 동사원형으로 쓰세요.

1. (read / I / it / not / suggest)

   "Look! Here's Marie's diary." " _I suggest not reading it_____ . She'll be very upset."

2. (for / it / her / is / get up / difficult)

   "Why is Janet always late?" "I think _____ in the morning."

3. (you / decide / did / study / not)

   "I'm not taking Japanese classes." "Why not? _____ in Japan?"

4. (are / busy / they / prepare)

   I haven't seen Tom and Sarah for days. _____ for their wedding.

5. (order / the last train / in / not / miss)

   You should leave soon _____ .

6. (you / would / make / not / mind)

   _____ so much noise? Jessica is sleeping.

 괄호 안에 주어진 동사를 사용하여 문장을 완성하세요. -ing나 being + 과거분사 또는 to + 동사원형이나 to be + 과거분사로 쓰세요.

7. (retire) "Do you hope _to be retired_____ when you're 60?" "Yes, I do."

8. (sing) I'm too shy. I can't imagine _____ at a party.

9. (wash) My pants are so dirty. They need _____ .

10. (quit) "Jake promised _____ smoking." "That's good news."

11. (catch) The thieves avoided _____ , so they got away with the money.

12. (choose) "Dan looks depressed." "He failed _____ as the captain of the hockey team."

 괄호 안에 주어진 단어들을 적절한 형태로 사용하여 문장을 완성하세요. 현재 시제로 쓰세요.

To	terryallen@fastmail.com
From	dawncollins@fastmail.com

Hi Terry. Thank you for your e-mail.

13. (want, lose) If you _want to lose_____ some weight, the Tango is your best option.

14. (invite, you, attend) So we _____ one of our three new Tango classes this fall.

15. (recommend, take) If you're a beginner, we _____ the Tuesday night class. No experience is necessary for that one.

16. (consider, sign) If you already have some experience, then _____ up for our class on Wednesday night. That one is taught by Ms. Wright.

17. (decide, join) If you _____ her class, you'll receive a 10% discount.

18. (remember, register) Please _____ before August 20 if you want to start in September.

And yes, we are open on Sundays.

19. (learn) You can visit our website _____ more about these great opportunities.

Best wishes,
Dawn Collins, Uptown Dance Studios

20. "It was a pleasure _____ you." "Me too. Let's meet again soon."
    a) for meeting   b) meet   c) to meet   d) to meeting

21. "I'll _____ me up after work. You don't have to give me a ride." "Oh, OK."
    a) get Sharon pick   b) get Sharon picked
    c) get Sharon picking   d) get Sharon to pick

22. "What is that man doing on the roof?" "He appears _____ something."
    a) to be fixed   b) to be fixing   c) being fixed   d) being fixing

23. I have a cold, but it isn't bad. It won't stop me _____ out tonight.
    a) going   b) to go   c) of going   d) from going

24. Something was wrong with my computer, so I _____ at it for me.
    a) had Steven looking   b) had Steven looked
    c) had Steven look   d) had Steven to look

25. The boy admitted _____ the vase. He promised to be more careful.
    a) having broken   b) having breaking   c) to have broken   d) to break

26. "Is it _____ the cookies out of the oven?" "Not yet."
    a) time taking   b) time to take   c) to take time   d) taking time

보기 중 틀린 것을 고르세요.

27. "I'm not sure where hanging this picture." "I feel like hanging it on that wall."
           a)   b)   c)   d)

28. I bought this knife to cut vegetables, but it isn't very good for cut them.
        a)   b)   c)   d)

29. "Did you get the wall paint?" "Yes. It took two days to get it done.
        a)   b)   c)   d)

30. I always set my alarm before going to bed not to oversleep in the morning.
        a)   b)   c)   d)

31. "I couldn't help to notice your dress. It's beautiful." "It's very kind of you to say that."
        a)   b)   c)   d)

32. We can't afford to having breakfast today. We need to attend a meeting at 7 a.m.
        a)   b)   c)   d)

정답 p.331

틀리거나 확실하지 않은 문제는 아래의 표를 확인하여 해당 Lesson으로 돌아가 복습하세요.

문제	1	2	3	4	5	6	7	8	9	10	11	12	13	14	15	16
Lesson	37	43	38	46	42	37	38	37	39	38	37	38	38	40	37	37
문제	17	18	19	20	21	22	23	24	25	26	27	28	29	30	31	32
Lesson	38	39	42	36	41	38	40	41	37	42	44	45	41	42	46	46

괄호 안에 주어진 표현들을 적절히 배열하여 현재 시제 문장을 완성하세요. 필요한 경우 단어를 적절한 형태로 바꾸어 쓰세요.

1. (person / visit / many)
   Busan is one of the most beautiful places in Korea. _Many people visit_ _____ the city every year.

2. (hair / a few / be)
   "_____ on the floor." "Really? I'll vacuum the floor then."

3. (help / the news)
   I like watching the news. _____ us understand what is happening in the world.

4. (cost / of / two / cake / piece)
   This bakery is so expensive. _____ $15.

5. (wood / be)
   _____ used to make many kinds of furniture.

6. (some / contain / juice)
   _____ a lot of sugar. For example, grape juice is sweeter than orange juice.

 주어진 명사를 사용하여 문장을 완성하세요. 필요한 경우 a/an을 함께 쓰거나 복수로 쓰세요.

article	flower	furniture	picture	~~travel~~

7. Jason and I really enjoy _travel_ _____. We take many _____ of the sights we visit.

8. Jim gave us _____ for our wedding gift. He bought us a bed and two chairs.

9. There's _____ about gardening in this magazine. It explains how to grow _____.

assignment	glass	e-mail	ice	team

10. "May I have _____ of water, please?" "Sure. Do you want some _____ in it?"

11. My _____ won first prize in the competition. We received congratulations from many people.

12. I got _____ from Jenny. I haven't replied to it yet because I have a lot of _____ to do.

다음 신문 기사를 읽고 틀린 부분이 있으면 바르게 고치세요. 틀린 부분이 없으면 ○로 표시하세요.

The Daily News

Robbery at the Lakeview Mall

13. Two ~~thief~~ _thieves_ broke into the Lakeview Mall last weekend.

14. The robbery happened when the staffs had already gone home.

15. The thieves stole a lot of money and some jewelries.

16. They also took an antique lamp and a pair of binoculars.

17. Fortunately, the thieves were caught by the polices yesterday.

18. And the stolen items was found in a room in their house.

October 15, 2018

19. "Why are you so late?"   "_____ on the road."
    a) There were too much traffic   b) There were too much traffics
    c) There was too much traffic   d) There was too much traffics

20. "Does our room have _____ of the beach?" "Yes, it does."
    a) view   b) a view   c) a scenery   d) sceneries

21. "Was Kathy interested in _____ from an early age?" "Not really."
    a) politic   b) a politic   c) some politics   d) politics

22. Julie added _____ to the mixing bowl to make some cookies.
    a) three cups of flours   b) three cup of flours   c) three cup of flour   d) three cups of flour

23. "_____ on this website might be helpful for your essay." "Thanks. I'll check it out."
    a) the information   b) an information   c) informations   d) the informations

24. _____ very important for growing plants. They can't grow without it.
    a) Lights are   b) A light are   c) Light is   d) A Light is

25. "_____ very soft and comfortable." "They are. They're made of cotton."
    a) Your pajamas look   b) Your pajama look   c) Your pajamas looks   d) Your pajama looks

보기 중 틀린 것을 고르세요.

26. "Do you have any baggages, sir?" "Yes. I have two small suitcases."
          a)   b)   c)   d)

27. It's easy to learn vocabularies, but it's hard to speak complete sentences fluently.
                    a)   b)   c)   d)

28. "What did you buy at the mall yesterday?" "I bought two pairs of pant."
                a)   b)   c)   d)

29. Frank didn't have times to repair his glasses.
              a)   b)   c)   d)

30. The beautiful surrounding of Mount Fuji are great for taking photos.
        a)   b)   c)   d)

31. The audiences cheered at the concert while the rock band was performing its music.
        a)   b)   c)   d)

32. Don't forget your belonging in the airport. Cell phones are often left behind.
                    a)   b)   c)   d)

정답 p.332

틀리거나 확실하지 않은 문제는 아래의 표를 확인하여 해당 Lesson으로 돌아가 복습하세요.

문제	1	2	3	4	5	6	7	8	9	10	11	12	13	14	15	16
Lesson	47	48	48	48	48	47	49/47	49	49/47	48	50	49	47	50	49	50
문제	17	18	19	20	21	22	23	24	25	26	27	28	29	30	31	32
Lesson	50	47	47	49	48	48	48	48	50	49	49	50	48	50	50	50

 주어진 명사와 a/an 또는 the를 사용하여 문장을 완성하세요.

| essay | manager | pharmacist | radio | table | ~~umbrella~~ |

1. It's raining heavily outside. Did you bring _an umbrella_____ ?
2. "Are you listening to _____?"　"No. You can turn it off."
3. _____ is someone who sells medicine.
4. "Who is _____ of your department?"　"His name is Peter West."
5. "What are you writing?"　"It's _____. It's for my English class."
6. Sarah bought me _____. I think I'll use it in my dining room.

 괄호 안에 주어진 표현들을 적절히 배열하여 문장을 완성하세요. 필요한 경우 the를 함께 사용하세요.

7. (on / fell / ground) A lot of trees _fell on the ground_____ because of the storm.
8. (TV / watch) I usually _____ on Sundays, but I'm seeing a friend tonight.
9. (that hotel / at / rooms) _____ were very clean. I'd like to go there again.
10. (breakfast / some cereal / for) Jane had _____ this morning.
11. (were / my neighbors / Smiths) _____ until last month. Now they live in Seattle.
12. (church / attend) I didn't use to _____ very often, but I go every week now.

 틀린 부분이 있으면 바르게 고치세요. 틀린 부분이 없으면 ○로 표시하세요.

| To | sallyscott@fastmail.com |
| From | tinaevans@fastmail.com |

✉ Hi, Sally!

I haven't heard from you in a long time. How are you?

　　　　　a friend
13. I met ~~the friend~~ on the street yesterday by chance.

14. We used to go to a same school.

15. She's the engineer and works for the government.

16. We decided to go to movies tomorrow. Do you want to go with us?

17. And what are you doing on Saturday?

18. I'm planning to go downtown to buy the present for my mother.

Her birthday is next week. If you can go with me, let me know.

Tina

19. Scientists disagree on how _____ formed. It's still a mystery.
    a) universe   (b) the universe   c) a universe   d) an universe

20. "Did the thief get caught?" "Yes. He's in _____ now."
    a) prison   b) the prison   c) a prison   d) prisons

21. I don't have any brothers or sisters. I'm _____ in my family.
    a) only child   b) a only child   c) the only child   d) child only

22. "How do people celebrate _____ in Korea?" "We spend time with our family."
    a) a New year's Day   b) New Year Day   c) the New Year's Day   d) New Year's Day

23. When I _____ from work, there was a package on the doorstep.
    a) came home   b) came a home   c) came to home   d) came the home

24. "I bought a laptop yesterday." "What model is _____? Is it a good one?"
    a) a laptop   b) the laptop   c) laptop   d) laptops

25. _____ consists of 12 months, which is 365 days.
    a) The year   b) Year   c) A year   d) Years

26. "Do you go to the work by bus?" "Yes. It's the most convenient way."
    (a)   b)   c)   d)

27. "I need money to pay the parking fee. Where is nearest bank?" "It's just around the corner."
         a)   b)   c)   d)

28. A health is very important to me, so I eat right and go to the gym every day.
    a)   b)   c)   d)

29. Jack always visits his grandparents in a summer. They live in Toronto.
         a)   b)   c)   d)

30. "Nate will be joining an army in June." "Really? Is he the first soldier in your family?"
                            a)   b)   c)   d)

31. Cello is a string instrument like a violin. It makes a lower sound than the violin.
    a)   b)   c)   d)

32. "Is Jenny in the bed already?" "Yes. She was tired from school."
    a)   b)   c)   d)

정답 p.332

틀리거나 확실하지 않은 문제는 아래의 표를 확인하여 해당 Lesson으로 돌아가 복습하세요.

문제	1	2	3	4	5	6	7	8	9	10	11	12	13	14	15	16
Lesson	51	53	52	51	52	51	53	53	51	54	54	54	51	53	52	53
문제	17	18	19	20	21	22	23	24	25	26	27	28	29	30	31	32
Lesson	54	51	53	54	53	54	54	51	52	54	53	51	54	53	52	54

 셋 중 맞는 것을 고르세요.

1. Have you seen (mine / my / me) phone? I think I've lost it.
2. "Which shoes are yours?" "The (some / ones / them) over there."
3. "I found this umbrella by the door." "Melissa has one like that. I think it's (her / she / hers)."
4. "Can you recommend a watch for my mom's birthday present?" "This pink (ones / one / it) is very popular."
5. We've cooked plenty of food for everyone, so please help (yourselves / yours / you).
6. "I hope Pete remembers the meeting time."
   "Laura sits next to Pete. I'm sure she will remind (him / herself / himself)."

 괄호 안에 주어진 단어들을 적절히 배열하여 문장을 완성하세요. -'s 또는 of를 함께 사용하세요.

7. (this poem / the title) _The title of this poem_ is "A Summer in Tokyo."
8. (this month / magazine) My article will be published in _____. I'm so excited!
9. (classmate / mine / a) _____ won a national art contest.
10. (our house / the roof) _____ was leaking, so we had it repaired.
11. (husband / Katie) _____ is a doctor. He's a very nice man.
12. (my / necklace / sister) "I like your jewelry!" "Thank you. This is _____."

괄호 안에 주어진 표현과 her/him 등 또는 herself/himself 등을 함께 사용하여 문장을 완성하세요. 가능한 경우 herself/himself 등을 생략하고 쓰세요.

Success Through Hard Work

By Cathy Lewis

You can be successful!

When Mark Davis was growing up, his family was very poor.
13. (take care of) His parents were always working, so he had to
   take care of himself .
14. (look after, cared for) His sister was too young to _____, so
   he _____ too.
After high school, he was accepted into college. But his parents couldn't afford the tuition.
15. (paid for school) So he found a part-time job and _____.
Even though his life wasn't easy, he never gave up.
Today, he is a famous speaker. He travels around the world giving presentations to teenagers.
16. (helped) He says the hardships _____ to become successful.
He even met the president.
17. (gave him an award) He _____ for inspiring young people.
18. (believe in) At the awards ceremony, he said, "If you _____,
   you can be successful too!"

19. Mary has to leave work early this afternoon. She has to go to _____.
    a) dentist's office   b) the dentist's   c) the dentist office   d) dentist

20. "Have fun on your honeymoon!" "Thanks. I'm sure we'll _____."
    a) enjoy ourselves   b) enjoy themselves   c) enjoy us   d) enjoy yourselves

21. I wanted to drink some milk, but we didn't have _____ in the fridge.
    a) one   b) it   c) any   d) its

22. "Did you travel to Florida _____?" "Yes. I went alone."
    a) yourself   b) by yourself   c) all yourself   d) yourselves

23. My new apartment has _____. It's very convenient.
    a) own its parking space   b) its parking space own
    c) parking space own its   d) its own parking space

24. The old paintings in this museum are OK, but I prefer _____ the other museum.
    a) the modern ones in   b) the ones modern in   c) modern ones in   d) modern the ones in

25. "Is that Ryan and Helen's suitcase?" "No. _____ black, but that one is brown."
    a) Theirs are   b) Theirs is   c) Their is   d) Their are

26. "I like your new table." "Thanks. My parents bought it for we."
          a)   b)   c)   d)

27. Cats can be easier to keep than dogs because they can clean them.
          a)   b)   c)   d)

28. A your car is blocking the road. Can you move it, please?
          a)   b)   c)   d)

29. When we were in Bolivia, we visited La Paz. It is Bolivia capital city.
          a)   b)   c)   d)

30. "The Lees bought a house downtown. I've seen theirs house and it's huge." "I'd like to see it myself."
          a)   b)   c)   d)

31. Those pants don't look good on Joel. I think he should wear his black one.
          a)   b)   c)   d)

32. "Whose briefcase is that? Is it Mr. Roberts?" "I don't know. I'll ask him."
          a)   b)   c)   d)

정답 **p.332**

틀리거나 확실하지 않은 문제는 아래의 표를 확인하여 해당 Lesson으로 돌아가 복습하세요.

문제	1	2	3	4	5	6	7	8	9	10	11	12	13	14	15	16
Lesson	55	58	55	58	57	57	56	56	56	56	56	56	57	57	57	57
문제	17	18	19	20	21	22	23	24	25	26	27	28	29	30	31	32
Lesson	57	57	56	57	58	57	55	58	55	55	57	55	56	55	58	56

 주어진 명사와 some/any/no를 사용하여 문장을 완성하세요.

advice	milk	movies	plans	room	~~students~~

1. There are _some students_____ on the playground. They are playing football.
2. Katie bought me a new sofa, but my house has _____ for it.
3. "We don't have _____ for the cereal." "Really? I'll go to the store and get some."
4. _____ seemed interesting, so we decided not to watch one.
5. "Have you made _____ for the holidays?" "Yes. I'm visiting my parents."
6. I really need your opinion. Could you give me _____?

 괄호 안에 주어진 표현들을 적절한 형태로 사용하여 현재 시제 문장을 완성하세요. 필요한 경우 of를 함께 쓰세요.

7. (every, car, need)
   _Every car needs_____ a parking pass to park in this garage.
8. (either, the parks, seem)
   _____ perfect for our picnic. I like both.
9. (all, paper, come)
   "_____ from trees, right?" "Actually, that's not true."
10. (half, them, be)
    I bought these apples today, but _____ spoiled.
11. (both, my children, go)
    _____ to that high school.
12. (each, these boxes, cost)
    "_____ $10." "OK. I'll take two of them, please."

 셋 중 맞는 것을 고르세요.

The First Sports News

Big Game Next Weekend

13. ((Many) / Any / Much) people are looking forward to the game between the Panthers and the Bears.
It's going to be a great game because they're the strongest teams.
14. (Both / Neither / Either) of them has lost a game this season.
15. So it seems that (either / both / neither) team could win.
16. Unfortunately, (each / every / some) of the players from the Bears are injured.
17. But Bears fans don't have (some / any / no) doubt that the Bears will win.
The tickets are selling fast.
18. If you want to see this game, you must hurry because (few / some / little) tickets remain.

April 06, 2019

19. "If you have any problems, you can call me _____." "That's so nice of you."
    a) some time   b) any time   c) no time   d) both time

20. Ronald bought two pairs of shoes, and he paid $50 for _____.
    a) each   b) many   c) no   d) much

21. _____ was in the swimming pool, so we couldn't swim.
    a) Not any water   b) No water   c) Not water   d) None water

22. When Sam arrived at the birthday party, we had already eaten _____.
    a) none cake   b) any cake   c) most cake   d) most of the cake

23. My wife and I come to this café _____. It's our favorite.
    a) a lot of   b) lots of   c) a lot   d) a lots of

24. "I left my phone _____, and I don't remember where." "Did you check in your car?"
    a) somewhere   b) anywhere   c) nowhere   d) everywhere

25. _____ in the store is on sale, but most products are.
    a) Not everything   b) Nothing   c) No one   d) Not everyone

26. You eat salad for breakfast every day. You should try different something.
          a)   b)   c)   d)

27. There are over a hundred applicants for the job and each of them are well qualified.
                          a)   b)   c)   d)

28. Tim missed the meeting because nobody didn't tell him about it.
                  a)   b)   c)   d)

29. We have gotten hardly some rain in weeks. A lot of farmers are worried.
                          a)   b)   c)   d)

30. I had two exams today, but I didn't do well on neither. Both were so difficult.
          a)   b)   c)   d)

31. Judy has to travel a lot on business. That's why she has none pets.
                    a)   b)   c)   d)

32. "We have few cheese left. There's not enough for a sandwich." "I ate most of it yesterday."
          a)   b)   c)   d)

정답 p.333

틀리거나 확실하지 않은 문제는 아래의 표를 확인하여 해당 Lesson으로 돌아가 복습하세요.

문제	1	2	3	4	5	6	7	8	9	10	11	12	13	14	15	16
Lesson	59	60	59	60	59	59	61	64	61	63	64	63	62	64	64	63
문제	17	18	19	20	21	22	23	24	25	26	27	28	29	30	31	32
Lesson	59	62	59	61	60	63	62	59	61	59	63	60	59	64	60	63

주어진 단어를 사용하여 문장을 완성하세요. 필요한 경우 형용사를 부사로 바꾸어 쓰세요.

| ~~expensive~~ | melting | outdoor | perfect | sudden | surprised |

1 "That purse looks _expensive_ !" "Actually, it was cheap."

2. "Alice didn't expect to receive the award, but she did." "She must have been very _____."

3. The pianist performed the music _____, so everyone in the audience was impressed.

4. "Do you enjoy playing soccer?" "Not really. I don't like _____ sports."

5. Scientists warn that the _____ ice will cause sea levels to rise.

6. "Where's Cathy?" "I don't know. She left the room _____."

주어진 단어들을 적절히 배열하여 문장을 완성하세요. 필요한 경우 형용사를 부사로 바꾸어 쓰세요.

7. (you / warm / enough / for)
   "Is the room _warm enough for you_ ?" "Actually, I feel a little cold."

8. (us / go / for / too / heavy / to)
   It's raining _____ on a picnic today. Let's go tomorrow.

9. (garden / beautiful / such / a)
   "You have _____, Ms. Taylor." "Thank you."

10. (that / want / didn't / deep / so / I)
    Kevin was sleeping _____ to wake him up.

11 (long / to / too / Katie / for / wear)
   I think this skirt is _____. Do you have any shorter ones?

12. (polite / always / Ellie / so / talks)
    "_____ to everyone." "I know. She's never been rude to anyone."

틀린 부분이 있으면 바르게 고치세요. 틀린 부분이 없으면 ○로 표시하세요.

| To | toddbaker@fastmail.com |
| From | samadams@fastmail.com |

Hello Mr. Baker,

I bought a sofa from your store last year.

13. It has been an ~~excellently~~ *excellent* sofa for me. Also, I liked your staff too.

14. I have never met so friendly staff!

15. So the experience was highly satisfied.

16. Anyway, I'm looking for a new table for my dining room.

17. Could you recommend me a suitably table for me?

Oh, and if I decide to buy one, can you deliver it on the weekend?

18. I'm asking this because I usually am at work on weekdays.

I hope I hear from you soon.

Sincerely,

Sam Adams

보기 중 맞는 것을 고르세요.

19. "Look at that _____ sports car!" "Wow. That seems very expensive!"
    a) red nice   b) nice red   c) red nicely   d) nicely red

20. "Do you know who _____ is?" "Yes. That's Emily Brown."
    a) the girl singing on the stage   b) the singing on the stage girl
    c) the girl sung on the stage   d) singing the girl on the stage

21. I'm a twin, but I look _____ from my twin brother.
    a) complete different   b) different complete
    c) differently complete   d) completely different

22. It is _____ by yourself. I'll drive you home.
    a) to walk too dark   b) too walk to dark   c) too dark to walk   c) too darkly to walk

23. "I'm looking for Ms. Green." "She's gone out for lunch. She'll _____."
    a) be soon here   b) be here soon   c) here soon be   d) soon here be

24. I can't study here because there is _____.
    a) too much noise   b) too many noise   c) very much noise   d) very many noise

25. "How was your exam?" "It was _____. Everyone got an A."
    a) so easily test   b) so easy test   c) so easy   d) so easily

보기 중 틀린 것을 고르세요.

26. "Jake works so good that I don't need to train him." "That's very convenient."
       a) b)   c)   d)

27. "Did you receive the signing contract from the buyer?" "Yes. I got it late last night."
        a)   b)   c)   d)

28. Mr. Jones usually lets us speak free during class discussions.
             a)   b)   c)   d)

29. "You don't look happily. Is something wrong?" "I'm just too tired."
       a)   b)   c)   d)

30. I accidentally spilled red wine on the carpet. Bring me a towel fastly.
       a)   b)   c)   d)

31. "Did you have time enough to finish the test?" "No. The test was so long."
              a)   b)   c) d)

32. Our old house was too small, so we moved to a bigger house recent.
        a)   b)   c)   d)

정답 **p.333**

틀리거나 확실하지 않은 문제는 아래의 표를 확인하여 해당 Lesson으로 돌아가 복습하세요.

문제	1	2	3	4	5	6	7	8	9	10	11	12	13	14	15	16
Lesson	69	67	68	65	66	68	72	72	73	73	72	73	69	73	67	65
문제	17	18	19	20	21	22	23	24	25	26	27	28	29	30	31	32
Lesson	69	71	65	66	68	72	71	72	73	70	66	70	69	70	72	68

 주어진 단어를 사용하여 문장을 완성하세요. 형용사/부사를 비교급 또는 최상급으로 쓰거나 as를 함께 쓰세요.

cold	exciting	little	~~polite~~	smoothly	soon

1. You are _the politest_ person I know. You're always kind to everyone.
2. "Which car should I buy?" "The red car. It runs a lot _____ than the black one."
3. Mary cooks with _____ salt than before. She is trying to eat healthy.
4. You'd better finish the report _____ you can, or you won't meet the deadline.
5. My trip to Alaska was fun, but it was _____ place I've ever been to.
6. The end of the musical wasn't _____ the beginning. I was a little disappointed.

 괄호 안에 주어진 표현들을 적절히 배열하여 문장을 완성하세요.

7. (than / a little / tidier / usual)
   "Your room looks _a little tidier than usual_____." "I cleaned it this morning."
8. (the smartest / one / animals / of) The dolphin is _____ in the world.
9. (as / calls / many / as) The office received _____ it normally do.
10. (the most / experience / amazing)
    Riding an elephant was by far _____ I've ever had.
11. (the other days / twice / as / crowded / as)
    There are so many people at the restaurant today. It is _____.
12. (you / the more / will sing / the better / practice / you)
    "I want to be good at singing." "_____."

 괄호 안에 주어진 단어를 사용하여 문장을 완성하세요. 필요한 경우 형용사/부사를 비교급 또는 최상급으로 쓰세요.

To	samadams@fastmail.com
From	toddbaker@fastmail.com

Hello Mr. Adams,

As you wanted me to recommend a table, I picked three different tables for you.

	TABLE 1	TABLE 2	TABLE 3
Size	1.5m X 1m	1.2m X 1m	1.4m X 1m
Price	$300	$250	$500
Material	wood	plastic	steel

13. (cheap) If price is most important to you, table 2 is _(the) cheapest_ of all.
14. (small) However, it's slightly _____ than the other two tables. And it's made of plastic.
15. (expensive) Table 3 is stronger than the others as it's made of steel, but it's much _____.
16. (much) If you want a cheaper one, table 1 doesn't cost as _____ as table 3.
17. (large) And it is _____ in our store.
18. (heavy) Also, it's not as _____ as table 3 because it's made of wood.

Please call me if you need any more information.

Sincerely,
Todd Baker, Sales Manager

19. Our neighbors are _____ people in the neighborhood. They have loud parties every night.
    a) the noisiest   b) the noisier   c) the most noisy   d) noisiest

20. I arrived at the café _____ than Tom, so I ordered our drinks.
    a) a bit early   b) a bit earlier   c) by far early   d) by far earliest

21. I can run almost _____ as Jack, but he always wins the races.
    a) faster   b) fastest   c) as fast   d) quickly

22. "Who scored _____ during the soccer game?" "I did."
    a) most goals   b) the more goals   c) the most many goals   d) the most goals

23. Our town was chosen as _____ city in the country.
    a) the third safest   b) the third safe   c) third the safest   d) the third most safe

24. "Where did you get that wallet? It's _____." "Janet gave it to me for my birthday."
    a) the same than mine   b) the same mine as   c) the mine same as   d) the same as mine

25. Mr. Jones is popular among students because he's _____ the other teachers.
    a) less strict as   b) less stricter as   c) less strict than   d) less stricter than

보기 중 틀린 것을 고르세요.

26. The sunflowers in my garden have grown very taller than my son. They used to be very short.
    a)   b)   c)   d)

27. "The math test was as just easy as the science test." "Really? I thought it was more difficult."
    a)   b)   c)   d)

28. Jamie can speak Chinese, English, and Korean, but she speaks Chinese the less fluently of all.
    a)   b)   c)   d)

29. "Did you enjoy your trip?" "Yes. It was the best vacation in my life."
    a)   b)   c)   d)

30. The weather gets warm and warm as spring comes nearer.
    a)   b)   c)   d)

31. "Is tomorrow's meeting at the same time than the last one?" "No. It starts an hour earlier."
    a)   b)   c)   d)

32. The supermarket is having a sale. Food prices are slightly lowest than last week.
    a)   b)   c)   d)

정답 p.333

틀리거나 확실하지 않은 문제는 아래의 표를 확인하여 해당 Lesson으로 돌아가 복습하세요.

문제	1	2	3	4	5	6	7	8	9	10	11	12	13	14	15	16
Lesson	77	74	74	79	77	78	75	77	78	77	79	75	76	75	75	78
문제	17	18	19	20	21	22	23	24	25	26	27	28	29	30	31	32
Lesson	76	78	77	75	78	76	77	78	74	75	79	77	77	75	78	75

괄호 안에 주어진 표현들과 **at/on/in**을 함께 적절히 배열하여 문장을 완성하세요.

1. (the world / great places)
   There are many _great places in the world_____.
2. (dinner / anything)
   Janet didn't say _____. Is something wrong with her?
3. (Friday / the baseball game)
   "Do you want to watch _____?" "Sure. What time is the game?"
4. (something / my face)
   Is there _____? People keep looking at me.
5. (the hairdresser's / her)
   "Where did you see Sherry yesterday?" "I saw _____."
6. (my hometown / years)
   "I haven't visited _____." "Why not? Is it far from here?"

 주어진 단어들을 하나씩 사용하여 문장을 완성하세요.

concerned	~~difference~~	excellent		about	after	at
look	replied	search	**+**	~~between~~	for	to

7. "Is there any _difference between_____ these two shirts?" "No. They're the same."
8. Is Sarah busy these days? She hasn't _____ my e-mails for days.
9. Jerry has been sick for a week. We're very _____ him.
10. "Would you _____ my baby while I'm away?" "Sure. I'll take care of him."
11. The _____ the missing dog has been going on for three days.
12. Robin is _____ learning languages. She speaks five languages now.

 셋 중 맞는 것을 고르세요.

Welcome to Pan Music School!

13. Are you wondering what to do ((during) / with / by) summer vacation?
Come and learn to play the guitar at Pan Music School!

14. You will perform like a professional (at / within / until) two months.

15. (Thanks to / In spite of / By) our great instructors, many of our students have been able to play the guitar after only four weeks of training!

16. Or if you want to learn a different instrument (despite / instead / instead of), we'll find a perfect class for you!

17. If you apply for a class (until / by / in) the end of this month, you'll get a 10 percent discount.

18. So hurry! This offer is only available (till / by / on) August 31.
For directions to our location, please visit www.panmusic.com/location.

19. We are easy to find, and you can come here (in / by / with) bus or subway.

---

20. Is someone cooking _____ the kitchen? I smell something delicious.
    a) at   b) on   c) in   d) within

21. Katie was late for the meeting. She must not have been aware _____ the meeting time.
    a) about   b) at   c) for   d) of

22. I didn't _____ before going to bed last night. I was so sleepy.
    a) turn my clothes on   b) turn my clothes down
    c) take my clothes off   d) put my clothes off

23. "I think the cost _____ entrance to the zoo was $20." "It's $30 now."
    a) between   b) for   c) in   d) of

24. Jim shouted on the phone _____ anger. He might have been fighting with someone.
    a) by   b) with   c) to   d) for

25. "What did you complain _____ at the restaurant?" "The waiter was so rude to me."
    a) about   b) at   c) by   d) to

26. I'd like to go shopping on the weekend _____ watching a movie.
    a) instead of   b) instead   c) due to   d) because of

27. "I like that guy singing on the middle of the stage." "Oh, I saw him on TV!"
              a)   b)   c)   d)

28. "Do you exercise at the gym on every evening?" "No. Every morning."
                 a)   b)   c)   d)

29. Timothy came to my wedding despite of his broken leg.
            a) b)   c)   d)

30. I wasn't good for painting before taking lessons in the summer.
                 a)   b)   c)   d)

31. When we entered to the church, we could see a huge cross on the wall.
    a)   b)   c)   d)

32. "Where are my old toys?" "I threw away them. You're too old to play with them."
     a)   b)   c)   d)

.... 정답 **p.333**

틀리거나 확실하지 않은 문제는 아래의 표를 확인하여 해당 Lesson으로 돌아가 복습하세요.

문제	1	2	3	4	5	6	7	8	9	10	11	12	13	14	15	16
Lesson	81	82	82	80	81	83	90	87	89	87	90	89	84	84	86	86
문제	17	18	19	20	21	22	23	24	25	26	27	28	29	30	31	32
Lesson	84	84	85	80	89	88	90	85	87	86	81	82	86	89	87	88

주어진 표현들을 적절히 배열하여 예시와 같이 문장을 완성하세요.

~~as~~	as	by the time	even though	so that	until

1. (got / the holidays / closer)

   I become more excited _as the holidays get closer_____ .

2. (sit down / can / I)

   "Would you move your bag _____?" "Oh, sorry. Have a seat."

3. (on a diet / Lisa / was)

   _____ , she ate lots of food. She was so hungry.

4. (set / the sun)

   "Why do the children look so tired?" "They played in the park _____."

5. (Christmas presents / I / buy)

   _____ for everyone, I won't have much money left.

6. (on the phone / was / Tim / talking)

   _____ , the doorbell rang.

주어진 표현을 -ing로 사용하여 문장을 완성하세요. 필요한 경우 not을 함께 쓰세요.

be scared	know how to cook curry	~~live with my sister~~
travel in Europe	want to gain any more weight	watch the animal show

7. _Living with my sister_____ , I usually have dinner with her.

8. _____ , I visited many cities. Paris was the most exciting.

9. Heather joined a running club, _____ .

10. _____ of heights, I didn't go skydiving with my friends.

11. "We had a good time _____ at the zoo." "Did you take pictures?"

12. _____ , I searched the Internet to find a recipe.

틀린 부분이 있으면 바르게 고치세요. 틀린 부분이 없으면 ○로 표시하세요.

Follow Your Dreams

By Timothy White

Mary Williams has always been interested in fashion.

13. However, she majored in education ~~while~~ _during_ college, and she became a teacher.

14. Despite she was successful as a teacher, she decided to quit and study fashion.

15. By she graduated Parsons Fashion School, she had opened her first fashion design business.

16. As her brother majored in marketing, he helped her to start the business.

17. Mary is busy so that she stays at her office until midnight these days.

18. However, she seems very happy when design clothes.

19. By the time this year will end, she'll start her second business.

20. _____ Kenneth was walking in the forest, he saw a snake.
    a) Until   b) By the time   c) Although   (d) While

21. _____ a bicycle, you should wear a helmet.
    a) While ride   b) Not riding   c) When riding   d) When ride

22. _____ the hot weather, we went hiking.
    a) Until   b) In spite of   c) During   c) Although

23. "Could you check the oven _____ the table?" "OK."
    a) though I set   b) while I set   c) while I'll set d) though I'll set

24. _____ the teacher told us yesterday, we don't have class today.
    a) While   b) When   c) By the time   d) As

25. "How does Matt like college?" "He enjoys it _____ he says it's hard."
    a) in spite of   b) despite   c) although   d) while

26. Sharon is very angry at me. Should I keep apologizing _____ me?
    a) until she forgives   b) until she'll forgive
    c) by the time she forgives   d) by the time she'll forgive

보기 중 틀린 것을 고르세요.

27. I read many books while my vacation because I had a lot of free time.
       a)   (b)   c)   d)

28. By Jasmine woke up, everybody had gone out. She watched TV until they came back.
    a)   b)   c)   d)

29. Can you look for spelling mistakes as you will check the reports?
              a)   b)   c)   d)

30. Charlie's shoes are dirty so that you can't see what color they actually are.
                      a)   b)   c)   d)

31. There was some traffic as we were going to work. We weren't late, although.
    a)   b)   c)   d)

32. This money is so that paying the rent. I didn't spend it although I wanted to buy a new bag.
            a)   b)   c)   d)

정답 p.334

틀리거나 확실하지 않은 문제는 아래의 표를 확인하여 해당 Lesson으로 돌아가 복습하세요.

문제	1	2	3	4	5	6	7	8	9	10	11	12	13	14	15	16
Lesson	92	93	94	91	91	92	95	95	95	95	95	95	91	94	91	92
문제	17	18	19	20	21	22	23	24	25	26	27	28	29	30	31	32
Lesson	93	95	91	91	95	94	91	92	94	91	91	91	92	93	94	93

괄호 안에 주어진 표현들을 적절한 형태로 사용하여 문장을 완성하세요. 필요한 경우 will을 함께 쓰세요.

1. (not find, buy) Michael lost his wallet. If he _doesn't find_ it, he _'ll buy_ a new one.
2. (have, book) We _____ to wait a long time unless we _____ a table. That restaurant is very popular.
3. (catch, drink) If Jamie _____ cold, she always _____ lemon tea.
4. (ask, accept) If Ted _____ me on a date, I _____ his offer. I have a boyfriend.
5. (make, be) "I'm hungry." "I _____ you some toast if there _____ some bread."
6. (not go, not feel) "_____ to the party if you _____ well."
   "Well, I might feel better later."

주어진 문장을 보고 예시와 같이 문장을 완성하세요.

7. I didn't bring my jacket, so I feel cold.
   → _I wouldn't feel cold_ if _I had brought my jacket_ .
8. I won't go jogging because it's snowing.
   → If _____, _____.
9. Brian forgot about the meeting because I didn't remind him.
   → _____ if _____.
10. We can't send Sam a wedding gift because we don't know his address.
    → _____ if _____.
11. Angela broke her leg, so she is at the hospital.
    → If _____, _____.
12. Timothy didn't study hard, so he couldn't pass the English test.
    → If _____, _____.

괄호 안에 주어진 표현들을 적절한 형태로 사용하여 문장을 완성하세요. 필요한 경우 will 또는 would를 함께 쓰세요.

Hello Kathy,

I'm in Osaka now. I'll be here for a couple of days.
I almost missed my flight this morning because I arrived at the airport late.
13. (not stay, not wake) If I _hadn't stayed_ up so late, I _____ up late.
14. (not call, miss) If my dad _____ me, I _____ my flight!
15. (not rain, visit) Anyway, if it _____ tomorrow, I _____ the Osaka Market.
16. (buy, go) I _____ you a present if I _____ there.
By the way, I ate sushi for dinner. It was very good.
17. (come, like) If you _____ with me, you _____ it too.
18. (be) I wish we _____ here together. There are lots of interesting places in Osaka.
I hope you have a nice holiday too.

Julia

19. "Ken _____ this show if he watched it." "I think so too. It's very funny."
    a) will enjoy   b) enjoy   c) would have enjoyed   (d) would enjoy

20. If _____ the president, what would you say?
    a) you will meet   b) you meet   c) you met   d) you had met

21. I'll ask Jennifer to help me with my assignment if _____ busy.
    a) she isn't   b) she wasn't   c) she won't be   d) she hadn't been

22. Exercise more _____ to be healthier.
    a) if you wanted   b) if you want   c) if you will want   d) if you had wanted

23. I wish I _____ Spanish. It's a very beautiful language.
    a) spoke   b) speak   c) will speak   d) had spoken

24. If your office were closer to mine, I _____ you a ride every morning. But it's far away.
    a) can give   b) could give   c) could have given   d) give

25. If I _____ a nightmare last night, I could have slept well.
    a) had had   b) didn't have   c) don't have   d) hadn't had

26. If you'll wash the dishes, I'll do the laundry.
    (a)   b)   c)   d)

27. Unless the salad isn't fresh, I won't eat it.
         a)   b)   c)   d)

28. It's very hot in here because the air conditioner is broken. If only I had it fixed in advance.
          a)   b) c)   d)

29. If Chloe visited her parents last month, they could have celebrated her birthday together.
    a)   b)   c)   d)

30. I wish I attended class yesterday. I think Mr. Thomson said something important about the exam.
    a)   b)   c)   d)

31. Tom would make fewer mistakes if he listens to his brother's advice.
         a)   b)   c)   d)

32. "If you're free Saturday night, will you have joined us for dinner?" "Sure."
    a) b)   c)   d)

정답 p.334

틀리거나 확실하지 않은 문제는 아래의 표를 확인하여 해당 Lesson으로 돌아가 복습하세요.

문제	1	2	3	4	5	6	7	8	9	10	11	12	13	14	15	16
Lesson	96	96	96	96	96	96	98	97	98	97	98	98	98	98	96	96
문제	17	18	19	20	21	22	23	24	25	26	27	28	29	30	31	32
Lesson	98	99	97	97	96	96	99	97	98	96	96	99	98	99	97	96

주어진 표현들을 적절히 배열하여 문장을 완성하세요.

1. (studies / her cousin / who)

   Kim introduced me to _her cousin who studies_____ in New York.

2. (can / a restaurant / we / have / where)

   "Would you recommend _____ both seafood and steak?"

   "There's one on 6th Avenue."

3. (stories / I / whose / the novelist / like)

   "I sent a letter to _____ so much." "Who is that?"

4. (makes / what / angry / me)

   _____ is Tom's behavior. He's being very rude these days.

5. (from / I / the library / borrowed / which)

   _____ this book is too far. Can you drive me there?

6. (the way / cook / I)

   Jack likes _____ pasta. I put a lot of garlic and pepper in it.

 주어진 표현과 who/which/that/what을 함께 사용하여 문장을 완성하세요. 필요한 경우 콤마를 함께 쓰세요.

| caused the fire | ~~Christine gave to me~~ | I went to Paris |
| still live in my hometown | stole your bag | was very fun |

7. This cup _, which Christine gave to me_____, is my favorite. I always use it for coffee.

8. "Do you know _____?" "I heard lightning started it."

9. "Did you find the thief _____?" "Not yet."

10. Yesterday, I took my kids to the amusement park _____.

11. Aaron and Ken _____, are my oldest friends.

12. "The time _____ was exciting." "What did you do there?"

 틀린 부분이 있으면 바르게 고치세요. 틀린 부분이 없으면 ○로 표시하세요.

Hello Jennifer,

13. Yesterday, I found an old photo ~~which took~~ *which we took* together years ago.

Since I saw it, I've missed you so much.

14. And that's the reason I'm writing this letter.

15. Do you remember the river we went fishing?

16. We met a man which name was Patrick. He was really good at fishing.

17. And the woman came with Patrick was a really good cook.

18. I can't forget the delicious fish which she cooked it. Let's go fishing again when you have time.

Love,

Sharon

AIR MAIL

보기 중 맞는 것을 고르세요.

19 "Is that the dancer _____ the first prize in the dance contest?" "Yes. His name is Jonny."
   a) which won   b) which he won   c) who won   d) who he won

20. The man _____ last week for the manager position was really impressive.
   a) whom I interviewed   b) whom interviewed   c) who interviewed   d) which I interviewed

21. The city _____ my childhood has a great night view.
   a) which I spent   b) in which I spent   c) in I spent   d) I spent

22. "What's this?" "It's _____ I bought my mom for her birthday. Do you think she'll like it?"
   a) who   b) which   c) that   d) what

23. Ms. Collins, _____ me Japanese, is getting married next month.
   a) who taught   b) that taught   c) who she taught   d) that she taught

24. Can you tell me _____ I can turn on this air conditioner? It's very hot in here.
   a) the way how   b) how   c) the way what   d) which

25. The little girl _____ eyes are brown is very cute.
   a) who   b) whom   c) whose   d) that

보기 중 틀린 것을 고르세요.

26 This is the briefcase, that was in the conference room. Whose is it?
   a)   b)   c)   d)

27. I know two brothers whose father work as an editor at this company. They also want to become editors.
   a)   b)   c)   d)

28. Did you see the man to who I was talking earlier? That's Professor Anderson.
               a)   b) c)   d)

29. The thing what the mailman delivered this morning is a postcard Jake sent from LA.
   a)   b)   c)   d)

30. I own a house which it has five rooms. It's big enough for our family.
         a)   b)   c) d)

31. The way how Terry deals with customers is rude. Some people who shopped here complained.
   a)   b)   c)   d)

32. Karen has the flu, which stop her from going to school.
       a)   b)   c)   d)

정답 p.334

틀리거나 확실하지 않은 문제는 아래의 표를 확인하여 해당 Lesson으로 돌아가 복습하세요.

문제	1	2	3	4	5	6	7	8	9	10	11	12	13	14	15	16
Lesson	100	104	102	102	101	104	103	102	100	103	103	104	101	104	104	102
문제	17	18	19	20	21	22	23	24	25	26	27	28	29	30	31	32
Lesson	100	101	100	101	101	102	103	104	102	103	102	101	102	100	104	103

주어진 문장을 보고 괄호 안의 동사를 사용하여 각 사람의 말을 예시와 같이 전달해보세요. 필요한 경우 if를 함께 쓰세요.

1. SARAH: "Tim passed the driving test."
   YOU: (said) *Sarah said (that) Tim passed (OR had passed) the driving test*   .

2. DR. TURNER: "Nancy, you'll feel much better."
   YOU: (told) _____ .

3. RICHARD: "Is the bathroom on the first floor?"
   YOU: (asked) _____ .

4. JAKE: "Annie, I'm writing a letter to John."
   YOU: (told) _____ .

5. HELEN: "Can I use the computer?"
   YOU: (asked) _____ .

6. JEFF: "I haven't tried bungee jumping."
   YOU: (said) _____ .

 괄호 안에 주어진 동사를 사용하여 예시와 같이 Vicky의 말을 전달해보세요. 필요한 경우 not을 함께 쓰세요.

7. Bill, please don't touch my phone.	(told) *She told Bill not to touch her phone* .
8. Lisa, could you make some toast for me?	(asked) _____ .
9. Mike, stop playing video games.	(told) _____ .
10. Sam, please don't talk loudly.	(asked) _____ .
11. Janice, don't be late for class.	(told) _____ .
12. Kim, would you lend me some money?	(asked) _____ .

VICKY

괄호 안에 주어진 표현들을 적절히 배열하여 문장을 완성하세요. 필요한 경우 to나 that을 함께 쓰세요.

Amazing Animal Behaviors

Some animal behaviors are so amazing.

13. (are / lay / some birds / known)
For example, *some birds are known to lay* _____ their eggs in another bird's nest.

14. (cows / face / believed / are)
And _____ north while eating in the field.

15. (some penguins / is / known / dance / it)
In addition, _____ when they are trying to attract females.

16. (thought / like / cats / are)
And, _____ people who don't like them.

17. (eating stones / it / said / helps / is)
Also, _____ crocodiles swim.

18. (don't / is / it / sleep / believed / dolphins)
Finally, _____ for months after their babies are born.

It's hard not to be surprised by these behaviors. So, next time you see an animal, watch it carefully.

19. Don't get onions on the pizza. Daniel said his daughter _____ onions.
    a) is hating   b) hated   c) to hate   d) hate

20. Professor Lim _____ be very strict to his students.
    a) is known to   b) is known   c) know to   d) know

21. Jennifer _____ not good at math. So I decided to teach her.
    a) told she was   b) told she is   c) said she was   d) said to she was

22. Mr. Young asked _____ help him paint the wall.
    a) whether could I   b) whether I could c) that I could   d) to

23. In that restaurant, it is _____ only in cash.
    a) expected customers pay   b) expected to customers pay
    c) expected customers that pay   d) expected that customers pay

24. Whenever Karen is angry with me, I always _____ first.
    a) say sorry to her   b) say sorry her   c) told sorry to her d) told sorry her

25. Ronald _____ he was practicing dancing.
    a) told that   b) said me   c) told me that   d) said me that

26. "Ms. Carter said her husband that she wanted to buy a new car." "Did they buy one?"
        a)   b)   c)   d)

27. Betty said she lives in Hong Kong before she moved to Beijing a few years ago.
        a)   b)   c)   d)

28. The president is speaking at the seminar. He is expected that he will arrive soon.
                                    a)   b)   c)   d)

29. "Donna wondered why George calls her last night." "I have no idea. I'll ask him."
            a)   b)   c)   d)

30. It is said to that Mt. Everest is very hard to climb.
        a)   b)   c)   d)

31. "I like dogs." "Me too. They believed to understand people's feelings very well."
        a)   b)   c)   d)

32. Michael asked to Jessie go camping with him last weekend, but she was too busy then.
                    a)   b)   c)   d)

정답 p.335

틀리거나 확실하지 않은 문제는 아래의 표를 확인하여 해당 Lesson으로 돌아가 복습하세요.

문제	1	2	3	4	5	6	7	8	9	10	11	12	13	14	15	16
Lesson	105	106	106	106	106	105	106	106	106	106	106	106	107	107	107	107
문제	17	18	19	20	21	22	23	24	25	26	27	28	29	30	31	32
Lesson	107	107	105	107	106	106	107	106	106	106	105	107	106	107	107	106

괄호 안에 주어진 표현들과 so/neither/not을 함께 사용하여 대화를 완성하세요.

1. I've never watched that TV show before.
2. I'm hungry. Is there anything to eat?
3. Sarah can speak Spanish very well.
4. Is our boss in his office?
5. My parents didn't let me go to the party.
6. Are you going to get vacation time in August?

(I) _Neither have I_ . But Janice said it's funny.
(I'm afraid) _____ . Let's order a pizza.
(Jake) _____ . He can also speak Italian.
(I think) _____ . It's lunchtime now.
(mine) _____ . So I stayed home.
(I hope) _____ . I want to go to Cebu City this summer.

 괄호 안에 주어진 표현들을 적절히 배열하여 문장을 완성하세요. 필요한 경우 not을 함께 쓰세요.

7. (space / there / be / might / some)
"Where should I put these boxes?" " _There might be some space_ in the garage."

8. (so / do / I / think)
"Is Tony working hard these days?" "_____ . He's being a little lazy."

9. (eggs / are / enough / there)
_____ in the fridge? We will need three to make the cookies.

10. (have / any / new employees / been / there)
_____ at the company for years. But they're hiring some this year.

11. (Aaron / were / we / asked / surprised / that)
_____ Sharon to marry him. We thought they were just friends.

12. (was / much / there / traffic)
_____ on the road, so it took less time than usual to get here.

 주어진 동사를 적절한 형태로 사용하여 문장을 완성하세요. 필요한 경우 not을 함께 쓰세요.

~~be~~ be go join miss read talk

Tips for Freshmen from the President of the Student Council

13. Some freshmen think that getting good grade _is_ difficult.
So here are some tips for doing well in your first year.

14. First, it's essential that students _____ any classes.

15. And I suggest you _____ with your professors if you have any problems.

16. Also, I recommend that you _____ study groups on campus, which can be helpful.

17. And it's important that college students _____ as many books as possible.

18. Lastly, I advise that you _____ to too many parties. Many students' grades have dropped for this reason.

19. I hope that these tips _____ helpful for you.

---

20. "Have the Andersons come back from Japan?" "I _____. I called but nobody answered."
    a) don't believe   (b) don't believe so   c) believe so   d) don't believe not

21. "_____ coins on the desk. Have you seen them?" "Kathy might have taken them."
    a) There is some   b) There are some   c) There was some   d) There were some

22. We demand that _____ in the river. It's very dangerous.
    a) kids don't swim   b) kids swim   c) kids not swim   d) kids swim not

23. "I might not be able to go to your wedding." "_____? Will you be out of town?"
    a) Why no   b) Why so   c) Why not   d) Not why

24. Was Carol _____ a teacher?
    a) proud that Jill became   b) proud that became Jill
    c) proud became Jill   d) proud Jill became that

25. "I have my haircut at the Alexis Hair Salon downtown." "_____."
    a) Neither have I   b) Neither do I   c) So have I   d) So do I

26. Are you driving to school tomorrow? _____, let's take the bus together.
    a) If so   b) If not   c) If neither   d) If don't

27. When <u>you're</u> pregnant, <u>it's important</u> you <u>don't be</u> upset. It's <u>harmful</u> to your baby.
          a)   b)   (c)   d)

28. There <u>be should</u> <u>enough</u> <u>sunlight</u> for plants, or they <u>might</u> die.
    a)   b)   c)   d)

29. "Is it essential <u>that</u> <u>we finish</u> this essay today?" "I <u>don't hope so</u>. I have another assignment."
          a)   b)   c)   d)

30. "I'm <u>surprised</u> <u>that</u> Jim <u>get</u> a scholarship." "<u>So am I</u>. He didn't study very hard."
          a)   b)   c)   d)

31. "The fireman <u>insisted</u> that everyone <u>went</u> outside quickly." "<u>I suppose</u> <u>there was</u> a big fire."
                    a)   b)   c)   d)

32. "I have <u>been</u> very busy these days." "<u>So was I</u>. I'm afraid I haven't slept for two days."
          a)   b) c)   d)

정답 p.335

틀리거나 확실하지 않은 문제는 아래의 표를 확인하여 해당 Lesson으로 돌아가 복습하세요.

문제	1	2	3	4	5	6	7	8	9	10	11	12	13	14	15	16
Lesson	109	109	109	109	109	109	108	109	108	108	110	108	110	110	110	110
문제	17	18	19	20	21	22	23	24	25	26	27	28	29	30	31	32
Lesson	110	110	110	109	108	110	109	110	109	109	110	108	109	110	110	109

GRAMMAR
GATEWAY
INTERMEDIATE

www.Hackers.co.kr

Appendix

Lesson에서 다룬 사항을 정리한 내용과 영어 공부의 기본이 되는 사항들,
익혀두면 유용한 실용적인 표현들을 부록에 담았습니다.
보다 효과적인 학습을 위해 필요한 내용을 찾아 공부하세요.

1. 영어의 문장 성분

영어 문장에는 주어, 동사 등과 같이 반드시 들어가야 하는 필수 요소와 그 외에 부가 요소인 수식어가 있습니다.
다음 설명과 예문을 보면서 문장을 구성하는 요소들을 익혀보세요.

A. 주어와 동사

주어 + 동사

She drives. 그녀가 운전한다.
주어　동사

영어 문장에는 주어와 동사가 꼭 필요합니다. **주어**는 어떤 행동이나 상태의 주체가 되는 말로 우리말의 '누가' 또는 '무엇이'에
해당합니다. **동사**는 행동이나 상태를 나타내는 말로 우리말의 '~하다, ~이다'에 해당합니다. 위의 문장에서 **주어**는 **She**이고,
동사는 **drives**입니다.

주어와 동사의 수 일치

A bird is in the tree. 새가 나무에 있다.
단수명사　단수동사

Water flows under the bridge. 물이 다리 아래로 흐른다.
셀 수 없는 명사　단수동사

Three cows are in the field. 소 세 마리가 들판에 있다.
복수명사　복수동사

영어 문장에서 **단수명사** 또는 **셀 수 없는 명사**를 주어로 쓸 때는 **단수동사**를 쓰고, **복수명사**를 주어로 쓸 때는 **복수동사**를 씁니
다. 위의 문장들에서 단수명사 **A bird**, 셀 수 없는 명사 **Water**를 주어로 썼기 때문에 단수동사 **is**와 **flows**를 썼고, 복수명사
Three cows를 주어로 썼기 때문에 복수동사 **are**를 썼습니다.

B. 목적어

주어 + 동사 + 목적어

He teaches math. 그는 수학을 가르친다.
주어　동사　목적어

She drives와 같이 주어와 동사만으로 완전한 문장이 되는 경우도 있지만, 동사 뒤에 목적어가 필요한 문장도 있습니다.
목적어는 동사가 나타내는 행동의 대상이 되는 말로 우리말의 '~을/를'에 해당합니다. 위의 문장에서 그가 무엇을 가르치는지 말
하기 위해 동사 teaches 뒤에 **목적어 math**를 썼습니다.

주어 + 동사 + 간접목적어 + 직접목적어

She gave the girl a present. 그녀는 소녀에게 선물을 주었다.
주어 　동사　간접목적어　　　직접목적어

하나의 목적어가 필요한 경우도 있지만, 두 개의 목적어가 필요한 문장도 있습니다. **간접목적어**는 우리말의 '～에게'에 해당하고,
직접목적어는 우리말의 '～을/를'에 해당합니다. 위의 문장에서 그녀가 누구에게 무엇을 주었는지 말하기 위해 동사 gave 뒤에
간접목적어 the girl과 **직접목적어 a present**를 썼습니다.

C. 보어

주어 + 동사 + 보어

He is a police officer. 그는 경찰관이다.
주어 동사　　　보어

목적어가 필요한 문장도 있지만, 보어가 필요한 문장도 있습니다. **보어**는 주어가 무엇인지, 어떤 상태인지 등을 설명해주는 말입
니다. 위의 문장에서는 그가 무엇인지 설명하기 위해 동사 **is** 뒤에 **보어 a police officer**를 썼습니다.

주어 + 동사 + 목적어 + 보어

The story made her sad. 그 이야기가 그녀를 슬프게 했다.
　주어　　　동사　목적어　보어

보어는 목적어가 무엇인지, 어떤 상태인지 등을 보충 설명할 수도 있습니다. 위의 문장에서는 목적어인 그녀가 어떤 상태인지 설
명하기 위해 목적어 **her** 뒤에 **보어 sad**를 썼습니다.

D. 수식어

Every evening, he watches TV. 그는 저녁마다 TV를 본다.
　　수식어　　　　　주어　　동사　목적어

He watches TV **with Helen.** 그는 Helen과 TV를 본다.
주어　　동사　　목적어　　수식어

문장을 구성하는 요소에는 주어, 동사, 목적어, 보어와 같은 필수 요소 외에 수식어도 있습니다. **수식어**는 문장을 구성할 때 없어
도 되는 부가 요소지만, 다른 요소를 꾸며주어 문장을 더 풍부하게 하는 말입니다. 첫 번째 문장에서는 언제 TV를 보는지 나타
내기 위해 **수식어 Every evening**을 썼습니다. 두 번째 문장에서는 누구와 TV를 보는지 나타내기 위해 **수식어 with Helen**
을 썼습니다.

2. be동사와 일반동사

우리는 앞에서 be동사와 일반동사를 사용하여 다양하게 말하는 방법을 배웠습니다. 다음 설명과 예문을 보면서 be동사와 일반동사를 사용하는 법을 비교해서 익혀보세요.

A. 긍정

be동사

(현재)	주어	**am/is/are**
(과거)		**was/were**

- I**'m** a children's doctor. I take care of kids.
- The singers **were** nervous during their first performance.

일반동사

(현재)	주어	**want(s)/call(s)** 등
(과거)		**wanted/called** 등

- Nick **wants** to stay healthy, so he **exercises** every day.
- I **called** Jenny yesterday to ask about her trip.

일반동사를 사용한 긍정문에서는 **work(s)/visit(s)** 등의 앞에 **am/is/are** 등을 쓰지 않는 것에 주의합니다.

- I **work** Monday through Friday, but I'm off on weekends. (am work로 쓸 수 없음)
- My cousins **visited** me last weekend. (were visited로 쓸 수 없음)

B. 부정

be동사

(현재)	주어	**am/is/are**	**not**
(과거)		**was/were**	

- My neighbors **aren't** home. I think they're on vacation.
- The new book by my favorite author **wasn't** interesting.

일반동사

(현재)	주어	**do(es)n't**	동사원형
(과거)		**didn't**	(own/bring 등)

- We **don't own** a car because gas is too expensive.
- "Can I borrow your phone?" "I **didn't bring** it."

일반동사를 사용한 부정문에서는 **like/come** 등의 동사원형 앞에 **do(es)n't/didn't**를 씁니다. **am/is/are not** 등을 쓰지 않는 것에 주의합니다.

- "Michelle **doesn't like** scary movies." "I **don't either.**" (isn't like로 쓸 수 없음)
- Brad **didn't come** to work today. He's sick. (wasn't come으로 쓸 수 없음)

C. 의문

be동사

(현재)	am/is/are	주어	... ?
(과거)	was/were		

- "**Is this umbrella** yours?" "Yes it is."
- "How **was the movie?**" "It was interesting."

일반동사

(현재)	do(es)	주어	동사원형 (work/buy 등)	?
(과거)	did			

- I need to make some copies. **Does that printer work?**
- "What **did you buy** at the mall?" "A necklace."

일반동사를 사용한 의문문에서는 주어 앞에 **do(es)/did**를 씁니다. **am/is/are** 등을 쓰지 않는 것에 주의합니다.

- "**Do you have** roommates?" "No. I live alone." (Are you have로 쓸 수 없음)
- "**Did Marcia win** her tennis match?" "Yes. She played very well." (Was Marcia win으로 쓸 수 없음)

D. be동사 + -ing/과거분사

be동사 뒤에 동사원형은 쓸 수 없지만, **-ing**와 과거분사는 쓸 수 있습니다.

진행 시제

am/is/are	-ing
was/were	(studying, raining 등)

- "Where are Brian and Lisa?"
  "They**'re studying** in the library right now." (They're study로 쓸 수 없음)
- It **was raining** when I left home this morning. (It was rain으로 쓸 수 없음)

수동태

am/is/are	과거분사
was/were	(packed, painted 등)

- "Are you ready for your trip?"
  "Yes. All of our bags **are packed.**" (All of our bags are pack으로 쓸 수 없음)
- "That picture **was painted** by one of my friends." "It's beautiful." (That picture was paint로 쓸 수 없음)

3. 주의해야 할 형태 변화

영어의 동사, 명사, 형용사는 경우에 따라 형태가 다양하게 변합니다. 다음 표를 보면서 그 규칙을 익혀보세요.

A. 동사의 형태 변화 (Lesson 2 - 20, 33, 36)

동사에 (e)s를 붙일 때 (주어가 he/she/it 등인 경우)

+ s	speak → speaks laugh → laughs	care → cares know → knows	clean → cleans ride → rides
-ss/-sh/-ch/-x + es	miss → misses rush → rushes mix → mixes	pass → passes touch → touches fix → fixes	wash → washes catch → catches relax → relaxes
-o + es	go → goes	do → does	
자음 + y → y를 i로 바꾸고 + es	worry → worries reply → replies	fly → flies rely → relies	hurry → hurries dry → dries
모음 + y → + s	stay → stays	pay → pays	buy → buys

동사에 ing를 붙일 때

+ ing	cook → cooking	grow → growing	join → joining
-e → e를 빼고 + ing	dance → dancing use → using change → changing	drive → driving hope → hoping save → saving	write → writing decide → deciding invite → inviting
-ee + ing	agree → agreeing	see → seeing	
-ie → ie를 y로 바꾸고 + ing	die → dying	lie → lying	tie → tying
단모음 + 단자음으로 끝날 때	1음절 단어는 끝에 오는 자음을 한 번 더 쓰고 ing를 씁니다. stop → stopping 　　 knit → knitting 　　 rub → rubbing plan → planning 　　 dip → dipping 　　 run → running get → getting 　　 chat → chatting 　　 jog → jogging 2음절 이상의 단어는 강세가 마지막에 있는 경우에만 끝에 오는 자음을 한 번 더 쓰고 ing를 씁니다. begin [bigín] → beginning 　　 refer [rifə́ːr] → referring permit [pərmít] → permitting 　　 prefer [prifə́ːr] → preferring admit [ædmít] → admitting 　　 regret [rigrét] → regretting

동사에 (e)d를 붙일 때

+ ed	ask → ask**ed**	allow → allow**ed**	order → order**ed**
	reach → reach**ed**	call → call**ed**	rain → rain**ed**
-e/-ee/-ie + d	create → create**d**	believe → believe**d**	agree → agree**d**
	die → die**d**	tie → tie**d**	lie → lie**d**
자음 + y → y를 i로 바꾸고 + ed	try → tr**ied**	apply → appl**ied**	study → stud**ied**
	bury → bur**ied**	copy → cop**ied**	carry → carr**ied**
모음 + y → + ed	enjoy → enjoy**ed**	delay → delay**ed**	stay → stay**ed**
	예외) pay → pa**id**	lay → la**id**	say → sa**id**

단모음 + 단자음으로 끝날 때	1음절 단어는 끝에 오는 자음을 한 번 더 쓰고 ed를 씁니다. drop → drop**ped** beg → beg**ged** rub → rub**bed** jog → jog**ged** grab → grab**bed** shop → shop**ped** 2음절 이상의 단어는 강세가 마지막에 있는 경우에만 끝에 오는 자음을 한 번 더 쓰고 ed를 씁니다. occur [əkə́ːr] → occur**red** equip [ikwíp] → equip**ped** permit [pərmít] → permit**ted** prefer [prifə́ːr] → prefer**red** regret [rigrét] → regret**ted** control [kəntróul] → control**led**

B. 명사의 형태 변화 (Lesson 47, 56)

명사에 s를 붙일 때 (명사의 복수형)

+ s	idea → idea**s**	museum → museum**s**	street → street**s**
-s/-ss/-sh/-ch/-x + es	bus → bus**es**	dress → dress**es**	brush → brush**es**
	match → match**es**	lunch → lunch**es**	box → box**es**
-f(e) → f를 v로 바꾸고 + es	leaf → lea**ves**	wolf → wol**ves**	shelf → shel**ves**
	thief → thie**ves**	life → li**ves**	knife → kni**ves**
자음 + y → y를 i로 바꾸고 + es	lady → lad**ies**	family → famil**ies**	story → stor**ies**
	city → cit**ies**	penny → penn**ies**	secretary → secretar**ies**
모음 + y → + s	holiday → holiday**s**	toy → toy**s**	journey → journey**s**
자음 + o → + es	potato → potato**es**	tomato → tomato**es**	hero → hero**es**
	예외) kilo → kilo**s**	piano → piano**s**	photo → photo**s**
모음 + o → + s	video → video**s**	radio → radio**s**	zoo → zoo**s**

명사에 's를 붙일 때 (명사의 소유격)

단수명사 + 's	the **doctor's office** my **boss's car**	the **bird's nest** the **elephant's nose**	**John's address** **Charles's birthday**
-s로 끝나지 않는 복수명사 + 's	the **women's clothes**	the **children's books**	the **people's feelings**
-s로 끝나는 복수명사 + '	the **clients' needs**	the **dogs' houses**	the **giraffes' necks**

C. 형용사/부사의 형태 변화 (Lesson 68, 74 - 77)

형용사에 ly를 붙여 부사로 만들 때

+ ly	cheap → cheap**ly** safe → safe**ly**	careful → careful**ly** extreme → extreme**ly**	excited → excited**ly** similar → similar**ly**
-y → y를 i로 바꾸고 + ly	lazy → laz**ily** hungry → hungr**ily**	noisy → nois**ily** happy → happ**ily**	heavy → heav**ily** easy → eas**ily**
-le → e를 빼고 + y	proba**ble** → proba**bly** possi**ble** → possi**bly**	incredi**ble** → incredi**bly** sim**ple** → sim**ply**	terri**ble** → terri**bly** reasona**ble** → reasona**bly**
-ic + ally	fantast**ic** → fantastic**ally** automat**ic** → automatic**ally**		romant**ic** → romantic**ally** dramat**ic** → dramatic**ally**

형용사/부사 뒤에 (e)r/(e)st를 붙일 때

1음절 형용사/부사 → **+ er/est**	deep - deep**er** - the deep**est** bright - bright**er** - the bright**est** 예외) fun - **more** fun - the **most** fun	fast - fast**er** - the fast**est** hard - hard**er** - the hard**est**
-e로 끝나는 1음절 형용사/부사 → **+ r/st**	large - larg**er** - the larg**est** safe - saf**er** - the saf**est**	wide - wid**er** - the wid**est** late - lat**er** - the lat**est**
단모음 + 단자음으로 끝나는 1음절 형용사/부사 → 자음 한 번 더 쓰고 **+ er/est**	hot - hot**ter** - the hot**test** fit - fit**ter** - the fit**test**	fat - fat**ter** - the fat**test** sad - sad**der** - the sad**dest**
-y로 끝나는 2음절 형용사/부사 → y를 i로 바꾸고 **+ er/est**	funny - funn**ier** - the funn**iest** angry - angr**ier** - the angr**iest**	dirty - dirt**ier** - the dirt**iest** early - earl**ier** - the earl**iest**

형용사/부사 앞에 more/most를 쓸 때

2음절 이상 형용사/부사	famous - **more** famous - the **most** famous quickly - **more** quickly - the **most** quickly	popular - **more** popular - the **most** popular clearly - **more** clearly - the **most** clearly
-ing/-ed로 끝나는 형용사	boring - **more** boring - the **most** boring tired - **more** tired - the **most** tired	relaxing - **more** relaxing - the **most** relaxing annoyed - **more** annoyed - the **most** annoyed

4. 불규칙 동사 (Lesson 6, 10-15, 20, 33)

 eat의 과거는 ate, 과거분사는 eaten인 것처럼 영어의 동사 중에는 -(e)d를 붙이지 않고 과거, 과거분사를 만드는 불규칙 동사가 있습니다. 다음 표를 보면서 다양한 불규칙 동사를 익혀보세요.

현재	과거	과거분사	현재	과거	과거분사
am/is/are (be동사)	was/were	been	drink	drank	drunk
arise	arose	arisen	drive	drove	driven
awake	awoke	awoken	eat	ate	eaten
beat	beat	beaten	fall	fell	fallen
become	became	become	feed	fed	fed
begin	began	begun	feel	felt	felt
bend	bent	bent	fight	fought	fought
bite	bit	bitten	find	found	found
blow	blew	blown	fit	fit	fit
break	broke	broken	fly	flew	flown
bring	brought	brought	forbid	forbade	forbidden
build	built	built	forget	forgot	forgotten
burn	burned/burnt	burned/burnt	forgive	forgave	forgiven
burst	burst	burst	freeze	froze	frozen
buy	bought	bought	get	got	got/gotten
catch	caught	caught	give	gave	given
choose	chose	chosen	go	went	gone
come	came	come	grow	grew	grown
cost	cost	cost	hang	hung	hung
cut	cut	cut	have	had	had
deal	dealt	dealt	hear	heard	heard
dig	dug	dug	hide	hid	hidden
dive	dived/dove	dived	hit	hit	hit
do	did	done	hold	held	held
draw	drew	drawn	hurt	hurt	hurt
dream	dreamed/dreamt	dreamed/dreamt	keep	kept	kept
			know	knew	known

현재	과거	과거분사
lay	laid	laid
lead	led	led
lean	leaned/leant	leaned/leant
learn	learned/learnt	learned/learnt
leave	left	left
lend	lent	lent
let	let	let
lie	lay	lain
light	lit	lit
lose	lost	lost
make	made	made
mean	meant	meant
meet	met	met
pay	paid	paid
prove	proved	proved/proven
put	put	put
quit	quit	quit
read [riːd]	read [red]	read [red]
ride	rode	ridden
ring	rang	rung
rise	rose	risen
run	ran	run
say	said	said
see	saw	seen
seek	sought	sought
sell	sold	sold
send	sent	sent
set	set	set
shake	shook	shaken
shine	shined/shone	shined/shone
shoot	shot	shot
show	showed	showed/shown

현재	과거	과거분사
shut	shut	shut
sing	sang	sung
sit	sat	sat
sleep	slept	slept
slide	slid	slid
speak	spoke	spoken
spell	spelled/spelt	spelled/spelt
spend	spent	spent
spill	spilled/spilt	spilled/spilt
spin	spun	spun
split	split	split
spread	spread	spread
spring	sprang	sprung
stand	stood	stood
steal	stole	stolen
stick	stuck	stuck
strike	struck	struck
sweep	swept	swept
swim	swam	swum
swing	swung	swung
take	took	taken
teach	taught	taught
tear	tore	torn
tell	told	told
think	thought	thought
throw	threw	thrown
understand	understood	understood
upset	upset	upset
wake	woke	woken
wear	wore	worn
win	won	won
write	wrote	written

5. 시제 (Lesson 2 - 20)

우리는 앞에서 다양한 시제로 말하는 방법을 배웠습니다. 다음 표를 보면서 시제에 따라 문장의 동사가 어떻게 변하는지 간단히 정리해서 익혀보세요.

A. 현재

	긍정	부정	의문
현재 시제 **do/does**	Tom **exercises.**	Tom **doesn't exercise.**	**Does** Tom **exercise?**
현재진행 시제 **am/is/are doing**	Tom **is exercising.**	Tom **isn't exercising.**	**Is** Tom **exercising?**
현재완료 시제 **have/has done**	Tom **has exercised.**	Tom **hasn't exercised.**	**Has** Tom **exercised?**
현재완료진행 시제 **have/has been doing**	Tom **has been exercising.**	Tom **hasn't been exercising.**	**Has** Tom **been exercising?**

B. 과거

	긍정	부정	의문
과거 시제 **did**	Tom **exercised.**	Tom **didn't exercise.**	**Did** Tom **exercise?**
과거진행 시제 **was/were doing**	Tom **was exercising.**	Tom **wasn't exercising.**	**Was** Tom **exercising?**
과거완료 시제 **had done**	Tom **had exercised.**	Tom **hadn't exercised.**	**Had** Tom **exercised?**

C. 미래

	긍정	부정	의문
미래 시제 **will do** 또는 **am/is/are going to do**	Tom **will exercise.** 또는 Tom **is going to exercise.**	Tom **won't exercise.** 또는 Tom **isn't going to exercise.**	**Will** Tom **exercise?** 또는 **Is** Tom **going to exercise?**
미래진행 시제 **will be doing**	Tom **will be exercising.**	Tom **won't be exercising.**	**Will** Tom **be exercising?**
미래완료 시제 **will have done**	Tom **will have exercised.**	Tom **won't have exercised.**	**Will** Tom **have exercised?**

6. 축약형

영어 문장을 말할 때는 He is, We cannot 대신 He's, We can't와 같이 짧게 줄인 축약형을 자주 씁니다. 다음 표를 보면서 다양한 축약형을 익혀보세요.

	긍정	부정
be **(am/is/are, was/were)**	am → **'m** is → **'s** are → **'re**	am not → **'m not** is not → **'s not** 또는 **isn't** are not → **'re not** 또는 **aren't**
	-	was not → **wasn't** were not → **weren't**
do **(do/does/did)**	-	do not → **don't** does not → **doesn't** did not → **didn't**
have **(have/has/had)**	have → **'ve** has → **'s** had → **'d**	have not → **'ve not** 또는 **haven't** has not → **'s not** 또는 **hasn't** had not → **'d not** 또는 **hadn't**
will/would	will → **'ll** would → **'d**	will not → **'ll not** 또는 **won't** would not → **'d not** 또는 **wouldn't**
조동사	-	cannot → **can't** could not → **couldn't** might not → **mightn't** must not → **mustn't** should not → **shouldn't**

is 또는 **has**는 **'s**로 줄여 쓰지만, **was**와 **were**는 줄여 쓰지 않는 것에 주의합니다.

● Kelly**'s** good at Spanish because she**'s** lived in Mexico. (= Kelly is good at Spanish because she has lived in Mexico.)
● Jack **was** sleeping while we **were** watching TV. (Jack's sleeping while we're watching TV로 쓸 수 없음)

had 또는 **would**는 **'d**로 줄여 씁니다.

● Sara wasn't at the party when we arrived. She**'d** already left. (= She had already left.)
● If I won the lottery, I**'d** buy a new car. (= I would buy a new car.)

yes를 써서 의문문에 짧게 답할 때는 축약형을 사용하지 않는 것에 주의합니다.

● "Is Mr. Bradley in his office?" "Yes, **he is**." (Yes, he's로 쓸 수 없음)
● "Are these shoes on sale?" "Yes, **they are**." (Yes, they're로 쓸 수 없음)

7. 조동사 (Lesson 22-28)

우리는 앞에서 다양한 조동사를 배웠습니다. 다음 표를 보면서 각 조동사의 의미와 형태를 간단히 정리해서 익혀보세요.

A. 조동사 + 동사원형

능력 · 가능성

can ~할 수 있다	● Melissa **can play** the piano very well.
can't ~할 수 없다	● My grandmother **can't see** without her glasses.
could (과거에) ~할 수 있었다	● I **could run** fast when I was young.
couldn't (과거에) ~할 수 없었다	● Henry **couldn't drive** a motorcycle, so I taught him.

추측

might/may ~할지도 모른다	● Be quiet! You **might wake** the baby.
might/may not ~하지 않을지도 모른다	● I **might not move** to Miami. I just got a job offer in Dallas.
could ~할지도 모른다	● It's cloudy and cold today, so it **could snow**.
couldn't/can't ~할 리 없다	● This sweater **couldn't fit** Maria. It's too big.
must 분명히 ~할 것이다	● Larry worked all night. He **must be** tired.
must not 분명히 ~하지 않을 것이다	● Tim never plays cards with us. He **must not enjoy** it.

의무

must 반드시 ~해야 한다	● You **must fill** out this form to register for the course.
must not ~해서는 안 된다	● "Excuse me, sir. You **must not smoke** here." "Oh. Sorry."
have/has to ~해야 한다	● I **have to write** an essay for my history class.
don't/doesn't have to ~할 필요가 없다	● I did the dishes. You **don't have to do** them.

충고 · 제안

should ~하는 것이 좋겠다	● We **should try** that new restaurant. My friend said it's great.
shouldn't ~하지 않는 것이 좋겠다	● The floor is very slippery. You **shouldn't run**.
had better ~하는 것이 좋겠다	● I**'d better go** to bed soon. I have an interview tomorrow morning.
had better not ~하지 않는 것이 좋겠다	● You**'d better not be** late or you'll miss your flight.

B. 조동사 + have + 과거분사

could have + 과거분사 (과거에) ~할 수도 있었다 (그러나 하지 않았다) (과거에) ~했을지도 모른다	• Eric **could have baked** a cake, but he bought one instead. • "Joe is not answering his doorbell." "He **could have left** home."
couldn't/can't have + 과거분사 (과거에) ~했을 리 없다	• Rita **couldn't/can't have gone** to the wedding. She had to work that day.
might/may have + 과거분사 (과거에) ~했을지도 모른다	• "I can't find my purse." "You **might have lost** it."
might/may not have + 과거분사 (과거에) ~하지 않았을지도 모른다	• Mr. Porter wasn't at the meeting. He **might not have known** about it.
must have + 과거분사 (과거에) 분명히 ~했을 것이다	• All of the cookies are gone. Somebody **must have eaten** them.
must not have + 과거분사 (과거에) 분명히 ~하지 않았을 것이다	• The mailbox is empty. The mailman **must not have come** yet.
should have + 과거분사 (과거에) ~했어야 했다 (그러나 하지 않았다)	• My computer crashed. I **should have saved** the files I was working on.
shouldn't have + 과거분사 (과거에) ~하지 말았어야 했다 (그러나 했다)	• I **shouldn't have drunk** so much wine. I have a headache now.

8. 주의해야 할 장소 이름 (Lesson 53-54)

> 어떤 장소 이름 앞에는 the를 쓰지만, 어떤 장소 이름 앞에는 the를 쓰지 않습니다. 다음 설명과 표를 보면서 the를 쓰는 장소 이름과 the를 쓰지 않는 장소 이름을 익혀보세요.

도시, 섬, 나라, 대륙 이름 앞에는 보통 **the**를 쓰지 않습니다.

도시, 섬	Tokyo	Washington DC	Prague	Long Island	Jeju Island	Bermuda
나라, 대륙	Brazil	Russia		Canada	Europe	Africa	Asia

- When we were living in **Tokyo**, we visited many sushi restaurants.
- "Have you ever been to **Brazil**?" "No. But I plan to go next year."
- **Russia** is the largest country in **Europe**.

단, **Republic, Kingdom, States**가 포함된 나라 이름과 복수형 나라 이름 앞에는 **the**를 씁니다.

the Czech Republic	the United Kingdom	the United States of America	the United Arab Emirates

- "Is Prague the capital of **the Czech Republic**?" "Yes, that's right."
- **The United Arab Emirates** has the tallest building in the world.

산 이름 앞에는 보통 **the**를 쓰지 않지만, 산맥 이름 앞에는 **the**를 씁니다.

산	Mount St. Helens	Mount Everest	Mount Fuji	Mount Seorak
산맥	the Himalayas	the Rocky Mountains	the Alps	the Andes

- **Mount St. Helens** is an active volcano. It is between Portland and Seattle.
- I've never been to **the Himalayas**, but I want to go someday.

호수 이름 앞에는 보통 **the**를 쓰지 않지만, 강, 바다, 대양 이름 앞에는 **the**를 씁니다.

호수	Lake Superior	Lake Michigan	Lake Victoria	Lake Titicaca
강	the Thames	the Nile	the Amazon	
바다, 대양	the Caribbean	the Mediterranean	the Pacific	the Arctic

- "Have you ever been ice fishing?" "Yes. I tried it once at **Lake Superior**."
- We relaxed by **the Thames** after a long day of sightseeing.
- **The Caribbean** is famous for its clear water. It's popular among scuba divers.

공공건물과 대학교 이름 앞에는 보통 **the**를 쓰지 않습니다.

공공건물	Waterloo Station	Union Station	Narita Airport	JFK Airport
대학교	Harvard University	Oxford University		

- Meet me at **Union Station** at 4 p.m. My train will arrive then.
- **Harvard University** was founded in 1636. It is one of the oldest universities in North America.

단, **형용사** 또는 **of**가 포함된 공공건물과 대학교 이름 앞에는 **the**를 씁니다.

the White House	the Open University	the University of Florida

- Our history class toured **the White House** last year. It was very interesting.
- Do you know anyone who attends **the University of Florida**?

도로, 거리, 공원, 광장 이름 앞에는 보통 **the**를 쓰지 않습니다.

도로, 거리	76th Street	Main Road	Park Avenue	Wilshire Boulevard	
공원, 광장	Central Park	Hyde Park	Stanley Park	Times Square	Trafalgar Square

- We live near **Central Park**. Our house is on **76th Street**.

9. 익혀두면 유용한 동사 표현 (Lesson 87, 88)

'~에 대해 말하다'라는 의미로 말할 때 동사 talk 뒤에 전치사 about을 쓰는 것처럼 영어에는 동사 뒤에 특정한 전치사나 부사를 쓰는 경우가 있습니다. 지금부터 다양한 동사 표현을 예문과 함께 익혀보세요.

A. 두 단어로 이루어진 동사 표현

about	**bring about** ~을 불러일으키다	• The invention of the train **brought about** a huge change in transportation.
	care about ~에 대해 관심이 있다	• I don't **care about** celebrity gossip.
	come about 발생하다	• "How did the accident **come about**?" "The other car didn't stop at the red light."
after	**go after** ~를 뒤쫓다	• My cat saw a mouse and **went after** it.
	take after ~를 닮다	• Ted **takes after** his father. Their personalities are very similar.
along	**come along** 도착하다/나타나다	• The train already left, but another one will **come along** soon.
apart	**tell apart** (~을) 구별하다	• The twins are difficult to **tell apart**. They look just alike.
around	**move around** ~을 움직이다	• My suitcase is easy to **move around**. It has four wheels.
	play around 놀다	• "Can we **play around** in the pool for a while?" "Sure."
	turn around 돌아서다	• There's Katie over there. Let's wave at her if she **turns around**.
at	**aim at** ~을 목적으로 하다	• The store **aims at** increasing sales this year.
	glance at ~을 힐끗 보다	• Scott **glanced at** his watch many times during the meeting.
	grin at ~에게 활짝 웃다	• I like when Tina **grins at** me. She has a beautiful smile.
	shoot at ~을 겨냥하여 쏘다	• The hunter **shot at** the bird, but it flew away too fast.
away	**drive away** (차를 타고) 떠나다	• Mark tried to **drive away**, but he couldn't start his car.
	fly away 날아가다	• Oh no! My balloon is **flying away**!
	give away ~을 기부하다	• The rich man **gave away** most of his money to charity.
	go away 떠나다/사라지다	• Why did Jeff **go away**? I had a question for him.
	put away ~을 치우다/집어넣다	• Your room is so messy! **Put away** all your clothes that are on the floor.
back	**answer back** (~에게) 말대꾸하다	• Mrs. Lee's children are well behaved and never **answer back**.
	bring back ~을 돌려주다	• You must **bring back** this book by next week.
	call back (~에게) 다시 전화를 하다	• Henry isn't in the office right now. Please **call back** later.
	cut back (~을) 줄이다, 삭감하다	• "I've been drinking too much coffee lately." "I agree. You should **cut back**."

back	get back 돌아오다	• Dad **gets back** from China tomorrow. He's been gone a week.
	go back 돌아가다	• Jan was born in France. She wants to **go back** someday.
	pay back (빌린 돈)을 갚다	• When I graduate from university, I will **pay back** my loans.
	put back ~을 다시 제자리에 갖다 놓다	• "Did you **put back** the milk?" "Yes. It's in the fridge."
	sit back 편히 앉다	• Tom **sat back** in his chair and relaxed as the movie began.
	take back ~을 되찾다/회수하다	• I **took back** my headphones that Mike borrowed.
	walk back 걸어서 돌아가다	• I forgot to lock the door. Can you **walk back** home and lock it?
	wave back 손을 흔들어 답하다	• The people on the boat waved, so I **waved back**.
	write back (~에게) 답장을 쓰다	• Liz wrote me a letter, but I haven't **written back** yet.
behind	fall behind (~에) 뒤처지다/낙오하다	• Max studies hard so that he doesn't **fall behind** in school.
down	bend down 몸을 굽히다	• Kim **bent down** and picked a flower from the garden.
	blow down ~을 불어 넘어뜨리다	• The wind **blew down** the old bridge.
	break down 고장 나다	• "Why were you late this morning?" "My car **broke down**."
	bring down ~을 낮추다/내리다	• Emily took medicine to **bring down** her fever.
	burn down 불에 타다	• There was a fire last night and two houses **burned down**.
	close down 폐업하다/폐쇄하다	• I was sorry to see that my favorite café had **closed down**.
	cut down ~을 잘라 넘어뜨리다	• My dad **cut down** the maple tree in the yard.
	fall down 넘어지다	• Mr. Harris **fell down** on the ice. Thankfully, he's OK.
	go down (가격, 기온 등이) 내려가다/낮아지다	• The price of gas has **gone down** a lot recently.
	knock down ~을 쓰러뜨리다	• The goal in bowling is to **knock down** all the pins.
	let down ~를 실망시키다	• I can't be late for dinner. I don't want to **let down** my wife.
	put down ~을 내려놓다	• Christina finished her drink and **put down** the glass.
	slow down 속도를 줄이다	• **Slow down**! You're driving too fast.
	take down ~을 치우다	• After the garage sale was over, I **took down** the posters.
	tear down (건물 등)을 허물다	• The workers **tore down** the old factory to build a gallery.
	write down ~을 적다/기록하다	• "Let me **write down** my phone number for you." "Thanks."
for	fall for ~에 속아 넘어가다	• "Did you **fall for** the trick?" "Yes. It was very clever."
	feel for ~를 가여워하다	• Diane lost all of her money. I really **felt for** her, so I let her borrow some.
	qualify for ~의 자격을 얻다	• A friend of mine **qualified for** the Olympics. We're so proud of her.
	search for ~을 찾다	• I **searched for** a good cookbook at the bookstore.

for	**stand for** ~을 나타내다/의미하다	● ASAP **stands for** "as soon as possible."
	believe in ~이 존재함을 믿다	● My little sister **believes in** Santa Claus.
	bring in (밖에서 안으로) ~을 들여오다	● It's raining, so we had better **bring in** the laundry.
	call in (전화해서) ~를 부르다	● Phil couldn't fix his computer, so he **called in** a technician.
	check in (투숙, 탑승) 수속을 밟다	● Bob went to the hotel's front desk to **check in**.
	come in 도착하다/들어오다	● Our flight **came in** 30 minutes early.
	fill in ~을 채우다/메우다	● You need to **fill in** all the blanks on the form to apply for a credit card.
	fit in (~와) 어울리다	● "Do you like your new school?" "Yes. At first it was hard to **fit in**, but now I really enjoy it."
	get in ~의 안으로 들어가다, ~에 타다	● I'll give you a ride. **Get in** the car.
	give in 항복하다	● Henry tried to win the chess game, but after several hours he just **gave in**.
	hand in ~을 제출하다	● Please **hand in** your reports on Friday.
	join in (~에) 참여하다	● There were some people playing volleyball on the beach, so we **joined in**.
in	**let in** ~을 들어오게 하다	● Close the window! You'll **let in** mosquitoes!
	look in ~의 안을 들여다보다	● "I can't find my coat." "Did you **look in** the closet?"
	move in 이사를 오다	● The new neighbors **moved in** last month.
	plug in ~의 플러그를 꽂다	● You should **plug in** the laptop because the battery is low.
	result in (결과적으로) ~을 야기하다	● The flood in New Orleans **resulted in** a lot of damage.
	specialize in ~을 전문으로 하다	● This restaurant **specializes in** sushi.
	stay in (나가지 않고) 집에 머물다	● "Let's **stay in** tonight. I'll cook for us." "OK. That sounds good."
	succeed in ~에 성공하다	● Mr. Lee gave me some advice about how to **succeed in** business.
	take in ~을 섭취하다	● Our bodies need to **take in** vitamins every day.
	turn in ~을 제출하다	● Please **turn in** your résumé when you apply for the job.
	break into ~에 침입하다	● An alarm rang when someone **broke into** the building.
	bump into ~과 부딪치다	● While Dave was playing in his room, he **bumped into** the wall and hurt his head.
into	**crash into** ~과 충돌하다	● The Titanic **crashed into** an iceberg and sank to the bottom of the ocean.
	get into ~에 들어가다	● After graduating from college, Emily **got into** a good company.
	look into ~을 주의 깊게 살피다	● My uncle will **look into** the problem with the kitchen sink.

into	**run into** ~와 우연히 만나다	• I **ran into** my friend from high school at the mall.
	turn into ~로 변하다	• During heavy rain, small streams can **turn into** large rivers.
like	**feel like** ~을 하고 싶다 ~을 먹고 싶다	• I don't **feel like** going shopping. I'll just stay home. • I'm tired of my usual lunch. I **feel like** a pizza today.
	look like ~처럼 보이다	• The students decorated the gym to **look like** a dance hall.
of	**approve of** ~을 받아들이다	• Lena's parents don't **approve of** her new boyfriend.
	complain of ~을 불평하다	• Some passengers on the flight **complained of** bad service.
	consist of ~으로 구성되다	• The US **consisted of** 13 states when it was formed in 1776.
	die of ~으로 죽다	• The movie director passed away. He **died of** cancer.
	dream of ~을 꿈꾸다	• Beth **dreams of** having a long vacation. She has worked overtime a lot lately.
	hear of ~에 대해 듣다	• "Do you know Dave Akers, the author?" "No. I've never **heard of** him before."
	talk of ~에 대해 이야기하다	• The factory workers **talked of** asking for higher pay.
	think of ~을 생각하다/떠올리다	• "I miss Mary." "Me too. I **think of** her often."
off	**call off** ~을 취소하다	• The weather was bad, so we **called off** the baseball game.
	cut off ~을 자르다	• Do you have any scissors? I want to **cut off** the tag of my new shirt.
	doze off 졸다	• I **dozed off** during the lecture. It was quite boring.
	drive off 떠나다	• The bus **drove off** after all the tourists were seated.
	drop off (사람, 짐 등)을 내려주다	• Ms. Smith **drops off** her kids at school every morning.
	fall off ~에서 떨어지다	• All of the books **fell off** the shelf during the earthquake.
	get off (~에서) 내리다	• "Is this the stop for the museum?" "No. You should **get off** at the next stop."
	lay off ~를 해고하다	• Five employees were **laid off** after the management changed.
	let off ~을 터뜨리다/발사하다	• The city **let off** fireworks during the parade. They were beautiful.
	nod off 꾸벅꾸벅 졸다	• William was so tired that he **nodded off** during the movie.
	pay off ~을 다 갚다 성과를 올리다/성공하다	• Janet **paid off** her credit card bill this morning. • My team's hard work **paid off**. We won the championship.
	set off 출발하다	• "Let's leave for the beach early in the morning." "OK. What time shall we **set off**?"
	show off ~을 자랑하다	• Tracy **showed off** her new dress to her friends.
	shut off (기계 등)의 전원을 끄다	• "Did you remember to **shut off** the stove?" "Of course."
	stop off 잠시 들르다, 머무르다	• We **stopped off** at a local coffee shop on our way home.

off	**switch off** (기계 등)의 스위치를 끄다	●	**Switch off** the light when you leave the room.
	tear off ~을 잡아 찢다	●	Jake **tore off** the wrapping paper to get to his present.
	wear off (효과 등이) 서서히 사라지다	●	The pain medicine is **wearing off**. My leg is hurting again.
	work off ~을 빼다/해소하다	●	Running is a great way to **work off** extra calories.
on	**add on** ~을 추가하다	●	When Sally and Ron had a baby, they had to **add on** a room to the house.
	carry on ~을 계속하다	●	Pat **carried on** studying despite the noise.
	catch on (~을) 이해하다	●	The teacher tried explaining the lesson clearly, but the students didn't **catch on**.
	come on 시작하다/등장하다	●	When I turned on the TV, the evening news **came on**.
	concentrate on ~에 집중하다	●	Please be quiet. I can't **concentrate on** my homework.
	count on ~를 믿다/기대하다	●	I will finish the assignment before the deadline. You can **count on** me.
	decide on ~을 결정하다	●	Mia and John haven't **decided on** a date for their wedding yet.
	depend on ~에게 의존하다	●	Children **depend on** their parents for food and clothing.
	drive on 차를 몰고 계속 가다	●	My son wanted me to stop at the toy store, but I **drove on**.
	get on ~을 타다	●	Tom and Rick **got on** the train at the Low Valley station.
	go on 계속하다	●	Susie's story sounded interesting, so I asked her to **go on**.
	insist on ~을 주장하다, 고집하다	●	Beth wanted to leave the party early, but Dawn **insisted on** staying.
	keep on ~을 계속하다, 유지하다	●	Lena **kept on** practicing the piano. She improved a lot.
	leave on ~을 입은 채로 있다	●	"May I **leave on** my shoes in the house?" "Sure."
	live on 계속 존재하다	●	My grandmother died years ago, but her memory **lives on**.
	move on (새로운 일, 주제로) 옮기다	●	After 12 years at the law office, Peter decided to **move on** and do something new.
	pass on ~을 전달하다	●	"Mr. Smith wants to see Jack." "OK. I'll **pass on** the message."
	plan on ~을 계획하다	●	"Do you **plan on** going to Jill's wedding?" "Yes. What about you?"
	play on (경기를) 계속하다	●	Tim hurt his ankle during the game, but he **played on**.
	rely on ~에게 의존하다	●	Many people **rely on** public transportation.
	settle on (생각 끝에) ~로 정하다	●	I've **settled on** the black car. It looks nicer than the red one.
	spend on ~에 소비하다	●	"How much money did you **spend on** those clothes?" "Around $500."
	switch on (기계 등)의 스위치를 켜다	●	I can't see in here. Please **switch on** the light.

on	**take on** (일)을 맡다. (책임)을 지다	●	I'm too busy to **take on** any extra work.
out	**ask out** ~에게 데이트를 신청하다	●	"Kyle **asked out** my sister." "Really? Is she going to go out with him?"
	block out (빛, 소리 등)을 차단하다	●	I use curtains to **block out** the light in my room.
	blow out ~을 불어서 끄다	●	**Blow out** the candles on your cake and make a wish.
	break out 발생하다	●	"Did you hear about the fight at school?" "Yes. It **broke out** at lunch."
	carry out ~을 실행하다	●	We need to **carry out** our plan to clean the basement.
	check out (호텔 등에서) 나오다 ~을 대출하다	● ●	The tourists **checked out** and went to the airport. I'm going to **check out** this book from the library.
	come out (사실, 진실 등이) 밝혀지다	●	It **came out** that Mary will become the department manager.
	cross out 선을 그어 ~을 지우다	●	Just **cross out** the wrong word and write in the correct one.
	cut out ~을 배제하다	●	My doctor told me to **cut out** red meat from my diet.
	drop out (~을) 그만두다/탈퇴하다	●	Tom didn't have enough time to practice for the singing contest, so he **dropped out**.
	empty out ~을 비우다	●	The fire department **emptied out** the building because of a gas leak.
	fall out 떨어지다	●	My keys were in my pocket earlier, but I think they **fell out**.
	figure out ~을 알아내다	●	Something is wrong with my car, but the mechanic can't **figure out** the problem.
	fill out ~을 작성하다/기입하다	●	Donna **filled out** the form to register for the tennis class.
	find out ~을 알아내다	●	"Did you **find out** when the exam starts?" "Yes. It's at 2:30."
	give out ~을 나누어 주다	●	The grocery store **gave out** free samples of cheese.
	hand out ~을 나누어 주다. 배포하다	●	The restaurant **handed out** coupons to the first 100 customers.
	help out ~를 도와주다	●	I **help out** my grandparents with their garden every Sunday.
	keep out ~이 들어가지 않게 하다	●	We got our windows repaired in order to **keep out** the flies in the summer.
	knock out ~를 나가떨어지게 하다	●	The fighter **knocked out** the other boxer with one punch.
	lay out ~을 펼쳐놓다	●	Lucy **laid out** all the fruit and let the guests help themselves.
	leave out ~을 빼다. 제외하다	●	I thought I'd invited everyone to the party, but I **left out** Ben!
	let out (울음소리, 신음소리 등)을 내다	●	Julie **let out** a scream when the bee flew toward her.
	lock out (문을) 잠가서 들어가지 못하게 하다	●	My sister had to bring an extra set of keys because I left mine in the car and got **locked out**.
	look out 조심하다/주의하다	●	**Look out!** There's a dog running across the road.

out	**move out** 이사를 나가다	• "Doesn't Lily live next to you?" "No. She **moved out**."
	pass out 의식을 잃다	• Tim's fever became so high that he **passed out**.
	pick out ~을 고르다	• I have to **pick out** the perfect gift for our anniversary.
	print out ~을 출력하다	• I **printed out** the list of words so I could study at home.
	put out (불 등)을 끄다	• The firemen **put out** the fire. They saved the building.
	run out 다 쓰다/다 떨어지다	• "Is there any tea left?" "No, we **ran out** yesterday."
	send out ~을 보내다	• Gina **sent out** invitations to her wedding last month.
	set out 출발하다/시작하다	• I packed a lunch and **set out** for a hike up the mountain.
	sort out ~을 (분류해서) 정리하다	• You have to **sort out** the bottles from the cans for recycling.
	take out ~을 가져가다	• Please **take out** the trash. The trash can is full.
	tear out ~을 잘라내다, 잡아 뜯다	• Alison **tore out** a photo from the magazine. It was a picture of her favorite actor.
	throw out ~을 버리다	• I bought some new towels, so I **threw out** my old ones.
	turn out 나타나다/모습을 드러내다	• A large crowd **turned out** for the parade.
	watch out 조심하다, 주의하다	• **Watch out**! You're about to step in a puddle.
over	**check over** ~을 자세히 살피다	• My mom used to **check over** my homework before bedtime.
	get over ~을 극복하다/회복하다	• It took two weeks for Megan to **get over** the flu.
	go over ~을 점검하다/검토하다	• You should **go over** used cars carefully before you buy them.
	hand over ~을 넘겨주다	• I felt sad when we **handed over** the keys to our old house. I had lived there all my life.
	look over ~을 살펴보다	• Mary always **looks over** her reports very carefully.
	run over (사람, 동물 등)을 치다	• If you drive too fast, you might **run over** a pedestrian.
	start over 다시 시작하다	• The computer crashed and I forgot to save my file. Now I have to **start over**.
	talk over ~에 대해 이야기를 나누다	• Let's **talk over** our options with the salesperson.
	think over ~을 심사숙고하다	• We're still **thinking over** the contract. We haven't signed it yet.
	turn over ~을 뒤집다	• Don't forget to **turn over** the form. There's writing on the back side, too.
through	**get through** ~을 끝내다 (전화 등으로) 연결되다	• We finally **got through** all of our exams. Let's celebrate! • I tried to call Jackie twice earlier, but I didn't **get through**.
	see through ~을 꿰뚫어 보다	• I can **see through** Kelly's lies. Her story is clearly false.
to	**admit to** ~을 인정하다	• Rick **admitted to** the mistake and said he caused the car accident.
	apologize to ~에게 사과하다	• The server **apologized to** us for spilling the wine.

to	**get to** ~에 도착하다/이르다	●	I **got to** the bus stop just as the bus was arriving.
together	**get together** ~을 모으다/합치다	●	Jeremy **got together** all his tools to fix the fence.
	put together (이것저것을 모아) ~을 만들다	●	"I **put together** a list of my favorite movies." "Great. Let's watch some of them."
up	**back up** 후진하다, ~를 지지하다	● ●	If you see a snake, **back up** slowly so you don't scare it. Nobody **backed up** Ed's proposal. It wasn't a good idea.
	bring up (문제 등)을 제기하다, ~을 기르다	● ●	I hate to **bring up** the issue, but you still owe me money. I want to **bring up** my children in the country.
	cover up ~을 숨기다/완전히 가리다	●	Lenny tried to **cover up** the fact that he didn't go to class.
	dress up 꾸미다, 옷을 갖춰 입다	●	Let's **dress up** and go to a dance club tonight!
	end up 결국 ~하게 되다	●	It's cold outside. You should wear your coat or you might **end up** sick.
	fill up ~을 가득 채우다	●	"Did you **fill up** the tank with gas?" "Yes. I stopped at the gas station after work."
	give up (~을) 포기하다	●	You can finish the race, Steve! Don't **give up**!
	go up (가격, 기온 등이) 오르다, (건물이) 올라가다, 들어서다	● ●	The temperature has **gone up** a lot since this morning. A new apartment will **go up** on this street. It'll get busy.
	hang up ~을 걸다	●	Every Christmas, my kids **hang up** stockings on the fireplace.
	hurry up 서두르다	●	**Hurry up** or we're going to be late for the concert.
	keep up 계속되다	●	The heavy snow **kept up** for several days.
	look up ~을 찾아보다	●	Kathy **looked up** Alex's phone number in the phone book, but it wasn't in there.
	set up ~을 설치하다, 세우다	●	I've **set up** the chess board and I'm ready to play now.
	sign up 등록하다, 가입하다	●	"There's an art class starting next week." "Are you going to **sign up**?"
	speak up 더 크게 말하다	●	Please **speak up**. We can't hear you.
	split up ~을 나누다	●	The two owners of the shop **split up** the profits every month.
	stay up 자지 않고 깨어있다	●	I want to **stay up** until 11:00 so I can watch the show.
	turn up ~의 소리를 높이다	●	**Turn up** the sound on the television. I can't hear it.
	use up ~을 다 쓰다	●	Jennifer **used up** all the butter to bake her cake.
	walk up ~을 걸어 올라가다	●	You have to **walk up** a lot of stairs to get to Jim's apartment.
with	**deal with** ~을 처리하다/다루다	●	"Who handles refund requests?" "Maria **deals with** those."
with	**stick with** ~을 계속하다	●	Although Fred wasn't good at basketball at first, he decided to **stick with** it.

B. 세 단어로 이루어진 동사 표현

break out of ~에서 탈출하다	● The prisoners tried to **break out of** jail, but the guards caught them.
catch up with ~를 따라잡다	● The runner tried to **catch up with** the people in front of him.
come down with (병)에 걸리다	● I've **come down with** a terrible cold, so I'm staying in bed today.
come up with (생각 등)을 내놓다	● How do you **come up with** your brilliant fashion designs?
cut back on ~을 줄이다	● I have to **cut back on** my spending if I want to buy a new car.
cut down on ~을 줄이다	● Larry's eyes get tired easily. He should **cut down on** computer time.
do away with ~을 그만두다	● I'm going to **do away with** all my bad habits and make a fresh start.
drop out of ~에서 중도 하차하다	● Tom **dropped out of** band and decided to play soccer instead.
end up with 결국 ~하게 되다	● Gina barely studied, so she **ended up with** a bad score on the exam.
get away with ~을 훔쳐 달아나다	● The thieves **got away with** lots of expensive jewelry.
go up to ~으로 가까이 가다	● We should **go up to** the pop star and ask for an autograph.
hang on to ~을 꽉 붙잡다	● Can you **hang on to** my bag? I need to tie my shoes.
hold on to ~을 계속 보유하다	● I don't need that book, so you can **hold on to** it.
keep away from ~을 가까이하지 않다	● Please **keep away from** the fire. It's dangerous.
live up to ~을 지키다 　　　　~에 부응하다	● You need to finish college and **live up to** the promise you made. ● The comedian's show definitely **live up to** our expectations.
look forward to ~을 고대하다	● Everyone in class was **looking forward to** summer vacation.
look out over ~을 건너다보다	● From the top of the hill, you can **look out over** the whole village.
make up for ~에 대해 보상하다	● To **make up for** missing your graduation, I'll take you out for dinner.
miss out on ~을 놓치다	● Karen **missed out on** Bill's surprise party.
put up with ~을 참다/참고 견디다	● I can't **put up with** Mike's bad attitude. He never seems happy.
run away from ~에서 도망치다	● "Jeremy **ran away from** home." "His parents must be worried."
step down from (지위 등)에서 내려오다	● Mr. Park **stepped down from** his position as the CEO of the company.
watch out for ~을 주의하다	● **Watch out for** children on the road. We're near a school.

10. 익혀두면 유용한 형용사 + 전치사 표현 (Lesson 89)

'~에게 친절한'이라는 의미로 말할 때 형용사 kind 뒤에 전치사 to를 쓰는 것처럼 영어에는 형용사 뒤에 특정한 전치사를 쓰는 경우가 있습니다. 지금부터 다양한 형용사 + 전치사 표현을 예문과 함께 익혀보세요.

about	**angry about** ~에 대해 화가 난	Mr. Meyer is **angry about** the mistakes in the report.
	excited about ~에 대해 흥분한	"Are you **excited about** your trip to Europe?" "Yes! I've never been there before."
	nervous about ~에 긴장되는	"Are you **nervous about** your first day at work?" "Not really."
	sad about ~에 대해 슬퍼하는	Kristy is **sad about** moving. She'll miss her friends.
	sorry about ~에 대해 미안한/유감스러운	"Excuse me, I'm still waiting for my food. It's been an hour." "**Sorry about** that. I'll go and ask the chef."
	sure about ~에 대해 확신하는	I asked how much the car was, but the salesman wasn't **sure about** the price.
	upset about ~에 대해 화가 난	We had a party, and our neighbors were **upset about** the noise.
	worried about ~에 대해 걱정하는	"I can't sleep." "Why? Are you **worried about** something?"
at	**amazed at** ~에 깜짝 놀란	We were **amazed at** your performance. Your voice is beautiful.
	angry at ~에게 화가 난	I'm **angry at** Betty for ignoring my phone calls.
	mad at ~에게 화가 난	My wife is **mad at** me for forgetting our anniversary.
	surprised at ~에 놀란	John hadn't studied at all, so he was **surprised at** his high score on the test.
for	**bad for** (건강 등)에 나쁜	"Is sugar **bad for** health?" "Only if you eat too much."
	crazy for ~을 매우 좋아하는	Monica is absolutely **crazy for** romance novels.
	famous for ~으로 유명한	This restaurant has become **famous for** its wonderful desserts.
	prepared for ~에 대해 준비가 된	Thomas did so well during the interview because he was **prepared for** it.
from	**different from** ~와 다른	"How is this apartment **different from** the other one?" "This one has an extra bathroom."
in	**dressed in** ~을 입은	All of the men were **dressed in** tuxedos at the party.
	interested in ~에 관심 있는	I'm **interested in** art, so I often go to galleries.
	involved in ~에 관련된	Jacob is very busy because he's **involved in** many school activities.

of	**afraid of** ~을 두려워하는	• You don't have to be **afraid of** my dog. He won't bite.
	ashamed of ~을 부끄러워하는	• I was **ashamed of** Bill's behavior. He was rude to the waitress.
	certain of ~을 확신하는	• Erica loves me. I'm **certain of** it.
	conscious of ~을 의식하는	• Drivers need to be **conscious of** people crossing the street.
	convinced of ~을 확신하는	• A lot of people take vitamins these days. They seem **convinced of** their benefits.
	guilty of ~으로 유죄인	• The man wasn't **guilty of** theft. He didn't have to go to jail.
	jealous of ~를 질투하는	• A lot of people are **jealous of** Kenny. He's so popular.
	proud of ~를 자랑스럽게 여기는	• I'm so **proud of** you for winning the tennis tournament.
	sick of ~에 싫증이 난	• I'm **sick of** the snow. I wish it would stop.
	terrified of ~을 무서워하는	• Hannah is **terrified of** spiders.
	tired of ~에 지친/싫증이 난	• Brent was **tired of** waiting for his friend, so he went home.
to	**accustomed to** ~에 익숙한	• Dorothy isn't **accustomed to** living with roommates.
	clear to ~에게 분명한	• "The instructions for my new camera aren't **clear to** me." "Let me see them. Maybe I can explain them to you."
	dedicated to ~에 헌신하는	• Tony is a hard worker. He is very **dedicated to** his job.
	engaged to ~와 약혼한	• Jackie is **engaged to** my younger brother.
	equal to ~와 동일한	• A mile is **equal to** 1.6 kilometers.
	identical to ~와 똑같은	• "What do you think of this new cap?" "It looks **identical to** the one that Jim has."
	married to ~와 결혼한	• Jeff has been **married to** his wife for six years.
	nice to ~에게 잘해주는	• Matt, you should be **nice to** your younger sister.
	opposed to ~에 반대하는	• My wife is **opposed to** taking a vacation this summer.
with	**angry with** ~에게 화가 난	• I'm sorry I broke your glasses. Please don't be **angry with** me.
	careful with ~을 조심하는	• Be **careful with** that plate. It's hot.
	crowded with ~으로 꽉 찬	• The stadium was **crowded with** people who were excited to see the boxing match.
	happy with ~에 대해 행복해하는	• Thomas is very **happy with** his new bicycle.
	impressed with ~에 감동을 받은	• All of the guests were **impressed with** Danny's speech.
	pleased with ~에 대해 기뻐하는	• Rita was **pleased with** her exam results. She did a good job.
	satisfied with ~에 만족하는	• I'm **satisfied with** our president. He's leading the country well.
	wrong with ~에 문제가 있는	• What's **wrong with** the TV? It's not turning on.

11. 익혀두면 유용한 명사 + 전치사 표현 (Lesson 90)

'~의 이유'라는 의미로 말할 때 명사 reason 뒤에 전치사 for를 쓰는 것처럼 영어에는 명사 뒤에 특정한 전치사를 쓰는 경우가 있습니다. 지금부터 다양한 명사 + 전치사 표현을 예문과 함께 익혀보세요.

about	**argument about** ~에 대한 논쟁	● My parents and I had an **argument about** staying up late.
	discussion about ~에 대한 논의	● Let's have a **discussion about** the new marketing project.
	information about ~에 대한 정보	● "Do you have any **information about** tours in London?" "Yes. I'll give you some brochures."
between	**connection between** ~의 관련	● There's a **connection between** hard work and success.
	link between ~의 관련	● The professor discussed the **link between** history and culture.
for	**advertisement for** ~에 대한 광고	● I saw an **advertisement for** the art exhibit in the paper. Why don't we go tomorrow?
	cure for ~에 대한 치료법	● Researchers are working hard to find a **cure for** AIDS.
	hope for ~에 대한 희망/기대	● There's still **hope for** the patient. His condition has improved recently.
	recipe for ~의 요리법	● Could you give me the **recipe for** this pasta? It's so good!
	sympathy for ~에 대한 동정	● I feel a lot of **sympathy for** Eric. He's had a difficult year.
in	**difficulty in** ~의 어려움	● My grandfather has some **difficulty in** remembering names.
	drop in ~의 감소/하락	● There will be a **drop in** temperature later today, so don't forget your coats.
	reduction in ~의 감소/인하	● The **reduction in** tuition made all of the students very happy.
	rise in ~의 증가/인상	● I'm expecting a **rise in** income next year.
of	**beginning of** ~의 초기/시작	● School will start around the **beginning of** August.
	experience of ~의 경험	● I've never had the **experience of** bungee jumping.
	importance of ~의 중요성	● I teach my children the **importance of** saving money.
	method of ~의 방법	● My company is looking for a new **method of** attracting customers.
	opinion of ~에 대한 의견	● "What's your **opinion of** Jeffery?" "I think he's very nice."
	plan of ~에 대한 계획	● Ken's **plan of** traveling across Mexico sounds fun!
	price of ~의 가격	● The **prices of** airline flights are going up. I'm glad I bought my ticket last month.
on	**advice on** ~에 대한 조언	● This article has some good **advice on** how to prepare for a new baby.

on	**agreement on** ~에 대한 합의/동의	●	After many hours, we finally reached an **agreement on** the contract.
	attack on ~에 대한 공격	●	David took photos of the tiger's **attack on** the deer.
	comment on ~에 대한 언급/논평	●	Randy didn't make any **comments on** my article.
	decision on ~에 대한 결정	●	I haven't made a **decision on** a name for my new business yet.
	effect on ~에 대한 영향	●	Exercising every day has a good **effect on** my health.
	expert on ~에 대한 전문가	●	Professor Williams is an **expert on** Russian history.
to	**approach to** ~에 대한 접근	●	My friend Lisa has a very positive **approach to** life.
	introduction to ~에 대한 소개	●	Have you read the **introduction to** the book? It's interesting.
	invitation to ~에 대한 초대(장)	●	Did you get an **invitation to** Erin's birthday dinner?
with	**contact with** ~와의 연락/접촉	●	I lost **contact with** Jessica. I wonder how she is.
	conversation with ~와의 대화	●	Jim enjoys having **conversations with** his grandfather.
	problem with ~의 문제	●	There's a **problem with** the printer. It's out of ink.
	trouble with ~의 문제	●	I'm having **trouble with** my phone. Can I borrow yours?

GRAMMAR
GATEWAY
INTERMEDIATE

www.Hackers.co.kr

Answers

PRACTICE Answers

Check-Up Test Answers

PRACTICE Answers

Lesson 1

A

2. Sarah and Julia are nurses. They're in a cafeteria OR They are in a cafeteria
3. Betty is a reporter. She's in a helicopter OR She is in a helicopter
4. Marvin is a soldier. He's at the airport OR He is at the airport
5. Jim and Alan are baseball players. They're on a bench OR They are on a bench

B

2. 're not in my bag OR aren't in my bag OR are not in my bag
3. 'm not happy OR am not happy
4. is at the theater
5. are twins
6. isn't Chinese OR is not Chinese

C

2. Johnny and Robert are in Seattle
3. is the bathroom
4. I'm not familiar OR I am not familiar
5. Are you a photographer
6. This necklace isn't expensive OR This necklace is not expensive

D

2. Is; in his room
3. 's busy OR is busy
4. is at school; isn't back from the library OR is not back from the library
5. Are; hungry
6. 'm OK OR am OK

Lesson 2

A

2. is reading a book
3. is holding a cup
4. are riding bikes
5. are moving a plant
6. is cleaning the desk

7. is fixing a photocopier
8. are standing at the door

B

2. I'm not acting OR I am not acting
3. I'm taking OR I am taking
4. are you doing
5. I'm teaching OR I am teaching
6. Is he studying
7. he's not attending OR he isn't attending OR he is not attending
8. He's learning OR He is learning

C

2. I'm listening OR I am listening
3. Are they dating
4. She's not sleeping OR She isn't sleeping OR She is not sleeping
5. we're not hiring OR we aren't hiring OR we are not hiring
6. Is Mom baking
7. I'm not spending OR I am not spending
8. The leaves are changing

Lesson 3

A

2. see
3. wake
4. travels
5. cost
6. teaches
7. fixes
8. eat

B

2. don't have flowers OR do not have flowers
3. doesn't mix with water OR does not mix with water
4. falls in the rainforest
5. fly south in the winter

C

1. I bring
2. do you and your friends go
3. Does this bus stop; It turns
4. Does Jennifer enjoy

5. do you spell
6. Does Peter send; he calls

D

2. usually helps
3. often answers
4. Does; like
5. doesn't talk OR does not talk
6. always meets

Lesson 4

A

2. don't agree
3. 's planting
4. Does; have
5. are; going
6. doesn't belong
7. isn't lying
8. are having

B

2. sounds
3. Do; feel OR Are; feeling
4. doesn't taste
5. don't smell
6. is tasting

C

2. have → are having
3. ○
4. tastes → is tasting
5. ○
6. I'm not believing → I don't believe
7. is possessing → possesses
8. ○

D

2. know
3. look OR 're looking
4. are; doing
5. 'm searching
6. sounds

Lesson 5

A

2. Do; bring
3. Is; shopping
4. runs

5. are singing
6. Does; smoke
7. freezes
8. Are; looking

B

2. 'm practicing
3. see
4. 's growing
5. 're staying
6. plays

C

2. are
3. is being
4. 's
5. 're being
6. 'm being

D

2. 'm watching
3. meet
4. 're taking
5. want
6. 'm being

Lesson 6

A

2. exercised at a gym
3. got a haircut
4. watched a movie
5. went to a restaurant

B

2. joined
3. didn't hear *OR* did not hear
4. were
5. didn't swim *OR* did not swim
6. wrote
7. wasn't *OR* was not

C

1. Was it
2. Were you; I arrived
3. Did Roy play; he was
4. I worked; did you leave

D

2. was
3. met; fell
4. didn't give up *OR* did not give up
5. got
6. live; visit

Lesson 7

A

2. was attending
3. was holding
4. wasn't giving *OR* was not giving
5. were sitting
6. was talking
7. was looking
8. weren't eating *OR* were not eating

B

2. weren't wearing *OR* were not wearing
3. wasn't paying *OR* was not paying
4. were; carrying
5. was arguing
6. Was; hiding

C

1. He was meeting
2. Were you driving; I was going
3. You weren't exercising *OR* You were not exercising; I was walking
4. Did you know; We were
5. did you turn; Were you watching
6. Did you show; They liked

D

2. was reading
3. came; wanted
4. didn't hear
5. was listening
6. were sleeping

Lesson 8

A

2. jumped; was swimming
3. paid; left
4. lost; was jogging
5. landed; got
6. was snowing; went

B

2. got; was cooking
3. was preparing; put
4. was sleeping; went
5. was ringing
6. had

C

2. while I was giving my presentation
3. when the rain stopped
4. While I was parking
5. while we were watching TV
6. When Maria woke up
7. when his computer shut down
8. When the child dropped the glass

Lesson 9

A

2. didn't use to wear
3. used to be
4. didn't use to grow

B

2. Did; use to drink
3. didn't use to have
4. used to bake
5. Did; use to be
6. didn't use to check
7. used to belong

C

2. 'm used to running
3. used to be
4. 'm used to taking
5. used to ski

D

2. used to spend
3. costs
4. have
5. used to take
6. miss
7. need

Lesson 10

A

2. Has; worked
3. 've not visited *OR* haven't visited *OR* have not visited
4. have made
5. hasn't checked *OR* has not checked
6. have; had

B

2. 've not brushed my hair since last week *OR* haven't brushed

my hair since last week *OR* have not brushed my hair since last week
3. 's taught here since last semester *OR* has taught here since last semester
4. 've not done the laundry for a month *OR* haven't done the laundry for a month *OR* have not done the laundry for a month
5. hasn't come for 30 minutes *OR* has not come for 30 minutes
6. 's driven that car since 1995 *OR* has driven that car since 1995

C
1. 's become *OR* has become
2. 've not gone *OR* haven't gone *OR* have not gone
3. have been; was
4. 's sold *OR* has sold
5. 've not listened *OR* haven't listened *OR* have not listened; broke

D
2. hasn't smoked since he got married *OR* has not smoked since he got married
3. 've met many people since we moved to LA *OR* have met many people since we moved to LA
4. haven't spoken since they had an argument *OR* have not spoken since they had an argument

Lesson 11

A
2. hasn't lived
3. Have; listened
4. haven't used
5. 's received
6. Has; given

B
2. I've (never) broken a bone
3. I've (never) tried scuba diving
4. I've (never) made bread at home
5. Have you ever studied Chinese

6. Have you ever broken a bone
7. Have you ever tried scuba diving
8. Have you ever made bread at home

C
2. 's gone
3. Have; been
4. Have; gone
5. 's been

D
2. Have you ever done
3. I've volunteered
4. I've been to Africa once
5. I've ever had
6. I've never thought

Lesson 12

A
2. Has; lost
3. woke
4. visited
5. Did; paint
6. has wanted
7. have; played
8. did; go

B
2. Have you chosen a wedding dress yet *OR* Did you choose a wedding dress yet
3. I bought
4. Have you already found a place *OR* Did you already find a place
5. We've just made reservations *OR* We just made reservations

C
2. exercised → have exercised
3. ○
4. didn't smoke → hasn't smoked
5. ○
6. Have you gone → Did you go

D
2. were
3. have; worked
4. started
5. haven't told *OR* didn't tell

Lesson 13

A
2. have been listening to
3. has been cleaning the windows
4. has been painting a picture
5. has been sitting
6. have been running

B
2. She's been cooking dinner since 5 o'clock *OR* She has been cooking dinner since 5 o'clock
3. They've been building a bridge for six months *OR* They have been building a bridge for six months
4. They've been playing tennis since noon *OR* They have been playing tennis since noon
5. He's been using his laptop for an hour *OR* He has been using his laptop for an hour

C
2. 've been climbing *OR* have been climbing
3. 's been sleeping *OR* has been sleeping
4. 's been swimming *OR* has been swimming
5. 've been packing *OR* have been packing

D
2. How long have you been watching
3. Where has John been staying
4. Have you been enjoying
5. How long has Lucy been planning

Lesson 14

A
2. 's driven 90 miles
3. 've baked eight muffins
4. 's picked a basket of oranges
5. 's had three cups of coffee

B
2. 's been keeping a diary since she was 10
3. have been sleeping for an hour
4. 's been wearing glasses for five

years
5. have been renovating the house since May

C
2. I've called her
3. I've read this book
4. It's sold *OR* It's been selling
5. Sandra has spent *OR* Sandra has been spending
6. Sue has visited
7. Ken and Mark haven't worked *OR* Ken and Mark haven't been working
8. They've had
9. have you gone out for drinks
10. have you been designing clothes

Lesson 15

A
2. had broken the lamp
3. had gone to bed
4. had left a note
5. had eaten all the cookies

B
2. 'd not seen *OR* hadn't seen *OR* had not seen
3. had ordered
4. 'd not expected *OR* hadn't expected *OR* had not expected
5. hadn't opened *OR* had not opened
6. 'd practiced *OR* had practiced

C
2. had answered
3. 'd saved *OR* had saved
4. watched
5. reached
6. 'd gone *OR* had gone

D
2. arrived; had already left
3. got; 'd already gone *OR* had already gone
4. did; get
5. drank *OR* 'd drunk *OR* had drunk

Lesson 16

A
2. will call
3. Will; be
4. won't hurt *OR* will not hurt
5. will have
6. will; arrive
7. 'll help *OR* will help
8. won't buy *OR* will not buy

B
2. won't play *OR* will not play
3. won't eat *OR* will not eat
4. 'll explain *OR* will explain

C
2. I (don't) think I'll get a haircut next week
3. I (don't) think I'll see a movie next weekend
4. I (don't) think I'll travel abroad next year
5. I (don't) think I'll go to the beach next summer

D
2. I'm sure you'll become *OR* I'm sure you will become
3. Will you take
4. I guess I'll study *OR* I guess I will study
5. You won't be *OR* You will not be
6. I'll think *OR* I will think

Lesson 17

A
2. are going to fall into the box
3. 's going to sleep on the sofa
4. 're going to wash the dog
5. is going to melt

B
2. 'll help *OR* 's going to help
3. 's going to have
4. 'll find *OR* 're going to find
5. 'll learn *OR* 'm going to learn
6. 're going to complete

C
2. He's going to visit
3. I'll be
4. I won't order
5. She's not going to be

D
2. were going to give
3. was going to attend
4. were going to wait

Lesson 18

A
2. They're meeting
3. She's opening a bakery
4. He's running in a marathon
5. They're getting married

B
2. arrives at 11:40 a.m.
3. starts at 7:00
4. departs on February 5
5. play on Thursday

C
2. The class begins
3. she's not joining
4. does the musical end
5. Alex and I are going
6. The bus doesn't leave

D
2. is about to close
3. 'm about to check
4. is about to break
5. are about to announce

Lesson 19

A
2. 'll be packing
3. 'll be painting the new house
4. 'll be buying some furniture
5. 'll be moving into the new house

B
2. won't remember
3. Will; be sleeping
4. 'll go
5. 'll be preparing
6. won't be attending
7. Will; show
8. will be playing

C
2. won't be coming
3. 'll be volunteering
4. will; be staying

D

2. I won't be going
3. will you be doing
4. I'll be having
5. I won't be doing
6. I'll be waiting

Lesson 20

A

2. will have saved
3. will have produced
4. will have dropped
5. will have lost

B

1. finds
2. won't have finished
3. 'll have melted; get
4. reach; 'll have walked
5. won't have read; return
6. 'll have waited

C

2. Will; pass
3. 'll call
4. 'll have cleaned
5. will have lived
6. 'll pay

D

2. I'll have completed college
3. I'll have directed several movies
4. I'll have won a big award

Lesson 21

A

2. When I move to New York City
3. when he gets a bonus next month
4. when Lisa and Jake feel hungry
5. When Mr. Harris retires next year

B

1. make
2. don't pay; will charge
3. travel; 'll study
4. 'll be; doesn't come
5. buys; 'll give
6. won't start; arrive
7. Will; become; receives

C

2. ○
3. won't be using → isn't using
4. ○
5. will return → returns
6. will have completed → have completed

D

1. leave
2. fixes; 'll pick
3. Will; stop; go
4. have; will; do
5. 'll ask; comes

Lesson 22

A

2. can't reach
3. Can; do
4. can play
5. Can; pay
6. can't eat

B

2. I could type
3. they couldn't get
4. I can't run
5. he can throw
6. Josh can't afford
7. You could read
8. Kelly couldn't ski

C

2. was able to
3. couldn't OR weren't able to
4. were able to
5. couldn't OR wasn't able to
6. could OR was able to

D

2. can OR 'm able to speak
3. been able to learn
4. couldn't understand OR wasn't able to understand
5. be able to sing

Lesson 23

A

2. couldn't see
3. could have
4. could tell
5. couldn't join

6. could be

B

2. couldn't fly
3. couldn't have done
4. couldn't know
5. couldn't have written
6. couldn't have gotten
7. couldn't eat
8. couldn't have arrived

C

2. We could have visited the Great Wall
3. Bill and Helen could have sold their old car
4. You could have gone shopping with me

D

2. could have dropped
3. couldn't have done
4. could belong

Lesson 24

A

2. She might not help Jo with her presentation
3. He might not buy that shirt
4. The package might arrive today
5. She might not go to the festival next week
6. They might have dinner with Tom

B

2. might know
3. might not wear
4. might not have heard
5. might have ordered
6. might not attend
7. might have missed
8. might not have left

C

2. might not have felt
3. couldn't be
4. couldn't have
5. might not provide
6. couldn't have begun
7. might not work
8. might not have woken

Lesson 25

A

2. must not cook
3. must know
4. must play
5. must not be
6. must have

B

2. must have gotten
3. must enjoy
4. must exercise
5. must have come
6. must have drunk

C

2. She must not like chicken
3. He must not have slept enough
4. They must have learned Italian there
5. She must not be married
6. He must have ridden it to school

D

2. must not
3. might
4. might not
5. must
6. must not

Lesson 26

A

2. must not touch
3. must wear
4. must show
5. must not drive
6. must take

B

2. She doesn't have to take
3. Do we have to work
4. Does the mayor have to give
5. You don't have to walk
6. He has to pass

C

2. don't have to bring
3. must not fish
4. don't have to carry
5. don't have to pay
6. must not feed

D

2. have to teach
3. didn't have to apologize
4. must tell *OR* have to tell
5. had to move
6. Did; have to revise
7. didn't have to sleep
8. must hire *OR* have to hire

Lesson 27

A

2. shouldn't worry
3. shouldn't give
4. should listen
5. should leave
6. shouldn't open

B

2. should I meet
3. should I hang
4. should I order
5. Should I throw
6. should I plan

C

2. Jack shouldn't have played
3. I should have asked you first
4. We should have helped her
5. She shouldn't have sold it
6. you shouldn't have scared your little sister
7. You should have come with us

D

2. shouldn't have eaten
3. shouldn't have ordered
4. should take
5. shouldn't have stopped
6. shouldn't be

Lesson 28

A

2. 'd better stay away *OR* had better stay away
3. 'd better slow down *OR* had better slow down
4. 'd better close the window *OR* had better close the window
5. 'd better keep quiet here *OR* had better keep quiet here
6. 'd better wash your hands *OR* had better wash your hands

B

2. 'd better sweep
3. 'd better not play
4. 'd better register
5. 'd better not arrive
6. 'd better not forget
7. 'd better turn
8. 'd better not quit

C

2. We'd better not go outside *OR* We had better not go outside
3. We'd better put the vase on the top shelf *OR* We had better put the vase on the top shelf
4. You'd better not miss the deadline *OR* You had better not miss the deadline
5. You'd better not spend a lot of money this month *OR* You had better not spend a lot of money this month

Lesson 29

A

2. When will you return home
3. Has Jenny sent the documents
4. Does your neighbor have
5. Are your friends graduating
6. Where have you traveled
7. Who did Sarah visit

B

2. Whose idea
3. What languages
4. How often
5. Whose car
6. how much

C

2. What is he apologizing for
3. What is she hiding from
4. What are they laughing at
5. What are you reaching for
6. What are they arguing about

D

2. What is your roommate like
3. What was your first date like
4. What was the cake for
5. What is this big bowl for

Lesson 30

A

2. Who did Craig tell the secret
3. Who beat the Bears
4. Who did the Owls beat

B

2. Who is going to visit Jane
3. What happened downtown
4. What will Tim order for lunch
5. What keeps dropping from the ceiling
6. Who have the police arrested
7. What did Erica print for the meeting
8. Who called this morning

C

2. Who invited you
3. How many people are coming
4. What should I give her
5. Which will she like

Lesson 31

A

2. why she looks worried
3. where I can buy that laptop
4. who that singer is

B

2. what was in Lucy's backpack
3. how the thief got into
4. who left this file
5. where you stayed in LA
6. which sandwich Laura wanted

C

2. if/whether these shoes are on sale
3. if/whether I told you about the art exhibit
4. if/whether someone is sitting here
5. if/whether the bus to Oak Park stops here

D

2. Do you know what it is called
3. I don't know if/whether I should believe her
4. Can you tell me when my suit will be ready
5. I don't remember if/whether it

was a dog or a cat
6. I wonder who Christine called

Lesson 32

A

2. shouldn't we
3. can you
4. haven't you
5. do you

B

2. You can't take me to the concert, can you
3. Melissa rides her bike to work, doesn't she
4. Chad is going on a business trip, isn't he
5. We haven't gone hiking together, have we

C

2. Wasn't Lucas waiting for his sister at the airport
3. Don't I look good in blue jeans
4. Didn't Melanie leave for work yet
5. Won't we have fun at the beach
6. Hasn't Roger had a girlfriend before

D

2. No
3. No
4. Yes
5. No
6. Yes

Lesson 33

A

2. The juice was spilled
3. The onion was cut
4. The windows were washed
5. The letters were sent

B

2. joined
3. be canceled
4. carry
5. is known
6. be cooked
7. wears
8. were included

C

2. were being planted
3. aren't being used
4. wasn't being cleaned
5. are being developed
6. was being performed
7. isn't being helped
8. were being printed

D

2. North America hadn't been discovered
3. my purse had been taken
4. it has been updated
5. we've been introduced
6. The ring had been sold
7. It has been closed
8. All of the things have been packed

Lesson 34

A

2. is baked
3. was caused by a tornado
4. were delivered
5. are prepared by Antonio Bruno
6. was arrested

B

2. photographers → by photographers
3. was appeared → appeared
4. O
5. O
6. isn't belonged → doesn't belong
7. O
8. delayed → were delayed

C

2. is married *OR* got married
3. was lost
4. be done *OR* be finished
5. be born

D

2. got broken
3. Did; get caught
4. didn't get hurt
5. Did; get dressed
6. didn't get fired

Lesson 35

A
2. was given some medicine
3. were given cards
4. was given a good grade
5. were given some cookies
6. was given a package
7. were given balloons
8. was given a gold medal

B
2. I was paid $50 (by Bob)
3. Money is lent to foreign residents
4. Visitors will be shown the gardens (by Ms. Sanders)
5. The story was told to his grandchildren
6. We were offered a discount
7. Students are taught yoga
8. Some questions will be asked to the movie star (by the reporter)

C
2. will be paid to the driver
3. must be shown passports
4. are taught manners by their parents
5. was sent to the girl by Ned

Lesson 36

A
2. Sharing a room
3. Cooking a meal at home
4. Finding a job
5. Parking on this road
6. Seeing the singer on stage

B
2. Drinking coffee is
3. Sitting close to the TV leads
4. Eating fruits doesn't affect
5. Wearing a hat causes

C
2. Taking care of children; requires
3. Reviewing the article again; doesn't seem
4. Becoming a famous actress; is
5. Riding an elephant; doesn't sound
6. Speaking in front of people;

doesn't make

D
2. It's comfortable to sleep on a sofa *OR* It's uncomfortable to sleep on a sofa
3. It's necessary to have a cell phone *OR* It's unnecessary to have a cell phone
4. It's convenient to take the bus *OR* It's inconvenient to take the bus
5. It's fun to watch movies alone *OR* It's boring to watch movies alone

Lesson 37

A
2. risk losing
3. deny meeting
4. keep walking
5. finish eating
6. suggest taking
7. give up skating

B
2. putting sugar in his coffee
3. not locking the door
4. studying Spanish
5. not going to Susie's party

C
2. living
3. being photographed
4. being taught
5. spending
6. being injured

D
2. read → reading
3. ○
4. having rented → renting
5. ○
6. carrying not → not carrying

Lesson 38

A
2. to catch
3. living
4. moving
5. to finish
6. shopping

7. to allow

B
2. expected to arrive
3. promised not to watch
4. offered to share
5. decided not to ride
6. agreed not to hide
7. intended to call

C
2. to be built
3. to provide
4. to use
5. to be recognized
6. to be amazed

D
2. to have fixed
3. to be growing
4. to have stopped
5. to have changed
6. to be listening

Lesson 39

A
2. to quit
3. working *OR* to work
4. making
5. to keep
6. rising *OR* to rise

B
2. remember going
3. Remember to pick
4. regret buying
5. forget visiting
6. regret to announce
7. forget to pack

C
2. tried to make an omelet
3. tried to call Sarah
4. try studying with a partner
5. Try following the recipe
6. try sending her a text message

D
2. stop to check
3. stop spending
4. need signing
5. Stop changing
6. need to take
7. need updating

Lesson 40

A

2. wants me to sell it to him
3. wants me to take him
4. want me to move back
5. wants me to meet her

B

2. told Cori to prepare for the presentation
3. invited Kevin to go out for drinks tonight
4. allowed Denise to go home early
5. advised Jane to call the customer soon
6. encouraged Steve to attend the seminar

C

2. him joining
3. it from spreading
4. her saying
5. them waiting
6. us from taking
7. me laughing

D

2. to live
3. them going
4. to study
5. her taking
6. him to apologize
7. playing
8. us to do

Lesson 41

A

2. He let her play outside
3. She had him sign the form
4. He made them wait in line
5. She let him use her scissors

B

2. made me fall
3. get them to read
4. get him to take
5. had your eyes tested
6. let Phil ride
7. get a tooth pulled

C

2. help us (to) solve

3. help you (to) feel
4. help me (to) bake

D

2. listened to him speak
3. saw her leave
4. heard them call
5. saw him finish
6. felt it shake

Lesson 42

A

2. went to the park to fly kites
3. went to the hall to listen to the speech
4. went to the restaurant to deliver groceries
5. went to the bank to get some cash

B

2. so that we won't get hungry later
3. so that I can look at the stars at night
4. so that I wouldn't forget
5. so that you don't injure yourself
6. so that an old lady could sit there

C

2. for a conference
3. to enter the National Museum
4. to wish her good luck
5. for a hammer
6. to help the environment
7. for my cousin's wedding
8. for a drink

D

2. letter to send
3. dress to wear
4. decision to make
5. chance to listen
6. movies to watch

Lesson 43

A

2. Maria was sorry to miss the phone call
3. I was relieved to find my credit card

4. I was surprised to get so many presents for my birthday
5. Don was glad to help his wife with the housework

B

2. are (OR aren't) difficult to learn
3. is (OR isn't) expensive to own
4. is (OR isn't) hard to get
5. are (OR aren't) easy to grow
7. It is (OR isn't) difficult to learn languages
8. It is (OR isn't) expensive to own a car
9. It is (OR isn't) hard to get a good job
10. It is (OR isn't) easy to grow plants

C

2. cheap for me to get
3. impossible for us to carry
4. generous of him to lend
5. dangerous for beginners to try
6. selfish of Evan to eat

D

2. happy to be
3. difficult for you to get
4. hard for me to find
5. relieved to hear
6. nice of you to invite

Lesson 44

A

2. who to date
3. where to hang
4. when to meet
5. how to change

B

2. where to put
3. how to play
4. when to come
5. who to hire
6. whether to join

C

2. whose story to believe
3. which book to read
4. what color to paint the wall
5. which way to go
6. whose advice to follow

D

2. where to have
3. who to invite
4. whether to buy
5. how to cook
6. what to do

Lesson 45

A

2. for cleaning
3. without leaving
4. at cooking
5. by calling
6. on making

B

2. As a result of training
3. in favor of changing
4. In addition to offering
5. in spite of having
6. instead of celebrating

C

2. 's used to speaking
3. object to staying
4. when it comes to building
5. looking forward to taking

D

2. have → having
3. ○
4. by ask → by asking
5. start → starting
6. ○

Lesson 46

A

2. felt like having
3. Do you mind pushing
4. was busy cleaning
5. have difficulty understanding
6. was worth reading

B

2. spent a lot of money fixing my car
3. is busy preparing for her presentation
4. can't help worrying about their children all the time
5. has trouble/difficulty seeing without her glasses

C

2. It took her three weeks to make
3. It cost her $500 to buy
4. It took them two hours to watch
5. It cost them $68 to see
6. It cost him $25 to get

D

2. can't wait to leave
3. can't help feeling
4. can't help laughing
5. can afford to stay
6. can't wait to meet

Lesson 47

A

2. There's a bicycle
3. There are four birds
4. There are three books
5. There's an umbrella
6. There's a calendar

B

2. tourists
3. a table
4. air
5. athletes
6. rain
7. an apartment
8. novels

C

2. movies look
3. juice contains
4. museum displays
5. cookies have
6. delivery truck brings

D

2. Music aren't → Music isn't
3. baby → a baby
4. A people → People
5. ○
6. rices → rice
7. ○
8. game → games
9. This street have → This street has

Lesson 48

A

2. an engineer
3. ice
4. a tie
5. news
6. an envelope
7. politics
8. a picture
9. meat
10. information

B

2. three jars of jam
3. a bar of soap
4. A kilo of cheese
5. two bottles of beer

C

2. paper
3. times
4. time
5. lights
6. light
7. glass
8. glasses
9. a room
10. room
11. a hair
12. hair

Lesson 49

A

1. earrings; bracelets; jewelry
2. money; coins; pennies
3. table; chairs; furniture
4. mail; regular letters; postcards
5. luggage; brown suitcase; backpacks

B

2. words
3. a suggestion
4. Travel
5. news
6. a big meal

C

2. work
3. articles
4. job
5. trips
6. scenery

Lesson 50

A
1. two pairs of pants
2. a pair of sunglasses; two skirts
3. four shirts; a pair of pants
4. three caps; one skirt; three pairs of shorts

B
2. Binoculars help
3. My vocabulary improves
4. The surroundings are
5. Do these pants seem
6. A museum ticket costs
7. Pajamas feel
8. Time is
9. My son plays
10. These shoes make
11. Personal belongings need
12. Your steak smells

C
2. Congratulation → Congratulations
3. ○
4. is → are
5. ○
6. hasn't → haven't
7. a pair of glass → a pair of glasses
8. a shorts → a pair of shorts OR shorts
9. good → goods
10. ○

Lesson 51

A
2. a newspaper
3. the dream
4. The bike
5. an umbrella
6. the vase
7. an old man
8. a store

B
1. the
2. a; the; the
3. an; the
4. a; the
5. the; the
6. a; the

C
2. a bathrooms → bathrooms
3. A mayor → The mayor
4. ○
5. a sugar → sugar
6. ○
7. the idea → an idea

D
2. a superhero
3. a city
4. a motorcycle
5. an enemy
6. the city
7. the enemy

Lesson 52

A
2. Muffins are great for breakfast or as a snack
3. Garages provide space to park cars
4. Cell phones help you keep in touch with friends
5. Nouns are words for people, places, or things
6. Sailors travel on ships

B
2. -
3. A
4. The
5. an
6. -
7. -
8. a
9. The
10. the

C
2. The blue whale OR Blue whales
3. the microscope OR microscopes
4. Bones
5. the tiles
6. judges

D
2. The tomato is a vegetable
3. Todd is an excellent singer
4. Judy is a lawyer in Florida
5. This is an old desk
6. The cactus is a tough plant

Lesson 53

A
2. **The** TV uses a lot of electricity.
3. In 2010, China had **the** largest population in **the** world.
4. **The** sky is beautiful. There are so many stars.
5. We go to **the** movies a lot. We enjoy it.
6. I use **the** Internet everyday for research.
7. Do you prefer listening to **the** radio or watching TV?
8. "I hope **the** rain stops soon." "I do too."
9. **The** government passed a new child protection law.
10. Ronald and I went fishing in **the** ocean yesterday.

B
2. the cinema
3. books
4. Flour
5. The wind
6. the universe
7. TV
8. songs

C
2. April is the fourth month
3. Who is the oldest child
4. Brad's Café serves the best coffee
5. I'm the only person in my class
6. Matthew has lived in the same house

D
2. It is very important to save **the** environment.
3. Plants and animals living on the land and in **the** ocean need a clean environment, too.
4. Recycling is **the** first thing we can do.
5. **The** second thing is reducing pollution.
6. There are many ways to help, but **the** best way is to do something right now before it's too late.

Lesson 54

A
2. the sea
3. home
4. the theater
5. bed
6. the universe
7. work
8. the earth
9. home
10. bed

B
2. Alex is at the school
3. Tony and Bob are in jail
4. Beth is at the church
5. Lynn and Ray are at church

C
2. Saturday
3. dinner
4. home
5. the winter *OR* winter
6. the best party
7. the Jacksons
8. Mrs. Carson

Lesson 55

A
1. it
2. I
3. you; them
4. you
5. us
6. they; me
7. He
8. her

B
2. Her
3. yours
4. their
5. our
6. mine

C
2. O
3. Their → Theirs *OR* Their hotel
4. is → are
5. mine briefcase → mine *OR* my briefcase
6. a your date → your date
7. were → was

8. The ours → Ours

D
2. We
3. her
4. us; your
5. they
6. Mine
7. yours
8. you

Lesson 56

A
2. the owner of this truck
3. the director of that movie
4. last night's concert
5. the ingredients of the food
6. A turtle's shell
7. next month's election
8. the roof of the building

B
2. Angela's
3. yesterday's picnic
4. Brazil's president
5. Ron's
6. the hairdresser's
7. rabbit's hair
8. my neighbor's

C
2. one of his coworkers
3. Some toys of my brother's *OR* Some of my brother's toys
4. one of my goals
5. some classmates of Rita's *OR* some of Rita's classmates
6. a tradition of ours
7. Some of their drinks
8. A hobby of Melinda's

D
2. the end of the show
3. the magician's name
4. A friend of mine
5. the manager of that theater

Lesson 57

A
2. her
3. yourself
4. us

5. themselves
6. me
7. himself
8. yourselves

B
2. Did; pack everything themselves
3. didn't bake this pie ourselves
4. made them myself
5. booked all of the tickets herself
6. Did; fix the sink yourself

C
2. see himself
3. make yourself
4. trust ourselves
5. Behave yourselves
6. help themselves
7. turn itself

D
2. by yourself
3. yourself
4. yourself
5. by yourself
6. yourself

Lesson 58

A
2. them
3. ones
4. They
5. it
6. one
7. ones

B
2. My blue one
3. some wild ones
4. a dry one
5. his best ones
6. the wrong ones

C
2. that expensive one
3. these
4. This brown one

D
2. the gold ones
3. the cozy one on the hill
4. the big ones
5. the spicy one with chicken

6. The ones near the entrance

Lesson 59

A
2. some forms
3. any wind
4. some pills
5. some time
6. any children

B
2. some apple juice
3. any drugstores
4. any candles
5. some salt
6. some suggestions

C
2. something
3. any
4. some
5. anyone OR anybody
6. someone OR somebody
7. some
8. anywhere
9. any
10. somewhere
11. anything
12. any

D
2. Any customer OR Any customers
3. any items
4. Some sofas
5. any trouble
6. any question OR any questions

Lesson 60

A
2. any problem
3. no mistakes
4. any advice
5. no snow
6. no secrets
7. no energy
8. any alcohol

B
2. This highway has no gas stations
3. I didn't plan anything for today

4. Aaron didn't do any homework all afternoon
5. There was nobody at the gym this morning
6. I went nowhere last night

C
2. O
3. Not any → No
4. isn't nothing → is nothing OR isn't anything
5. O
6. no → none OR no movies
7. don't know nobody → know nobody OR don't know anybody

D
1. any
2. some
3. none
4. no
5. some
6. any
7. no

Lesson 61

A
2. All luggage
3. every age group
4. All paintings
5. Every worker
6. all schools

B
2. Each chapter includes
3. Each piece of chocolate is
4. Each band member plays
5. Each can contains

C
2. all staff members get
3. Each guest receives
4. every dish looks
5. All bags need
6. each seat turns
7. Every neighborhood has
8. all perfume smells

D
2. No one OR Nobody
3. Not everyone OR Not everybody
4. everywhere

5. nothing
6. nowhere
7. Not everything

Lesson 62

A
2. much work
3. many clients
4. Many birds
5. much advice
6. many magazines

B
2. a lot of
3. A lot
4. much
5. much OR a lot of
6. a lot of
7. a lot

C
2. Few items
3. a few friends
4. a little salad
5. little noise
6. a few blocks
7. a little soup
8. few trains

D
2. so many
3. a lot of
4. much
5. little
6. a little

Lesson 63

A
2. None of the girls
3. Most of the players
4. Some of the main dishes
5. None of the appetizers
6. All of the desserts

B
2. some of us
3. a little of it
4. any of you
5. half of it
6. Most of them

C

2. All fish live in water
3. a little ice cream with my pie
4. Most of us don't know Jenny
5. Some people don't have a mobile phone
6. a few of them made mistakes
7. Half (of) the cup is filled

D

2. (of) the snow; melts
3. of the bedrooms; has
4. of my friends; own
5. of their earrings; cost
6. (of) his fridge; is

Lesson 64

A

2. either
3. both
4. Either
5. Neither
6. Both
7. neither
8. Either
9. both
10. neither

B

2. either test
3. Neither jacket
4. either drawing
5. Both cameras
6. Neither girl
7. either house
8. both toys

C

2. Neither of the subway lines; goes *OR* go
3. Both of us; look
4. Either of them; is *OR* are
5. Neither suit; fits
6. Both (of) these flashlights; need
7. Either event sounds
8. neither of us; plays *OR* play

Lesson 65

A

2. tastes sweet

3. Large families
4. wrong answer
5. got dirty
6. is true
7. long hair
8. sounds familiar
9. looks fresh
10. strong wind

B

2. I wasn't alone
3. Is this the only train
4. I feel sorry
5. *The Beatles* became famous
6. The hotel doesn't have an outdoor pool
7. The snake is alive
8. The company's main office moved
9. I'm glad to meet you
10. Tomorrow is an important day

C

2. beautiful pink roses
3. large white table
4. cute little puppies
5. nice new gray suit

Lesson 66

A

2. stolen
3. sleeping
4. barking
5. signed
6. renovated

B

2. The boy climbing the tree
3. All the songs performed by the band
4. the motorbike parked over there
5. The woman speaking right now
6. the flowers growing in your garden

C

2. used computer
3. woman staring
4. guided tour
5. cheering crowd
6. characters described

D

2. photo taken
3. crying baby
4. broken toy
5. girl laughing

Lesson 67

A

1. amazing
2. disappointing; disappointed
3. confusing; confused
4. frightened; frightening

B

2. tired; relaxing
3. embarrassed
4. boring
5. puzzling; puzzled
6. depressing
7. shocking
8. interesting; bored
9. depressed
10. excited; interested

C

2. exciting
3. surprising
4. shocked
5. disappointing
6. satisfied

Lesson 68

A

2. dramatically
3. lazily
4. kindly
5. carefully
6. responsibly

B

2. completely normal
3. church regularly
4. totally differently
5. really loud
6. the window tightly
7. the new mall surprisingly rapidly
8. amazingly cheap

C

2. closely the instructions → the instructions closely

3. absolute → absolutely
4. O
5. smoothly relatively→ relatively smoothly
6. angry → angrily
7. gently the furniture → the furniture gently
8. O

D

2. immediately
3. slightly
4. patiently
5. Hopefully

Lesson 69

A

2. surprisingly strong
3. getting hungry
4. famous speakers
5. extremely rapidly
6. normally busy
7. became popular
8. open automatically

B

2. acted bravely
3. smells sweet
4. look sharp
5. waited anxiously
6. looked closely

C

2. accurate
3. incorrect; immediately
4. glad
5. shortly
6. carefully

D

2. deliciously → delicious
3. proper → properly
4. easily → easy
5. angrily → angry
6. extreme → extremely
7. O

Lesson 70

A

2. long
3. comfortably
4. near

5. early
6. silent
7. hardly
8. high

B

1. lately
2. late
3. nearly
4. high
5. immediately
6. Surprisingly
7. happily

C

2. free
3. good
4. well
5. freely
6. well
7. free

D

2. O
3. high → highly
4. longly → long
5. good → well
6. O
7. lately → late
8. freely → free

Lesson 71

A

2. left it there yesterday
3. waiting for you downstairs
4. have a doctor's appointment tomorrow
5. can meet you then
6. move this sofa upstairs now
7. sit outside today

B

〈샘플 정답〉
2. I usually use public transportation *OR* I rarely use public transportation
3. I always brush my teeth after meals *OR* I often brush my teeth after meals
4. I sometimes go jogging in the morning *OR* I never go jogging in the morning
5. I rarely travel to foreign

countries *OR* I sometimes travel to foreign countries
6. I always watch TV on weekends *OR* I never watch TV on weekends

C

2. just arrived
3. isn't usually friendly
4. has already gone to work
5. can sometimes help a cold
6. have hardly seen him lately
7. don't often go skiing in the winter
8. always had to study a lot in college

D

2. never used to go
3. doing anything outside
4. really hate
5. should often exercise
6. going to the mall tomorrow
7. meet there then

Lesson 72

A

2. too dirty
3. enough milk
4. high enough
5. too slowly
6. long enough
7. too small
8. enough beds

B

2. comfortable enough
3. too many mistakes
4. carefully enough
5. too much homework
6. enough cash
7. too suddenly
8. way too short
9. enough games
10. far too early

C

2. well enough for you
3. enough time for me to go
4. too dark to read
5. enough sunlight to survive
6. too loudly for us to have
7. safe enough for you to walk

8. too big for our living room

Lesson 73

A
2. so much pain
3. so different
4. so often
5. so many animals
6. so funny

B
2. such an old song
3. so excited
4. such polite children
5. such a strange dream
6. so well
7. such great news
8. so heavily

C
2. such a hobby
3. Such knowledge
4. such accidents
5. such an age

D
2. I was so sick that I couldn't go to work
3. The service was so slow that we left the café
4. It was such an impressive movie that people clapped at the end
5. Michelle left so quickly that I didn't have a chance to say goodbye
6. Rudy has such great style that people dress like him

Lesson 74

A
2. less difficult
3. quieter *OR* more quiet
4. hungrier
5. less regularly
6. more carefully
7. less painful
8. more surprised

B
2. faster than our previous models

3. fitter than ever before
4. cooler than any other air conditioners
5. more powerful than its competitors
6. more easily than in other beds

C
2. more customers than
3. less clothes than
4. more traffic than
5. more children than
6. less wine than

D
2. less busier → less busy
3. ○
4. simple → simpler *OR* more simple
5. many mistakes → more mistakes
6. ○

Lesson 75

A
1. much higher
2. a bit bigger; even lighter
3. far younger; much older
4. a little farther *OR* a little further; a lot longer

B
2. taller and taller
3. more and more afraid
4. closer and closer
5. more and more quickly

C
2. the more successful we will be
3. the more valuable it becomes
4. the faster they fall asleep
5. the more carefully people invest

D
2. The sweeter the better
3. The scarier the better
4. The more the better
5. The easier the better

Lesson 76

A
2. The most popular song
3. the warmest day
4. the most people
5. the highest score

B
2. more comfortably
3. the earliest
4. darker
5. older
6. most polluted
7. least
8. the saddest

C
2. the shortest
3. (the) closest
4. (the) most frequently
5. the politest *OR* the most polite
6. The least common
7. (the) least often
8. the least heavy

D
2. the most experience
3. the least interest
4. the least money
5. the most votes
6. the least damage

Lesson 77

A
2. the quietest street in town *OR* the most quiet street in town
3. the most relaxing holiday I've ever had
4. the hardest of all materials
5. the most honest person I know
6. the most famous composer of the 18th century
7. the healthiest student in our class
8. the slowest of all
9. the most ancient paintings in our museum
10. The most expensive gift I've ever received

B
2. by far the most loudly
3. easily the biggest

4. by far the funniest
5. easily the most dangerous

C
2. the largest
3. the second most expensive
4. The newest
5. the third oldest
6. the second most

D
2. one of the noisiest neighbors
3. one of the most boring meetings
4. one of the greatest artists
5. one of the most important jobs

Lesson 78

A
2. as often as Kevin
3. as heavy as they look
4. as famous as the others in the city
5. as calmly as I could
6. as badly as we had feared

B
2. The Golden Gate Bridge isn't as old as the Brooklyn Bridge
3. The Brooklyn Bridge isn't as wide as the Golden Gate Bridge
4. The Golden Gate Bridge is longer than the Brooklyn Bridge
5. The Brooklyn Bridge is older than the Golden Gate Bridge
6. The Golden Gate Bridge is wider than the Brooklyn Bridge

C
2. as many women as men
3. as much cash as Ted
4. as much light as my brother's room
5. as many seats as the new theater

D
2. the same school as you
3. the same time as her
4. the same height as you
5. the same day as yours
6. the same city as them

Lesson 79

A
2. just as important as
3. nearly as terribly as
4. almost as hungry as
5. nearly as well as
6. just as confused as

B
2. twice as big as
3. three times as expensive as
4. twice as long as
5. four times as fast as
6. three times as heavy as

C
2. as unique as possible
3. as truthfully as possible
4. as soon as you can
5. as loudly as I can
6. as often as he can

D
2. As far as I remember, Donna is coming back from her trip tomorrow
3. As far as I'm concerned, the red dress looks best
4. As far as I know, Mr. Brown is in his office

Lesson 80

A
2. at
3. at
4. on
5. in; in
6. in
7. on; on
8. at

B
2. in the tent
3. on the car
4. on the door
5. at the desk
6. on the desk
7. at the bus stop
8. in the car
9. at the crosswalk
10. at the door
11. on their faces
12. in their bags

C
1. at the door
2. on the carpet; on the sofa
3. at the mall
4. in the library; on the grass
5. on the floor; in the yard
6. in his office

Lesson 81

A
2. on
3. at
4. on
5. in
6. at
7. in
8. on

B
2. at the eye doctor's
3. in the car
4. on the menu
5. in rows
6. at Carrie's house
7. on the bus
8. in the ocean

C
2. in the middle of the table
3. at the bottom of the ladder
4. on the left side of the door
5. at the top of the poster

D
2. at the 15th floor → on the 15th floor
3. In the plane → On the plane
4. in the party → at the party
5. in her home → at her home
6. in a map → on a map
7. on the world → in the world

Lesson 82

A
1. at; at
2. on; at; on
3. in; On; at
4. in; in; on
5. on; at; in
6. at; in; at; at

B

2. in the 19th century
3. at lunch
4. (on) March 8
5. in the future
6. in the winter
7. at night

C

2. in
3. -
4. - *OR* on
5. at
6. - *OR* on
7. at; in

Lesson 83

A

2. in the meantime
3. at the moment
4. in years
5. at once
6. at the latest

B

2. At the same time
3. in advance
4. In the end
5. At first

C

2. on time
3. at the end of
4. In the end
5. on time
6. in time

D

2. in time
3. at that time
4. in years
5. in advance

Lesson 84

A

2. for
3. during
4. for
5. for
6. during
7. during

B

2. until 9 o'clock
3. by dinnertime
4. until next Saturday
5. until the beginning of July
6. by August
7. by the end of the week

C

2. won't be submitted until this Friday
3. doesn't pay the staff until the last day of every month
4. wasn't chosen until 5 o'clock
5. didn't receive the test results until yesterday

D

2. After
3. During
4. within
5. in
6. until

Lesson 85

A

2. in boots
3. by taxi
4. with glasses *OR* in glasses
5. with a tour guide
6. in capital letters
7. by phone
8. in shorts
9. in love
10. with chopsticks

B

2. for
3. in
4. by
5. with
6. on

C

2. with anger
3. in use
4. by fax
5. on (the) air

D

2. in a hurry
3. on sale
4. by check
5. by e-mail

Lesson 86

A

2. Because of her headache, Maria had to go home early
3. Because of their bad hearing, my grandparents rarely hear the phone ring
4. Thanks to her computer class, Betty knows computers better than I do
5. Thanks to their reservation, Helen and Ryan didn't have to wait
6. Thanks to the map, Jim was able to find his hotel without any problem

B

2. Instead of
3. instead
4. instead of
5. instead of
6. Instead

C

2. In spite of washing my shirt
3. in spite of her busy schedule
4. In spite of the darkness
5. in spite of being nervous
6. In spite of taking vitamins

D

2. because of
3. instead
4. instead of
5. Despite

Lesson 87

A

2. 're learning about geography
3. 's pointing at a sign
4. 's paying for the newspaper
5. 's thinking about chocolate cake
6. 're waving at the cameras

B

2. leads to many health problems
3. shouted at each other
4. apologized for losing

5. belong to Monica
6. forgets about appointments

C
2. look at
3. ask about
4. ask for
5. look after
6. look for

D
2. answer to → answer
3. ○
4. married with → married
5. Look after → Look at
6. ○
7. replied for → replied to
8. call to → call

Lesson 88

A
2. calm down
3. show up
4. hold on
5. work out

B
2. 's taking off
3. 're cleaning up
4. 's running away
5. 's turning down

C
2. run out of
3. get along with
4. break up with
5. got out of
6. signed up for

D
2. Why did you turn the TV on *OR* Why did you turn on the TV
3. she made it up
4. You have to try these shoes on *OR* You have to try on these shoes
5. I want to throw it away
6. You can't just take them away
7. Susan pointed out the mistake *OR* pointed the mistake out

Lesson 89

A
2. close to
3. related to
4. terrible at
5. suitable for
6. fond of
7. eager for
8. curious about

B
2. shocked at the news
3. responsible for sales
4. similar to limes
5. concerned about Sue's performance
6. scared of the noise
7. full of people

C
2. good for
3. familiar with
4. good to
5. familiar to

D
2. excellent at
3. capable of
4. kind to
5. late for

Lesson 90

A
2. in
3. of; to
4. to; to
5. between
6. of
7. in

B
2. cost of
3. key to
4. responsibility for
5. example of
6. difference between
7. change in

C
2. A good way of thanking people
3. Belief in Santa Claus
4. a desire for wealth
5. Mary's reply to your suggestion

6. the conversation between Chuck and Arnold
7. a request for a vegetarian meal

D
1. a great need for
2. an answer to
3. The search for; knowledge of
4. The demand for; an increase in
5. The lack of; the reason for

Lesson 91

A
2. While he brushed his teeth, he watched the news. *OR* He brushed his teeth while he watched the news
3. He fell while he was snowboarding
4. While she played the guitar, she sang *OR* She played the guitar while she sang
5. While they were walking in the forest, they saw a deer

B
2. By the time Frank called Julie back, she was already asleep
3. Max applied for jobs until he finally got one
4. Hans kept studying Russian until he became fluent
5. We were already back in the hotel by the time it began to rain
6. By the time our seminar ended, everyone was pleased with it

C
1. 'll let
2. won't order; arrive
3. hear; 'll be
4. Will; feed; am
5. meet
6. returns; will; tell

D
2. ○
3. By → By the time
4. you are going to be → you are
5. during → while
6. ○

A
2. as she was looking through her bag
3. as he crossed the finish line
4. as she was pouring it
5. as they introduced themselves

B
2. as gas becomes more expensive
3. As Melissa drank more water
4. As the population grows
5. as we went up the mountain

C
2. As the sign says, you can't park your car
3. As I promised, I bought my wife
4. As I mentioned on the phone, Sandra is giving
5. As I explained in the e-mail, Mr. Jennings has

D
2. As this area has a warm climate
3. As the elevator was broken
4. As Claire didn't understand the instructions
5. As our products are high quality

Lesson 93

A
2. so that she won't gain any more weight
3. so that she can speak it fluently
4. so that he will get a promotion
5. so that she can have more space for her children
6. so that he won't be late for school again

B
2. to make some extra money
3. for running
4. so that your hands don't get cold
5. for drinks
6. to send Mom's birthday card
7. so that I won't forget

C
2. so loud that I couldn't concentrate
3. so that he can get
4. so bright that I need
5. so thin that we couldn't skate
6. so that we won't be

Lesson 94

A
2. Although my computer is old, it works perfectly
3. Although I washed my sneakers twice, the smell didn't disappear
4. Although I didn't put much salt on the food, Sam said it was too salty
5. Although Greg is just a beginner, he plays golf really well
6. Although my grandparents are over 70 years old, they're still very active

B
2. in spite of the flight's delayed departure
3. Although Terry practiced his speech many times
4. despite failing the test
5. even though she isn't famous
6. In spite of the fact that I've been on a diet for a month

C
2. though
3. In spite of
4. although OR though
5. though
6. in spite of

Lesson 95

A
2. putting pepper in her soup
3. Opening the window
4. Receiving the award
5. looking at himself in the mirror

B
2. Needing to borrow a blouse for

an interview, Shelly asked her sister
3. Noticing the smoke from the building, we called 911
4. Eating his burger, Max dropped some ketchup on his pants
5. Being married to a pilot, I don't see my husband every day
6. Riding my bicycle around the neighborhood, I saw many of my friends

C
2. not owning my house
3. Feeling refreshed after our vacation
4. not wanting to argue anymore
5. Riding on the boat
6. being stuck
7. Not being old enough

Lesson 96

A
2. if he doesn't reply
3. If Emma gets a scholarship
4. if there's nothing interesting on TV
5. if I don't pay the electricity bill
6. If we hurry to the theater

B
2. If I become a doctor, I'll open a children's hospital
3. If I move to France, I'll learn to paint
4. If I learn to paint, I'll have an exhibit
5. If I graduate college, I'll work at the UN

C
1. won't take
2. Send; travel
3. open; 'll eat
4. lock; leave
5. mix; don't get
6. don't order; won't be
7. Take; hurt
8. pour; sinks

D
2. Unless Sarah has an important appointment, she doesn't wear

makeup
3. You can't borrow new DVDs unless you return the old ones first
4. Unless Rick calls his mom back, she will keep worrying
5. Unless you are interested, I'm not going to ask you again

Lesson 97

A
2. if you didn't live near me
3. if I weren't (*OR* wasn't) so shy
4. If I drew well
5. If he didn't own a garden
6. if she had glasses

B
2. Daniel would read many books; he didn't play so many video games
3. Eric weren't *OR* wasn't on a business trip; he would attend the wedding
4. our heater turned on; we wouldn't have to call the repairman
5. Cindy would go dancing tonight; she had a partner

C
1. would do
2. take; won't be
3. will; arrive; mail
4. wouldn't ask; weren't *OR* wasn't
5. would have; went
6. get; 'll give

D
1. would be
2. would love; tasted
3. 'll go; have
4. visit
5. weren't; would feel

Lesson 98

A
2. if he hadn't studied business in college
3. If we had worked hard
4. If Tom hadn't scored three

goals
5. if I hadn't had a bad dream
6. If we had returned the book on time

B
2. If Lucy had practiced enough, she would have done well in her speech
3. If Greg hadn't drunk too much wine, he wouldn't have gotten a headache
4. If Mike and Jenny hadn't run on the icy sidewalk, they wouldn't have fallen
5. If we had known about Claire's birthday, we would have sent her a present
6. If my computer hadn't broken, I would have completed my report

C
1. would have given
2. had locked; wouldn't have gotten
3. knew; 'd tell
4. hadn't been; would've come
5. had; I'd buy
6. wouldn't use; were *OR* was

D
2. he had gone to the bank, he would have cash
3. he hadn't grown up in Spain, he couldn't cook Spanish food well
4. he hadn't had a big lunch, he would feel hungry
5. he hadn't forgotten his keys, he could get in his car

Lesson 99

A
2. I wish we had more space
3. I wish I could ski like him
4. I wish I were (*OR* was) stronger
5. I wish I weren't (*OR* wasn't) alone
6. I wish he weren't (*OR* wasn't) so busy

B
2. visited
3. had gone
4. lived
5. weren't *OR* wasn't
6. hadn't read

C
2. I hope
3. I wish
4. I wish
5. I hope
6. I wish

D
2. If only he had been nice to Judy
3. If only I hadn't left the cookies in the oven too long
4. If only he weren't (*OR* wasn't) so scared
5. If only we had visited her in the hospital
6. If only I didn't have a stomachache

Lesson 100

A
2. which cost $500
3. who was born in 1992
4. who doesn't like roller coasters
5. which might not get fixed

B
2. who don't want
3. who plays
4. which are
5. which goes
6. who doesn't lie
7. which don't have
8. who understands

C
2. have a leather bag that doesn't get dirty easily
3. is the music album that has sold over one million copies
4. brought Samantha a shirt that wasn't her size
6. that provides the best view is on the top floor
7. that won the big award has only been in two movies

8. that are chefs invited us to dinner on Friday

Lesson 101

A

2. that William can cook
3. that she hasn't met before
4. that you might wear
5. that we attended today
6. that I've ever seen

B

2. A person you can get medicine from
3. a plant you can make beer with
4. A place you can wash your clothes at
5. a tool you can open a wine bottle with

C

2. are photos which were taken last week
3. has two sisters she shares a bedroom with
4. who write to him are traveling abroad
5. is a VIP member of the gym he exercises at *OR* is a VIP member of the gym at which he exercises
6. Christina got on was crowded

D

2. O
3. in I am living → in which I am living *OR* which(*OR* that) I'm living in *OR* I'm living in
4. makes them → makes
5. O
6. with that → with whom
7. a park had → a park which(*OR* that) had

Lesson 102

A

2. the teacher; whose school trained all of the fighters
3. the pilot; whose parents Malachi killed
4. the warrior; whose leg was

injured during battle
5. the princess; whose planet Malachi attacked

B

2. a garden whose flowers look
3. a vegetable whose seeds have
4. a country whose oil industry is
5. A company whose employees aren't
6. a store whose furniture doesn't cost

C

2. What attracts me to Jenny
3. What you wear
4. what she learned
5. what caused Kevin's illness
6. What scares Patrick

D

2. whose
3. that
4. What
5. what
6. that
7. whose
8. what

Lesson 103

A

2. My English professor, who I won't ever forget, is very intelligent and friendly
3. Tracey had already decorated a room for her twins, who weren't born yet
4. Everyone enjoyed Annie's chocolate cookies, which she baked yesterday
5. Matt owns that small car, which his friends always joke about
6. Kevin's parents, who have been working as lawyers, will retire soon

B

2. My neighbors painted their fence yellow, which made their garden look bright
3. Lisa didn't eat anything at the family dinner, which worried her whole family

4. Kevin showed up late for the meeting, which isn't normal for him
5. The final match was canceled due to rain, which wasn't good news for the fans
6. I took a vacation last week, which was very relaxing for me

C

2. , who
3. , who
4. , which
5. which *OR* that
6. , who
7. , which
8. , which
9. who *OR* that

Lesson 104

A

2. why Andy didn't take
3. where a lot of accidents happen
4. why she's so tired all the time
5. when my daughter was born
6. where I buy my groceries

B

2. the restaurant where you can get the city's best pizza
3. the day (when) summer vacation begins
4. the reason (why) the concert is canceled
5. the beach where swimming is not allowed
6. the time (when) some animals start to hunt

C

2. the day which → the day when(*OR* that)
3. O
4. the stadium → the stadium where
5. the way how → the way (that) *OR* how
6. O

D

2. when
3. who

4. which
5. where
6. why

Lesson 105

A

2. He said that he was trying to lose weight
3. He said that his parents hadn't been to Europe
4. He said that he didn't like the food at that restaurant
5. He said that his neighbor's dogs barked too much
6. He said that Cindy and Julie weren't paying their rent

B

2. She said she couldn't watch scary movies alone
3. He said he needed to buy a new wallet
4. She said she would call Derek later
5. He said the mall wouldn't be open this month
6. They said they had lived in Toronto for 10 years
7. He said Monica could sing beautifully
8. She said Max and Sue weren't dating anymore

C

2. Jane said Robert doesn't/didn't like jazz music
3. Dana said she studied English literature in college
4. Bill said he wouldn't be attending Joel's presentation
5. Sylvia said her office is/was too small
6. Ted said Roger can/could draw portraits well
7. Mr. Phillips said the clock wasn't broken when he left

Lesson 106

A

2. He told them they looked like twins

3. She told him he couldn't smoke in the building
4. They told her they hadn't cleaned the bathroom yet
5. She told me she was learning to cook Thai food

B

2. said goodbye to his brother
3. told Joey he should wait
4. said nothing to me
5. told Nate that it was snowing
6. said that the concert had been canceled

C

2. She told Harry not to turn on the radio
3. She asked Laura to take out the garbage
4. She told Beth to get some rest
5. She told Christine not to open the present yet
6. She asked Roy not to leave too early

D

2. wanted to know who my favorite actor was
3. asked if I had any hobbies
4. wanted to know where I was from
5. wondered if I was interested in sports

Lesson 107

A

2. it is believed that a broken dish brings good fortune
3. it is said that brides wearing pearls will have bad marriages
4. it is thought that whistling inside a building will cause you to lose money
5. it is believed that people with big ears live longer

B

2. Dogs are believed to feel emotions
3. Exercise is known to reduce stress levels
4. Carrots are thought to be good

for eyesight
5. That house on the hill is said to belong to a famous singer
6. The rose is thought to be the flower of love

C

2. said that he likes
3. thought to be
4. believed that Mr. Crow will soon decide
5. expected that he will tell
6. said to have lived

Lesson 108

A

2. There haven't been
3. there isn't
4. Are there
5. there weren't
6. there has been
7. there were
8. Was there

B

2. There may not be enough copies
3. Will there be any live music
4. There used to be cheap clothes
5. There couldn't be much snow
6. There must be a fire
7. There used to be many fish

C

2. There seem to be some problems with the project
3. There appears to be a concert at city hall
4. There seem to be flowers on your desk
5. There appears to be no mail today

D

2. there were a lot of
3. there aren't any
4. there won't be any
5. There was no
6. There might be some

Lesson 109

A

2. Neither have we
3. So does my son
4. Neither are my kids
5. So has my husband
6. Neither did my family
7. So should I
8. Neither can I

B

2. I'm afraid so
3. I hope not
4. I believe not *OR* I don't believe so
5. I guess so
6. I'm afraid not
7. I suppose so

C

2. Neither
3. not
4. So
5. so
6. so
7. not

Lesson 110

A

2. He supposes (that) Jake will win the race
3. They feel (that) the restaurant is too crowded
4. She knows (that) the bookstore opens at 9 o'clock
5. He believes (that) what Jen said isn't true

B

2. She insisted (that) they invite Sam and Liz
3. She demanded (that) he not smoke in her car
4. He proposed (that) he cook dinner tonight
5. She suggested (that) we not go to the exhibit
6. He advised (that) I not leave my bag there

C

2. I'm disappointed that Lesley canceled our date

3. Pam is glad that the music festival isn't sold out
4. It's important that you drink enough water
5. It's vital that schools teach history
6. It's essential that people exercise regularly

D

2. not miss
3. not climb
4. learn
5. lower
6. not wait

Check-Up Test Answers

TEST 1

2. I don't wear socks
3. Are they in the kitchen
4. Mike and Kim are preparing
5. Do you always eat breakfast
6. It isn't raining
8. are you learning
9. I don't go
10. He lives
11. Does she speak
12. I'm not working
14. She's visiting
15. Jamie and I don't see
16. we talk
17. I'm listening
18. Do you know
19. His voice sounds
21. c)   22. c)
23. b)   24. a)
25. a)   26. b)
27. c) (doesn't → isn't)
28. a) (isn't tasting → doesn't taste)
29. c) (plan → planning)
30. a) (Are → Do)
31. d) (has → is having)
32. b) (be → being)

TEST 2

1. She was dancing
2. You weren't working; was having
3. Did you get; I didn't check
4. did you turn off; Were you listening
5. I met; Was she shopping
6. Mark didn't visit; He wanted
8. prepares
9. didn't use to wear OR never used to wear
10. Does; play
11. don't drink
12. Did; use to spend
14. did → was doing
15. She's used to jogging → She used to jog
16. was making → made
17. O
18. was wanting → wanted
19. O
21. d)   22. a)
23. c)   24. d)
25. b)   26. d)

27. c) (traveled → was traveling)
28. d) (wasn't believing → didn't believe)
29. c) (walked → were walking)
30. c) (were → did)
31. a) (Did → Were)
32. d) (was buying → bought)

TEST 3

2. I've played
3. Did you read
4. It hasn't rained
5. Mr. Young hurt
6. She hasn't eaten OR She didn't eat
8. Jack has worked OR Jack has been working
9. have you stayed
10. I haven't studied OR I haven't been studying
11. have you lived OR have you been living
12. I haven't traveled
14. had arrived
15. met
16. had moved
17. took
18. did; had
19. returned; had left
21. a)   22. d)
23. d)   24. c)
25. a)   26. b)
27. b) (had → have)
28. a) (haven't → hadn't)
29. a) (didn't spend → hasn't been spending OR hasn't spent)
30. d) (have graduated → graduated)
31. c) (been → gone)
32. d) (I ever taste → I've ever tasted)

TEST 4

2. After we watch the fashion show
3. I won't take the children
4. until he loses 10 pounds
5. Will you tell me
6. If the restaurant doesn't sell red wine
8. I'll eat
9. I'll be driving
10. Will you be swimming
11. we won't know
12. Mr. Perez won't teach OR Mr. Perez won't be teaching
14. I'll graduate

15. I'll have studied
16. We'll get
17. We'll have dated
18. Eric and I will have left
19. I'll send
21. b)   22. c)
23. c)   24. a)
25. b)   26. d)
27. d) (do you watch → are you watching *OR* are you going to watch)
28. a) (wasn't → isn't)
29. b) (be believing → believe)
30. c) (will be → was)
31. b) (going to make → making)
32. c) (have joined → be joining)

TEST 5

2. Do I have to submit my résumé
3. I'll be able to ride a bike
4. should we meet
5. Has Tony been able to spend much time
6. We'd better not open the windows
8. was able to; was able to pass
9. should; should buy
10. could; couldn't be
11. must; must turn off
12. have to; doesn't have to get up
14. might have made
15. Should; ask
16. must not have read
17. shouldn't forget
18. might get
19. could have started
21. b)   22. a)
23. c)   24. c)
25. a)   26. d)
27. a) (could → couldn't *OR* wasn't able to)
28. c) (may → should)
29. b) (clean → have cleaned)
30. b) (must → have to)
31. b) (leave → have left)
32. a) (don't have to → must not)

TEST 6

2. What did you study
3. Do you come
4. When does the bank open
5. Did I call
6. Where do you go
8. Who should we give

9. Which computer is yours
10. What are you going to order
11. Who helped you
12. Which sport does Tom enjoy
14. whose class I should take
15. What kind of dance does she teach
16. if her class will be
17. when must I register
18. Are you open
20. b)   21. d)
22. a)   23. b)
24. a)   25. c)
26. b) (you did stay → did you stay)
27. b) (do you want → wants)
28. c) (does he → did he)
29. c) (Yes → No)
30. a) (To where → Where)
31. a) (How → How often)
32. d) (did he go → he went)

TEST 7

2. 's married
3. wasn't asked
4. cleans
5. were built
6. doesn't arrive
8. Is the package being shipped
9. The meeting had been arranged
10. The renovations won't be completed
11. Menus were being handed
12. Have all of today's games been postponed
14. Various classes are offered to
15. The students are taught
16. Some scholarships are given to
17. the school sends
18. The intern isn't paid
19. Mr. Miller hopes
21. a)   22. b)
23. a)   24. c)
25. b)   26. c)
27. d) (of → by)
28. c) (didn't write → wasn't written)
29. d) (are belonged → belong)
30. a) (be → get)
31. a) (didn't know → wasn't known)
32. c) (did → 'm done)

TEST 8

2. it's difficult for her to get up
3. Did you decide not to study

4. They're busy preparing
5. in order not to miss the last train
6. Would you mind not making
8. singing
9. washing *OR* to be washed
10. to quit
11. being caught
12. to be chosen
14. invite you to attend
15. recommend taking
16. consider signing
17. decide to join
18. remember to register
19. to learn
21. d)   22. b)
23. d)   24. c)
25. a)   26. b)
27. b) (hanging → to hang)
28. d) (cut → cutting)
29. b) (paint → painted)
30. d) (not to oversleep → in order not to oversleep)
31. b) (to notice → noticing)
32. b) (to having → to have)

2. A few hairs are
3. The news helps
4. Two pieces of cake cost
5. Wood is
6. Some juice contains
7. pictures
8. furniture
9. an article; flowers
10. a glass; ice
11. team
12. an e-mail; assignments
14. staffs → staff
15. jewelries → jewelry
16. O
17. polices → police
18. was → were
20. b)   21. d)
22. d)   23. a)
24. c)   25. a)
26. b) (baggages → baggage)
27. a) (vocabularies → vocabulary)
28. d) (pant → pants)
29. b) (times → time)
30. b) (surrounding → surroundings)
31. a) (audiences → audience)
32. a) (belonging → belongings)

2. the radio
3. A pharmacist
4. the manager
5. an essay
6. a table
8. watch TV
9. The rooms at that hotel
10. some cereal for breakfast
11. The Smiths were my neighbors
12. attend church
14. a same → the same
15. the engineer → an engineer
16. movies → the movies
17. O
18. the present → a present
20. a)   21. c)
22. d)   23. a)
24. b)   25. c)
26. a) (the → 삭제)
27. c) (nearest bank → the nearest bank)
28. a) (A health → Health)
29. c) (a summer → summer *OR* the summer)
30. a) (an army → the army)
31. a) (Cello → A cello *OR* The cello)
32. b) (the bed → bed)

2. ones
3. hers
4. one
5. yourselves
6. him
8. this month's magazine
9. A classmate of mine
10. The roof of our house
11. Katie's husband
12. my sister's necklace
14. look after herself; cared for her
15. paid for school (himself)
16. helped him
17. gave him an award (himself)
18. believe in yourself *OR* believe in yourselves
20. a)   21. c)
22. b)   23. d)
24. a)   25. b)
26. d) (we → us)
27. d) (them → themselves)
28. a) (A your car → Your car)
29. c) (Bolivia → Bolivia's)
30. c) (theirs → their)

31. d) (his black one → his black ones)
32. c) (Mr. Roberts → Mr. Roberts')

TEST 12

2. no room
3. any milk
4. No movies
5. any plans
6. some advice
8. Either of the parks seems OR Either of the parks seem
9. All paper comes
10. half of them are
11. Both (of) my children go
12. Each of these boxes costs
14. Neither
15. either
16. some
17. any
18. few
20. a)   21. b)
22. d)   23. c)
24. a)   25. a)
26. d) (different something → something different)
27. c) (are → is)
28. b) (didn't tell → told)
29. a) (some → any)
30. c) (neither → either)
31. d) (none → no)
32. a) (few → little)

TEST 13

2. surprised
3. perfectly
4. outdoor
5. melting
6. suddenly
8. too heavily for us to go
9. such a beautiful garden
10. so deeply that I didn't want
11. too long for Katie to wear
12. Ellie always talks so politely
14. so → such
15. satisfied → satisfying
16. O
17. suitably → suitable
18. I usually am → I'm usually
20. a)   21. d)
22. c)   23. b)
24. a)   25. c)

26. b) (good → well)
27. b) (signing → signed)
28. c) (free → freely)
29. b) (happily → happy)
30. d) (fastly → fast)
31. a) (time enough → enough time)
32. d) (recent → recently)

TEST 14

2. more smoothly
3. less
4. as soon as
5. the coldest
6. as exciting as
8. one of the smartest animals
9. as many calls as
10. the most amazing experience
11. twice as crowded as the other days
12. The more you practice, the better you'll sing
14. smaller
15. more expensive
16. much
17. (the) largest
18. heavy
20. b)   21. c)
22. d)   23. a)
24. d)   25. c)
26. b) (very → much OR even OR a lot)
27. a) (as just → just as)
28. c) (the less → the least)
29. d) (in → of)
30. b) (warm and warm → warmer and warmer)
31. b) (than → as)
32. c) (lowest → lower)

TEST 15

2. anything at dinner
3. the baseball game on Friday
4. something on my face
5. her at the hairdresser's
6. my hometown in years
8. replied to
9. concerned about
10. look after
11. search for
12. excellent at
14. within
15. Thanks to
16. instead
17. by

18. till
19. by
21. d)　　22. c)
23. d)　　24. b)
25. a)　　26. a)
27. b) (on → in)
28. b) (on every → every)
29. c) (despite of → despite OR in spite of)
30. a) (for → at)
31. b) (to → 삭제)
32. b) (away them → them away)

TEST 16

2. so that I can sit down
3. Even though Lisa was on a diet
4. until the sun set
5. By the time I buy Christmas presents
6. As Tim was talking on the phone
8. Traveling in Europe
9. not wanting to gain any more weight
10. Being scared
11. watching the animal show
12. Not knowing how to cook curry
14. Despite → Despite the fact that OR In spite of the fact that OR Though OR Although OR Even though
15. By → By the time
16. O
17. busy so that → so busy that
18. when design → when designing
19. will end → ends
21. c)　　22. b)
23. b)　　24. d)
25. c)　　26. a)
27. b) (while → during)
28. a) (By → By the time)
29. d) (will check → check)
30. a) (dirty so → so dirty)
31. d) (although → though)
32. b) (so that → for)

TEST 17

2. 'll have; book
3. catches; drinks
4. asks; won't accept
5. 'll make; is
6. Don't go; don't feel
8. it weren't (OR wasn't) snowing; I would go jogging
9. Brian wouldn't have forgotten about the meeting; I had reminded him
10. We could send Sam a wedding gift; we knew his

address
11. Angela hadn't broken her leg; she wouldn't be at the hospital
12. Timothy had studied hard; he could have passed the English test
13. wouldn't have woken
14. hadn't called; would have missed
15. doesn't rain; 'll visit
16. 'll buy; go
17. had come; would have liked
18. were
20. c)　　21. a)
22. b)　　23. a)
24. b)　　25. d)
26. a) (you'll → you)
27. b) (isn't → is)
28. d) (had → had had)
29. b) (visited → had visited)
30. b) (attended → had attended)
31. d) (listens → listened)
32. d) (have joined → join)

TEST 18

2. a restaurant where we can have
3. the novelist whose stories I like
4. What makes me angry
5. The library from which I borrowed
6. the way I cook
8. what caused the fire
9. who stole your bag
10. , which was very fun
11. , who still live in my hometown
12. that I went to Paris
14. O
15. the river → the river where
16. which name → whose name
17. came → who(OR that) came
18. cooked it → cooked
20. a)　　21. b)
22. d)　　23. a)
24. b)　　25. c)
26. c) (that → which)
27. d) (work → works)
28. c) (who → whom)
29. a) (The thing → 삭제)
30. c) (it → 삭제)
31. a) (The way how → The way (that) OR How)
32. d) (stop → stops)

2. Dr. Turner told Nancy (that) she would feel much better
3. Richard asked if the bathroom was on the first floor
4. Jake told Annie (that) he was writing a letter to John
5. Helen asked if she could use the computer
6. Jeff said (that) he hadn't tried bungee jumping
8. She asked Lisa to make some toast for her
9. She told Mike to stop playing video games
10. She asked Sam not to talk loudly
11. She told Janice not to be late for class
12. She asked Kim to lend her some money
14. cows are believed to face
15. it is known that some penguins dance
16. cats are thought to like
17. it is said that eating stones helps
18. it is believed that dolphins don't sleep
20. a)   21. c)
22. b)   23. d)
24. a)   25. c)
26. a) (said → told)
27. b) (lives → lived OR had lived)
28. a) (He → It)
29. c) (calls → called)
30. b) (to → 삭제)
31. c) (They → They're)
32. a) (to Jessie → Jessie to)

29. d) (don't hope so → hope not)
30. c) (get → got)
31. b) (went → go)
32. c) (was I → have I)

2. I'm afraid not
3. So can Jake
4. I think not
5. Neither did mine
6. I hope so
8. I don't think so
9. Are there enough eggs
10. There haven't been any new employees
11. We were surprised that Aaron asked
12. There wasn't much traffic
14. not miss
15. talk
16. join
17. read
18. not go
19. are
21. d)   22. c)
23. c)   24. a)
25. d)   26. b)
27. c) (don't → not)
28. b) (be should → should be)

GRAMMAR
GATEWAY
INTERMEDIATE

www.Hackers.co.kr

Index

영문 Index
한글 Index

영문 Index

한글 Index

Index에 있는 숫자는 Lesson 번호입니다. 괄호 안에 있는 숫자는 Lesson 내 섹션 번호입니다.

영어가 쉬워지는 기초 영문법

초판 23쇄 발행 2025년 1월 6일
초판 1쇄 발행 2014년 9월 1일

지은이	해커스 어학연구소
펴낸곳	㈜해커스 어학연구소
펴낸이	해커스 어학연구소 출판팀

주소	서울특별시 서초구 강남대로61길 23 ㈜해커스 어학연구소
고객센터	02-537-5000
교재 관련 문의	publishing@hackers.com
동영상강의	HackersIngang.com

ISBN	978-89-6542-077-4 (13740)
Serial Number	01-23-01

외국어인강 1위,
해커스인강(HackersIngang.com)

해커스인강

· 예문 해석 및 교재 정답 자료
· 교재에 수록된 예문을 듣고 따라하는 **예문 음성 MP3**
· 해커스 스타강사의 **본 교재 인강**

영어 전문 포털,
해커스영어(Hackers.co.kr)

해커스영어

· 영어의 기본원리가 이해되는 **본 교재 핵심포인트 무료 인강**
· 누구나 쉽게 학습할 수 있는 **말하기/듣기/읽기/쓰기 무료 학습자료**

'영어회화 인강' 1위,
해커스톡(HackersTalk.co.kr)

왕초보영어 탈출
해커스톡

· 쉽고 재미있게 학습하는 **기초 영어회화 동영상강의**
· **데일리 무료 복습 콘텐츠, 무료 레벨테스트** 등 다양한 무료 학습 콘텐츠